Shakespeare for the
Modern Reader

Shakespeare for the Modern Reader

A User-friendly Introduction

Henry I. Christ

Writer's Showcase
San Jose New York Lincoln Shanghai

Shakespeare for the Modern Reader
A User-friendly Introduction

Writer's Showcase
an imprint of iUniverse, Inc.

For information address:
iUniverse, Inc.
5220 S. 16th St., Suite 200
Lincoln, NE 68512
www.iuniverse.com

Cover by Tom Christ

ISBN: 0-595-19356-0

Printed in the United States of America

Contents

Introduction

Most people would like to know more about Shakespeare but find the subject forbidding. Where would someone begin? The prospect is daunting; yet not to become at least a bit familiar with this greatest of writers is to miss out on one of life's most satisfying pleasures.

There has never been a better time for enjoying Shakespeare's plays. Before the electronic revolution, audiences were limited to the performances of the moment. Now, with the growing storehouse of videotapes, the great performances of the past are available to today's audiences. We needn't talk wistfully about the Hamlets of Laurence, Mel Gibson, or Kenneth Branagh. They are available on tape for viewing whenever enthusiasm dictates.

Shakespeare for the Modern Reader is intended for the literate, curious, intelligent adult, motivated to learn more about Shakespeare in an informal, user-friendly way. It is intended to arouse the same love and enthusiasm for Shakespeare that I have experienced ever since a charismatic college professor introduced me to Shakespeare, Marlowe, Jonson, Fletcher and the rest of that incredible group.

The book is divided into three parts, followed by an Afterword. The first part, dealing with Shakespeare's life and theater, examines the known facts and the environment in which Shakespeare lived. The second part explores his genius, isolating, and illuminating elements that reveal his versatility. Each chapter in Parts 1 and 2 begins with a relevant Shakespearean quotation to introduce the topic.

Part Three introduces the individual plays. For each play, a brief summary of the main plot is included along with critical commentary to set the play in the context of its time and the Shakespeare canon. Each report provides enough information for a prospective theatergoer to understand the action and for a prospective reader to get the gist. Each group of plays is introduced with a brief explanation to place the plays in that productive career.

There was a strong temptation to label this section "Shakespeare Play by Play!" There are abundant cross-references throughout the text, linking the earlier parts with Part Three. Of course, Part Three may be read for its own sake to suggest the scope of Shakespeare's achievements.

In a final tribute to Shakespeare, the Afterword considers the fascinating question, "What if?" Editions of Shakespeare vary. For purposes of quotation identification, this book uses the Cambridge University Press edition. Printed by permission.

Acknowledgments

I wish to thank John and Dorothy Adams, Stewart and Betsy Holmes, Douglas and Essie Palmer, Roger and Nancy Sinclair for reading portions of the manuscript and providing input and encouragement. Sylvia Carlin and Sylvia Ponemon persuaded me that a user-friendly book about Shakespeare is needed. Martin Gardner, Jack and Lila Lowenherz contributed…many clippings and reviews that they had discovered in their wide reading.

I am deeply grateful to my sons Bob, Bill, and Tom for the major role they played at every step of the way in the production of this book. Their unfailing patience, good humor, and encouragement sustained me throughout. My daughter-in-law Robin made a significant contribution at a crucial stage of production.

Shakespeare for the Modern Reader is dedicated to my wife Marie, partner in my writing and my life:

> Age cannot wither her, nor custom stale
> Her Infinite variety.

Henry I. Christ

Part One

The Life and the Stage

1

Shakespeare, the Man

His life was gentle, and the elements
So mixed in him that Nature might stand up
And say to all the world, "This was a man!"

Julius Caesar, V, 5, 73-75

Mark Antony's tribute to Brutus might be Shakespeare's own epitaph. From all we know about Shakespeare the man, he was a gentle, sociable, amiable person, able to get along with a wide variety of people. Acting companies were a hotbed of intrigues, jealousies, even backbiting, but Shakespeare apparently got along with these nervous, high-spirited actors. His longevity as a writer with the same group says a great deal about his personality. Perhaps the strongest clue we have is the publication of the First Folio (p 85) of his plays seven years after his death, by his fellow actors. In a prologue to the collection, his former colleagues pay warm tribute to this "happie imitator of Nature…a most gentle expresser of it." Then follow two poems of praise, one by Shakespeare's rival Ben Jonson.

Critics complain that there just isn't as much known about Shakespeare as they'd like. The reality is that more is known about Shakespeare than about most of his contemporaries and rivals. Of course, political figures like Henry VIII, Elizabeth I, and Mary Stuart are well documented in the diaries, recollections, and biographies of the day. Players were second-class citizens in the eyes of the aristocracy. Shakespeare himself may not have had any idea that his plays would survive. They were written for the moment and served their purpose.

The facts about Shakespeare's life are found in the criticisms and praises of his fellow playwrights, in various legal documents and church records. We know when he was born, when he was married, when he returned to his birthplace, Stratford, and there lived the good life. Above all, we have his plays. They tell us much about the man, the creative genius. The images (p135) he used reveal the inner man and reflect the experiences he had. We believe we know for example, where he stood when he described the dangers of crossing tidal waters in a Kentish Estuary.

The story of his life is a gigantic jigsaw puzzle, with a great many pieces clearly present. Many of the other pieces can be inferred from what we know about life in Stratford during his lifetime and from what we know of his friends and especially his extended family.

Park Honan in *Shakespeare: a Life* presents An amazingly complete picture of what it was like to be born into the Shakespeare family, to grow up in Stratford, to leave for London and the ultimate acclaim and literary immortality.

Shakespeare's Parents

A great deal is known about Shakespeare's parents. His father, John Shakespeare, was a leading citizen of Stratford, fairly affluent even before he became prominent as a town official. He was chosen alderman in July, 1565, the year after Shakespeare's birth. John was a successful glover, probably with three or four stitchers in his employ. As bailiff, he presided over Stratford in October, 1568. Often called upon to arbitrate disputes, John was known for his tact.

Until Shakespeare's thirteenth year, John served as a trusted alderman, justice of the peace for a year, and town official in many capacities. William was undoubtedly influenced by the strength and prestige of his father. In *A Mid-summer Night's Dream* (I, 1, 47) Theseus warns Hermia, "To you your father should be as a god."

John's father, Richard, Shakespeare's grandfather, had been a modestly successful farmer. John administered Richard's estate after Richard's death. John spent seven years as a glover's apprentice and became sufficiently skilled to strike out successfully on his own. Shakespeare's plays have many glowing images of the artisan's skill. Many images include gloves.

Later economic misfortunes toppled John from his lofty perch, but even in adversity his friends on the town council helped him in a variety of ways, a tribute to his popularity. John's uncertain fortunes are reflected in Shakespeare's plays, when rapid turns of fortune (as in *Richard II* and *King Lear*) are dramatized.

John's mother, born Mary Arden, was the daughter of a respectable farmer. She had been born about 1540, the youngest of eight daughters. Mary's mother died young, and her father, Robert Arden, took a second wife, Agnes Hill. She had two boys and two girls of her own, suggesting a crowded household. Without sons of his own (remember those eight daughters!), Robert found farming life hard. His daughters married one by one, leaving the still unmarried Mary. Robert doted on Mary, making her one of the two executors of his will, despite her youth. Perhaps Robert didn't trust his own wife in carrying out the provisions of the will.

Mary Arden and John Shakespeare were married, probably in 1557. This was a union of two well-respected families. At best, life was hard and infant mortality was high. Their first child, Joan, evidently died in infancy. Margaret, the second child was baptized on December 2, 1562. A victim of childhood diseases, she was buried in April, 1563.

The Early Years

With two infants already lost, Mary became pregnant in 1563. William was born in April, 1564. The exact date is unknown, though April 21, 22, and 23 all have their advocates. The most popular date, April 23, coincides with the recorded date of his death April, 23, 1616. April 23 is also St. George's Day, the day of England's patron saint. Mary was certainly worried. Having buried two children, she agonized over William. An added worry was the plague (p 25).

The plague seemed to close in on Stratford. It broke out at Leicester in June and then Coventry. By July 11, the plague had reached Stratford. It struck the heart of the city, killing Thomas Deege's apprentice and Deege's wife. The plague was threatening every inhabitant, but John Shakespeare, as an officer of the council, did not leave town. It was unlikely that he'd allow Mary to leave either.

Black rats lived in the wattle-and-daub houses, in thatch or walls. The transmitting fleas accompanied their hosts and were able to infect even those supposedly secure in their homes. Entire households perished. Then the plague began to die away, and the town came to life again. Mary Arden brought her precious son through this chilling episode and probably gave to him a sense of security that could sustain him in later life.

As the child of a prominent, well-to-do citizen, Shakespeare would have the benefits of a good education. A "grammar boy" was special. As an alderman's son, William would have been pressured to succeed, to be a credit to his father. Teaching techniques of the time relied heavily on memorizing. From 7 to 15, William probably memorized Latin almost daily. This experience probably helped shape his writing style.

School was essentially seven days a week. Students had to account for sermons heard on Sundays. The Bible and Latin authors like Ovid were familiar tools for these young minds.

Social Uncertainty

At the time of Shakespeare's birth, the country was divided. Only thirty-one years separated the marriage of King Henry VIII (p255) to Anne Boleyn from the birth of Shakespeare. In those years, England suffered through a painful readjustment to a new church. Henry had originally married Katherine of Aragon as a Roman Catholic prince, but when Katherine failed to bear him a male heir, Henry sought to divorce her so that he could marry another woman, who might provide the male heir.

The Pope refused to allow the divorce on the grounds that the marriage was a sacrament, not to be flouted. As the secular head of the church, Henry declared his marriage to Katherine invalid and married Anne Boleyn. He declared the Church of England a separate body of faith, no longer under Papal control. As part of the break, Henry began suppressing the monasteries and appropriating land and treasure.

After Anne Boleyn was executed for infidelity, Henry married his third wife, Jane Seymour, who bore Henry a son. When Henry died in 1547, that son became Edward VI. He reigned under the control of Protectors but died of tuberculosis in 1553. Without other male heirs to choose, the country went through a brief period of uncertainty. An unfortunate young woman, Lady Jane Grey was made queen, but after nine days she was overthrown and later executed (p256).

Henry had two surviving children: Mary, daughter of Katherine, and Elizabeth, daughter of Anne Boleyn. As the elder, Katherine was anointed queen in 1533. A true daughter of Katherine, Mary was a devout Roman Catholic. She and her followers attempted to restore the old ties with Rome. She also sought to strengthen England's ties with Catholic Spain. She married Philip in 1554, but the marriage was not popular with many of her subjects. Mary may have hoped for a close relationship with Philip, but he stayed in England briefly and returned to Spain. Mary was heart-broken.

In her zeal to reestablish the old faith, Mary was accused of persecuting Protestants. She was called "Bloody Mary," though her personal part in tortures or executions has never been proved.

What of Elizabeth, her surviving half-sister? At the beginning of Mary's short reign, Elizabeth was imprisoned and accused of conspiracy. The charges were false. Elizabeth was a faithful subject and was allowed to live. Mary died in 1558, childless, ill, and broken in spirit.

Elizabeth ascended the throne at a very dangerous time. The old factions, Protestant and Catholic, were hostile toward each other. To some Catholics Elizabeth was a demon, undeserving of the throne. Even some Protestants doubted the ability of an untested young woman to rule the restless country. Elizabeth proved to be a shrewd and strong ruler. She formally established the Anglican Church and set England's course in the future as a Protestant nation. Her long reign, from 1558 to 1603 is sometimes called England's Golden Age.

All the reversals caused turmoil throughout the land. People reared in the Catholic faith found it difficult to change religious allegiances. Some unyielding Catholics were executed. Others outwardly conformed to the new religion while quietly observing the old in their private lives. Younger folk adhered to the new faith more easily.

This world of ferment was Shakespeare's world, especially in his early years. Shakespeare's own religious beliefs have been the subject of volumes. There is no definitive answer. Shakespeare certainly was familiar with Catholic rituals, but whether he himself secretly observed the old faith is unclear. Shakespeare reveals a great deal about himself in his plays, especially in his images (p135), but his genius conceals the ultimate mysteries of his life, loves, and career.

Marriage

Many tongues have wagged and winks have passed because Shakespeare's first child, Susanna, was born approximately six months after his wedding. Was Shakespeare forced into an unwelcome marriage? There is no proof for such a supposition. The best guess is that he loved Anne Hathaway and entered into the marriage with good will. Anne came from a good family and was an entirely appropriate bride for the young man. The parents probably welcomed the marriage. Anne, eight years older than William, brought stability and love into the Shakespeare household. The young married were expected to live with the parents. As a well brought-up homemaker, Anne could be expected to be an asset in the Shakespeare household, a helper for Mary. John Shakespeare would have been happy at the possibility of having another male heir to carry on the name and family fortunes.

Exact dates are sometimes elusive, but it is probable that the two were married December 1, 1582. Their daughter, Susanna, was baptized May 26, 1583, a firm date. Twins, Hamnet and Judith, were christened on February 2, 1585.

Why, at a time of large families, did Shakespeare have only three children? Again, all kinds of speculation have suggested that the marriage was a good/bad one, that Shakespeare loved/disliked Anne, that he hated/loved the small-town life in Stratford.

Nobody knows for sure, but some elements are there for all to see. First of all, there was never any hint that he tired of Anne, that he wanted a divorce, that life in Stratford was so unhappy, he couldn't stay there.

Secondly, there is his inscrutable attitude toward marriage. The Capulets in *Romeo and Juliet* are by no means an ideal couple, but there are friendly marriages in *The Merry Wives of Windsor*. In *King Lear*, the marriage of Cornwall and Regan is an exercise in villainy, but in the same play, the King of France marries Cordelia for herself, not for her missing dowry. In *Macbeth*, Lady Macbeth loves her husband perhaps too well, but the affection is there. How did Shakespeare feel about his marriage? We don't know. Through wills and legal documents, we surmise that Shakespeare was often annoyed with Anne's relatives, the Hathaways, but we have no way of knowing that this annoyance was transferred to Anne herself.

As for not having more children: perhaps she couldn't. One good conjecture is that having twins ended her childbearing possibilities. The statistics are unsettling. Between 1560 and 1600, there were 32 instances of twin births in Stratford. In only 18 cases did both children survive after the first three months of infancy. In 8 cases involving twins, the mothers bore no later children. The barber-surgeons, with their unsterilized instruments, might have harmed the mothers.

The next decade has fostered all kinds of stories about Shakespeare, but until he surfaces in London ten years later, we can only surmise. One possible story is that he acted as schoolmaster for a time. He had to support a wife and children, so he must have earned a living. He was not destined to be a farmer, a glover, or an artisan. His art was to be words.

London

London was a city of paradoxes. The heart of Elizabethan England, it boasted flourishing markets, the parliament, royal palaces, and even the royal mint. It was a city throbbing with life and energy, but it was also a city of the impoverished. As Park Honan reports, "More people died in

London than were born there," but the city continued to grow with a constant influx of workers seeking their fortune in the great metropolis. Shakespeare was one of those.

With so many people of diverse backgrounds thrown together, there were inevitable brawls, robberies, and occasional civic unrest. The greatest threat, however, was from the plague (p 25). The epidemics impacted everyone, rich and poor; the rich were more able to flee infection...but not always successfully. The theaters were almost fatally affected, closing for long periods. Acting companies left the dangerous city and toured the provinces, There they were not always welcome, partly because their morals were suspect by the virtuous, and partly because they were considered potential plague carriers.

It was a challenging society that Shakespeare came to, and he had to earn a living by his skill with words. By the time he arrived in London, companies of players were competing to survive (p 26). Some of the intense competition is suggested in the film *Shakespeare in Love*. The theater pictured there is the Rose, an important predecessor of the Globe. Like the rebuilt Globe, the restoration of the Rose is planned on the site where the historic theater once stood. We are reasonably certain that *Henry VI, Part One*, was presented at the Rose in 1592, a date that puts Shakespeare already in London.

Biographical surmise for the next decade is based largely on the plays, though there are comments by other actors and critics that help us determine how things were going.

Shakespeare sought to be part of a group. Mutual help and support sustained the players through difficult times. The actors didn't think of a play as Shakespeare's or Marlowe's or Ben Jonson's. A play was the company's. The writer played an important role, of course, but equally important were all the other people who made the play a success...or failure. It is a measure of Shakespeare's greatness that his fellow actors went further with his plays than was usual at the time. The First Folio, published in 1623, towered over the Folio publications presenting the works of Ben Jonson and John Fletcher, the only other 17th-century dramatists so honored.

Historians enjoy inferring from the plays events in Shakespeare's life. He uses names of friends and relatives as fictional names. Undoubtedly his treatment at the hands of the nobility, fellow actors, and everyday tradespeople shaped his characterizations.

We sense the interaction of playwrights, each learning from the others. Christopher Marlowe's influence on Shakespeare can be traced to *The Merchant of Venice*, a parallel story to Marlowe's *The Jew of Malta*, (p 51). *Titus Andronicus* owes a great deal to Thomas Kyd's *The Spanish Tragedy* (p 52). There is one surprising link that has stirred scholarly conjecture. In *As You Like It*, the shepherdess Phoebe says, "Who ever loved that loved not at first sight?" (III, 5, 82). This is an exact quotation of a line in Marlowe's *Hero and Leander*. Is Shakespeare here paying tribute to a gallant rival? Shakespeare may also have learned from Marlowe the device of mixing tragedy and farce. Both *Doctor Faustus* and *The Jew of Malta* blend serious scenes with broad humor. That blending may have been called for by the heterogeneous audiences. University scholars, nobility, even royal personages sat in different boxes, but they saw the same performances as the groundlings (p 106). There had to be "something for everyone," stretches of magnificent poetry in close proximity to slapstick. The porter scene in *Macbeth*, after the murder of Duncan by Macbeth (p297), is admittedly low humor. It had a dual purpose, however. It tickled the fancy of the groundlings, but it provided a necessary relief after grueling scenes preceding it. Even the sophisticated lords welcomed this change of pace.

Some time in the early 1590s, Shakespeare began devoting his energy to poetry (p323), undoubtedly taking time from his playwriting. There seems to have been a good reason. In 1592, the plague struck London with cruel intensity. About 14% of the total population died. To make a living, poets wrote lengthy poems and dedicated them to various noblemen, in the hope that the dedication would bring some financial help. Shakespeare, for example, dedicated *Venus and Adonis* and *The Rape of Lucrece* to the young Earl of Southampton.

Problems

The companies of players were surprisingly resilient. When the plague subsided, they opened the theaters, but the door wasn't wide open. Plays had to be licensed by the Master of the Revels, an official censor. The office originally related to entertainments at court only, but gradually the power and responsibility increased, until the stamp of approval became matter of life and death for plays. This was an added burden and worry for the harassed companies. The power of the office actually increased after Shakespeare's time until 1642, when the theaters were closed by order of the Puritans. After the Restoration of King Charles in 1660, there was an unsuccessful attempt to revive the censorship office.

Some persons associated with the theater found creative ways to make a living during plague times. James Burbage, father of the great Richard Burbage (p30), had an empty theater on his hands. He sold food illegally though receiving summonses from 1591-1594. He apparently had friends in high places, as did other theater people.

In the spring of 1594, southern England had relief from the plague. It was a cold, dismal spring when the actors returned. Shakespeare apparently decided that his career would fare better writing plays rather than poetry. His patron, the Earl of Southampton, was not in a position to provide much help. Poetry's loss was drama's gain, especially since the plays themselves are filled with poetry.

Productive Years

The next years were unbelievably busy. Play followed play with reassuring regularity...reassuring because Shakespeare's company relied on him for playable dramas. During this period, Shakespeare also managed to act in some of his company's plays. We are reasonably certain that he played old Adam in *As You Like It* and the Ghost in *Hamlet*. Undoubtedly he took other parts as he was needed. Recent computer studies have come up with a surprising number of roles for the busy playwright, including Antonio in *Twelfth Night* and Friar Laurence in *Romeo and Juliet*. The conjecture is that he preferred smaller roles, especially old men. Shakespeare's grasp of what makes a play work on the stage strongly supports the idea that he was an actor as well as a playwright.

Though exact dating of all the plays is impossible, scholarly research has placed the plays in a reasonable timetable. Some dates of performance are secure. Contemporary visitors to London reported seeing some of the plays. Internal evidence also helps date a play. The shipwreck in *The Tempest*, for example, may have been partially inspired by the wreck of the *Sea Venture* in the Bermudas in 1609. This, along with other evidence, suggests that *The Tempest* is a late play, perhaps 1611-1612. Scholars have also traced a greater skill and sophistication as Shakespeare honed his craft through the years.

In the period following the plague, the acting companies competed vigorously for the audiences. Both Shakespeare's men and the Admiral's had competing plays on *Henry V*, *King John*, or *Troilus and Cressida*. The Admiral's presentations were more traditional; Shakespeare's plays were more radical and subtle. *Romeo and Juliet*, for example, was more than a traditional love story. Juliet displays an unmaidenly ardor in her thoughts about Romeo. It is her passion that moves the play. Though much older than Juliet, Romeo is a lovesick adolescent.

A Midsummer Night's Dream develops scenes familiar to Shakespeare in his Stratford childhood. The play put on by Bottom and his fellow artisans recalls scenes of Midsummer Eve in Stratford. Even the "wall" in the play may have stirred memories of the deteriorating wall outside the Stratford grammar school. The artisans themselves, though humorous in their self-importance, are presented with nostalgia and compassion.

The history plays that followed show Shakespeare's developing powers. The first, *Richard II*, almost ruined the company. It shows the deposition and death of a king, a risky subject for Elizabeth at a time of uncertainties. Like Richard, Elizabeth had no direct heir. The parallels were dangerous. The deposition 'scene was never printed while the Queen was alive, but the play was actually staged. The Earl of Essex and his men had paid handsomely for the production to aid their conspiracy against the Queen. Essex was beheaded, but the company squeaked through, pleading naiveté. Portions of the play pleased Elizabeth.

By 1596, Shakespeare was fairly well-to-do. His name was sent to the Exchequer because he had failed to pay a small tax, probably an oversight. In all probability, he returned to Stratford for visits. He had no intention of breaking his connection with his childhood town. He sought to buy property. There are court records noting that he recovered debts owed him. He took local debtors to court twice.

What of his relationship with Anne Shakespeare at this time? We have only conjecture. Anne was undoubtedly a faithful wife, heavily involved in household chores and the raising of their three children. Nearly 40 in 1596, she would have shown the results of hard work in face and hands. In *As You Like It,* Rosalind says of Phoebe,

> She has a leathern hand,
> A free-stone coloured hand. I verily did think
> That her old gloves were on, but 'twas her hands.
> She has a housewife's hand.
>
> IV, 3, 24-27

Though seemingly heartless in the thoughtless comment of a young girl, this quotation has a touch of sadness and sympathy. Elsewhere in the play, Shakespeare shows sympathy for older women. At Stratford, he had his aging mother and industrious wife to greet him.

Personal Notes

One secure date is August 11, 1596. On that date, Shakespeare's only son Hamnet, twin of Judith, was buried at Holy Trinity Church, where Shakespeare was buried in 1616. Shakespeare was not a stranger to personal loss. He had three brothers and survived them all, though they were all younger.

Gilbert, the oldest of Shakespeare's brothers, apparently followed his older brother to London. He left little mark on life and was buried at Stratford on February 3, 1612. Richard, the second younger brother, outlived Gilbert by only a year. He was buried at Stratford on February 4, 1613.

The youngest brother, Edmund, became an actor. An actor's life was often undisciplined and rash. Edmund was imprudent. He fathered a son, who died after a month. Edmund barely survived his son. He was buried in December 31, 1607, at St. Saviour's church, Southwark.

During 1596, Shakespeare was apparently involved in securing a coat of arms for his family. John Shakespeare had applied previously but had been turned down. In the 1580s, John's fortunes had taken a turn for the worse. When he reapplied in 1596, the request was granted. The money and prestige of his son undoubtedly had something to do with the successful petition. William, his daughter, and son-in-law used the coat of arms.

Another clue to Shakespeare's rising fortune is the purchase of a sumptuous house in Stratford. Though in London for a good part of his adult life, Shakespeare never forgot the town of his birth. He retired to Stratford after a busy career and was buried there, in the Holy Trinity church. Stratford had not been without problems. Bitter legal disputes and a murder took some of the sheen off Stratford's blissful image. Richard Quiney, Stratford bailiff, had been killed in office, while trying to break up a brawl. Quiney's third son, Thomas, later married Shakespeare's daughter Judith. However distressed Shakespeare may have been by the partial social disintegration, he nevertheless considered Stratford home. On May 4, 1597, Shakespeare bought the second largest mansion in Stratford for a substantial sum. The house brought with it local prestige, as well as a sense of spaciousness. New Place, as it was called, had a frontage of over 60 feet, a depth along the lane of 70 feet, and a height of 28 feet at its northern gable. This was the home of a gentleman, a title applied to the successful Shakespeare.

After repairing the house, Shakespeare settled his wife and daughters there. When he visited from London, he stayed there. When he finally retired from London about 1611, he lived at New Place till his death, a wealthy, respected member of the community. All the events described had an impact on Shakespeare. Scholars enjoy selecting passages from the poems or plays and saying, for example, "Aha, here is a reference to

Shakespeare's lawsuit." Shakespeare is so universal, however, that he defies easy pigeonholing.

During the last decade of the century, Shakespeare's plays began to appear in quarto form, another recognition of his genius by his country-men. A quarto is a fourth of a full sheet. When a full sheet is folded twice, the result is the quarto, about 7 inches by 9. Even the poems *Venus and Adonis* and *The Rape of Lucrece* (p 325) appeared a number of times in the decade and even into the years following the turn of the century.

The quartos of the plays had long been considered almost worthless by scholars when they were compared with the "definitive" text of the First Folio. Recent scholarship, however, has discovered that these early versions often contain textual clues that can settle annoying questions raised by the Folio.

There were no copyright laws then. Literary pirates could try to copy the plays they had listened to. Sometimes the companies sold playbooks to raise cash. In 1597 and 1598, Shakespeare's company sold the playbooks of *Richard III, Richard II, Henry IV, Part One*, and *Love's Labour's Lost*. These subsequently appeared as quartos.

The history of the *Hamlet* quartos suggests some of the looseness of printing at that time. *Hamlet* was probably composed and produced about 1601. Within a few years, two quartos appeared. The First Quarto, often called the "Bad Quarto," appeared in 1603. This was probably recon-structed from actors' memories of the play. The Second Quarto, often called the "Good Quarto," appeared a year later. This was probably based largely on the author's manuscript.

The First Folio of 1623 provided a text at some variance with that of the quartos. Perhaps the Folio contains later revisions. At any rate, schol-ars tried to fathom Shakespeare's intentions, incorporating those emenda-tions that presumably were Shakespeare's. Even today there is no final text, assured in every detail. Current published texts often do not correspond line for line with each other.

Shakespeare's father was buried at Holy Trinity on September 8, 1601, a date closely associated with the composition of *Hamlet*. John left no sur-viving legal will, but William inherited two houses on Henley Street.

Hamlet had brought financial success to the acting company, and Shakespeare apparently had many offers for investing his money. There are records of various investments; Shakespeare was a shrewd businessman. He made two purchases in 1602, for example, including 107 acres in open fields north and east of the town. Shakespeare was aware of the town's prejudices against actors and acting companies. As a respectable landowner, however, he was not rejected. When he was buried in the church, his effigy was that of a poet, not an actor.

During these years, Shakespeare grew in stature as a playwright, taking on more and more challenges. A comparison of *Julius Caesar* and *Hamlet* shows Shakespeare's increasing mastery of technique and maturity of outlook, though but a few years separate their creation. Park Honan has these comments. *Julius Caesar* is "neatly well-mannered, almost timid." But with its wealth of meaning, ambiguities, high-handed contradictions and supreme and troubling beauty, *Hamlet* is nearly a chaos."

It established Shakespeare's place as the world's greatest writer of tragedies. It also made his star, Richard Burbage, the toast of the age. The popularity of *Hamlet* was immediate and enduring. Within a few years of its London production, Captain Keeling's men aboard the Dragon acted *Hamlet* off the coast of Sierra Leone. Sir Thomas Smith, an envoy to the court of Czar Boris Godunov in Moscow, compared events there to *Hamlet*.

Some authors are famous for a single work. The modern writer J.D. Salinger established his reputation with one slender novel, *The Catcher in the Rye*. If Shakespeare had created just one play, *Hamlet*, his place in literature would be assured. Incredibly, he kept on writing plays in the years ahead. Though the exact dating of each play is elusive, the total is not. Within eight years, he created at least eight major plays: comedies, like *All's Well That Ends Well* and tragedies, like *Othello*, *King Lear*, and *Macbeth*. The later comedies show a more mature understanding of the darker side of life. Sometimes called the "dark comedies," they are more complex, more ambivalent, more paradoxical than earlier comedies like *The Taming of the Shrew* and *The Comedy of Errors*.

How did Shakespeare manage this outpouring of genius? In all probability, he occasionally left the stresses of London to visit his family in the beautiful, spacious house he had provided for them. His accurate depiction of family life in the plays suggests that he renewed his ties and replenished hi strength. Though more conspicuous by his absences from New Place, he'd nevertheless play a role in Stratford life, through his investments and his legal activities.

King James I

When Elizabeth died in 1603 without children, James VI, king of Scotland, ascended the English throne as James I, the first Stuart king of England. He was the son of Mary, Queen of Scots, who had been beheaded in 1586 because of treason against Elizabeth. Mary Stuart felt that she had an even better claim to the English throne than Elizabeth. This was her justification.

Both Elizabeth and Mary were descendants of the first Tudor king, Henry VII. Mary was the daughter of James V of Scotland, who was the son of James IV. James IV had married Margaret Tudor, daughter of Henry VII. Thus, Mary's grandmother was a Tudor and her great-grandfather king of England. Why did Mary consider her more distant claim to the throne more powerful than Elizabeth's? After all, although Mary's great-grandfather had been king of England, Elizabeth's father, Henry VIII, had been king. Mary based her "stronger" claim on Elizabeth's possible illegitimacy. Elizabeth was the daughter of Henry and Anne Boleyn, who had been charged with treason and beheaded. Elizabeth's uneasiness was understandable.

Thus, James I was a reasonable claimant to the throne. His mother, who had married Henry Stuart, Lord Darnley, was a direct descendant. Even his father, the dissolute Henry Stuart, was a grandson of that same Margaret Tudor. The fortunes of England and Scotland were intertwined in love and in hate through many centuries and many marriages.

Although the Stuart line ended with the revolution of 1688 and the deposing of James II, the Stuarts kept their claims alive for generations. The last Stuart claimant to the English throne was Charles Stuart, called by the Scots "Bonny Prince Charlie" and by the English the "Young Pretender." In 1746, his defeat at Culloden in northern Scotland ended all Stuart threats to the throne of England.

The problems of writing under intense pressure often resulted in "confused time-schemes, blatant contradictions, changed names, 'ghost' characters who loom up to be forgotten by the author, and other minor faults" as Park Honan points out. Shakespeare learned from experience, however, so that each new play was built upon the foundations of those performances he had already witnessed.

Shakespeare's Family

After the death of Hamnet, Shakespeare had two surviving children: Susanna and Judith, who had been Hamnet's twin. Susanna, his favorite, married Dr. John Hall on June 5, 1607. When the plays explored the loving relationship between a father and a daughter, Shakespeare may have been giving voice to his own feelings about his daughters, especially Susanna.

In 1616, the youngest daughter, Judith, married Thomas Quincy, a young man less reliable than Shakespeare's other son-in-law, John Hall. Despite an inauspicious beginning, the marriage survived. At 77, Judith outlived Susanna by thirteen years. Three of her sons died without issue, one in infancy, the other at 21 and 19.

Susanna had a daughter Elizabeth, who had two marriages but no children. Thus, Shakespeare had no direct descendants. There were many collateral descendants, however. His sister married William Hart. They had five children. From son Thomas's marriage came five other children. The names of those who descended from Shakespeare's nephew Thomas Hart fill a page, a listing taken down only to the sale of the Shakespeare birthplace in 1806.

Shakespeare's mother, Mary Shakespeare, was buried on September 9, 1608. Shakespeare's relationship with his mother has tantalized scholars for centuries. She was apparently an alert, intelligent, strong-minded woman who played a major role in the managing of properties at her original home and at the home in Stratford. One hint that Shakespeare may have feared her more puritanical judgments: he kept the Sonnets out of print until after her death.

The Final Days

In all probability, Shakespeare did not suddenly disappear from the London scene and return irrevocably to Stratford. As would be expected, he kept contact with London and his former fellow players. He even became a partner in the purchase of the Blackfriars Theater gatehouse (p27). This theater shared performances with the Globe. As an indoor theater, it could host performances even in winter.

By the end of 1613, Shakespeare's writing career was over, though he may have acted occasionally. In the quiet Stratford life, he may have had withdrawal symptoms, now and then, away from the hectic life of the London theater. Life in Stratford, was not always serene, however. Though several disputes of various kinds erupted in Stratford, Shakespeare tried to keep neutral or aloof, even when both daughters were involved in controversies.

During the later years, Shakespeare was concerned about his estate, a considerable one for his times. He took several steps to enlarge and preserve it. When illness struck in March, 1616, he took special care in revising his will to suit his decisions.

The illness lingered for a month. Shakespeare became progressively more feeble, and the disease was terminal. When he died on April 23, he had had the best of care at the time, but his family knew the outcome. He was diagnosed with a "fever," an all-encompassing word for a variety of ailments. Some scholars believe it was typhoid. A polluted stream ran beside New Place, a possible source of the infection. His final illness corresponds with the usual symptoms and timeline for typhoid deaths.

The Will

"I give unto my wife my second-best bed with the furniture." By making this strange bequest, Shakespeare effectively cut Anne off from control of the estate. The bequest has generated as much controversy as his feelings toward this wife eight years his senior. Critics who sneer at Shakespeare's marrying an "old maid" have been corrected by the actual statistics. Anne's age, 26, was a fairly common one for first marriages. Shakespeare would not have been considered her last chance.

Those same critics suggest that the "second-best bed" is Shakespeare's final slap at a wife he neither loved nor respected. Another group dismisses such inferences with the simple "We just don't know." It does seem clear that one purpose of the request is to deny Anne of power. There are many possible reasons. He may have loved her but deemed her too inexperienced to manage the legacy. We knew that she would always be cared for by Susanna and John. He may also have distrusted her Hathaway relatives, who may previously have exploited their relationship to Shakespeare. This apparent slight may well have been a protection for a woman inexperienced in handling large sums of money.

Shakespeare's will is complicated, with many legatees. He shows favoritism to Susanna over his daughter Judith, but Judith's husband, Thomas Quincy, had been in and out of difficulties in Shakespeare's later years. He shows his respect for his son-in-law John Hall by making him co-executor with Susanna. He looks into the future and makes some of his bequests dependent on children yet to be born.

Through the years, Shakespeare had collected art objects, bowls, plate, even a sword. These objects were bequeathed to various friends, along with various small sums. By omission from the will, Shakespeare shows his feelings toward individuals like Thomas Quiney, Judith's husband, and Richard Hathaway, Anne's brother. Stoically accepting disappointments in life, Shakespeare after death silently rebuked those who had displeased him. Shakespeare's bequests might have made a play worthy of the dramatist's talents. Perhaps the will is his final play.

2

Shakespeare and the Theater

Can this cockpit hold
The vasty fields of France? Or may we cram
Within this wooden O the very casques (helmets)
That did affright the air at Agincourt?

Henry V, **Prologue, 11-13**

In this introduction to *Henry V*, the actor playing the Prologue urges the players to use their imaginations. The "wooden O," the theater stage, must become the fields at the battle of Agincourt. And why not?

Every performance of any play requires a "willing suspension of disbelief." Theatergoers must forget that they are looking on a bare platform variously decorated and often changed. The stage is not really a mountaintop, as in *The Sound of Music*. It is not the Paris Opera, as in the Phantom of the Opera. It's all make-believe. The playwright and the audience have made an agreement to imagine a bachelor's quarters, as in *My Fair Lady* or a prairie scene, as in *Oklahoma*. It's all light and shadow. When a room scene is represented on the stage, we're looking through a fourth wall, eavesdropping and prying.

The trend in the modern theater is toward ever more spectacular sets: a panicky city with a helicopter overhead in *Miss Saigon* and a sinking ocean liner in the musical *Titanic*.

Shakespeare had no worries about sets. A balcony might represent Juliet's house and a trapdoor might represent the door to the Underworld, but scene 3, of *The Winter's Tale* opens on a seacoast of Bohemia. What did it matter if Bohemia had no seacoast? Shakespeare informs us in the opening words, delivered by Antigonus: "Thou art perfect then, our ship hath touched upon the deserts of Bohemia?" The ship has landed on a deserted coast in Bohemia. It's all there. It's all magic anyway.

The Shakespearean stage relied on costumes and props to set the scene. Two opponents dueling with a scurrying of players back and forth clearly identified a battle scene. More important, though, was the language.

Shakespeare carefully paints or suggests the scene by the magic of his language.

Try These Shakespearean Settings

What scene is Shakespeare painting for us in each of the following selections? Match the selections with the identifications just below. Answers on page 29.

A.	quiet woodland	F.	battlefield
B.	storm at sea	G.	middle of the night
C.	frigid exterior	H.	Italian city
D.	sunset	I.	river procession
E.	peaceful country garden	J.	attractive castle

1. LORENZO. How sweet the moonlight sleeps upon this bank!
   Here will we sit, and let the sounds of music
   Creep in our ears; soft stillness and the night
   Becomes the touches of sweet harmony.
   The Merchant of Venice, V,

1, 55-59

2. HAMLET.   The air bites shrewdly; it is very cold.
HORATIO.   It is a nipping and an eager air.

Hamlet, I, 4, 1-2

3. DUNCAN.   This castle hath a pleasant seat; the air nimbly and sweetly recommends itself unto our gentle senses.

Macbeth, I, 6, 1-2

4. KING RICHARD.   Here pitch our tents, even here in Bosworth Field.
My Lord of Surrey, why look you so sad?

Richard III, V, 3, 1-3

5. BOATSWAIN.   Down with the topmast! yare! lower! Bring her to try with main-course. (A cry within.) A plague upon this howling! They are louder than the weather of our office.

The Tempest, I, 1, 35-38

6. DUKE.   Now, my co-mates and brothers in exile,
Hath not old custom made this life more sweet
Then that of painted pomp? Are not these woods
More free from peril than the envious court?

As You Like It, II, 1, 1-4

7. ENOBARBUS.   The barge she sat in, like a burnished throne, burned on the water.

Antony and Cleopatra, II, 2 191-192

8. EGLAMOUR.   The sun begins to gild the western sky, And
now it is about the very hour That Silvia at
Friar Patrick's cell should meet me.
The Two Gentlemen of Verona, V, 1, 1-3

9. BRUTUS.   What Lucius! ho!
I cannot by the progress of the stars,
Give guess how near to day. Lucius, I say!
I would it were my fault to sleep so soundly.
When,Lucius, when! Awake, I say!
Julius Caesar, II, 1, 1-5

10. LUCENTIO.   Tranio, since for the great desire I had
To see fair Padua, nursery of arts.
I am arrived for fruitful Lombardy,
The pleasant garden of great Italy
The Taming of the Shrew, I, 1, 1-4

A Brief History

When the dying Marcutio says to Romeo in *Romeo and Juliet*. "A plague o' both your houses!" the word plague had an especially sinister ring to Shakespearean audiences. The recurring plague outbreaks were a fact of life for Elizabethan playgoers. The bubonic plague was transmitted to human beings by fleas from infected rats, Authorities did recognize the infectious nature of the disease and took steps to contain the outbreaks. But mortality was high, and attempts to isolate the infectious areas were not always successful. There were major outbreaks in London during the Shakespearean period. Public assemblies were banned in 1563, 1574, 1577, 1578, 1581, 1593, 1603, 1625, and 1636. Smaller outbreaks led to a restraint on plays in 1580, 1583, 1586, 1587, 1594, and 1605. When registered deaths reached 40 in any week, theaters were ordered closed. Since the hot summer months caused a rise in deaths from the plague, actors were often idle during the period of greatest demand. The plague was worst in London, but in 1564, the year of Shakespeare's birth, the country town of Stratford-Upon-Avon lost a quarter of its population to the plague.

Few playhouses have had as many obstacles to overcome as those of the Shakespearean period. The plague was only one problem. Getting plays approved for production was a difficult task at best. Without a royal patron, the going was often rough.

Shakespeare's company was lucky. Formed in 1594, the players had the patronage of the Lord Chamberlain. This was a profit-sharing company. By 1597, six of the group held shares in the company. The great tragic actor Richard Burbage (p 27) and the comic actor Will Kempe (p 31) owned shares. The other shares were held by John Heminge, Thomas Pope, Augustine Phillips, and William Shakespeare.

The major competitor of the company was the Admiral's Men. Their leading actor, Edward Alleyn, brilliantly played the tragedies of Christopher Marlowe (p 49), one of Shakespeare's strongest early competitors. Plays needed theaters, and those were built to accommodate the popular drama. The names of some of these have come down to us: the Theatre, the Curtain, the Rose, the Swan, the Hope, and the Fortune. The most famous of these is the Globe, the theater most closely associated with Shakespeare.

No one is quite certain what the Globe actually looked like, but scholars have made some reasonable guesses. In 1997, a replica of the supposed Globe opened in London. The original Globe had a large uncovered area, since plays were ordinarily produced during the day.

When Elizabeth died and James VI of Scotland became James I of England, the political and theatrical picture changed. Shakespeare's company had the resourcefulness and good fortune to secure the patronage of James I, successor to Queen Elizabeth. They became known as the King's Men. Though the Globe is traditionally the theater most closely associated with Shakespeare, another theater played a role in the later years.

Just as the available actors influenced the plays that Shakespeare wrote, so the physical theater itself played a role in the form and function of the plays themselves. Large theaters lend themselves to plays on a large canvas.

Smaller theaters accommodate more intimate plays. Such a smaller theater, known as Blackfriars, was a suite of rooms within the precincts of the dissolved Blackfriars monastery. In 1575, the site was leased for the presentation of plays featuring children. Difficulties in 1580 interrupted such use until 1596, when James Burbage, father of Richard, bought a section of the building for conversion into a theater. Neighbors protested the inclusion of the theater into a residential area.

James Burbage died in 1597, and it wasn't until 1600 that his son Richard got around the neighbors' objections. A new group, the Children of the Chapel, performed for five years. The company was suspended in 1605 for performing a satire, *Eastward Ho*, which somehow gave offense to the Scots. Since James I was a Scot, the play was an imprudent selection. A new company was formed, again with children. It ran into difficulties with the French, and the company was suppressed.

Here was a theater ready for use, but without a tenant. Ever enterprising, Richard Burbage induced leading players of the King's Men to use Blackfriars alternately with the Globe. The theater survived until 1642, when Oliver Cromwell's orders closed the theaters. One of the members of that new association was William Shakespeare, ever ready for a promising business arrangement. Plays performed at the more intimate Blackfriars Theater tended to appeal to a smaller, more select audience. Shakespeare's later plays reflected these subtle changes. Blackfriars continued long after Shakespeare's death, producing plays by the popular Beaumont and Fletcher (p 56).

Those children's theaters mentioned above were the bane of the adult professional companies. In Act II, scene 2, Rosencrantz tells Hamlet about the companies of children who are putting adult players out of work. These little "eyases" (young hawks) speak shrilly but are wildly applauded for their immature talents.

Hamlet comments wryly that when they grow to become adult players they'll find that their jobs have been destroyed by themselves. They "exclaim against their own succession." Hamlet and the two courtiers converse at length about their growing problem suggesting that the King's Men and others were worried by the success of these young competitors.

The Elizabethan theater was perfect for its times. It grew out of plays performed in inn yards. It encouraged Elizabethan playwrights to create sets by the magic of their verse. It served its purpose but was replaced during the Restoration of King Charles II by a theater more closely resembling our own, with a curtain and elaborate sets. Some contemporary theaters look back to the Elizabethan stage for inspiration.

==

Answers to "Try These Shakespearean Settings"-Pages

1E   2C   3J   4F   5B   6A   7I   8D   9G   10H

3

Shakespeare and His Players

All the world's a stage,
And all the men and women merely players.

As You Like It, II, 7, 139-140

When Scott Rudin, producer of *The Truman Show*, offered the leading role to Jim Carrey, he admitted that he had chosen the script with Jim Carrey in mind as Truman. Over and over again, we learn that plays and films are selected with a specific actor in mind. Indeed, sometimes the material is written visualizing a certain actor in the leading role.

Modern writers, directors, and producers have an easier task than Shakespeare. There are hundreds, thousands of talented actors available to fill nearly any role. Shakespeare had a relative handful.

The actors available shaped the plays that Shakeseare wrote. When he had a giant talent like Richard Burbage, Shakespeare was able to write *Hamlet*, *Macbeth*, *Othello*, and *King Lear*. Without Burbage, Shakespeare's talents would undoubtedly have been channeled in other directions.

Although we can match few actors' names with characters in Shakespeare's plays, we can be reasonably sure that Shakespeare would not write a part if he had no living actor to interpret it on the stage. Here's an example. Certain Welsh comic parts call for an accomplished actor who could manage an acceptable Welsh accent. Glendower, in *Henry IV, Part*

One, and Fluellen, in *Henry V*, add broad Welsh accents and a comic touch to soldiering. We can almost imagine Shakespeare saying, "That actor has a marvelous Welsh accent. I must find a way to use him."

Certain macho male roles appear throughout the plays: Benedick in *Much Ado about Nothing*, Hotspur in *Henry IV, Part One*, and Petruchio in *The Taming of the Shrew* all have a certain masculinity that might have tempted a modern actor like Mel Gibson. Clearly Shakespeare had an actor who could carry these roles effectively.

The clowns in Shakespeare play an important role, not only as humorous commentators, but sometimes as major players. At the beginning of Shakespeare's career, Richard Tarlton was a major comic actor. He established the popular style of stage clown. His performances were intentionally comically confused, awkward, perhaps like the roles Jerry Lewis once played. Though Tarlton himself had died before Shakespeare's plays appeared, his influence undoubtedly helped shape the clowns in Shakespeare's early plays.

A successor to Tarlton, Will Kempe, interpreted great clown parts in Shakespeare's first decade of writing. Kempe probably helped create the comic talents of Bottom in *A Midsummer Night's Dream*. As Dogberry in *Much Ado about Nothing*, he gave comic life to Shakespeare's amusing script. He also probably played Falstaff in *Henry IV, Parts One* and *Two*. His mastery of the role may explain one of the mysteries in Shakespeare.

In an Epilogue at the end of *Henry IV, Part Two*, the speaker says. "Our humble author will continue the story, with Sir John in it." *Sir John* is Sir John Falstaff, who successfully carries the comic action of the two *Henry IV* plays. Falstaff is perhaps Shakespeare's greatest comic creation. Why not include him as promised, in the cast of *Henry V*, the sequel to the *Henry IV* plays?

One explanation offered is that Will Kempe left Shakespeare's company in 1599, selling his share in the company to Shakespeare himself. And so, in *Henry V*, Falstaff does not appear. We hear his death described by the Hostess of the Boar's Head Tavern, Falstaff's favorite hangout. Did Shakespeare feel that a true Falstaff without Will Kempe would be impossible? Or did he feel that the plot of *Henry V* would be strengthened without the overwhelming presence of Falstaff?

Sir John does appear later in a comedy supposedly requested by Queen Elizabeth: *The Merry Wives of Windsor*. But the role of Falstaff in this play calls for different acting abilities from those demonstrated in the two *Henry IV* plays. Falstaff has become a figure of mockery.

Will Kempe's departure from the company in 1599 may have been a blessing in disguise. Robert Armin began to take on the roles of fools, clowns, comic characters. Will Kempe was a big man who specialized in physical humor, perhaps like Kramer in the *Seinfeld* series. By contrast, Robert Armin was a small man, whose talents were more verbal than physical. Except for Falstaff, Kempe played more simple clowns; Armin played complex ones. Shakespeare had found gold in his company. He began to write parts for Armin, Instead of bumbling physical clowns, he created characters like the philosophical Touchstone in *As You Like It* and the clever Feste in *Twelfth Night*. The plays we admire were created to match the available talent.

On the Elizabethan stage, boys played the roles of women. Probably boys of different ages played the various feminine roles. More mature young men would be needed for the heavily dramatic roles of Lady Macbeth and Cleopatra. Again Shakespeare probably wrote these great roles with specific players in mind. Except for a few like Richard Burbage and Robert Armin, these great actors remain nameless.

The Oscar winning film, *Shakespeare in Love*, imagines what Shakespeare's life might have been like about the time he wrote *Romeo and Juliet*. The play takes great liberties with the known facts about Shakespeare but creates a charming picture of what life was like in Shakespeare's London. The play imagines that Shakespeare met a dazzling young lady with whom he fell violently in love. This love affects Shakespeare's poetry and, especially, his creation of *Romeo and Juliet*, first titled *Romeo and Ethel*, the *Pirate's Daughter*! Part of the fun is putting this lovely young lady on the stage in the first performance of the completed *Romeo and Juliet*.

Of all the imaginative touches in the film, this is the most unlikely. The plot touch makes a dazzling conclusion, but it just never happened.

Shakespeare had to tailor his plays to the size of his company. A large canvas like *Hamlet* calls for more players than Shakespeare had available, and so he had to do what many modern acting companies do; have actors play multiple roles. Some Shakespearean characters appear early and then disappear. Other characters first appear late in the plays. Shakespeare was able to double up.

The character Reynaldo in *Hamlet* appears in Act II only. Then Polonius, father of Laertes and Ophelia, sends Reynaldo off to Paris to spy on his son. Reynaldo then disappears from the play, but during this brief scene, we learn a little about Reynaldo and a great deal about Polonius. Nothing is wasted. Osric, a nobleman in the court of King Claudius, appears in Act V as a courtier that Hamlet enjoys mocking. The roles of Reynaldo and Osric are minor and can easily be played by a single actor. They are sufficiently different to give the chosen actor an opportunity to display his versatility.

Throughout the Shakespearean plays there are many opportunities for doubling and even tripling. These opportunities suggest the resourcefulness of the playwright working with a limited company.

We have some idea of the resourcefulness of actors' companies in the play scene in *Hamlet*. The arrival of the traveling players has given Hamlet the idea to stage a murder scene so similar to the actual murder of his father that the guilty uncle, King Claudius, will reveal his guilt. This play-within-a-play performance can be handled by just three actors. These three are essential to play the staged murder; the Player King, the Player Queen, and the murderer, Lucianus. The First Player recites the monologue about Pyrrhus. He can also play the Player King, and earlier receive Hamlet's opinions on acting. "Speak the speech I pray you..." These actors playing these roles could also appear as soldiers, courtiers, or secondary characters like the Captain in Fortinbras's army.

The names of a few actors in Shakespeare's company have survived, but we don't know what roles they played. Of course, all actors appeared in other plays than Shakespeare's. Among the actors whose names have come down to us are Henry Condell, John Heminge, Augustine Philllps, and Richard Cowley. Condell and Heminge performed a service that the theater will always be grateful, for in 1623, seven years after Shakespeare's death, they published the First Folio, a collection of 36 plays. Though some of these had already appeared in short editions called quartos, eighteen of the 36 plays would probably have been lost without the First Folio. These fortunate survivors include such popular plays as *As You Like It*, *The Comedy of Errors*, *Julius Caesar*, *Macbeth*, *The Taming of the Shrew*, and *Twelfth Night*.

It's especially interesting to learn that Shakespeare, as an actor, may have played roles in his greatest plays. Tradition suggests that he took the role of the faithful old servant Adam in *As You Like It* and the Ghost in *Hamlet*. Whatever his abilities as an actor may have been, Shakespeare's colleagues wanted him to spend his time writing plays, not acting in them. We also learn that he was business director of the Lord Chamberlain's Men, later the King's Men (p 27).

In Shakespeare's day, the actors, the playwrights, and the theater owners knew each other well. The acting companies were a harassed group, often scorned, frequently idled by the plague (p 25). They kept working at their craft through financial troubles, fires, and unpredictable disasters. The world is fortunate that they persisted. They didn't know or care that they were creating masterpieces for ages to come. They were just trying to make a living.

4

Directing and Staging

> Speak the speech, I pray you, as I pronounced it to you, trippingly
> on the tongue, but if you mouth it as many of your players do, I had
> as lief the town-crier spoke my lines. Nor do not saw the air too
> much with your hand thus, but use all gently, for in the very torrent,
> tempest, and as I may say whirlwind of your passion, you must
> acquire and beget a temperance that may give it smoothness.
>
> *Hamlet*, III, 2, 1-8

In the four centuries since *Hamlet*, directors have been giving players the
same advice. Standards of good acting don't change very much, but productions do. Shakespeare's bare stage was in the round, with the audience
on three sides. Played in the open air during daylight, the plays relied
upon the playwright's words to set the stage (p 22). By contrast, contemporary directors can call upon a great many stage settings and illusions to
create the desired mood. The danger is overkill, with the display overshad-
owing the words.

The plays of Shakespeare have never been off the stage for extended
periods of time. Through the four centuries, the plays have been interpreted in accordance with the standards and morality of the times.
Shakespeare would not have recognized some of the productions bearing
his name.

In 1660, the triumphant return of Charles II to the English throne after the Cromwell years marked a watershed in theatrical history. Theaters reopened jubilantly. Women took the roles formerly played by boys and young men. Movable scenery accompanied the play's action. The plays were staged indoors away from the weather. Gone were the groundlings. Plays were aimed at a more homogeneous courtly audience. The period, called the *Restoration*, brought an explosion in new plays as well as revivals of the old.

Shakespeare "Improved"

Shakespeare was revived often, but with a difference. Actors, directors, and producers "improved" Shakespeare, removing and adding lines and characters, smoothing over the "rough" spots, changing endings, and still relying on the prestige of the Shakespeare name. Plays were made into "shows." In Sir William Davenant's production of *Macbeth*, the witches sang, flew, and danced, yielding some of their ominous impact to the spectacle.

The desecration of *The Tempest* is even more pronounced. Retitled *The Tempest, or, The Enchanted Isle*, the Shakespearean play is changed almost beyond recognition. Miranda has a male counterpart, Ippolito, also kept secretly on the isle by Prospero. Miranda also has a sister, Dorinda. Ariel has a soul mate called Milcha. Caliban has a sister Sycorax, named after his mother. Comic characters are added. Though Shakespeare relied on his words to create the storm, this staging, and many others, used elaborate special effects to show the ship sinking midst a shower of fire, all accompanied by lightning and thunder. This version was a great success in its day, 1674, but it was a substantial departure from Shakespeare.

The greatest changes tended to be in characterization. John Dryden, a major poet and dramatist of the Restoration, wrote a play, *All for Love*, about the tragic love affair of *Antony and Cleopatra*. Though it parallels Shakespeare's *Antony and Cleopatra*, it diverges from it in the character studies of the two principals. Although not a strict redoing of *Antony and Cleopatra*, *All for Love* helps to clarify the Restoration attitude toward tragedy, different from Shakespeare's.

As noted in a discussion of characters (p 91), Shakespeare's characters are not easily explained. They are complicated and send ambiguous messages. Are they right or wrong in their actions? Shakespeare doesn't tell us. Dryden does. *All for Love* makes clear that Antony and Cleopatra broke the moral law and must suffer. To Shakespeare, the tragedy is not that simple.

Shakespeare was often too painful for Restoration audiences. The poet and dramatist Nahum Tate produced *The History of King Lear*, based upon the Shakespeare tragedy. Tate was so impressed by Shakespeare's play, that he called the tragedy "a heap of jewels, unstrung and unpolished; yet so dazzling in their disorder, that I soon perceived I had seized a treasure." Tate then proceeded to "polish" the jewel! He developed a love plot between Cordelia and Edgar. Cordelia survives and marries Edgar. Lear and Gloucester also survive. Characters are omitted or added, and the tragedy ends in a promise of bliss.

Shakespeare for Every Age

Each era seems to produce its own Shakespeare. The eighteenth century restored more of the original text, but actors continued to take liberties to enhance their own roles or feature their own special talents. Charles Macklln, James Quin, and David Garrick interpreted many of the Shakespearean roles. Contemporary descriptions of their art suggest that these interpretations were perhaps a bit too theatrical for modern tastes, but the actors were the stars of their own age.

The Kemble family produced five famous actors, including Sarah Kemble Siddons, whose performances straddled two centuries. The nineteenth century produced many other actors whose fame resonates through any history of Shakespearean performances: Edmund Kean, Henry Irving, William Charles Macready, Charles Kean, Ellen Terry, and Herbert Beerbohm Tree, America produced Edwin Forrest and Edmund Booth, whose brother John Wilkes Booth played a tragic role in American history.

All these actors put an individual spin on the roles they played. Sarah Siddons was famous for her sleepwalking scene in *Macbeth*, Edmund Kean for his Shylock, John Philip Kemble for his Coriolanus.

The twentieth century has brought forth actors too numerous to enumerate. Just to mention the interpreters of Hamlet requires a sizable list, among them John Barrymore, John Gielgud, Laurence Olivier, Richard Burton, Maurice Evans, Kenneth Branagh, and Mel Gibson. Shakespearean actresses like Maggie Smith, Judi Dench, and Joan Plowright have also conquered other roles in film.

Shakespeare has always been popular abroad, even in non-English-speaking countries. Though something is inevitably lost in any translation, enough content gets through to keep foreign audiences happy.

As the theaters grew larger, the spectacles tended to intrude on the poetry. In *Shakespeare on the Stage*, Robert Speaight declares, "From the beginning of the nineteenth century on into our own times, theaters were to get bigger and bigger, and progressively worse adapted for the performance of Shakespeare's plays," Still, Shakespeare has survived.

Shakespeare for Every Director

When faced with a Shakespearean play, directors and producers think, "How can we make this somewhat different from the usual, yet remain true to the spirit of Shakespeare's plays?" Unfortunately, the staging sometimes overwhelms the play. Even in the memory of a single playgoer, there are a great variety of settings and times. *Hamlet* has been played traditionally in Elizabethan costumes, in rehearsal clothes, in modern dress, in a nineteenth-century kingdom. *Much Ado about Nothing* has been set at the turn of the century. Constable Dogberry and his comical crew were dressed as the Keystone Cops of the early Mack Sennett movies. *A Midsummer Night's Dream* has been set in a lavish Hollywood "forest," a bare stage with gymnasium equipment, and a lovely Tuscan countryside. One production used a gauze at the front of the stage to give the mysterious feeling of fairyland. The fairies have been represented by beautiful women, mischievous children, and puppets.

A good director has a sense of the total desired effect and may even have his own favorite interpretations of key lines. If he is wise, however, he'll consider the actor's suggestions, even if ultimately he must reject them. When actors feel they have creative input, they tend to do a better job.

John Barton, outstanding director of Shakespeare for the Royal Shakespeare Company, invites his actors to provide their own interpretations. If they seem wide of the mark, he'll gently interject with a "Don't you think...?" The two then debate the merits of alternative interpretations before choosing one. John Barton is a facilitator, not a dictator.

The discussion inevitably involves stage business, too. An actor may bring a prop that ultimately finds its way into the performance. Apart from the nuances of a given line, there is the stage business that accompanies the lines. There is a temptation to pad a part with unnecessary and distracting gestures. (Remember Hamlet's advice to the players, quoted at the beginning of this chapter?)

In Act II, scene I, Hamlet berates Ophelia because he fears that she may be in league with the King and her father Polonius. Hamlet speaks bitterly, departs, returns and continues his tirade, ending with "to a nunnery go." Off he goes. Shakespeare stops there, but the director sometimes doesn't. In some staged versions, Hamlet returns to kiss Ophelia's hand before departing again. The director is thus taking a stand on the question of Hamlet's true feelings for the unfortunate Ophelia. This action may well be debated: does it "solve" the riddle of Hamlet's love for Ophelia? Shakespeare, however, keeps us guessing. Even in the graveyard scene later, when Hamlet wildly professes his love for Ophelia, we may discern in his outburst a touch of theatrical demonstrativeness. Ultimately Shakespeare doesn't commit himself totally on the question of Hamlet's true feelings toward Ophelia. That loving return to Ophelia's side is contradicted by the text itself. The King and Polonius have been spying on Hamlet and Ophelia. At the end of the painful episode, the King says, "Love! his affections do not that way tend." If the two men had seen Hamlet lovingly return to show his love for Ophelia, the King would not have made that dread pronouncement.

Directors can go further afield. In Herbert Beerbohm Tree's production, Ophelia collapsed on a couch. Hamlet sneaked back and, unseen by her, kissed one of the tresses of her hair! The spare and cruel beauty of the entire scene ends in a touch of pure sentimentality, out of character for Hamlet.

The Interpretation of Key Lines

The stage-business just described is different from the challenges of line interpretations. Here both director and actors can interpret in new and daring ways that still lie within the total effect of the play. When Macbeth comes down the stairs after murdering Duncan, Lady Macbeth has a simple exclamation: "My husband!" Macbeth is tottering, his arms bathed in blood, and the two daggers still clasped in his hands.

How does Lady Macbeth deliver those two simple words? What are her feelings?

Is she shocked, in spite of her seemingly exterior? Is she dismayed to find Macbeth with the incriminating evidence still in his hands? Is she proud that he has had the courage to do the deed? Is she suddenly nervously aware of the possible consequences of this bloody deed? Is she inquisitively asking about the deed? How does she feel at this point? Shakespeare doesn't tell us specifically. He relies on the total picture to help us make up our minds. If we don't agree, that's fine with him!

There's another line in *Macbeth* that has come in for critical evaluation over the centuries. In Act V, Lady Macbeth enters, reading a letter from Macbeth describing his meeting with the Three Witches. He writes, "When I burned in desire to question them further, they made themselves air, into which they vanished." This is a fairly straightforward sentence, not especially available to a dramatic reading, but Mrs. Siddons made history by pausing slightly before the word air; "made themselves...air." Critics picked up this reading and said it expressed "ten times the wonder with which Macbeth and Banquo actually beheld the vanishing of the witches." To this day, that interpretation is remembered as a creative triumph. Surely this is a minor variation, but it demonstrates how important the actor's interpretation can be. Shakespeare provides all those skeletons. The actors flesh out the bones.

The Soliloquies

When it comes to the great set pieces, like the soliloquies, interpretations vary considerably. A good example is the "To be or not to be" speech in Hamlet. Every actor approaches this soliloquy with nervous tremors. The speech is so famous that Winston Churchill is said to have mouthed the words, audibly, along with the actor. What shall Hamlet do with it? Is it a contemplation of suicide or something else altogether? What words should he emphasize? Should he speak in a conversational tone, or in a mood of heightened anxiety? Are some portions of the speech intended for emphasis? Should he pause thoughtfully after "Ay there's a rub," or should he keep the rhythm of the sentence intact. The speech is long, boring if recited without feeling, but always fascinating as a key to Hamlet's mind. Then there's the greeting to Ophelia at the end of this soliloquy. How shall Hamlet speak these lines? He has been interrupted in his reverie. Is he annoyed, indifferent, genuinely touched by finding his former love? All these considerations enter into the delivery of just this one speech. Then there's the rest of the play.

An even more challenging soliloquy occurs after Hamlet has heard the Players performing a piece about the fall of Troy (p287). Though the death of King Priam, husband of Hecuba means nothing to him, the First Player undergoes an emotional transformation. When the stage is clear, Hamlet says:

> Now I am alone.
> O, What a rogue and peasant slave am I!
> Is it not monstrous that this player here,
> But in a fiction, in a dream of passion,
> Could force his soul so to his own conceit
> That from her working all his visage wanned,
> Tears in his eyes, distraction in his aspect,
> A broken voice, and his whole function suiting
> With forms to his conceit; and all for nothing!
> For Hecuba!
> What's Hecuba to him, or he to Hecuba,
> That he should weep for her? What would he do,
> Had he the motive and the cue for passion
> That I have?
>
> *Hamlet*, II, 2, 552-565

The "to be" soliloquy is the one most closely associated with Hamlet, but this Hecuba speech may be even better: a gem, an actor's dream. In its 57 lines, it runs the gamut from rational deliberation to a wild outcry, close to lack of control. Line 585 has the cry "O, vengeance!" How shall this key line be rendered?

Fortunately, in this day of electronic reproduction, we have the voices of many great Hamlets, going all the way back to John Barrymore, whose voice was recorded on an old disc. Comparing the interpretations is an education in acting. The Barrymore interpretation, in keeping with the standards of another day, is somewhat exaggerated. He screams the words "0, vengeance!" in a way not attempted by modern Hamlets.

It is possible, on audiotape or videotape, to hear the interpretations of John Gielgud, Maurice Evans, Nicoll Williamson, Richard Burton, Paul Scofield, Laurence Olivier, Kevin Kline, Mel Gibson, and Kenneth Branagh. The interpretations are all different, as indeed they should be. Such a comparison is as good an introduction to the actor's art as can be found.

The Character as a Whole

Then there's the question of the character as a whole. The actor must develop a focus, an interpretation that gives life to the words. The actor who attempts Othello, for example, must determine the kind of image the central character projects. As one of the most consistently successful and popular of Shakespeare's plays, *Othello* has attracted the greatest actors of every period. Yet, according to the eyewitness accounts of the performances, the central interpretations have varied widely. In a recent filmed version, Lawrence Fishburn played a powerful military leader, a person of overwhelming presence. This is, perhaps, the favorite interpretation, but there have been Othellos who projected an earlier vulnerability that foreshadowed the tragedy at the end.

Othello and Iago are paired gems. Actors sometimes like to alternate roles. In 1881, Edmund Booth alternated playing Iago with Henry Irving. More recently, Ralph Richardson and Laurence Olivier played Othello and

Iago on succeeding nights, a treat for London theatergoers, who enjoyed the subtle differences in the way two great actors interpreted the roles. The directors must make decisions in every play. Consider the role of Queen Gertrude in *Hamlet*. Most actresses interpret Gertrude as a loving but rather superficial woman, easily swayed by others. There is, however, a decision that must be made about Gertrude's relationship with King Claudius. At the beginning of the play, she is unquestionably charmed by her new husband, entirely content with her new status as wife to Claudius. Hamlet, however, strikes a discordant note. In the closet scene, he berates his mother, actually accusing Claudius of murdering her former husband, Hamlet's father. This accusation should certainly turn Gertrude away from Claudius. But Shakespeare, as always, makes things complex. The Ghost appears only to Hamlet, not to Gertrude. She says:

> This the very coinage of your brain!
> The bodiless creation ecstasy
> Is very cunning in.
>
> *Hamlet*, III, 4, 137-139

She thinks Hamlet is mad and reports that madness to the King. Has Hamlet's tirade against her had an effect on her feelings toward the King? She realizes that she did marry quickly after the death of King Hamlet. Earlier, she had shown pangs of conscience during the reproach:

> O' Hamlet, speak no more,
> Thou turn'st my eyes into my very soul,
> And there I see such black and grained spots
> As will not leave their tinct.
>
> *Hamlet*, III, 4, 88-91

Should she show on the stage the effects of Hamlet's censure? Shakespeare doesn't help us decide. When Laertes bursts in later, threatening to kill the King, Gertrude defends Claudius, telling Laertes that it wasn't Claudius who killed Laertes' father. At this point she still seems to have some feelings for the King, but there is that conscience-stricken admission quoted above.

There comes a moment when the director must make a decision. In the scene just after Polonius's murder, Gertrude, Claudius, Rosencrantz and Guildenstern share the stage. Finally, the two courtiers depart, leaving the stage to Gertrude and Claudius. Then the stage directions in the First Folio say, "Exeunt": "They go out." How do they go? In one production, Gertrude went off to the left by herself. Claudius looked sadly at her departure and then went off to the right. This decision suggested that Gertrude had indeed been affected by Hamlet's words and the challenge of her relationship with Claudius. Is this decision justified? Is the director taking too much upon himself? There is nothing in the text to tilt the decision either way. The suggested alienation is possible. Does it retain the spirit of the play? Playgoers must decide for themselves.

Conventions of Another Day

Shakespeare's language was a bit different from our own (p119). The stage conventions were different, too, causing modern directors and text editors some headaches. A good example of a puzzle is the pronouncement of Lady Macbeth's death, as it was reported in the First Folio:

MACBETH.	What is that noise?
SEYTON.	It is the cry of women, my good lord.
MACBETH.	I have almost forgot the taste of fears:
	The time has been, my senses would have cooled
	To hear a night-shriek, and my fell of hair
	Would at a dismal treatise rouse and stir
	As life were in't: I have supped full with horrors;
	Direness, familiar to my slaughterous thoughts,
	Cannot once start me. Wherefore was that cry?
SEYTON.	The Queen, my lord, is dead.

Macbeth, V, 5, 7-15

Then follows the famous "Tomorrow, and tomorrow, and tomorrow" speech. But what is most interesting is how Seyton suddenly knows that the Queen is dead. To answer Macbeth's first question, he merely replied "The cry of women, my good lord."

Modern editors and directors assume that there is a missing stage direction. They usually have Seyton leave the stage after his first answer to find out what has happened. Then he returns just as Macbeth asks, "Wherefore was that cry?" This makes perfect sense in a logical, reasonable world. Alan C. Dessen, however, suggests that Seyton's uncanny knowledge emphasizes the mystery engendered by the Three Witches. "After all, how do the witches know what they know? Perhaps Shakespeare did not intend Seyton to inquire after the Queen. Perhaps Shakespeare preferred to nourish the sense of mystery.

Challenging Interpretations

Traditional interpretations are sometimes challenged to the delight of some critics and the dismay of others. In a 1982 production with Christopher Walken as Hamlet, Lisabeth Bartlett as Ophelia won the praise of stern drama critic Walter Kerr. He called her presence "penetrating and fiercely animated She's not wispy, wistful, self-pitying. She is in a fury." This is a far cry from the weak, pitiful Ophelias so often presented. Yet this different Ophelia didn't stray from Shakespeare's words.

Among the great "set pieces" is Portia's speech on mercy in *The Merchant of Venice*. It has often been quoted, sometimes used as a recitation piece for precocious children. If it is delivered mechanically with little change of emphasis, it falls flat. It doesn't stand alone in the play as a bit of Shakespearean philosophy. It is a direct answer to a question put by Shylock: "On what compulsion must I (be merciful)?"

Portia's first line can be misread. For an effective responsive reply, she pauses a moment, looks at Shylock almost imploringly, and says in a voice of reasonable explanation: "The quality of mercy is not strained." There is no compulsion involved. It is given freely, without thought of gain.

On the other hand, if Portia delivers the speech pompously and self-righteously, she becomes a smug, patronizing scold. An actor's interpretation is partially determined by the temper of the age in which the play is performed. Just as the productions of *Henry V* by Laurence Olivier and Kenneth Branagh (p 70) were influenced by external events, so the performance of every play carries the mark of its period. *The Taming of the Shrew* is a good example. In a male-dominated age, it can be played for crude laughs at the expense of hapless Katharina, finally getting her just deserts. But a clever cast can give a different tone to the play. In a feminist age, the battle of the sexes can be seen with a more sympathetic eye toward Katharina. It is true that Petruchio has some domineering lines early on, but even the strongest lines can be delivered with affectionate humor. Petruchio always speaks with courtesy and restraint. This "underlying delicacy," as it has been called, leaves Katharina some dignity and paves the way for the ultimate reconciliation. Sympathetic actors can suggest that the "taming" involves two characters possibly in love from their first meeting.

How can the final long speech of submission at the end of Act V satisfy a feminist age? Katharina has 44 lines in which to praise the man's role in a happy marriage and describe the woman's. She scolds her sister Bianca and the Widow for their lack of respect. This does indeed seem like complete capitulation to the demands of her husband, but a clever actress playing Katharina can suggest that the ideal marriage is one of mutual respect free of self-indulgence. Bianca, initially the prize for marriage, is shown as spoiled, not an ideal mate. Petruchio shows that he has been completely "tamed" also, when he says, "Come on, and kiss me, Kate."

"In Accents Yet Unknown", after the murder of Julius Caesar, Cassius declares:

> How many ages hence
> Shall this our lofty scene be acted over
> In states unborn and accents yet unknown!
> *Hamlet*, III, 1, 112-114

Of all the lines in Shakespeare, these are perhaps the most prophetic. That "lofty scene," along with the rest of Shakespeare, is indeed acted over and over again in nations that came to birth after Shakespeare's times. More than any other artist, Shakespeare has earned the label *universal.*

5

The Rivals of Shakespeare

I pray you all stand up.
I know you two are rival enemies:
How comes this gentle concord in the world,
That hatred is so far from jealousy
To sleep by hate, and fear no enmity?

A Midsummer Night's Dream, IV, 1,140-145

Theseus (p211) is amazed that former rivals have resolved their differences and become friends. So, we can imagine, Shakespeare and many of his rival playwrights ultimately became friends, sometimes even collaborators.

Robert Greene

Older than Shakespeare by six years, Robert Greene has given scholars the earliest literary reference to Shakespeare, an uncomplimentary comment about actors in general, a specific reference to an "upstart crow," usually identified with the newly popular William Shakespeare. As one of the University Wits, Greene popularized Elizabethan dramas in the 1580s and looked down his nose at those who were not university bred. Greene led a sad, dissolute life, dying at thirty-two.

After Greene's death, Henry Chettle, Greene's publisher, issued a public apology to Shakespeare. It is ironic that Greene wrote plays of his own, even wrote a romantic novel used by Shakespeare as his plot for *Measure for Measure* many years later.., but Greene is principally famous for making that derogatory comment about Shakespeare!

George Peele

Another University Wit, George Peele, is celebrated for a hit play, *The Old Wives' Tale*. Some critics believe that Peele also had a hand in several early Shakespeare plays, but the consensus now does not support that claim. Peele is remembered chiefly as one of Shakespeare's immediate predecessors.

A Noble Brood

Shakespeare was not an isolated genius. As the great critic William Hazlitt said, Shakespeare "was one of a race of giants-the tallest, the strongest, the most graceful and beautiful of them; but it was a noble brood." We can imagine that in the relatively limited world of the theater, the playwrights knew each other, competed for attention, cross-fertilized each other with creative ideas, socialized, quarreled, reconciled. Many careers overlapped. Marlowe, Kyd, and Shakespeare all had productions on the stage at the same time. After Marlowe and Kyd had gone, Ben Jonson came along to provide stimulating competition. As Jonson and Shakespeare were disappearing, other playwrights arrived on the scene, creating plays that still filled the theaters.

Christopher Marlowe

Of all of Shakespeare's rivals, Christopher Marlowe stands out, partly in dramatic contrast to Shakespeare. Born in the same year as Shakespeare, Marlowe was more precocious, achieving fame earlier than Shakespeare. His lifestyle was quite different from Shakespeare's. So far as can be gleaned from the sources, Shakespeare led a reasonably uneventful life for an actor. We know of no serious brawls, no passionate love affairs other than those uncertainly inferred from his work. He retired while still young and died, prematurely, of some disease, possibly typhoid.

Marlowe's life is a study in contradictions. He led a dissolute life, given to drunken brawls. Yet he created some of the most glorious poetry in all of English literature. At one time he was a soldier in the Netherlands, from which he was deported for counterfeiting gold coins. He took part in street fights, in one of which a man was killed. Most critics think he was a spy in the service of Queen Elizabeth. Possibly something went awry. He was mysteriously killed during this service by a government agent, who was immediately pardoned. The way the story is usually told is that he was killed in a tavern dispute over a bill, but the details are obscure. There is much of a romantic mystery about the life of Christopher Marlowe.

What is not in doubt is the extent of his abilities. In 1587, at the age of 23, he created the great tragedy *Tamburlaine*. A landmark in English literature, it established blank verse (p.) as the medium for drama, often called the "mighty line," Marlowe's blank verse was often imitated but seldom equaled. It took the maturing Shakespeare some time to challenge Marlowe on his own terms. In its grand design and scope, *Tamburlaine* invited other dramatists to meet Marlowe's brilliant challenge.

Marlowe's hero Tamburlaine (usually spelled *Tamerlane*) was a Mongol conqueror who ravished vast areas, from Turkey to India. A ruthless warrior, he is reputed to have slaughtered 80,000 defenders of Delhi and made a pyramid of their skulls. Marlowe takes this fearsome butcher and makes him a poet who expresses himself in action. Conquest after conquest is interspersed with scenes of tenderness toward his wife Zenocrate. The play is filled with excitement, passion, and heightened emotion. There are stretches of excellent poetry, many of those lines spoken by Tamburlaine himself. Audiences were overwhelmed.

Success encourages imitation. Robert Greene wrote *Alphonsus of Aragon* and George Peele wrote *Battle of Alcazar*, but these were pale copies. Meanwhile Marlowe moved ahead to a different battleground, that of the mind. He took an old medieval story of a magician who had sold his soul to the devil in exchange for supernatural powers. His play *Dr. Faustus* contains many celebrated lines, including his tribute to Helen of Troy, summoned by the devil at Dr. Faustus' command:

> Was this the face that launched a thousand ships,
> And burnt the topless towers of Ilium?

Sweet Helen, make me immortal with a kiss.

In *Troilus and Cressida*, Shakespeare has written lines reminiscent of Marlowe's tribute to Helen. Troilus tells the Trojan leader Hector:

> Why, she is a pearl
> Whose price hath launched above a thousand ships
> And turned crowned kings to merchants.
> *Troilus and Cressida*, II, 2, 81-83

Time passes. As the demons approach to take his soul, the doomed magician cries out for the dissolution of his immortal soul to save it from eternal damnation.

> O soul, be changed into little water-drops,
> And fall into the ocean—ne'er be found.

This was all heady stuff, and the audiences ate it up. So, too, did other playwrights. His effect on others, including Shakespeare, is profound. As noted above, Shakespeare pays tribute to Marlowe throughout his plays, actually quoting a line in *As You Like It* from Marlowe's poem *Hero and Leander* (p 11): "who ever loved that loved not at first sight?"

Marlowe's influence on Shakespeare can be traced in later plays. Shakespeare's *A Merchant of Venice* owes a debt to Marlowe's *The Jew of Malta*. Marlowe's history play *Edward II* has been compared favorably with Shakespeare's *Richard II* and *Richard III*. Marlowe had raised English drama to a new level. He had introduced great beauty into his plays. He had filled the stage with powerful personalities. He had presented scenes of great emotion and beauty. Who knows what Marlowe might have accomplished...but he was killed in his twenty-ninth year. In Shakespeare's twenty-ninth year, his greatness was still ahead of him. Had he died then, Shakespeare might have been considered a minor playwright, overshadowed by Marlowe.

Thomas Kyd

Outstanding playwright, along with Marlowe, when Shakespeare began his career, Thomas Kyd is most famous for a landmark play produced about 1588: *The Spanish Tragedy*. This new type, the revenge tragedy, like the horror films of our own day, was immensely popular for a long period. It featured retribution for evil, and the repayment included blood, murders, mutilations, and often insanity, or feigned insanity. Sometimes the supernatural was called in to stir the pot. Does this sound familiar? Except for mutilations, *Hamlet* includes all the other features. If *Hamlet* can loosely be called a kind of revenge tragedy, the type has been transformed by the genius of Shakespeare.

Shakespeare's early tragedy, *Titus Andronicus* (p219), was also influenced by the rousing success of *The Spanish Tragedy*. Even *Richard III*, *Julius Caesar*, and *Macbeth* include some elements of the type. Some critics also believe that Kyd had written by 1589 an early version of *Hamlet*, called the *Ur-Hamlet*. The text is lost, but it is conjectured that the major plot lines came from the same source as Shakespeare's *Hamlet*. What Shakespeare did with his sources (Chapter 17) reflects Shakespeare's genius.

Kyd was a close friend of Christopher Marlowe; he was arrested along with Marlowe for atheism and immorality. When he was tortured, he recanted, but his career was blunted. He died in poverty in 1594 a year after Marlowe. He was thirty-six.

Ben Jonson

O rare Ben Jonson!

This famous epitaph was paid for by Sir John Young, who was upset many years after Jonson's death at seeing his neglected grave. He gave a mason eighteen pence to carve the tribute. Since then, Jonson has been gradually restored as one of the great playwrights of the period, second only to Shakespeare.

Jonson's life reads like improbable fiction. Born nine years after Shakespeare, Jonson would play a major role in Shakespeare's life and career. His early life wasn't easy. After his father's death, Jonson's mother married a bricklayer. Jonson worked for a while in this trade, but he had as much respect for the job as his stepfather had for his writing. Always hotheaded and opinionated, Jonson found himself embroiled in many quarrels. His idealism and love of adventure motivated him to enlist with the English supporters of the Netherlands against Spain. During his service, he challenged a Spaniard to single combat and killed him.

Jonson was in London about 1592, trying to make a living by his pen. He married a woman whom he described as "a shrew yet honest," and became a father to a son he called "his best piece of poetry." Jonson was crushed when the plague killed that son at the age of seven.

Jonson's life in London didn't run smoothly. He quarreled with the actor Gabriel Spencer and killed him in a duel "with a blade ten inches shorter than Spencer's." He was imprisoned, but he benefited by an ancient law. Because he could read Latin, he was given "benefit of clergy" and released with a fine. His property was confiscated, however, and his thumb was branded with a T. This was a warning against future offenses. Thereafter, a similar capital crime would mean Tyburn: the gallows.

Jonson's recklessness was evidenced by another episode. In 1605, John Marston and George Chapman wrote *Eastward Ho*, a play deemed insulting to the new king, James I. Jonson voluntarily joined the two playwrights in prison, claiming equal responsibility for the play. The charge against them was serious, and they might have had their noses and ears clipped. Jonson's popularity saved the day, however, and the men were released. Jonson was fearless, often testing the limits of censorship.

At first, Jonson made a living by reworking the scripts of other playwrights. He doctored that old standby, *The Spanish Tragedy*, but he would not long continue to waste his talent and energy on other playwrights' works. He came into his own in 1598 with the production of his hit play *Every Man in His Humour*. Shakespeare probably had a major acting role in this production.

Jonson has been compared with Charles Dickens in his ability to accentuate character's humorous quirks. Shakespeare uses the same technique with his minor characters, like Pistol, Nym, and even Malvolio, but Jonson applied this artistry to his principal characters.

The title of the play needs a brief explanation. In medieval times, the four chief fluids of the human body were called humours (p119): blood, phlegm, black bile, and yellow bile. These humours were linked with the basic four elements: air (cold), fire (hot), water (moist), and earth (dry). Blood was hot and moist; yellow bile hot and dry; phlegm cold and moist; and black bile cold and dry. According to this philosophy, good health requires a balance of all elements. When one humor predominates, disease or misery follows. In Jonson's play, all the principal characters but one are driven by a special "humour." Plots, counterplots, absurd situations, all activated by eccentric characters, delighted Londoners and influenced the course of comedy.

As is so often true, Jonson wrote an unsuccessful sequel, *Every Man Out of His Humour*. The play contains a comment that some critics consider a veiled barb against Shakespeare, who had recently acquired a gentleman's coat of arms. Shakespeare's motto "non sanz droigt," meaning "not without right," may have been satirized in Jonson's "not without mustard."

The relationship between Jonson and Shakespeare has been evaluated, debated, and studied ever since. It is true that after Shakespeare's death, Jonson made a critical comment.

> I remember, the Players have often mentioned it as an honour to Shakespeare, that in his writing, whatsoever he penn'd, he never blotted out a line. My answer hath beene, would he have had blotted out a thousand.

But in the same notes, he wrote "I lov'd the man, and do honour his memory on this side Idolatry." Jonson evaluated Shakespeare's towering superiority more accurately than any other contemporary.

The two comments probably sum up their relationship. While it is true that they were rivals, competing for audiences, there are many stories-some verifiable, some mere legends-of their friendship. Shakespeare acted not only in the *Humour* play mentioned above but also in Jonson's major tragedy *Sejanus*. That role, in 1603, may have been Shakespeare's last appearance on stage. The ultimate proof of Jonson's affection for Shakespeare is the preface to the First Folio, which included this tribute: "He was not of an age, but for all time."

Jonson was an austere literary critic, perhaps the sharpest of the period. There is some evidence that Shakespeare made a slight revision in *Julius Caesar* as a result of a Jonson criticism. Jonson didn't spare any of his fellow playwrights. Shortly after the turn of the century, the celebrated "war of the theaters" began. Jonson objected to a caricature of him by the playwright John Marston in his play *Histriomastix*. Jonson countered by poking at Marston's style in *Every Man Out of His Humour*." The war was on. Other poets entered the fray, though there is no certain evidence that Shakespeare took any part in this battle of the wits.

Jonson wrote many more plays, popular on the London stage. *Volpone*, revived from time to time on our own stages, is a bitter satire on greed and hypocrisy. Though the theme of the play is grim and negative, there are many amusing touches that evoke laughter in modern audiences. *Volpone* is sometimes labeled a "dark comedy," like Shakespeare's *Measure for Measure*. Though comedy predominated in later years, Jonson managed to squeeze in a tragedy like *Catiline*. In his mastery of satirical comedy, he has been compared with George Bernard Shaw.

John Lyly

Ten years older than Shakespeare, John Lyly had the same short life span: 52 years. Because Lyly preceded Shakespeare, he was famous long before Shakespeare became a force in the London theater. His success prompted Shakespeare to imitate him, borrow ideas from him, and even parody the overblown style that Lyly affected.

Lyly was not part of the hectic scene that Marlowe, Shakespeare, and Jonson inhabited. His plays were aristocratic, intended for the pleasure of the upper classes. He courted royal favor and dreamt of becoming Master of the Revels (p 12), a position he never won. His plays are tales of idealized country life, love stories for the elite. Written in prose, unlike the blank verse (p110) of Marlowe and Shakespeare, the plays nevertheless include beautiful songs.

A comparison of Lyly and Shakespeare accentuates the superior artistry of Shakespeare. Though he was strongly influenced by Lyly's plays of pastoral life, Shakespeare escaped the narrow boundaries of mischievous cupids, beautiful nymphs, and other mythical trappings. His characters are human beings. Still, Lyly's influence on Shakespeare was profound. Not on Marlowe, however! His rugged, larger-than-life characters owe little or nothing to the delicate characters and settings of Lyly.

John Lyly also wrote plays for the children's companies, criticized by Hamlet when he gets news of the theater from Rosencrantz and Guildenstern.

Beaumont and Fletcher

One of the most famous effective collaborations in literary history is that of Beaumont and Fletcher. They wrote plays independently, but together their creations charmed London audiences from 1609 until Beaumont's retirement in 1613.

John Fletcher was born in 1579, fifteen years after Shakespeare. His career was a long and honorable one. Both he and Francis Beaumont came from the upper middle classes. They entered the theater scene during periods of change. During the last decade of the century, Shakespeare had been attempting to please a cross-section of the population of London. After the turn of the century, the audiences tended to be more select and homogeneous, as at the Blackfriars Theater (p 27). The composition and attitudes of the audience influenced the content and direction of the plays.

Francis Beaumont was five years younger than Fletcher. They came together for an inspired collaboration in 1609, with *The Knight of the Burning Pestle*, a kind of tragicomedy, with elements of both tragedy and comedy. *Philaster* and *The Maid's Tragedy* followed within a few years. Beaumont married and retired in 1613, leaving Fletcher to create plays on his own and to collaborate with other playwrights.

Shakespeare was the leading dramatist of the King's Men (p 27) until his retirement. After that, Fletcher assumed the role. His successor was Philip Massinger, who lasted almost until the closing of the theaters in 1642.

Fletcher's output was substantial. He, Shakespeare and Ben Jonson were the only poets honored with a Folio edition of their works. In 1647, they were labeled the "Triumvirate of Wit" and considered the major dramatists of their time. Shakespeare's influence upon Fletcher was probably strong. The reverse was also probably true. Indeed, a strong case can be made for the possibility that they collaborated, possibly on three plays, probably on one.

Of those three plays, one of them *Cardenio*, has been lost. More than a century later, the famous editor, Lewis Theobald, produced a play, presumably *Cardenio*, that he claimed to have found on an old manuscript. His claim has never been substantiated. The situation with *The Two Noble Kinsmen* is more complex. A substantial number of scholars insist that Shakespeare wrote portions of this play, helping the young Fletcher to turn out a usable manuscript. A blow to those who see in it the strong pen of Shakespeare is its omission from the First Folio.

A play that is included in the Folio is *Henry VIII*. There are all kinds of theories about the authorship. The case for Shakespeare's total authorship is growing, but there are still critics who assign various portions of the play to Fletcher. One critic even theorized that portions of the original manuscript were burned in the Globe fire of 1613 and that Fletcher had to insert some lines of his own to complete the play. Whatever the truth may be, John Fletcher was another giant of that glorious period.

George Chapman

Much have I travelled in the realms of gold…

This is the first line of a famous sonnet by John Keats. Titled "On First Looking into Chapman's Homer," it pays a glowing tribute to the man who translated the *Iliad* and the *Odyssey* for Shakespeare's contemporaries. In another day, George Chapman may not have written for the theater.

During his lifetime, the theater provided the major literary opportunity. Chapman had other talents, however. In 1598, the first printed portions of Chapman's *Homer* appeared. Through the following years, along with his plays, Chapman continued the task of translating the two Homeric epics. This is the masterwork for which he wished to be chiefly known.

Shakespeare and Chapman influenced each other. Looking for similarities of phrasing and imagery in their plays provides an interesting hobby, for Shakespeare enthusiasts. Chapman's influence upon *Troilus and Cressida* is well established. Whether or not the two playwrights were friends is uncertain, but in the narrow world of the London theater, everybody probably knew everybody.

John Webster

Called "the final Elizabethan," John Webster was a younger contemporary of Shakespeare's. He paid his dues. In the early 1600s, he collaborated with other playwrights. He came into his own, however, with two plays, classed with the greatest in the English language: *The White Devil* and *The Duchess of Malfi*. Unlike the plays of less-talented contemporaries, these two are sometimes played even today. Although Webster continued to collaborate and also to write his own plays, nothing quite reached the height of his two masterpieces.

Other Dramatists of the Period

Many other competent dramatists kept the theaters going after the deaths of Shakespeare and Marlowe. Lacking genius of the highest level, they nevertheless showed a competence that helped identify the period as a golden age of English literature. For more than fifty years, the theater had displayed a vitality rarely equaled in subsequent ages. Though the quality of plays suffered near the end of the period, now and then a memorable play was produced. The plays of Thomas Dekker, John Marston, Thomas

Middleton, Cyril Tourneur, Philip Massinger, Thomas Heywood, James Shirley, William Rowley, and John Ford continued to please audiences. When the theaters closed in 1642, darkness fell on the theaters and on English drama. Eighteen years later, with the Restoration of Charles II (p 36), the theater took on a new life, but it was a different life with a different kind of play. The age of Shakespeare had ended.

6

Music and the Opera

> If music be the food of love, play on,
> Give me excess of it; that, surfeiting,
> The appetite may sicken, and so die…

Twelfth Night, I, 1, 1-3

Here, lovesick Duke Orsino, pining for Olivia, hopes to cure his sickness with music. Throughout the plays, Shakespeare uses songs to entertain his audience and often further the plot. Many are versions of songs popular in his day. Some may have been written by others, but scholars generally agree that many of the most beautiful were created by Shakespeare himself.

Here are a few of the most beautiful and most famous:

"Who Is Sylvia?" (*The Two Gentlemen of Verona*)
"When Daisies Pied.." (*Love's Labour's Lost*)
"Tell Me Where Is Fancy Bred" (*The Merchant of Venice*)
"Sign No More, Ladies" (*Much Ado about Nothing*)
"It Was a Lover and His Lass" (*As You Like It*)
"O Mistress Mine" (*Twelfth Night*)

"Take, 0 Take Those Lips Away" (*Measure for Measure*)
"Hark, Hark, the Lark" (*Cymbeline*)
"Full Fadom Five Thy Father Lies" (*The Tempest*)
"Orpheus with His Lute" (*Henry VIII*)

The early songs provided a change of pace and a pleasing interlude, but the later songs were integrated more closely into the play, illuminating plot and character. When the new comic actor, Robert Armin, (p 32) joined the company in 1599, Shakespeare gave more prominence and significance to the songs. Armin apparently had a fine voice. The song of Touchstone in *As You Like It* is a good example.

Songs were used in tragedy as well as comedy. Armin probably played the Fool in *King Lear* and sang the songs essential to the plot. Perhaps the most famous song in the tragedies is Ophelia's mad song in *Hamlet*. It may have been based on a popular ballad.

What did Shakespeare's songs actually sound like? We can only conjecture. Little of the original music has survived. The tune of contemporary popular songs provided the melodies for some Shakespeare songs. We do have the names of some composers of the time: Robert Johnson, Thomas Morley, and John Wilson. Modern productions supply music for the songs, but it is not the original.

One of the most poignant songs is sung over the body of Cloten (p312), in *Cymbeline*.

GUIDERIUS.   Fear no more the heat o' th'sun,
Nor the furious winter's rages;
Thou thy worldly task hast done,
Home are gone and ta'en thy wages,
Golden lads and girls all must,
As chimney sweepers, come to dust.

ARVIRAGUS.   Fear no more the frown o'th'great;
                    Thou art past the tyrant's stroke;
                    Care no more to clothe and eat;
                    To thee the reed is as the oak.
                    The sceptre, learning, physic, must
                    All follow this and come to dust.
                              Cymbeline, IV, 2, 258-269

Shakespeare was well aware of the composer's task. He wrote short, rhymed lines of varying lengths, easy to set to music.

More recent composers have taken up the challenge. Eighteenth century composer Thomas Augustine Arne set a number of the Shakespearean songs to music; for example, "Under the Greenwood Tree" from *As You Like It* and "Where the Bee Sucks," from *The Tempest*. The great nineteenth century composer, Franz Schubert, turned his considerable talents to Shakespeare, with famous songs set to music: "Hark, the Lark" (*Cymbeline*) and "Who Is Sylvia?" (*Two Gentlemen of Verona*). Even Arthur Sullivan of Gilbert and Sullivan fame was tempted to write incidental music and accompaniments for several songs.

Shakespeare wrote in a highly competitive atmosphere. Just as a modern director keeps an eye on the competition when he guides the players through their lines, so the Elizabethan playwrights were very much aware of what their rivals were doing. The masque became a popular dramatic form, often imitated.

The Masque

The masque is a form of dramatic entertainment whose roots have been traced back to primitive fertility rites. The ordinary folk of Elizabethan times loved to dress up on festival days, especially Christmas. These mummers, as they were called, wore fantastic disguises and loved to serenade their neighbors, all in a spirit of great fun.

Among the aristocracy, the extreme elements of these festivities were muted, and the masques took on a courtly air. Starting as court masquerades, the masques gradually developed into theatrical presentations.

Courtiers often took part, with the help of professional dancers and musicians. Some of the major playwrights provided scripts; for example, Francis Beaumont, Samuel Daniel, and Ben Jonson. Queen Elizabeth enjoyed masques, and King James I encouraged their further development. Usually allegorical, the masque often contained mythological characters and represented virtues and vices. These productions were often requested at major events like noble marriages.

Shakespeare, always aware of current trends, introduced masque-like elements into his plays. Such elements appear in *Love's Labour's Lost* and *Much Ado about Nothing*. Romeo falls in love with Juliet at a masked ball. The betrothal masque in *The Tempest* adds grandeur to the impending marriage of Miranda and Ferdinand. In *The Winter's Tale*, a dance of twelve Satyrs enlivens the sheep-shearing festival. *A Midsummer Night's Dream* concludes with the dance of the Fairies, led by Oberon.

These masques were expensive, and cries of disapproval marked the later years. The masque did not survive the civil war that began in 1642.

Music Based on Shakespeare

Shakespeare's plays have inspired more music then the works of any other dramatist. Grove's *Dictionary of Music* lists some 800 works based on Shakespeare. This total does not include many unpublished pieces performed for a special occasion and then forgotten. Most major composers have tried their hand at music devoted to Shakespeare.

At the Restoration of King Charles II (p 36), many of Shakespeare's plays were transformed into a form called dramatic operas. These were not truly operas in the traditional sense. They did not resemble the newly created Italian operas but proved a dead end. Italian-style opera was to come later. Music continued to grow in importance and influence, however.

The Opera

The opera, as we know it, came into existence at the time when Shakespeare was creating *Hamlet*. Though this new form was contemporaneous with Shakespeare, it did not reach England until many years later.

The English had dramas accompanied by music, but not opera. An over-simplification might state that the English drama-with-music gave greater prominence to the words than the music. Opera tends to give greater prominence to the music. At the beginning of the 17th century, composers like Claudio Monteverdi began creating musical works now generally labeled *opera*. From these beginnings, opera has spread around the world, tempting some of the great composers to try their hand. Shakespeare's plays proved to be popular subjects.

Giuseppe Verdi composed three operas associated with Shakespeare's plays: *Macbeth*, *Otello*, and *Falstaff*. Forty years separated *Macbeth* from *Otello*, but critics especially admire *Otello* and *Falstaff*, the masterpieces of his old age. The two operas are different in tone. In its freshness, wit, and originality. *Falstaff* seems almost like the composition of a young man. *Otello*, a tragic work, contains some of Verdi's finest music. Both operas are close to Shakespeare.

Verdi's Falstaff is not the comic genius of the *Henry IV* plays but the hapless buffoon of *The Merry Wives of Windsor* (p215). In it, Falstaff, conniving as always, himself becomes the victim of his own greed. Verdi's *Otello* is also close to Shakespeare's play (p289). Part of the play's overwhelming success can be attributed to the libretto by Arrigo Boito. As he did for *Falstaff*, Boito retained much of Shakespeare's language, translated into Italian.

Otto Nicolai created another version of *The Merry Wives of Windsor*. Nicolai has achieved a measure of immortality because of this one popular opera. The plot follows Shakespeare's play, but many of the characters' names have been changed. The overture to this opera is a perennial concert favorite. Sadly, the opera was produced on March 11, 1849, just two days before the composer's death.

Falstaff is a tempting subject. Ralph Vaughan Williams also couldn't resist the challenge. His opera, *Sir John in Love*, incorporated the traditional song "Greensleeves."

A contrast to Verdi's *Falstaff* and *Otello* is *Hamlet*, by Ambroise Thomas. Though the music is beautiful, the opera has mutilated the plot of Shakespeare's play. One critic complained, "We find the Shakespearean names with their thoughts and deeds turned into operatic jargon." The worst mutilation is the ending. Hamlet kills Claudius at Ophelia's grave. He is elected King of Denmark on the spot, but his reign is short. He stabs himself on Ophelia's bier.

Charles Gounod's *Romeo and Juliet* follows Shakespeare fairly closely. The first act opens with the masked ball and moves relentlessly toward the tragic ending. The story also inspired Peter Ilyich Tchaikovsky to create one of his finest symphonic works: his *Romeo and Juliet*. Hector Berlioz provided a symphony based on the play. If the Tchaikovsky symphony is justly famous for the melodic overture, Berlioz has the famous and magical "Queen Mab Scherzo."

At the age of 17, Mendelssohn composed his first mature work, the Overture to *A Midsummer Night's Dream*. The music for the wedding of Theseus and Hippolyta in the play has given modern brides and grooms one of the two wedding marches used so often at the ceremonies. The other is from Richard Wagner's *Lohengrin*.

Opera, symphony, overture…what next? Sergei Prokofiev created a ballet score for *Romeo and Juliet*. But the possibilities are never exhausted. *Romeo and Juliet* became a Broadway musical, Leonard Bernstein's *West Side Story*. Instead of the rival noble families, Montagues and Capulets, *West Side Story* has the rival gangs, the Jets and the Sharks. The major plot line is honored. Tony (Romeo) and Maria (Juliet) fall in love at a dance. As members of rival groups, their love is challenged from the start. Episodes are changed and modernized, but the tragedy proceeds on its inexorable way, in this instance toward the death of Tony. As in Shakespeare's play, *West Side Story* ends with a sobering awareness of the deadly effects of hatred and division.

Back to opera. Hermann Goetz's *The Taming of the Shrew* is a fresh and witty musical dramatization of Shakespeare's comedy, Like Nicolai, Goetz died young, before the full maturing of his powers.

Hector Berlioz was attracted to Shakespeare again with his short opera *Beatrice and Benedict*. Based upon *Much Ado about Nothing*, the Berlioz opera concentrates on the two lovers, their quarrels, and their ultimate vows of eternal fidelity.

The works of Shakespeare are irresistible sources for songs, overtures, symphonies, operas, musicals, original scores for Shakespeare films, and incidental music. In music, in the study, and on the stage, Shakespeare is inexhaustible.

7

Films and Television

Dost thou love pictures? We will fetch thee straight
Adonis painted by a running brook,
And Cytherea all in sedges hid.

The Taming of the Shrew, **Induction, 2, 49-51**

In this quirky introduction to *The Taming of the Shrew* (p202), a lord and his servants play a trick on Christopher Sly, a poor tinker. Found in a drunken stupor, Sly is taken to a wealthy man's home by the practical jokers, dressed in rich clothing, and presented a "pleasant comedy" to entertain him. The comedy is *The Taming of the Shrew*. Oddly, the characters in this introductory playlet disappear from the scene and are not heard from again, except for a brief interruption by Sly.

The character of Sly is not essential to *The Taming of the Shrew*. His presence can perhaps be traced to an earlier, anonymous play, *The Taming of a Shrew*. In this play, Sly remains throughout, interrupting and making a nuisance of himself. Whether this play is an earlier version of Shakespeare's play or another entirely is a matter of debate. The tale of a poor man, tricked into believing he is rich and noble, goes back to *The Arabian Nights*. Whatever its source, Shakespeare evidently tired of that plot line and just let it die. The introductory quotation, however, makes a fitting introduction to this chapter.

For moviegoers and television viewers, the answer to "Dost thou love pictures?" is a resounding *yes*. When the new medium, the movies, took hold, the marriage with Shakespeare was inevitable. By the beginning of the new millennium, more than 300 film and television adaptations of his plays appeared on film or television.

Sometimes the resemblance is more subtle, less obvious. Versions of *The Tempest* have been set on a distant planet and on a lonely island during the Civil War. A movie like *10 Things I Hate about You* is a distant relative of *The Taming of the Shrew*. Most productions, however, are more recognizable attempts to put on a Shakespearean play.

A technological revolution has made a great many Shakespearean films of the past available to modern audiences. The videotape, the VCR and other recording devices bring most recent productions into the living room. It is possible to talk about the Hamlets of Laurence Olivier, Kenneth Branagh, and Mel Gibson soon after actually viewing these.

Shakespeare has always been popular with filmmakers. There are the obvious reasons, outlined throughout this book: Shakespeare's humanity, his insights into human nature, his dramatic plots, filled with sex, love, and violence. Professor James Shapiro of Columbia University says that he taps into "universal anxieties."

There are other less dramatic reasons for Shakespeare's popularity: availability, automatic name recognition, no problem with copyright, no up-front payment for the script. As for any problems of dating, modern directors often try to make their adaptations hip and sophisticated. Stars are often eager to play Shakespeare without demanding their usual high fees. Mel Gibson, one of the highest paid actors, took a much lesser fee for the privilege of playing *Hamlet*.

The first recorded example of Shakespeare on film is Herbert Beerbohm-Tree's *King John* in 1899. We can imagine exaggerated gestures and facial expressions to make up for the loss of Shakespeare's language. Movie captions cannot do justice to the majesty of Shakespeare's verse, of course, but this problem didn't deter other makers of silent films. Silent versions of Shake-speare's plays continued to be filmed.

When talking pictures arrived, Shakespeare came into his own on film. Within a year of each other, two cinematic blockbusters-*A Midsummer Night's Dream* and *Romeo and Juliet*-interpreted two of Shakespeare's most popular plays. Though sometimes criticized for being too heavily Hollywood and too little Shakespeare, the plays brought Shakespeare to a large, popular audience.

The famous Austrian composer Max Reinhardt was forced to flee from Nazi Germany in 1933. Within two years, he attempted a major film production in America: *A Midsummer Night's Dream*. Essentially true to the Shakespeare play, Reinhardt added elaborate scenes and costumes, with some of Mendelssohn's music as accompaniment. He made some amazing cast decisions, like the "hard-boiled" Jimmy Cagney as Bottom the Weaver. Mickey Rooney played an irrepressible (if sometimes irritating!) Puck. Olivia de Havilland made her screen debut. Because of its faithfulness to the spirit of Shakespeare's play, this was a landmark film.

A Midsummer Night's Dream has been revived frequently on films. A 1966 production was a recorded version of the New York City Ballet's presentation. In 1968, Diana Rigg, Judi Dench, lan Richardson, and others from the Royal Shakespeare Company presented their version. Then in 1999, Calista Flockhart, Michelle Pfeiffer, and Kevin Kline brought a new version to the screen. Set in Tuscany about the turn of the century, the film exploited cinematic possibilities by providing visualization of scenes only implied in the play. If Micky Rooney was an adolescent Puck, Stanley Tucci's Puck was more mature, more thoughtful, less frenzied.

A year after the Reinhardt version in 1936, the director George Cukor presented *Romeo and Juliet*, a star-studded well-acted version, true to Shakespeare's vision. Veteran actors John Barrymore, Edna May Oliver, C. Aubrey Smith, and Basil Rathbone supported the principals: Leslie Howard and Norma Shearer. The leads were really too old for the parts. Norma Shearer, 34, was playing fourteen-year-old Juliet. Leslie Howard, 43, was playing the young, impetuous Romeo. Still and all, said the critics, they both did a creditable job, with the assistance of Shakespeare's lines.

Romeo and Juliet has been a perennial favorite with movie producers. In 1954, Laurence Harvey and Susan Shentall played the young lovers. In

1966, Margot Fonteyn and Rudolf Nureyev performed a ballet version. A 1968 version narrated by Laurence Olivier won instant acclaim. In this version, the two leads, 17 and 15 were actually closer to the ages of the characters Shakespeare created. In 1996, Leonard DeCaprio and Claire Danes helped bring the play into the modern world. Set in Miami in the 90s, it helped introduce a youthful audience to Shakespeare. All versions are on videotape, as is the musical *West Side Story* (p 65), based on the play.

Two Henrys

Any stage or film version of Shakespeare is a product of its times. This statement is well demonstrated by comparing the *Henry V* of Laurence Olivier (1945) and the *Henry V* of Kenneth Branagh (1989). Filmed in wartime, Olivier's *Henry V* is intensely patriotic, stunningly beautiful in vibrant color. The battle scene at Agincourt is an electrifying representation of an overwhelming English victory. By emphasizing England's glorious past and bringing to life England's great warrior king, Olivier helped British morale at a time of national weariness. Olivier introduced a superb innovation. The play starts on a replica of the Globe and then moves on to the vaster world outside. Such a dramatic visualization is uniquely available to film, and Olivier took advantage of it.

Branagh's *Henry V* is quite different-visually and dramatically. Instead of the Globe replica, the actor playing the Chorus walks through a deserted movie set and then opens a door onto the revealing dialogue between the Archbishop of Canterbury and the Bishop of Ely. The greatest difference is in the tone. The battle scenes in Branagh's *Henry V* are grimy, gritty, muddy. There is little glory for the common soldiers dying in bloody hand-to-hand combat. In the Oliver production, the Battle of Agincourt is a glorious display of British superiority. The Branagh version is more grim.

Of course, there are many similarities. Every actor who has ever played Henry can testify to the sheer power of his exhortation to the troops.

We few, we happy few, we band of brothers;
For he today that sheds his blood with me
Shall be my brother.

Henry V, IV, 3, 60-63

At this point, Henry has a problem. His wanderings through camp the night before have shown the disillusionment of the common soldier facing superior numbers in the coming battle. He must find the words to rally these troops. Shakespeare provides them. Both Oliviver and Branagh loved that speech. At the time of the 1945 production, Olivier was speaking not only to the soldiers at Agincourt but to the British people.

The Challenge of *Hamlet*

If every Shakespeare play is a product of its time, it is also a product of the actors who interpret the lines. It is said that every serious actor yearns, at some time in his career, to play Hamlet. Perhaps *his* should be *his* or *her*, for some actresses have interpreted the part, including the great Sarah Bernhardt.

Probably, at this very moment, somewhere in the world a company is rehearsing or playing *Hamlet*. Even films have contributed to the vast history of *Hamlet*. By 1999, 41 screen adaptations had been made. Four excellent productions still available on videotape showcase the diversity and unique challenges of the play.

The first, Laurence Olivier's *Hamlet* of 1948, is ranked as the best by many critics. It thoroughly exploits the medium of film and enriches the text with brilliant camera work. The brooding quality of the opening castle scene sets the mood of the play, as the camera explores the vast and empty corridors. The use of voice-over for the first soliloquy adds a note of realism. Visualizing scenes that are only described by characters in the play adds a dimension impossible in a stage play. Ophelia's description of Hamlet's odd behavior, as well as the scene of her death, are actually dramatized in the movie version.

The Olivier version is unusual in other respects. Cutting Shakespeare's play to a running time of two or even three hours is always painful. In abridged versions, most of the First Player's long speech about Hecuba is usually eliminated. Minor characters like Reynaldo, Cornelius, and Voltimand may disappear. Trimming throughout increases the tempo.., and inevitably changes the play Shakespeare wrote. Oliver goes further, eliminating Rosencrantz and Guildenstern. These classmates of Hamlet introduce the Players, provide a sounding board for Hamlet's suspicions, and play a role throughout, until they go to their deaths in England (p288). After the play scene, they tell Hamlet to go to his mother's room. Olivier got around this by bringing Osric from Act V into this scene. Osric then makes the announcement made by Guildenstern in the text.

Nicoll Williamson in 1969 and Mel Gibson in 1990 presented Hamlets different in basic interpretation. The star power of Mel Gibson brought many young people into the Shakespearean fold and paved the way for the many Shakespearean films to come.

Kenneth Branagh attempted in 1996 to bring a complete, uncut Hamlet to the screen. This was a courageous gesture because of the great length. Would audiences be willing to sit for four hours of text, even with an intermission? Reactions were mixed, but Branagh gave lovers of Shakespeare a chance to hear all the lines, retain all the characters, an opportunity rarely available. Derek Jacobi played Claudius; Julie Christie, Gertrude; and Kate Winslet, Ophelia. As always, the director added many personal touches, like Hamlet's delivering his threatening speech to a mirror behind which Claudius and Polonius are crouching.

The Ethan Hawke 2000 production of *Hamlet* is set in contemporary corporate America, with Claudius as a CEO. Somehow the Shakespearean lines still work.

Other Films

As already noted, not all Shakespearean films present the plays more or less faithfully to the text. There are all kinds of varieties and derivatives. In

1947, *A Double Life* portrayed an actor whose stage performances spill over into his real life. He is chosen to play *Othello*, and the difficulties begin. In 1953, the musical *Kiss Me, Kate* brought *The Taming of the Shrew* up to date with a modern couple living out the situations of the play. In 1966, Orson Welles took sections of *Henry IV, Parts One* and *Two*, and *The Merry Wives of Windsor* and created *The Chimes at Midnight* for a robust portrayal of Sir John Falstaff.

In 1998, the hit movie *Shakespeare in Love* presented an imaginative depiction of the young Shakespeare near the beginning of his career. Though filled with intentional inaccuracies, it nevertheless showed what a Shakespearean performance looked like in the theater of the times. It won several Oscars, included that for best picture.

Shakespeare has been presented on foreign films, too. The most prestigious adapter of Shakespeare is the Japanese director Akira Kurosawa. In 1957, he adapted *Macbeth* as *The Throne of Blood*. The film is set in medieval Japan, not Scotland. In 1963, he presented a modern-day-Japan version of *Hamlet: The Bad Sleep Well*. In 1985, he adapted *King Lear*, with the title *Ran*, or *Chaos*. He set the film in medieval Japan and gave the Lear character three sons instead of three daughters.

Television

Though television has presented Shakespeare throughout the years, two series stand out. In the late 70s and early 80s, the British Broadcasting Company undertook to telecast all the Shakespearean plays. Competent, experienced Shakespearean actors played the principal roles, providing listeners an opportunity to see many plays that are rarely performed, like *Titus Andronicus* and *Timon of Athens*.

The second series goes back to 1971. *An Age of Kings* had a series of 15 broadcasts dealing with the Wars of the Roses (p226). The series carried the narrative from Richard II to Richard III: seven monarchs in eight plays. The same actors play the same characters in succeeding plays. Tom Fleming, for example, plays Bolingbroke in *Richard II*. As Henry IV, he plays in both *Henry IV* plays. This achieves a continuity rarely possible in separate plays.

The availability of videotapes has made it possible for the present generation to see the best of the past as well as the present, to compare productions, and to relish performances that only relatively few years ago would have been lost forever.

8

Shakespeare's Critics

O gentle lady, do not put me to't;
For I am nothing if not critical.

Othello, **II, 1, 118-119**

Iago's retort to Desdemona is part of a courtly play on words, passing the time until Othello arrives on the scene. Even in this wordplay, Shakespeare introduces a note of irony. Iago is self-confessed here; he is critical...in the extreme. That manner of judging almost fatally injures Cassio and ultimately brings about the death of Desdemona.

Criticism has been associated with Shakespeare from the beginning: much of it appreciative, some negative. Ben Jonson (p 52) accurately estimated the genius of Shakespeare, while pointing out occasional flaws. The steady stream of criticism has continued unabated to this day. *Criticism*, of course, is a broad term covering appreciation as well as faultfinding.

Shakespeare hasn't had only admirers without reservations. He's also had redoubtable detractors. The novelist Leo Tolstoy (p185) thought Shakespeare ruined the material he gleaned from perfectly good sources. The great playwright George Bernard Shaw coined the term *bardolatry* to make fun of Shakespeare lovers like the writer of this book. He professed to despise Shakespeare...some say to elevate his own position as a dramatist. Even Shaw had to admit grudgingly some of Shakespeare's good points. He called *As You Like It* a "cheap and pleasant falsehood," but he damned with faint praise, adding it is "one of the most affecting examples of romantic nonsense in existence."

Why Bother with Criticism?

"Every view of Shakespeare is imperfect," declared the critic-poet T. S. Eliot. "When a Poet is a great poet as Shakespeare is, we cannot judge of his greatness unaided; we need both the opinions of other poets and the diverse views of critics who were not poets, in order to help us understand."

Shakespeare has been closely examined, analyzed, subjected to conflicting theories of literature for four hundred years, but he still remains elusive.

The Seventeenth Century

John Dryden, the outstanding poet/dramatist of the Restoration (p 36), was conflicted when he wrote of Shakespeare. As a good classicist, he deplored Shakespeare's irregularities and lapses of good taste. Shakespeare was never bound by rules; a freedom that irked classically trained critics. But Dryden, despite the reservations, called Shakespeare "the man who of all modern and perhaps ancient poets had the largest and most comprehensive soul." Dryden's conception of what a good play should be is embodied in his own plays, like *All for Love*, a version of the Antony and Cleopatra story.

Thomas Rymer, a slightly younger contemporary of Dryden, was even more rigid in his criticism of Shakespeare's improbabilities and disregard of classical restraint. He called *Othello* a "Bloody Farce without salt or savor." He declared that using a handkerchief as a key element in the plot is beneath the dignity of tragedy.

The Eighteenth Century

After Dryden, Samuel Johnson was the preeminent Shakespearean critic. Johnson was a journalist, a poet, a lexicographer, an essayist, and even a novelist. An overpowering figure, physically and critically, Johnson dominated his period. The subject of a famous biography by James Boswell, Johnson is known to us in personal detail, with all the warts left on.

As a critic, Johnson paid Shakespeare the kind of tribute that only a gifted man of letters can give. As a creative artist himself, he understood Shakespeare's methods and realized his genius. He refuted the rigid boxes of classicism and freed Shakespeare from the limiting rules put forth by many earlier critics.

Shakespeare was often criticized for mixing comedy with tragedy, as in the Gravediggers' scene in *Hamlet*. Johnson said this about the First Folio (p 3), "The Players, who in their edition divided our author's work into comedies, histories, and tragedies, seem not to have defined the three kinds by any very exact or definite ideas." Like Shakespeare, Johnson sensed the ambiguities and paradoxes of life, realizing that *comedy* and *tragedy* are fluid terms.

The eighteenth century saw many other Shakespearean critics, but none were so influential and, to our eyes, so modern as Samuel Johnson. Foreign criticism abounded, with the French philosopher Voltaire a disparaging voice. The French, with their roots in classicism, tended to be negative; the German critics, positive.

The Nineteenth Century

Samuel Taylor Coleridge, famous for his romantic poetry, became one of the outstanding Shakespearean critics of his age. He refuted the claims of the neoclassicists. He hailed Shakespeare for a new kind of unity-not the unity of time and place but the unity of feeling. He considered Shakespeare the greatest artist of all time, the "ultimate philosopher of human nature."

The essayist Charles Lamb is noted more for the quality of his criticism than the quantity. He felt that some of Shakespeare's plays, notably *King Lear*, are too grand for the stage and are better appreciated in the library. With his sister Mary Ann, he wrote *Tales from Shakespeare*, which popularized the plots and characters of the plays.

Another essayist, William Hazlitt, wrote a penatrating critique: *The Characters of Shakespeare's Plays.* He was primarily concerned with human motivation and the complexity of human behavior.

Thomas De Quincey is immortal for a single essay; "On the Knocking at the Gate in *Macbeth.*" This short appraisal tells us more about the genius of Shakespeare than many lengthy tomes. De Quincey brushes aside the old criticism of introducing comedy into tragedy. Instead, he shows how Shakespeare artfully uses the scene as a breather after the horrifying events that preceded it, dramatically allowing the audience to catch its breath. It provides relief, a strengthening for the outrages to come.

Other writers turned their hand to criticism, in varying degrees: Thomas Carlyle, Matthew Arnold, Algernon Charles Swinburne, Walter Pater, and especially Edward Dowden and A.C. Bradley. In America, Edgar Allan Poe, Ralph Waldo Emerson, and James Russell Lowell couldn't resist issuing their own appraisals.

The Twentieth Century

A. C. Bradley, one of the most important of all Shakespearean critics, straddles both centuries. The Victorian novels of Dickens, Thackeray, Eliot, Brontes, and Hardy excelled in the depiction of character. Influenced perhaps by these writers, Bradley excelled in discussion of character, in his awareness of the complexities and profundities of Shakespeare's characters.

Modern-day critics, too numerous to list, have the benefit of all those who have gone before. Sometimes in an effort to find something new and modern, they come up with unique theories. Is *Hamlet* in many respects a Freudian play? Does Shakespeare espouse a particular political partisanship? Is Shakespeare essentially religious? Is Prospero a modern man "facing the timeless, existential despair so many of his generation have known," These barely scratch the surface of contemporary criticism, a constantly evolving approach to the plays, probing and weighing and enjoying. The study of Shakespeare has no end. Shakespeare resists "The Last Word".

Shakespeare's unique qualities have been brilliantly condensed in a single sentence by the critic Benedict Nightingale, in a review of Kevin Kline's performance of *Henry IV*. He says the interpretation is "inconsistent in a way the Elizabethans would have appreciated, but our age, which has lost the habit of creative self-contradiction, seems to find hard to understand."

Our fruitless attempts to put Shakespeare into a neat box of our own making has never been better put. *Creative self-contradiction*-those are pregnant words.

9

Who Wrote the Plays?

He wills you, in the name of God Almighty,
That you divest yourself, and lay apart
The borrowed glories that by gift of heaven,
By law of Nature, and of nations, 'longs
To him and to his heirs.

Henry V, II, 4, 7-81

The messenger of *Henry V* is here reporting to the King of France Henry's claim to portions of France. The same sentiment might be uttered by the scholars who claim that Shakespeare did not write the plays attributed to him, borrowing the glories of another.

The argument against Shakespeare's authorship runs something like this. Shakespeare was illiterate, from an illiterate family, without a university education or a position at court. How could this unrefined bumpkin write all those dazzling plays that show a knowledge of the world far beyond the reach of a poor Stratford lad? How could a simple country boy become so brilliant, so sophisticated, so wise in the ways of the world? The traditional answer is that Shakespeare was not a "simple country boy."

Sir Francis Bacon

The theory that Shakespeare did not write the plays is not new, but the suggested replacements have varied. The oldest and best-known candidate is Sir Francis Bacon: statesman, philosopher, and essayist. A contemporary of Shakespeare, he was born three years earlier and outlived Shakespeare by ten years. His rise to power and prominence was tainted in his final years by a charge of bribery.

Bacon was first suggested as the author of the plays by Herbert Lawrence in 1769. That claim was soon forgotten, but nearly eighty years later, Joseph C. Hart restated the hypothesis. The most famous case for Bacon was presented by Delia Bacon (no relation) shortly afterward. She considered Francis Bacon the presiding genius of a group that created the plays to advance his philosophy. Her theory rested upon numerology and ciphers built into the plays.

The theory did not die. In 1888, Ignatius Donnelly wrote *The Great Cryptogram*, which purported to show that Bacon had planted a revealing cipher into the First Folio. Donnelly claimed that Bacon wrote not only the Shakespeare plays, but also the plays of Christopher Marlowe, the essays of Montaigne, and Richard Burton's long tome *The Anatomy of Melancholy*. All of this was in addition to his own substantial writings! Donnelly had many converts, including Mark Twain.

Other Claimants

The Bacon controversy opened the floodgates for other candidates. *The Reader's Encyclopedia of Shakespeare* lists 58 other names of those who purportedly wrote the plays. Some of these are downright absurd; for example, Queen Elizabeth and Mary Queen of Scots, Four claimants have been taken more seriously: Christopher Marlowe, the Earl of Oxford, the Earl of Rutland, and the Earl of Derby.

The Earl of Oxford

The most persistent recent candidate is Edward de Vere, 17th Earl of Oxford. His claim to immortality was first put forth by J. Thomas Looney in 1920. His efforts resulted in the formation of the anti-Stratfordian brotherhood, devoted to disproving Shakespeare as the author of the plays. The publication of a biography of Oxford stimulated arguments suggesting links between Oxford's life and the plays. Since the Oxford supporters are the most recent and persistent of the forces against the traditional view, a sample of the arguments will show the basis for their claims.

Edward de Vere was a flamboyant young man, quite unlike the William Shakespeare of tradition. He lived life on the edge. A spendthrift and a dandy, he attracted attention at the court for his attractive personality and extravagant lifestyle. When she was 15, Anne, the daughter of Lord Burghley, one of the most powerful men in England, married the dashing Oxford. He was polished, attractive, high-spirited, and impetuous. His life was filled with excitement tempered with scandal, unplanned fatherhood, and a period in the Tower of London. Of course, he was, unlike Shakespeare, university educated.

Other arguments in his favor emphasize his experiences. In 1575, he had the Queen's permission to tour the Continent. He visited Padua and Verona, among many other cities. "Aha," say his supporters, "these are the settings for *The Taming of the Shrew, Romeo and Juliet,* and *Two Gentlemen of Verona.* He was there!" So far as we know, Shakespeare never traveled abroad.

Oxford's family had served the English monarchy since 1066. The young Earl would have had a special knowledge of historical incident and a special rapport with the problems of the nobility. His own life parallels many of the plots and characters of the plays. He is in a perfect position to write that vast body of treasure we assign to Shakespeare. But did he?

Oxford did have a literary bent. He wrote the introduction to *The Courtier,* a book combining romantic attitudes with lessons in manners. He wrote poems in Latin and English, and many of the latter still survive. To the ears of traditional scholars, however, the poems lack the spark of Shakespeare's poetry.

We know that Oxford was associated with the theater. He had inherited one company of players from his father and later had two of his own. The theater of the time was a magnet for creativity, and the young nobles were much attracted. Oxford himself was a patron of several writers. He *could* have written the plays, but did he?

If he wrote the plays, why didn't he take credit for them? Oxford's supporters insist that his position in court eliminated the possibility of associating his name with the plays. *His* plays would have been more severely censored than those by a poor actor. He might have been accused of using the plays to further his own ambitions. Court favorites might have seen themselves unfairly caricatured in the plays. Therefore, says Charlton Ogburn, a leading advocate of the Oxford claim, Oxford found the poorly educated William Shakespeare and paid him to assume authorship.

Oxonians, as they are sometimes called, have found other parallels in the life of Oxford and the characters in the plays. They continue to stir the waters, and Shakespeareans continue to rebut the Oxford claims. The vast bulk of modern scholarship supports the claim of William Shakespeare, not Oxford or any other. Why? What is the Shakespearean position?

The Author, William Shakespeare

Some of the charges against Shakespeare the man are just plain wrong. Shakespeare was not illiterate, nor did he come of an illiterate family. The Shakespeares were persons of substance in Stratford. At the time of Shakespeare's birth, his father was a town leader. John had married Mary Arden and thereby gained a good inheritance. As personages of some importance, his parents would have secured for their son William a good education (p   6). This education provided all the tools for an inquisitive, intellectual young man to read extensively and to learn on his own more than any university could provide. College graduates often affirm that they learned more after graduation than they learned while in school. A formal education provides the tools and the motivation to go on. It is fair to assume that Shakespeare was a voracious reader. The plots of his plays (p178) show a wide variety of sources used.

In all the twists and turns of the authorship controversy, one of the strangest arguments for Shakespeare as author suggests that the plays couldn't have been written by a university-trained writer! This is the reverse of the argument that Shakespeare didn't have enough schooling to write the plays. In this special pleading, Shakespeare made errors that a university-trained author would not have made!

These "errors," if they are such, are scattered throughout the plays. Geographical identifications are often faulty. Milan is far from the sea, but Prospero suggests that he and Miranda were kidnapped and put aboard a ship from Milan (*The Tempest*). Bohemia is landlocked, also far from the sea; yet Viola and her brother are shipwrecked on the seacoast of Bohemia (*Twelfth Night*).

There are occasional anachronisms, incidents out of place for their time. There were no church bells in ancient Rome; yet we hear "No mournful bell shall ring her burial" (*Titus Andronicus*). There were no striking clocks either, but Brutus says, "Peace! Count the clock" (*Julius Caesar*).

What shall we think of Shakespeare's occasional rewriting of history to suit his dramatic aims? Hotspur was actually 23 years older than Prince Hal, but for greater dramatic impact, Shakespeare makes him the same age as Hal (*Henry IV, Part One*) Shakespeare had read the chronicles. He knew the truth, but chose to embroider it a little. Modern historical dramas on film do the same thing.

What are we to think of these "errors"? Some say a university-educated writer wouldn't have made these mistakes. Therefore the author of the plays couldn't have been Oxford or Bacon. That may be debatable, but there is another explanation. Shakespeare was widely enough read to avoid some of these petty mistakes, but he didn't care. The worlds he was creating were his worlds. If he felt like importing some Elizabethan village folk into ancient Athens, so be it (*A Midsummer Night's Dream*).

It is not necessary to be a king to write about kings and imagine their emotions. It is not necessary to be a hotheaded zealot to create a Tybalt or a Laertes. It is not necessary to experience all the situations created for the plays. A creative artist, because of his genius, can live many lives and imagine many conflicting personalities.

Shakespeare knew two worlds: the world of the court and the world of the country village. The actors in Shakespeare's companies had noble and royal sponsorship and often moved on the fringes of the court. Shakespeare also knew well the life of the country village, as portrayed in so many of his plays, notably *A Midsummer Night's Dream* and *The Merry Wives of Windsor*. Oxford would have known the court but not the country experiences that Shakespeare brings to life in his plays.

Shakespeare himself did not take any pains to assure the preservation of his plays for posterity because once they were played, they were no longer his, but the company's. Fortunately, his popularity insured that many of the plays appeared in quarto (p 16) form, but these were not library editions for future generations. They were current bestsellers. Luckily many of these have survived.

There are a number of contemporary references to Shakespeare as an actor and a playwright. He earned the love and admiration of at least one major rival, Ben Jonson (p 52). It seems unlikely that Jonson would have revered a puppet of Oxford.

No one denies that Shakespeare was an actor. He is listed as Adam in *As You Like It* and as a character in Ben Jonson's *Every Man in His Humour*. That simple truth helps validate the Shakespearean claim.

"Only an actor could have written that poetry." This statement by a Shakespearean actor stresses the point that Shakespeare's plays are actor-friendly. The lines provide pauses to help the actor at a tense moment. They provide rhythms that make the lines easy to memorize. They show an intimate knowledge of actors and acting, as in Hamlet's "Advice to the Players." They are not quickly forgotten.

Seven years after Shakespeare's death, fellow actors published the First Folio (p   3), a compilation of the plays, many of which might otherwise have been lost. The Folio is a personal tribute, including a moving eulogy by Ben Jonson.

One of the strongest arguments for the Shakespeare claim was put forth by Caroline F. H. Spurgeon in her book *Shakespeare's Imagery* (p139). She analyzed all the images in the plays, classifying them and commenting on their relevance to the themes of the plays. She also analyzed the images of others like Marlowe and Bacon and found differences that make each writer's images unique. Marlowe's images, for example, are more classical. Shakespeare's depend more on personal observation.

Imagery is buried too deep in the psyche to be counterfeited. No two persons have exactly the same experiences and heredity. We all develop individual ways of speaking and thinking, of expressing these thoughts, of using figurative language. Our childhood experiences help determine the images we use. The impressions of a boy in Stratford found their way into mature writings. Scholars have pointed out some of these linkages.

Shakespeare was a prolific creator of images (p136). In an ironic dialogue with Polonius, Hamlet underscores the individual nature of images.

HAMLET.	Do you see yonder cloud that's almost in shape of a camel?
POLONIUS.	By th' mass and 'tis, like a camel indeed.
HAMLET.	Methinks it is like a weasel.
POLONIUS.	It is backed like a weasel.
HAMLET.	Or, like a whale?
POLONIUS.	Very like a whale.

Hamlet, III, 2, 379-384

When poets create images to describe anything, their results are instructively individual. Images of the moon, for example, are poetic favorites. The poet Shelley called it "that orbed maiden with white fire laden." Alfred Noyes called it a "ghostly galleon tossed upon cloudy seas." Robert Frost painted another picture: "Part of a moon was falling down the west, dragging the whole sky with it to the hills." For Walter de la Mare, "Softly, silently, now the moon walks the night in her silver shoon." Shakespeare likened the moon to a "silver bow." Shakespeare also called it "envious" (of the sun's rays), "pale-faced," "horned," "watery," "cold fruitless," "gracious," "noble and chaste," "modest," "blessed," "visiting," "fleeting," "mortal," and "inconstant." The last two refer to the moon's wandering through the sky, changing each night.

The moon's "unreliability" is immortalized by Juliet:

ROMEO. Lady, by yonder blessed moon I vow.
That tips with silver all these fruit-tree tops—
JULIET. O swear not by the moon, th'inconstant moon
That monthly changes in her circled orb
Lest that thy love prove likewise variable.
Romeo and Juliet, II, 2 107-110

There is at least one more strong case against Oxford as the author of the Shakespeare plays: the Earl died in 1604 before many of the great plays were written. The argument for faulty dating cannot hold when we note that *The Tempest*, created around 1610-1611, was based on a ship-wreck in 1609.

Balancing Inferences

Where direct evidence is lacking, we must depend upon inferences. We have no letter from Shakespeare to his wife Anne telling of his writing career. We can reasonably infer that such a letter was written, but we have no example.

Since we must depend upon inferences, we must base any claim on the reasonableness of the inferences we make. We must then balance ours against the inferences drawn by supporters of opposing claims. It is a reasonable inference that Shakespeare knew about the court from his personal experiences as an actor playing before the court. It is almost certain that his boyhood experiences in Stratford gave him expertise in depicting country life. Oxford, on the other hand, almost certainly had no intimate knowledge of country manners, celebrations, festivals, ways of speaking. In this single instance, inferences about Shakespeare far outweigh those about Oxford.

Why the Rival Claims?

An appreciator of the plays might well ask, "Why? Why all the attempts to take from the actor William Shakespeare the credit for those glorious plays?" Charlton Ogburn argues that "knowing about the real author's life could help us understand his work." Also, it is "a matter of elementary justice to give the man credit who produced Western culture's greatest literature."

The arguments will rage on. Since so much is shrouded in mystery, there is a continuing temptation to attack the problem like a giant puzzle waiting to be solved. Traditional scholars say that the effort is fruitless, a waste of time. Perhaps the British actor Ian McKellen had the final word. He said that the plays were written either by a man called Shakespeare or by a man calling himself Shakespeare. No matter. We have the plays.

Part Two

Shakespeare's Unique Genius

10

Shakespeare's Characters

There's no art
To find the mind's construction in the face:
He was a gentleman on whom I built
An absolute trust.

Macbeth, I, 4, 11-14

When King Duncan comments about the traitor Cawdor, he little realizes that an even more treacherous subject is about to enter: Macbeth. In *Othello*, Iago says, "I am not what I am." Throughout the Shakespearean plays, characters are not what they seem. Superficial appearances belie complexities of character, as in life itself. Shakespeare's characters are a cross-section of humanity.

Elusive Characters

In the creation of character, Shakespeare stands apart from many other writers. His characters seem less like literary creations than human beings snatched from real life. Many of the greatest Shakespearean characters defy analysis.

The most famous of Shakespeare's complex characters is Hamlet (p286). Hundreds of critics have "explained" Hamlet. Was his madness real or feigned? Was he basically a passive thinker or a man of action? Did he love

Ophelia or disdain her? Was his treatment of Rosencrantz and Guildenstern unnecessarily cruel or completely justified? These discussions are open-ended, with no certain resolutions. Hamlet the man and *Hamlet* the play are much too complex and elusive for any kind of pigeonholing. Writing and analyzing can be great fun as long as the writers realize that there are no final answers.

Our minds prefer an orderly universe, with everything manageable and classifiable, but life refuses rigid classifications. To survive and get along in the workaday world, we must act on the assumption that the boxes and maps we rely on are reliable. For most purposes, these boxes and maps can be valuable indeed. When we travel, for example, we assume that the road maps are accurate, as indeed they are…most of the time. But an accident or unexpected construction can make our maps useless.

When we enter the world of Shakespeare, we find some of our usual boxes and maps less than helpful. Things aren't what they seem. People aren't entirely what they appear to be. In much popular fiction and the movies, characters do not turn on us and surprise us. James Bond, for example, is always gallant, reliable, strong, charming, on the side of the angels. When we see a James Bond movie, we know what to expect, like getting a fast-food hamburger. Shakespeare scorns easy classifications.

The Greek philosopher Aristotle defined the tragic hero as a man "not pre-eminently virtuous and just, whose misfortune, however, is brought upon him not by vice and depravity but by some error of judgment." Sometimes the expression "tragic flaw" is used to explain the downfall of a tragic hero. Shakespeare goes beyond these commonsense explanations.

Paradox and Shakespeare

Paradox is an apparently self-contradictory statement. "I lie all the time" is a paradoxical statement. If I lie all the time, then the quotation is itself a lie. At the heart of paradox is a truth reconciling the conflict. "Apathy is our greatest problem-but who cares?" The central truth reveals that the speaker is not just stating the problem but is part of the problem. Paradox abounds in Shakespeare.

Hamlet is overwhelmed by conflicting demands. Suicide is not an option, as he cries out in agony:

> Or that the everlasting had not fixed
> His canon 'gainst self-slaughter.
> *Hamlet*, I, 2, 131-132

We know that Hamlet is religious, for he refrains from killing the King at his prayers. He believes in an afterlife at this moment but realizes that he himself is considering the crime of murder, a mortal sin. Through all his agonizing, he is burdened with the terrible command by the Ghost: "Revenge his foul and most unnatural murder." Hamlet's conflicting burdens provide the basic struggle in the play.

Hamlet can be *at the same time* bloody and restrained. He can be a tortured lover and a pitiless scorner almost simultaneously. He is many personalities at different times, sometimes almost at the same time. Though Hamlet is a pre-eminent example of Shakespeare's character contradictions, they abound elsewhere in the plays.

In *Julius Caesar* (p259), Brutus is another example of a man conflicted beyond endurance. Though labeled by Mark Antony at the end of the play as "the noblest Roman of them all," Brutus is a flawed hero, like others in the Shakespeare plays. Though Brutus prides himself on living by reason, he is often moved by irrational elements within himself. He joins the conspiracy against Caesar as much because of Cassius's insinuations as for any rational reason of his own. On the other hand, after the assassination, he shows his great-heartedness by allowing Mark Antony to live, a decision the conspirators come to regret.

The conspirators begin to fall out when Octavian and Mark Antony threaten. In one scene, Brutus argues with Cassius over money, as though it were an argument between two adolescents. The noble Brutus is here revealed as both petty and great, all within half a dozen lines. Why does Shakespeare show us this Brutus, the noblest Roman, with feet of clay? This contradiction is Shakespeare's greatest strength: his depiction of real people, with all their virtues and faults presented simultaneously.

A third example of a character impossible to pin down is Shylock in *The Merchant of Venice* (p213). Antonio, not Shylock, is the merchant in the title. Shylock himself appears in only five scenes and has fewer than 400 lines; yet he dominates the play. For four centuries, critics have attempted to come to grips with this fascinating character. He has been labeled all-too-human, bigoted, clownish, comic, crabbed, evil, fawning, greedy, hypocritical, inhuman, irreligious, malicious, pathetic, pitiful, religious, ridiculous, scheming, sensitive, vicious, vile, vindictive, weird—not necessarily in alphabetic order! Which one really applies? Only one? More than one? All? None? Shakespeare, being Shakespeare, lets us decide. He leaves us with a sense of ambiguity.

Shakespeare's Women

The three fascinating characters just considered are a tiny percentage of the rich personalities throughout the plays. Shakespeare's women, like his men, are complex, difficult to characterize. Lady Macbeth is a good example. At the end of *Macbeth* (p296), the new king, Malcolm, refers to Macbeth and his wife as "this dead butcher and his fiend-like queen." *Fiend-like* is an over-simplification. Lady Macbeth has indeed acquiesced in the evil deeds of her husband, but she is also repelled by them. She refuses to kill Duncan because he resembled her father. She begins to disintegrate as she surmises that Macbeth is bathing ever deeper in blood, and she is devastatingly conscience-stricken in the sleepwalking scene. She is no one-dimensional villain.

By contrast, in *King Lear* (p293), Cordelia is almost totally admirable, a heroine in every sense. It is difficult to find fault with any element of her personality. Yet, as some critics in a minority view have pointed out, Cordelia displays a stubborn streak that brings on the tragedy. As an intelligent woman, she realizes her father's weaknesses, his touches of senility. She may even guess what will happen if her two sisters gain complete control of the kingdom. Yet at the crucial moment of decision, she obstinately refuses to say what the old king wants to hear, thus opening the doors to the ensuing tragedy. Lear is repelled by what he labels Cordelia's pride; he divides his kingdom between Cordelia's sisters, Goneril and Regan.

Cordelia loves her father far more than her sisters do, but she won't say so. Does Shakespeare invite us to approve wholeheartedly of Cordelia's stubborn righteousness, or does he feel that there is a time for prudent compromise?

In *The Taming of the Shrew*, Katharina is the terror of her household, a wild, unmanageable spitfire. In the early scenes she displays qualities that make her a serious marital risk. Yet at the core of Katharina's personality are qualities of sweetness and amiability lost in the facade she has maintained. Like other Shakespeare characters, she is not a one-note personality.

A Sense of Balance

When Laurence Olivier produced his version of *Henry V* during the final years of World War II, he emphasized the greatness of King Henry, the patriotism of the English, and the glorious past all English shared. When Kenneth Branagh produced his version in 1989, he painted a darker picture, showing war at its grimmest. How is it possible to take the same text and produce such different interpretations? The answer lies in Shakespeare's all-embracing sense of balance.

Henry V is often considered one of the greatest of English kings. King Henry's achievements in France were incredible. His leadership was brilliant. His rallying of the soldiers before the Battle of Agincourt is gloriously portrayed by Shakespeare.

> We few, we happy few, we band of brothers:
> For he today that sheds his blood with me
> Shall be my brother: be he ne'er so vile,
> This day shall gentle his condition.
> And gentlemen in England, now a-bed,
> Shall think themselves accursed they were not here;
> And hold their manhoods cheap, whiles any speaks
> That fought with us upon Saint Crispin's day.
> *Henry V*, IV, 3, 60-67

This is indeed a high-souled commander worthy of our admiration, is it not? But Shakespeare shows us this same prince ordering the execution of captured French prisoners on uncertain grounds. Shakespeare also shows Henry threatening to slaughter all the men of the besieged town of Harfleur unless the citizens submit. He also draws a picture of children stabbed with pikes. Selective choices and emphases can paint different sides of Henry, another example of Shakespeare's avoidance of cardboard characters purely good or evil. Even Iago, in *Othello*, has a slim excuse for his actions, even though the reason doesn't justify the result. Besides Shakespeare has given Iago a certain devilish charm that makes his role popular with Shakespearean actors.

In *Henry V*, Shakespeare cannot resist showing another side of the war and England's role in it. Captain Macmorris is an Irish soldier in the English army. When Fluellen, a Welsh soldier, says, "There are not many of your nation…" Macmorris picks up the word *nation*: "Of my nation! What ish my nation? Ish a villain, and a bastard, and a knave, and a rascal. What ish my nation? Who talks of my nation?" By putting this nationalistic speech into the mouth of an Irish soldier, Shakespeare reveals his awareness of the Irish unhappiness under the English yoke.

In *The Tempest* (p315), Prospero is the protagonist, controlling the play's action and bringing events to a happy conclusion. Caliban is an unlovely, brutish slave of Prospero, a son of a devil and a witch. Caliban is taken into the home of Prospero and his daughter Miranda. Ungratefully, according to Prospero, he has attempted to rape Miranda. Later he even plots to murder Prospero. On the surface, this is an unsympathetic "thing of darkness." Yet Shakespeare cannot condemn Caliban totally. After all, Caliban has been enslaved, has lost his freedom, and is subject to the whims of Prospero. Any disapproval is tinged with sympathy. At the end, Caliban seeks to improve himself.

Almost as a planned way to balance the scales, Shakespeare gives to Caliban some of the finest poetry in the play. At one point, Caliban declares:

> Be not afeard-the isle is full of noises,
> Sounds and sweet airs, that give delight and hurt not:
> Sometimes a thousand twangling instruments
> Will hum about mine ears; and sometime voices,
> That, if I then had waked after long sleep,
> Will make me sleep again—and then, in dreaming,
> The clouds methought would open, and show riches
> Ready to drop upon me, that when I waked
> I cried to dream again.
>
> *The Tempest*, III, 2, 133-141

These are not the words of an insensible monster. Caliban, like so many of Shakespeare's characters, is difficult to pin down.

The Minor Characters

In *Hamlet*, (p286) Rosencrantz and Guildenstern have been summoned to spy on Hamlet for the King. Toward the end of their first audience, there is this dialogue:

KING.   Thanks Rosencrantz, and gentle Guildenstern.
QUEEN.   Thanks Guildenstern, and gentle Rosencrantz.

The Queen has reversed the order of salutation. Why? Some versions make a point of the reversal. The King has mixed up the two courtiers, and the Queen sets him straight with her own correct address. Is Shakespeare slyly making the point that these two unfortunate individuals are practically indistinguishable, puppets of the King's plans? Certainly they act in unison, always in each other's company. In the First Folio, Guildenstern enters four lines after Rosencrantz; otherwise they appear together.

In *Letters from an Actor*, William Redfield, who played the role of Guildenstern in Richard Burton's 1964 Broadway production of *Hamlet*, presents a fascinating picture of a Shakespeare play in production. An interesting component is his own effort to interpret his Guildenstern role, to give it some meaning and individuality.

It is interesting to compare the parts of these supposedly indistinguishable roles. First, there is a disparity in the number of lines assigned to each. Rosencrantz has approximately twice the number of lines as Guildenstern. Then, each actor has one face-to-face scene with Hamlet. When summoned to his mother's room, Hamlet takes Guildenstern aside and orders him to play the recorder. Obviously Guildenstern cannot, and Hamlet retorts, "You would play on me." This is a scene of some weight for a minor actor, a segment to be relished.

As always, for a sense of balance, Shakespeare gives Rosencrantz a similar scene. After the murder of Polonius, the courtiers want to know where Hamlet has hid the body. Rosencrantz carries the weight of the questioning. The two roles seem interchangeable, but a director can tilt the performances and individualize the roles, without changing the lines themselves. Surprisingly, though Rosencrantz seems the stronger role, in the Burton production, Redfield, the more seasoned actor, was given the role of Guildenstern.

An interesting postscript to the two roles: Tom Stoppard wrote a play, *Rosencrantz and Guildenstern Are Dead*, in which the two courtiers are the leads and Hamlet a minor actor. From time to time, Hamlet appears, muttering those soliloquies to the mystification of the two obsequious courtiers. In this play, they are innocent victims of the raging passions whirling around them.

Shakespeare's other minor characters are often fascinating in their own right. These often provide comic relief. The First Gravedigger in *Hamlet* is a comedian, useful for a bit of humor in the grim last act. In *The Two Gentlemen of Verona*, Launce has two hilarious scenes that parody the absurdities of the principal characters. In the two parts of *Henry IV*, the scruffy associates of Falstaff provide good acting moments for talented players. In *Measure for Measure*, Barnardine, a condemned criminal, decides not to appear for his execution for personal reasons and is eventually pardoned! The Nurse in *Romeo and Juliet* is a long-winded comical figure whose personality changes as the play progresses. Character change and development are part of Shakespeare's strategy.

Well-presented minor characters are not necessarily comic. When two murderers are sent by Richard to murder his brother Clarence, we might expect them to be uncontrasted, alike. Not so. Shakespeare clearly differentiates between the two murderers:

2 MURDERER.	What, shall I stab him as he sleeps ?
1 MURDERER.	No; he'll say 'twas done cowardly, when he wakes.
2 MURDERER.	Why, he shall never wake until the great judgment day.
1 MURDERER.	Why, then he'll say we stabbed him sleeping.
2 MURDERER	The urging of that word 'judgement' hath bred a kind of remorse in me.
1 MURDERER.	What, art thou afraid?
2 MURDERER.	Not to kill him, having a warrant; but to be damned for killing him, from the which no warrant can defend me.
1 MURDERER.	I thought thou hadst been resolute.
2 MURDERER.	So I am, to let him live.
1 MURDERER.	I'll back to the Duke of Gloucester, and tell him so.
2 MURDERER.	Nay, I prithee, stay a little: I hope this passionate humour of mine will change; it was wont to hold me but while one tells twenty.
1 MURDERER.	How dost thou feel thyself now ?
2 MURDERER.	Faith, some certain dregs of conscience are yet within me.
1 MURDERER.	Remember our reward when the deed's done.
2 MURDERER.	Zounds, he dies: I had forgot the reward.
1 MURDERER.	Where's thy conscience now ?
2 MURDERER.	O, in the Duke of Gloucester's purse.
I MURDERER.	When he opens his purse to give us our reward, thy conscience flies out.
2 MURDERER.	'Tis no matter, let it go; there's few or none will entertain it.

Richard III, I, 4, 101-132

The two murderers are not carbon copies of each other. Even in the brief excerpt above, the differences between the two men are apparent. Shakespeare goes further. In the ensuing dialogue, the Second Murderer does a turnabout and expounds the evils of having a conscience. During the murder scene itself, the murderers parry words with the doomed Clarence and reveal other aspects of their complicated personalities. After the deed, the Second Murderer says, in another reversal, "For I repent me that the duke is slain." As Hamlet said in a different context, "The native hue of resolution is sicklied o'er with the pale cast of thought." and these are only minor characters, mere instruments of Richard's evil designs, present in only two scenes. Shakespeare does not create dull stock characters. He has enough genius to expend on even minor characters.

Even the two gravediggers in *Hamlet* are clearly differentiated. The first Clown, as he is often labeled, is the comic. In modern show-business terms, the Second Clown is the second banana. He feeds the comic the lines, and the comic has the witty retorts. When Hamlet and Horatio arrive on the scene, the First Clown takes over completely and the Second Clown can retire, perhaps to become a courtier at the dueling scene later. Doubling up (p 33) was an essential strategy with a limited number of players.

Shakespeare's Style and Versification

Taffeta phrases, silken terms precise,
 Three-piled hyperboles, spruce affectation,
Figures pedantical-these summer-flies
 Have blown me full of maggot ostentation,
I do forswear them, and I here protest,
 By this white glove (how white the hand, God knows!)
Henceforth my wooing mind shall be expressed
 In russet yeas and honest kersey noes.

Love's Labour's Lost, V, 2, 406-413

In this speech, the young courtier Berowne (p206) confesses his previous ornate language and is resolving from then on to speak more simply and directly. Kersey is a simple, coarse-ribbed woolen cloth used for the clothing of the common people. Taffeta is a more showy, expensive cloth. The first four lines suggest Berowne's previous attempts to make an impression. The last line presents his resolve to give up affectation in the future and speak simply.

At this early stage in his career, Shakespeare seems to be giving advice, here on speaking. Later in his career Hamlet's advice to the players gives advice on acting. Throughout his plays Shakespeare is strong on style. He also reveals an ability to provide his characters with styles suitable to their roles in the plays.

If he chooses, Shakespeare can write the worst kind of jargon…but always appropriate to the speaker. In *Love's Labour's Lost*, the comical schoolmaster Holofernes, in an attempt to sound scholarly, speaks gibberish:

> This is a gift that I have, simple, simple; a foolish extravagant spirit, full of forms, figures, shapes, objects, ideas, apprehensions, motions, revolutions. These are begot in the ventricles of memory, nourished in the womb of pia mater, and delivered upon the mellowing of occasion. But the gift is good in those in whom it is acute, and I am thankful for it.
>
> *Love's Labour's Lost*, IV, 2, 71-77

In *Hamlet*, Polonius also tends to verbal excess. Though he doesn't misuse word meanings, as Holofernes does, he never uses one word where several can do. In the following speech, Polonius is trying to convince Claudus and Gertrude that Hamlet is mad for love of Ophelia:

> That he is made 'tis true, "tis true, 'tis pity,
> And pity 'tis 'tis true-a foolish figure,
> But farewell it, for I will use no art.
>
> *Hamlet*, II, 2, 97-99

Othello is a different kind of character: disciplined, martial in bearing, direct in speaking. Early in the play, Othello is accosted on the street by Desdemona's father and a force of officers. When a sword fight threatens, Othello says, "Keep up your bright swords, for the dew will rust them." It's a simple, direct, authoritative statement in keeping with the martial character of Othello. The statement has its desired effect.

By his choice of words and sentences rhythms, Shakespeare can suggest madness, as at the entrance of Lear on the heath:

Blow, winds, and crack your cheeks! rage! blow!
You cataracts and hurricanoes, spout
Till you have drenched our steeples, drown'd the cocks!
King Lear, III, 2, 1-3

Short sentences and lighthearted banter suggest the dialogue of a young couple in *As You Like It:*

ROSALIND.   O, my dear Orlando, how it grieves me to see thee wear thy heart in a scarf.
ORLANDO.   It is my arm.
ROSALIND.   I thought thy heart had been wounded with the claws of a lion.
ORLANDO.   Wounded it is, but with the eyes of a lady.
As You Like It, V, 2, 19-24

When the script calls for bitter, violent language, Shakespeare provides it. In the following excerpt from *Timon of Athens*, Timon bitterly denounces the false friends who deserted him at a time of need:

TIMON.   Live loathed and long,
Most smiling, smooth, detested parasites,
Courteous destroyers, affable wolves, meek bears,
You fools of fortune, trencher-friends, time's flies,
Cap-and-knee slaves, vapours, and minute-jacks!
Timon of Athens, III, 6, 92-96

When Coriolanus (p265) seems ready to attack his native city, Rome, his stern, unbending mother, Volumnia, must humble her pride to plead with him not to become a traitor. Her long speech is characterized by logic, emotion, and a steely acknowledgment of the situation as she sees it:

The end of war's uncertain; but this is certain,
That, if thou conquer Rome, the benefit

> Which thou shalt thereby reap is such a name
> Whose repetition will be dogged with curses;
> Whose chonricle thus writ: "The man was noble,
> But with his last attempt he wiped it out,
> Destroyed his country, and his name remains
> To th'ensuing age abhorred."
> *Coriolanus*, V, 3, 141-148

Despite the impending tragedy, Volumnia refuses to abase herself. With Coriolanus's wife and son, she kneels, but she refuses to humiliate herself further, saying, "We will home to Rome, and die among our neighbors." This is a haughty Roman matron, and the style of her discourse suggests that pride.

Against Type

Sometimes Shakespeare surprises by going against type, giving a key speech to a person least expected to deliver it, a character seemingly incapable of the content and the lyrical quality. One of Shakespeare's most beautiful tributes is given to Cleopatra by an unexpected admirer:

> The barge she sat in, like a burnish't throne
> Burned on the water: the poop was beaten gold;
> Purple the sails, and so perfumed that
> The winds were love-sick with them; the oars were silver,
> Which to the tune of flutes kept stroke and made
> The water which they beat to follow faster,
> As amorous of their strokes. For her own person,
> It beggared all description, she did lie
> In her pavilion, cloth-of-gold, of tissue,
> O'er picturing that Venus where we see
> The fancy outwork nature.
> *Antony and Cleopatra*, II, 2, 191-201

The praise goes on, adding more and more details to this alluring prospect. One might expect such a tribute to be delivered by a poet, a talented nobleman, or Antony himself. But no. The speech is delivered by Enobarbus, a fascinating and complex character. He is a crusty old warrior, gruff veteran of the civil wars. Assigning that magnificent speech to skeptical Enobarbus emphasizes the powerful attraction Cleopatra exerts on onlookers. It underlines the fatal attraction that Antony had for the Egyptian Queen and makes the tragedy both more complex and more understandable. It suggests an answer to the question "How could a mature, cynical, hardened politician like Antony fall into the trap that destroyed him?" Enobarbus's description suggests a reason why.

Levels of Usage

Speech is sometimes classified into broad groups; for example, slang, colloquial, informal, and formal, with considerable overlapping at each edge. Slang, sometimes called "the poetry of the streets," is characterized by inventiveness, punning, occasional coarseness, and new words. Most slang is perishable, though slang words sometimes enter standard English.

Colloquial English is the language of conversation. It is studded with contractions like "I'm" and is generally uncomplicated. Colloquial and informal English are sometimes grouped together, though some prefer to apply the label *informal* to the kind of prose generally used in this book.

Formal, or literary, English is the language of state, of legal documents, and of serious fiction or nonfiction. Formal English may contain words rarely used in informal English, like *relegate*, *precept*, and *discernment*. Shakespeare is a master of all levels.

Slang

Shakespeare's mastery of slang and the speech of everyday workers is demonstrated in *Henry IV, Part One*. Two carriers talk over events like two companionable workmen anywhere.

1 CARRIER.   I prithee, Tom, best Cut's saddle, put a few flocks in the point, poor jade is wrung in the withers out of all cess.

2 CARRIER.   Peas and beans are as dank here as a dog, and that is the best way to give poor jades the bots: this house is turned upside down since Robin Ostler died.

1 CARRIER.   Poor fellow never joyed since the price of oats rose, it was the death of him.

2 CARRIER.   I think this is the most villainous house in all London for fleas, I am stung like a tench.

Henry IV, Part One, II, 1, 5-13

Shakespeare's groundlings would have understood and appreciated every word. This is the way the lower classes spoke in Shakespeare's day, and Shakespeare has caught the words and the music. To understand what's been said, we should know that *flocks=wool*, *cess=measure*, *bots=worms*, and *tench=spotted* fish. Even without that knowledge, we can sense a friendly rapport between the carriers. The speeches go on, amusing the common folk in the theater, telling more about those villainous fleas and providing laughs for the common folk.

Dialect

Though not strictly a level of usage, dialect adds truth and color at times to the plays. Shakespeare seemed especially pleased to introduce Irish, Welsh, and Scottish dialect into his plays. In the so-called "international scene" of *Henry V*, Shakespeare introduces an Irish soldier, Macmorris; the Welsh Fluellen; and the Scottish captain, Jamy, who delivers the following lines in an almost impenetrable dialect!

By the mess, ere these eyes of mine take themselves to slomber, ay'll de gude service, or ay'll lig i'th'grund for it; ay, or go to death: and ay'll pay't as valorously as I may, that sal I suerly do, that is the breff and the long...Mary, I wad full pain hear some question tween you tway.

Henry V, III, 2, 111-115

This speech probably isn't outstanding for its clarity. We gather, in a general sort of way, that Jamy is here promising a valorous fight...to the death, if need be. No matter, the intent is to show that Henry's army was a diverse one, composed of subjects from throughout Henry's kingdom.

Colloquial and Informal English

Since plays are constructed of dialogue, Shakespeare's lines are often colloquial, conversational, informal. Of course, this is the colloquial English of Shakespeare's day, but it sounds easy and free to our modern ears. In this dialogue from *Twelfth Night* (p281), the reveler Sir Toby, uncle of the wealthy Olivia, is warned by the maid Maria that his niece is getting tired of his drinking and brawling. Maria also mentions another hanger-on, Sir Andrew Aguecheek, whose money is the source of his popularity with Sir Toby.

MARIA.   Ay, but you must confine yourself within the modest limits of order.

SIR TOBY.   Confine? I'll confine myself no finer than I am. These clothes are good enough to drink in, and so be these boots, too: an they be not, let them hang themselves in their own straps.

MARIA.   That quaffing and drinking will undo you: I heard my lady talk of it yesterday: and of a foolish knight, that you brought in one night here, to be her wooer.

SIR TORY.   Who? Sir Andrew Aguecheek?

MARIA.   Ay, he.

SIR TOBY.   He's as tall a man as any's in Illyria.

MARIA.   What's that to th' purpose?

SIR TOBY.   Why, he has three thousand ducats a year.

Twelfth Night, I, 3, 7-22

Formal English

Formal English is commonplace in the pronouncements of kings and other dignitaries of high station. For example, Lear makes his wishes known in rather formal English:

> LEAR.   Give me the map there. Know that we have divided
>   In three our kingdom, and 'tis our fast intent
>   To shake all cares and business from our age,
>   Conferring them on younger strength while we
>   Unburdened crawl toward death.
>   *King Lear*, I, 1, 137-41

Claudius, too, speaks rather formally in announcing his plans at the beginning of the second scene of *Hamlet*. At the beginning of *Henry V*, the Archbishop of Canterbury speaks at great, boring, almost comical length in setting forth a supposed legal reason for Henry to invade France. People of lower estate may also speak more formally at some time.

Many Levels

Shakespeare may include many levels of discourse in a simple play. *A Midsummer Night's Dream* is particularly interesting for its many levels of interest. Theseus, Hippolyta, and the Athenian court speak with dignity and formality:

> THESEUS. Now, fair Hippolyta, our nuptial hour
>   Draws on space: four happy days bring in
>   Another moon; but O! methinks, how slow
>   The old moon wanes.
>   *A Midsummer Night's Dream*, I, 1, 1-4

This is an impassioned love poem, but it is expressed with great restraint! The young lovers often speak in rhymed couplets:

LYSANDER.   Helen, to you our minds we will unfold.
            Tomorrow might, when Phoebe doth behold
            Her silver visage in the watery glass,
            Decking with liquid pearl the bladed grass,
            A time that lovers' flights doth still conceal,
            Through Athens' gate have we devised to steal.
                        A Midsummer Night's Dream, I, 1, 208-213

This sounds almost like greeting-card verse, a suggestion of the lovers' infatuations.

The working-class artisans speak prose, except in their play scenes. They begin preparations for presenting an entertainment for the wedding of Theseus and Hippolyta. They talk over the strategies involved in putting on this play about Pyramus and Thisbe:

BOTTOM.   Write me a prologue; and let the prologue seem to say, we will do no harm with our swords and that Pyramus is not killed indeed; and, for the more better assurance, tell them that I Pyramus are not Pyramus, but Bottom the weaver. This will put them out of fear.

QUINCE.   Well, we will have such a prologue; and it shall be written in eight and six.

BOTTOM.   No, make it two more; let it be written in eight and Eight.

SNOUT.   Will not the ladies be afeard of the lion?

STARVELING.   I fear it, I promise you.

BOTTOM.   Masters, you ought to consider with your selves: to bring in-(God shield me!)-a lion among ladies, is a most dreadful thing; for there is not a more fearful wild-fowl than your lion living; and we ought to look to it.

SNOUT.   Therefore another prologue must tell he is not a Lion.
                        A Midsummer Night's Dream, III, 1, 16-32

The episodes with the artisans may be Shakespeare's warm memories of such performances put on in Stratford during festival days.

When the artisans actually present their play to the wedding guests, they use pretentious, badly rhymed verse. Here Pyramus, played by Bottom, worries that Thisbe will not appear:

> PYRAMUS.   O grim-looked night! 0 night with hue so black!
> O night, which ever art when day is not.
> *A Midsummer Night's Dream*, V, 1, 169-170

The fairies' speech cannot be easily classified. They speak in a mixture of meters (below) and verse patterns. The lines are often shorter than the usual Shakespearean line, Sometimes the lines rhyme; sometimes, not. Here, a fairy answers Puck's question:

> PUCK.   How now, sprite! Whither wander you?
> FAIRY.   Over hill, over dale,
> Thorough bush, thorough brier,
> Over park, over pale,
> Thorough flood, thorough fire,
> I do wander everywhere.
> *A Midsummer Night's Dream*, II, 1, 1-6

Prose or Verse?

Comparing Theseus's opening speech with the dialogue involving the artisans reveals an obvious difference. The former is written in verse; the second, in prose. Throughout *A Midsummer Night's Dream* there are interludes of prose, though most of Shakespeare's lines here and elsewhere are written in verse.

How does Shakespeare's verse differ from his prose? In prose, sentences are run together. In verse, individual lines have a recurring pattern. These lines have an identifiable meter, a recurring pattern of stressed and unstressed syllables. The meter used by Shakespeare is called *blank verse*. This is sometimes defined as *iambic pentameter unrhymed*. A poetic foot usually consists of one stressed syllable and one or more unstressed syllables. There are four basic feet: *iambic-Marié*; *trochaic-Máry*; *anapestic-Gabriélle*; and *dactylic-Gábriel*. The ta-TUM meter of the iamb is basic to Shakespeare's verse, though variations often occur. If we put five ta-TUM feet together we have iambic pentameter. Here are several regular iambic pentameter lines:

> In time the savage bull doth bear the yoke.
> A little more than kin, and less than kind.
> So foul and fair a day I have not seen.

A succession of such lines would be monotonous. Shakespeare provides all kind of variations while still keeping the basic pattern. A glance back at the verse quotation opening this chapter shows both the basic pattern and the variation.

The last line is regular:

> In russet yeas and honest kersey noes.
> ta-TUM ta'TUM ta-TUM ta-TUM ta-TUM

The first line is not:

> Taffeta phrases, silken terms precise
> TUM-ta ta-TUM ta-TUM ta-TUM ta-TUM.

Blank verse resembles ordinary conversational speech. As director John Barton pointed out, "It's actually quite easy to pick up blank verse lines in everyday conversation, or in a book, a paper, or the telly." If blank verse resembles ordinary speech, why bother with it? The meter provides a pleasing pattern especially suited to the drama. Actors have commented that it is easier to memorize Shakespeare's lines than those of other playwrights.

Shakespeare often signals the end of a scene with a rhyming couplet, two lines that say, "The scene is over." When Malcolm urges his brother Donalbain to flee the castle after the murder of their father Duncan, he says:

> But shift; away; there's warrant in that theft
> Which steals itself when there's no mercy left.

The rhyming couplet may be used with two different speakers, as in this scene from *Henry VI, Part One*:

SOMERSET.   If he be dead, brave Talbot, then adieu!
LUCY.   His fame lives in the world, his shame with you.

A more unusual break in that rhyming couplet is this example from *Hamlet*, where the King completes Polonius's line:

POLONIUS.   Your wisdom best shall think.
KING.   It shall be so.
            Madness in great ones must not unwatched go.

Shakespeare at Play

In the years 1593-1596, Shakespeare was writing poetry to help earn a living during the plague years (p 25). He probably wrote most of his famous sonnets during this period. A sonnet is a fourteen-line poem, usually written in iambic pentameter, with a special rhyme scheme.

The two most common forms of the sonnet are the *Italian*, or *Petrarchan*, and the *Shakespearean*. The Italian sonnet is divided into two major parts: an eight-line section called the *octave* and a six-line section called the *sestet*. The rhyme scheme, usually designated by letters, is abbaabba cde cde. The rhyme scheme of the sestet varies. The Shakespearean sonnet has three four-line sections, called quatrains, and a rhyming pair called a couplet, at the end.

Each sonnet forms have a different effect. In the Italian form, the octave develops one thought. The sestet grows out of the octave, varying it and completing it. In the Shakespearean sonnet, each quatrain expresses a different idea, each related to the preceding. The couplet completes the development.

It's probable that Shakespeare was working on his famous sonnets at about the same time he wrote *Romeo and Juliet*. We can imagine him deciding to combine two projects by including a sonnet in *Romeo and Juliet*. And so he does. Perhaps no one noticed the clever touch, but Shakespeare probably chuckled at his achievement. When Romeo and Juliet first dance at the Capulet ball (p223), their dialogue is in the form of a sonnet :

ROMEO.   (takes Juliet's hand)
            If I profane with my unworthiest hand
            This holy shrine, the gentle pain is this:
            My lips, two blushing pilgrims, ready stand
            To smooth that rough touch with a tender kiss.
JULIET.   Good pilgrim, you do wrong your hand too much,
            Which mannerly devotion shows in this:
            For saints have hands that pilgrims' hands do touch
            And palm to palm is holy palmers' kiss.
ROMEO.   Have not saints lips, and holy palmers too?
JULIET.   Ay, pilgrim, lips that they must use in prayer,
ROMEO.   O then, dear saint, let lips do what hands do.
            They pray: grant thou, lest faith turns to despair
JULIET.   Saints do not move, though grant for prayers sake.
ROMEO.   Then move not, while my prayer's effect I take.
                                  Romeo and Juliet, I, 5, 93-106

Modern lovers might speak such heartfelt sentiments, though they are not likely to complete a sonnet in so doing! Romeo's "line" works, for after the next line he kisses Juliet.

Who Speaks Prose?

A common theory about the division of prose and verse in Shakespeare's plays assigns verse to the upper classes and prose to the lower. A superficial glance at the plays seems to bear this theory out. After all, in *A Midsummer Night's Dream*, members of the Athenian upper class speak verse. By contrast, the lower class artisans speak prose, except in their comical play of Pyramus and Thisbe.

The trouble with this theory is that it overlooks the occasional prose spoken by the upper classes. In a thoughtful statement to Guildenstern and Rosencrantz, Hamlet tries to explain his mood:

> I have of late, but wherefore I know not, lost all my mirth, forgone all custom of exercises; and indeed it goes so heavily with my disposition, that this goodly frame the earth, seems to me a sterile promontory, this most excellent canopy the air, look you, this brave o'erhanging firmament, this majestical roof fretted with golden fire, why it appeareth nothing to me but a foul and pestilent congregation of vapours...What a piece of work is man, how noble in reason, how infinite in faculties, in form and moving, how express and admirable in action, how like an angel in apprehension, how like a god: the beauty of the world, the paragon of animals; and yet to me, what is this quintessence of dust? Man delights not me.
>
> *Hamlet*, II, 2, 299-312

This gloriously poetic statement is written in prose, not verse. Actually, most of act 2, scene 2, is written in prose. Hamlet, Polonius, Rosencrantz, Guildenstern and the Queen all speak prose, but the First Player's recitation and Hamlet's brilliant soliloquy at the end of the scene return to verse, with stunning effect. Why? Prose can suggest a contrast, a change of pace, a shift in emotion. Prose also tends to be used for wit and satire. It is used for colloquial speech, relaxed moments. Since lower-class characters tend to speak informally and colloquially, prose fits their speech.

An example of prose used for wit is one of Rosalind's speeches in *As You Like It* (p278). Orlando tells the disguised Rosalind that he is in love. She says he's not, because he doesn't have the marks of a lovelorn lover:

ROSALIND.   A lean cheek, which! you have not: a blue eye and sunken, which you have not: an unquestionable spirit, which you have not: a beard neglected, which you have not, Then your hose should be ungartered, your bonnet unbanded, your sleeve unbuttoned, your shoes untied, and everything about you demonstrating a careless desolation: but you are no such man; you are rather point-device in your accoutrements, as loving yourself than seeming the lover of any other.

As You Like It, III, 2, 365-375

Rosalind, a duke's daughter, is certainly of the upper classes; yet she speaks prose here.

On the other hand, the lower classes sometimes speak excellent verse, if the occasion warrants. In *Richard II* (p230) two gardeners speak impressive blank verse discussing their gardening chores and comparing the responsibilities of gardening with those of running a kingdom. Richard has lost his supporters, all killed by Bolingbroke. Now Richard is in Bolingbroke's hands, doomed by his own mistakes.

GARDENER.   Bolingbroke
                   Hath seized the wasteful king. O! what pity is it
                   That he had not so trimmed and dressed his land,
                   As we this garden. We at time of year
                   Do wound the bark, the skin of our fruit-trees,
                   Lest being over-proud in sap and blood,
                   With too much riches it confound itself.
                   Had he done so to great and growing men,
                   They might have lived to bear, and he to taste,

> Their fruits of duty: superfluous branches
> We lop away, that bearing boughs may live:
> If he had done so, himself had borne the crown,
> Which waste of idle hours hath quite thrown down.
> *Richard II*, III, 4, 54-56

Shakespeare's choice of prose or verse is not simply a matter of observing class distinctions. He has the playwright's sense of what's appropriate at a particular moment in the play.

12

The Language of Shakespeare

Zounds: I was never so bethumped with words
Since I first called my brother's father Dad.

King John II, 1, 467-468

When Shakespeare began writing, English had moved from the Middle English of Chaucer to the beginning of Modern English in the Renaissance. Thus began a period of jubilant experimentation and expansion.

By then, English had come a long way from Old English and established itself as one of the world's great adventure stories. The incredible wealth of the English language is tied into its incredible history. Words like *druid, brother, Lincoln, candle, skirt, plaintiff, intellect, automobile, kimono, radar,* and *E-mail* tell the story of the English language and its people.

Early History of English

Little is known of the language of the Stone-Age people in England. When the Celts arrived some time before the beginning of the Common Era, they brought with them the first Indo-European tongue to be spoken in England. Today all the major languages of Europe are of Indo-European origin, except Finnish, Hungarian, and Basque.

Though the Celts occupied England for hundreds of years, there are relatively few Celtic words in the English language. These are mostly place names like *Avon* or *Dover* or names for peculiar Celtic customs, like *slogan* originally a "war cry," and *druid*, a "Celtic priest."

Roman armies came to Britain in 43 C.E. and stayed for nearly four centuries. Place names like *Lincoln* (from *colonia-*"colony") and *Lancaster* (*castra-*"camp") are reminders of that powerful presence, along with roads and other examples of Roman engineering.

When the Roman legions left for good, there followed turbulent years, with waves of invaders pillaging—and often settling, in Britain. The Celts in the south sought help to counteract the threats by northern Picts. They pursued alliances on the mainland. The warlike Saxons came, helped drive out the Picts, and then turned on the Celts. Another tribe, the Angles soon followed, forcing the Celts to flee westward to what is now Ireland and Wales. That Anglo-Saxon language is the backbone of modern English.

Latin entered the language a second time when Christianity spread throughout Britain. Many church words like *shrine, candle,* and *altar* are reminders of that influence.

Other invaders attacked the British coasts. The Danes marauded and then came to stay. Eventually, a Danish King ruled England. Danish words like *sky, rugged,* and *scrub* entered the language. Similar, related words often had different pronunciations. *Skirt* and *shirt* come from the same original root, but one is Danish and the other is Anglo-Saxon. The Saxons regained control of England in 1042, but their newfound freedom lasted just 24 years.

The next invaders also came from northern Europe. William the Conqueror's Norman armies defeated the Saxon in 1066 at the Battle of Hastings. This event had a profound and lasting impact on the language. French and Anglo-Saxon blended to give English a doubly rich vocabulary. French words like *plaintiff, jury, state,* and *mutton* entered the language. Pairs of words for the same object provided rich synonyms: *home-mansion, work-labor, speed-velocity, stir-agitate.*

The Renaissance

During the Renaissance, Latin and Greek were favorite sources for new English words. Writers eagerly searched the classics for words to express their thoughts more exactly. When Sir Thomas Elyot wanted to write a book on education, he had to make up such words as *maturity* and *dedicate*.

It was into this heady, exuberant linguistic society that Shakespeare was born. He was destined to become one of the most enduring influences on the growth and power of English.

Shakespeare's Vocabulary

Authorities have variously estimated the number of different words at about 27,000 for Shakespeare, with 8-14,000 for John Milton, and 7,000 for the King James Bible. Shakespeare not only used current words in new and resourceful ways; he also created what he needed.

A great many words he introduced are with us still, words like *agile, critical, demonstrate, emphasis, extract, horrid, meditate, modest,* and *vast.* Some words have changed their meanings since Shakespeare's time. To communicate, for example, then meant "To share or make common to many." Nowadays it means "to exchange information." The changes in meaning sometimes perplex modern readers or audiences who wonder at a word like humorous in the following quotation.

> RENVOLIO. Come, he hath hid himself among these trees
> To be consorted with the humorous night.
> Blind is his love, and best befits the dark.
> *Romeo and Juliet*, II, 1, 31-33

Humorous here doesn't mean "funny." It means "damp, moist." In Shakespeare's day, a humor was a "mood" or a "fluid"-black bile, phlegm, blood, and yellow bile-the four bodily fluids gave us *melancholy, phlegmatic, sanguine,* and *choleric.* In the sanguine person, the bodily fluid, blood, pre-dominated. Benvolio may here be referring to Romeo's mood, his *humor*, as well as the moisture in the night air.

Shakespeare's Method

What are some methods that Shakespeare used to bring new words into the language? English is a flexible, hospitable language that accepts word manipulation to create new concepts. One common device is using a word as a different part of speech. If a mother says to a child, "I don't want to hear any *buts*," she is using *but* as a noun rather than as a conjunction.

Some words enter the language immediately. Others take years to find acceptance. The English noun *contact*, probably entered the language after Shakespeare's death, some time around 1626. After a while, someone tired of saying *make contact with* and decided to use contact as a verb: *to contact*. This usage was first noted in 1834. Though this usage simplifies and streamlines communication, the usage was considered socially unacceptable. Even today some speakers avoid a sentence like this: "The voter contacted his Congressman." Their objections are ineffective. The language rolls relentless over those who try to set up roadblocks.

Shakespeare, of all writers, seemed to understand the genius of English best. He converted the verbs *embrace, glow, howl, resolve,* and *shudder* to nouns. He combined *marigold* and *bud* to make *maribud*. He created colorful new words like *bethumped*, quoted at the beginning of the chapter. Some of his creations are strikingly poetic. In *The Tempest* (I, 2, 49-50), Prospero is testing Miranda's memory (p316):

> What seest thou else
> In the dark backward and abysm of time?

Using the adjective *backward* as a noun here and linking it with *abysm* provides a colorful line.

Shakespeare liked to create new adjectives by adding *ed* to nouns. In *Cymbeline*, the Roman general Lucius suggests that Cloten (p311) be buried honorably:

> Let us
> Pick out the prettiest daisied plot we can

And make him with our pikes and partisans
A grave.
> *Cymbeline*, IV, 2, 399-402.

Shakespeare has taken the noun *daisy*, added the suffix *ed*, and made a colorful adjective of it. He liked the suffix *ment* as well, creating words like *amazement, bewitchment, excitement,* and *reinforcement*. The *ure* suffix provided *exposure*. Occasionally Shakespeare would add a suffix to help the meter of the line: *vasty, brisky, plumpy, steepy*.

Shakespeare created many new words with the prefix *un-*for example, *unchanging, unearthly, uneducated, unhappy, unhelpful, unpolluted, unpremeditated, unreal, unrival, unsolicited,* and *unsullied*. Very often, the negative proves especially effective, as in *Julius Caesar*. When Antony inflames the crowd by saying that Brutus's stab wound of Caesar was the final blow in Caesar's death, he doesn't call the blow "the cruelest cut." Instead, he uses the negative *unkindest* and combines it with another superlative, *most*.

For Brutus, as you know, was Caesar's angel.
Judge, 0 you gods, how dearly Caesar loved him.
That was the most unkindest cut of all.
> *Julius Caesar*, III, 2, 182-184

Unkind is an understatement, but in this context, it is powerful.

Shakespeare's Compound Epithets

Shakespeare's ability to create colorful compound descriptive epithets has provided some of his most memorable lines. A sample would include the following: *heaven-kissing hill, temple-haunting martlet, earth-treading stars, star-crossed lovers, cloud-capped towers,* and *tawny-finned fishes*. Each combines three elements in a striking combination.

The Enrichment of English

Trying to find out who first used a word is difficult, at best. Fortunately, the huge *Oxford English Dictionary* provides the first recorded use of the words included. The number of words attributed to Shakespeare reflects Shakespeare's inventiveness in transforming old words and treating new ones. The following is the barest sample:

accessible	distrustful	majestic
airless	domineering	motionless
auspicious	downstairs	negotiate
birthplace	employment	outbreak
characterless	fashionable	perplex
circumstantial	hostile	pious
cold-blooded	impartial	quarrelsome
courtless	inaudible	remorseless
courtship	lament	stealthy
dewdrop	laughable	tranquil

Shakespeare's Grammar and Usage

In the years since Shakespeare's time, many words have shifted their meanings. Modern versions of the King James Bible supply current words for those whose meanings have changed since the time of Shakespeare. Shakespeare's grammar, too, is somewhat different from our own. The Elizabethan period was a time of transition. Poets and dramatists gloried in the freedom afforded them: experimentation was common.

Some usages, acceptable in Shakespeare's time, are frowned upon today, like the double superlative on p121 and the double negative. In *Richard III* (I, 3, 90), Richard says to Queen Elizabeth, "You may deny that you were not the means of my Lord Hastings' late imprisonment." Modern usage would omit the *not*, but the Elizabethans preferred vigor of expression to logic.

Another such usage is the agreement of subject and verb, a must in modern English. In the battle scene in *Julius Caesar* (V, 1, 32-33), Cassius addresses his foe: "Antony, the posture of your blows are yet unknown." Modern standard usage would require *is*. This is another demonstration of the Elizabethan freedom from standard rules.

Those Familiar Quotations

"Shakespeare was very resourceful. He plagiarized so many common quotations." This old joke overlooks the truth that Shakespeare created those quotations. The following brief list gives some indication of Shakespeare's presence in modern English.

> All the world's a stage. (*As You Like It*)
> Bated breath (*The Merchant of Venice*)
> The better part of valor is discretion. (*Henry IV, Part One*)
> Breathe one's last (*Henry VI, Part One*)
> Brevity is the soul of wit. (*Hamlet*)
> Budge an inch (*The Taming of the Shrew*)
> Caviar to the general (*Hamlet*)
> He hath eaten me out of house and home. (*Henry IV, Part Two*)
> Fair play (*King John*)
> Flaming youth (*Hamlet*)
> For goodness' sake (*Henry VIII*)
> Foregone conclusion (*Othello*)
> Full circle (*King Lear*)
> Good riddance (*Troilus and Cressida*)
> The green-eyed monster (*Othello*)
> In my heart of hearts (*Hamlet*)
> Household words (*Henry V*)
> An itching palm (*Julius Caesar*)

Knock, knock: Who's there? (*Macbeth*)
Master of their fates (*Julius Caesar*)
The milk of human kindness (*Macbeth*)
In my mind's eye (*Hamlet*)
The play's the thing (*Hamlet*)
A sorry sight (*Macbeth*)
A spotless reputation (*Richard II*)
Strange bedfellows (*The Tempest*)
Sweets to the Sweet (*Hamlet*)
Too much of a good thing (*As You Like It*)
A tower of strength (*Richard III*)
Vale of tears (*Othello*)
What the Dickens (*The Merry Wives of Windsor*)
Wild-goose chase (*Romeo and Juliet*)

Not Invented by Shakespeare

Shakespeare has contributed far more to the English language than any other author who has written in English. Oddly enough, however, there are a few common expressions incorrectly attributed to Shakespeare, even though they originated elsewhere. Many of these were commonplace during Shakespeare's lifetime. Here's a sample.

Knit one's brow (Quoted in *Henry VI, Part Two*,
    but previously used by Geoffrey Chaucer)
Cold comfort (Used in *The Taming of the Shrew*
    and *King John*, but taken from the Book of Psalms)
Elbow room (used in *King John*, but traced to 1540)
Laughing stock (Used in *The Merry Wives of
    Windsor*, but traced to1533)
Fool's paradise (Used in *Love's Labour's Lost* and
    Romeo and Juliet, but traced to 1462)
In a pickle (Used in *The Tempest*, but previously
    used in a sermon by John Foxe)
Thereby hangs a tale, (Quoted in *The Taming of the*

Shrew, but previously used by the poet Thomas
Churchyard)
I have not slept a wink, (Used in *Cymbeline*, but
    traced back to the fourteenth century)

Titles from the Plays

When authors seek titles for their plays, they often mine the wealth of other writers. In his poem *Samson Agonistes*, John Milton describes the blinded Samson as "eyeless in Gaza, milling with slaves." The novelist Aldous Huxley chose *Eyeless in Gaza* as the title of a novel. He also chose a title from Shakespeare's *The Tempest*: *Brave New World*. There are numerous book titles taken from Shakespeare. John Steinbeck took *The Winter of Our Discontent* from *Richard III*. Ogden Nash took *The Primrose Path* from *Hamlet*. John Gunther took *Taken at the Flood* from *Julius Caesar*. Even King Hussein of Jordan picked an unusually appropriate title for his English language recollections: *Uneasy Lies the Head*, from *Richard II*). This brief listing barely scratches the surface.

13

Shakespeare's Strategy

For aught that I could ever read,
Could ever hear by tale or history,
The course of true love never did run smooth.

A Midsummer Night's Dream, I, 1, 132-134

How often have you heard the complaint about a situation comedy: "It's done by formula. You know exactly what's going to happen"? Sometimes the formula is so obvious that you know that a certain kind of scene will always be followed by another, specific kind of scene.

In a larger sense, plots in drama and fiction also follow a general formula. We've heard the oversimplification: "Boy meets girl. Boy loses girl. Boy gets girl." Nestled in plot is conflict. Something happens to upset the situation at the beginning. Boy may lose girl in one of a hundred different ways, but unless he loses the girl, at least temporarily, there is no conflict...and no plot.

Shakespeare was the master of conflict. All his plays contain a central conflict: a man against a shrewish woman; a lover against a hostile family; a son against a stepfather. Knowing the short attention span of the average audience, Shakespeare knew how to stir the pot in the opening scene. He had to capture his audience right away...or risk losing them.

Opening Lines

Notice how the following opening lines foreshadow the troubles to come and sketch out the probable source of conflict.

The Tempest-Men against the Sea

Enter a Ship Master and a Boatswain

MASTER.	Boatswain!
BOATSWAIN.	Here, master: What cheer?
MASTER.	Good, speak to the mariners. Fall to't yarely, or we run ourselves aground.

From the very first words, we realize that the ship is in a deadly storm. Shakespeare wastes no time getting into the middle of action. This foreshadows the essential conflict: a rightful duke of Milan against his brother, the usurping Duke. We can imagine one groundling elbowing his packed fellow observer and saying, "This is good already!"

Macbeth-Man against the Forces of Evil

Thunder and Lightning. Enter Three Witches.

FIRST WITCH.	When shall we three meet again
	In thunder lightning or in rain?
SECOND WITCH.	When the hurlyburly's done,
	When the battle's lost and won.
THIRD WITCH.	That will be ere the set of sun.
FIRST WTTCH.	Where the place?
SECOND WITCH.	Upon the heath.
THIRD WITCH.	There to meet with Macbeth.

When they conclude their comments with a joint "Fair is foul and foul is fair," the audience has been captured. In a few lines, Shakespeare has suggested the theme of the play. These supernatural creatures are somehow involved with Macbeth. Why? What have they to do with him? Is there an ultimate conflict here between Macbeth and the Witches, as sources of evil? Watch the play to find out.

There is a rhetorical device called foreshadowing, a suggestion of what's to come through carefully arranged incidents and conversations. The suggestion of evil in the witches' scene foreshadows the importance of evil in the deeds to come.

Julius Caesar-Man against Dictatorship

Enter Flavius, Marcellus, and certain Commoners
FLAVIUS.   Hence! home, you idle creatures, get you home;
              Is this a holiday? What, know you not,
              Being mechanical, you might not walk
              Upon a laboring day without the sign
              Of your profession? Speak, what trade art thou?
FIRST COMMONER. Why, sir a carpenter.
MARCELLUS. Where is thy leather apron, and thy rule?
What dost thou with thy best apparel on?

There is obviously trouble in the streets. Flavius and Marcellus, who are Roman tribunes, are objecting to the celebration of Julius Caesar's victories. Being supporters of the Roman General Pompey, they obviously hate seeing the masses supporting Pompey's rival. Already, the audience learns that there is unrest in Rome. There is hint here of conflict to come. The plot is set in motion.

Richard II-King against Usurper

Enter King Richard, John of Gaunt with Other Nobles and Attendants
KING RICHARD. Old John of Gaunt, time-honored Lancaster,
                 Hast thou, according to thy oath and hands,
                 Brought hither Henry Hereford thy bold son,

> Here to make good the boisterous late appeal,
> Which then our leisure would not let us hear,
> Against the Duke of Norfolk, Thomas Mowbray?

JOHN OF GAUNT.   I have, my liege.

With his opening words, King Richard reveals that there is trouble, a conflict between John of Gaunt's son and the powerful Duke of Norfolk. Within a few lines we meet the bitter enemies and watch the king make a fateful decision that will ultimately cost him his throne. Shakespeare loses no time in thrusting the audience into the middle of a deadly conflict.

There are other hints nestled in Richard's opening speech. He uses the unflattering words *bold* and *boisterous* in referring to Gaunt's son, who eventually overthrows Richard to become Henry IV. He also confesses that he couldn't hear young Henry's complaint because he was at "leisure." These lines provide a picture of a condescending King who is unaware of the fragility of his kingship.

As You Like It-Brother against Brother

Enter Orlando and Adam

ORLANDO. As I remember, Adam, it was upon this fashion bequeathed me by will but poor a thousand crowns; and, as though sayest, charged my brother on his blessing to breed me well; and there begins my sadness. My brother Jaques he keeps at school, and report speaks goldenly of his profit; for my part, he keeps me rustically at home, or, to speak more properly, stays me here at home unkept; for call you that keeping a gentleman of my birth that differs not from the stalling of an ox?

Orlando's opening complaint reveals that he has been treated shabbily. His brother Jaques has been pampered, while Orlando has been neglected. We quickly meet Oliver, the older brother, who is keeping Orlando down. Oliver is soon revealed as a villain, though he reforms later in the play. The theme of brother against brother is also suggested in the relationship between the banished Duke and his usurping brother, Frederick.

Strong Beginnings

So is it with the other plays. *Romeo and Juliet*, for example, begins with a street brawl. *Much Ado About Nothing* starts with indications of a battle of wits between Beatrice and Benedick, two bitter adversaries destined to fall in love, *King Lear* starts with an old king's foolish decision about the proper division of his kingdom. *Othello* starts at once with the plotting of Iago, one of Shakespeare's most evil villains. And so he goes. When a Shakespearean play starts, the audience must pay attention. There's no time wasted to allow latecomers to find their seats

Concluding Lines

No less important than the beginnings of Shakespeare's plays are the endings. The opening lines set the plot in motion, suggesting the conflicts to come. The concluding lines tie the threads together, resolving the conflicts and returning life to normal.

Here are the endings of the plays we've sampled in this chapter.

The Tempest

PROSPERO.   Now my charms are all o'erthrown,
            And what strength I have's mine own.

Prospero, whose magic has dominated the play, has relinquished his magic. Life has returned to normal.

Macbeth

MALCOLM.   So thanks to all at once and to each one,
                    Whom we invite to see us crown'd at Scone.

Malcolm, the son of the murdered Duncan, has rightfully claimed his throne. The murderer Macbeth is dead. His accomplices have all been defeated. Life has returned to normal

Julius Caesar

> OCTAVIUS CAESAR. According to his virtue let us use
> him, (Brutus)
>> With all respect and rites of burial.
>> Within my tent his bones tonight shall lie,
>> Most like a soldier, order'd honorably.
>> So call the field to rest; and let's away,
>> To part the glories of this happy day.

Caesar's assassins have been completely defeated. Mark Antony and Octavius Caesar have won. Brutus, "the noblest Roman of them all," is dead. Even Brutus's late foes pay tribute to his memory. With the words "happy day," Octavius Caesar returns life to normal.

Richard II

> BOLINGBROKE. I'll make a voyage to the Holy Land,
> To wash this blood off from my guilty hand.
> March sadly after; grace my mournings here,
> In weeping after his untimely bier.

Bolingbroke, now Henry IV, has triumphed, and life is returning to normal. There is a little difference here, though. The conquering Bolingbroke realizes that he has deposed an anointed king. His victory is tempered by a sense of guilt that will spread through the two succeeding plays: *Henry IV, Part One*, and *Henry IV, Part Two*.

As You Like It

DUKE SENIOR.   Proceed, proceed; we will begin these rites,
                 As we trust they'll end, in true delights.

All the complications have been smoothed out. Loving pairs have been united and all about to be wed. Villains have repented. Life has returned to normal.

Shakespeare's Suspense

One bit of advice often given to prospective storytellers is "Let 'em laugh; let 'em cry; let 'em wait." The third bit of advice deals with suspense, that most frequently used technique to keep people interested. The root of the word suspense is the Latin *pendere-*"to hang." Suspense keeps the reader or listener "hanging."

To keep his audience interested, Shakespeare used suspense. In old movie melodramas, the heroine might be placed on the railroad track. The camera shifts from the approaching train to the speeding hero, back and forth, back and forth. Of course, the audience knows that the hero will save the girl just in time, but despite this awareness, the suspense works.

Old movie serials put the hero or heroine in a most dangerous situation just at the end of each episode. "Come back next week to see how they get out...If they do." Current action movies use similar devices to keep the audience on edge.

The strategy is as old as storytelling, and Shakespeare knew it well. There are many suspenseful episodes scattered throughout the plays. In Act V of *Macbeth*, the final battle scenes are arranged in suspenseful order.

In Scene V, Macbeth at first decides to stay within the castle and let the attackers waste their strength in a futile assault. Then he learns that Birnam Wood is coming to Dunsinane, as the attackers take up bushes for camouflage. In a wild burst of anger, he resolves to fight outside the castle.

Scene VI takes us to the attackers' camp. Scene VII takes us to another part of the battlefield. We know that the final conflict is approaching, but

Shakespeare makes us wait, as Macbeth has some early success. But then he meets Macduff and his doom.

The opening scene of *Hamlet* tells the audience that a Ghost is walking the battlements of Elsinore Castle. The Ghost reappears briefly, enough to whet the audience's appetite for more. Then it disappears. By now the audience is dying to know more. What does Shakespeare do? He "lets 'em wait."

The Ghost doesn't reappear for a long time. Scene II is a brightly lit look at the King's revels. Though the Ghost is mentioned at the end of the scene, he doesn't appear. By now the audience is more eager than ever to see that Ghost again. What happens? Shakespeare introduces Scene III, a quiet look at domestic relations in the home of Polonius. No Ghost!

By now the audience is saying, "Will we ever see that Ghost again?" Just when the audience is getting a little irritated by the delay, Shakespeare finally brings the Ghost back in Scene IV—but not right away. The Ghost does reappear, finally, but he doesn't speak immediately. He draws Hamlet away and at last gives the details of his murder. Notice how Shakespeare has gotten tremendous mileage out of that Ghost. It may take half an hour to get the Ghost to speak, but that half hour isn't wasted.

Whose Plot Is It Anyway?

Scholars have pointed out that Shakespeare borrowed plots as bases of his plays. No source is known for *Love's Labour's Lost*, but this is an exception. Though Shakespeare may borrow the plot, what he does with that plot reveals his genius. *The Comedy of Errors* is based on a classical Latin play by Plautus: the *Menaechmi*, dealing with a set of twins and the errors caused by confusing the two characters. Shakespeare goes a step farther, introducing another set of twins. Thus the play has two sets of characters: master and bondsman, master and bondsman. The complications are doubled.

Shakespeare takes a simple, often crude tale and invents characters and new situations that breathe life into musty old legends. *Hamlet* is based on an old Danish saga. Though the outline of the "Amleth" story is similar to that of Hamlet, Shakespeare takes the rather primitive tale and creates one of the world's masterpieces.

Shakespeare is a master playwright. He learned his craft at first hand. He knew what worked.

14

Shakespeare's Imagery

Daffodils
That come before the swallow dares, and take
The winds of March with beauty.

The Winter's Tale, **IV, 4, 118-120**

Suppose you are asked to create a picture of spring in fifteen words. You are given three elements: daffodils, swallow, and March winds. How will you weave the three together to make a meaningful picture? In the quotation above, Shakespeare has done just that, effortlessly and brilliantly.

Don't let the simplicity of the image fool you. It creates a picture to flash into your mind's eye...economically. Another poet described spring in this way:

It is the season now to go
About the country high and low,
Among the lilacs hand in hand,
And two by two in fairy land.
Robert Louis Stevensen

This is a quiet, pleasing stanza, but it is quite different from Shakespeare's. It lacks the conciseness and vividness so characteristic of

135

Shakespeare. Shakespeare is not afraid to mix the concrete image of *daffodils* and *swallow* with the abstract term: *beauty*. He uses a key word, *take*, that is up to you to interpret.

Some editions suggest *charm* as the meaning of *take*, but the original meaning of *take* is much stronger: *take charge of, possess, control*. This interpretation suggests that March comes in, expecting to overcome everything but is controlled by the daffodils, by beauty.

In fifteen words, Shakespeare has created a minor miracle-a shivery picture of early March overwhelmed by the beauty of daffodils. How could the scene be better described?

Shakespeare's Images

Here follows a sample of Shakespearean imagery to show how varied and how effective such lines can be.

> How far the candle throws its beams!
> So shines a good deed in a naughty world.
> *The Merchant of Venice*, V, 1, 91-92

Portia (p214) sees the light burning in her home and is prompted to make a general comment on human morality—in a concise image.

> Within the hollow crown
> That rounds the mortal temples of a king
> Keeps Death his court.
> *Richard II*, III, 2, 160-162

King Richard (p230) has foolishly frittered away the kingship and has found himself at the mercy of Bolingbroke, soon to depose him. He is racked with self-pity as he contemplates the uncertainty of human destiny and the perils of kingship. The crown that kings wear is hollow. Instead of the royal court dominated by the king, there is a court inside that hollow crown...but here Death is the dominant figure.

> She never told her love,
> But let concealment, like a worm i' the bud,
> Feed on her damask cheek.
> *Twelfth Night*, II, 4, 110-112

Viola (p281), dressed as the page Cesario, is here confessing her love for her master, Duke Orsino, but he is so smitten with love for the unattainable Olivia that he isn't listening. Her failure to declare her love is feeding on her rosy cheek like a worm in a flowerbud.

> Say that she frown, I'll say she looks as clear
> As morning roses newly washed with dew.
> *The Taming of the Shrew*, II, 1, 172-173

Petruchie (p202) has come to Padua for a bride. Though his projected catch, Katharina, has a reputation as an unpleasant woman, Petruchio is prepared to win her by compliments, no matter how farfetched. "Morning roses newly washed with dew" is a pleasing compliment, no matter how ill-placed.

> Night's candles are burnt out, and jocund day
> Stands tiptoe on the misty mountain tops.
> *Romeo and Juliet*, III, 5, 9-10

In the morning, after a lover's meeting, Romeo (p222) fears to stay longer, for his life will be forfeit to the Capulets, enemies of his family, the Montagues. Juliet wants him to stay, saying it was the nightingale and not the lark, but Romeo knows that dawn has come. His description of the morning breaking over the mountains emphasizes the reasons for his departure.

Shakespeare has another beautiful morning image in *Hamlet*.

Look, the morning russet mantle clad
Walks o'er the dew of you high eastward hill.
Hamlet, I, 1 165-166

Here, Horatio (p286) is telling his companions, Marcellus and Bernardo, that it is time to leave, for the morning has come.

Golden lads and girls all must,
As chimney sweepers, come to dust.
Cymbeline, IV, 2, 262-263

Here, Guiderius and Arviragus (p310) are laying to rest the apparently lifeless Imogen. This song begins with the famous line "Fear no more the heat o'f the sun." Imogen is beyond mortal troubles. In choosing the *chimney sweeper* and the *dust*, is Shakespeare having a sly pun on the word *dust*?

Doubtful it stood;
As two spent swimmers, that do cling together
And choke their art.
Macbeth, I, 2, 7-9

The Captain is reporting to King Duncan the battle between his forces and those of the traitor Macdonwald. The two forces are destroying each other like two drowning swimmers until Macbeth saves the day.

The pleasant'st angling is to see the fish
Cut with her golden oars the silver stream
And greedily devour the treacherous bait.
Much Ado about Nothing, III, 1, 26-28

Benedick and Beatrice (p275), the two quarreling lovers, are being tricked into thinking the other is dying for love. Ursula, Hero's gentlewoman, is comparing the tricking of Benedick with an angler's catching a fish.

Shakespeare's Many Interests

In a major book, *Shakespeare's Imagery*, Caroline F. H. Spurgeon has analyzed the images in Shakespeare's plays and poems. Her study strongly supports the claims that Shakespeare is indeed the author of the plays (p 80). She also gives us insights into Shakespeare's life and many interests. We know, for example, that he was a keen observer of nature.

Those who live in the more northern states can appreciate Shakespeare's observations about the month of April.

> O, how this spring of love resembleth
> The uncertain glory of an April day,
> Which now shows all the beauty of the sun,
> And by and by a cloud takes all away.
> *The Two Gentlemen of Verona*, 1, 3, 84-87

Shakespeare creates many images from the sea, though he may never have gone to sea himself.

> Like a shifted wind unto a sail,
> It takes the course of thoughts to fetch about.
> *King John*, IV, 2, 23-24

The Earl of Salisbury (p227) compares a change of thought to a sail that has been forced to tack (*fetch about*).

Shakespeare uses images of cooking and the kitchen.

> Rudeness is a sauce to his good wit,
> Which gives men stomach to digest his words
> With better appetite.
> *Julius Caesar*, I, 2, 301-303

The conspirator, Casca (p259), has just told Brutus and Cassius of Caesar's manipulation of the crowd. When he leaves, Cassius has this to say about Casca's speech and personality.

Shakespeare was very much aware of gardening, its joys and disappointments.

> Like an untimely frost
> Upon the sweetest flower of all the field.
>
> *Romeo and Juliet*, IV, 5, 28-29

Juliet has feigned her death (p224) as part of the plan to rejoin Romeo later. When her father, Capulet, finds her, he pays tribute, in a gardener's image, to her beauty.

Childhood Memories

Tracing the effects of Shakespeare's early experiences on his writing is like a detective story. Sir Hugh Clopton built a fine bridge across the Avon at the end of the fifteenth century. A sturdy replacement for the old bridge, it nevertheless was subject to the occasional rampaging Avon. July 1588 was a wet and stormy month throughout England. The weather helped to destroy the Spanish Armada on its mission to crush England, but it also raised havoc with England itself. Three men who were crossing the Clopton Bridge were marooned when the new stone bridge was broken at both sides by flood. Shakespeare often saw the Avon's power in flood and used the flood image over and over again in his images. Caroline Spurgeon found fifty-nine river images in Shakespeare.

In one image, Shakespeare describes a rage that turns back on itself and returns to grief. The eighteenth arch of the Clopton Bridge causes a portion of the river to turn back on itself. Perhaps Shakespeare had this recollection in mind when he created the image.

Extended Images

Sometimes Shakespeare is not satisfied with a single image. Sometimes he piles image on image in rich profusion. In *Troilus and Cressida*, the battle for Troy, immortalized in Homer's *Iliad*, is dragging on. Achilles is sulking in his tent. He resents that he seems to be forgotten, while other warriors, like Ajax, have stolen Achilles' former limelight. The crafty Ulysses (Odysseus in Homer) makes clear that praise is bestowed on the hero *of the moment*. Many contemporary actors can vouch for the soundness of Ulysses' observations.

ULYSSES.   Time hath, my lord, a wallet at his back
             Wherein he puts alms for Oblivion,
             A great-siz'd monster of ingratitudes.
             Those scraps are good deeds past,
             Which are devour'd as fast as they are made,   5
             Forgot as soon as done. Perseverance, dear my lord,
             Keeps honor bright. To have done is to hang
             Quite out of fashion like a rusty mail,
             In monumental mock'ry. Take the instant way,
             For honor travels in a strait so narrow   10
             Where one but goes abreast. Keep then the path;
             For emulation hath a thousand sons
             That one by one pursue. If you give way
             Or hedge aside from the direct forthright,
             Like to an ent'red tide, they all rush by   15
             And leave you hindmost;
             Or like a gallant horse falne in the first rank
             Lie there for pavement to the abject [rear],
             O'errun and trampled on. Then what they do in present,
             Though less than yours in past, must o'ertop yours.
                                                                 20
             For Time is like a fashionable host
             That slightly shakes his parting guest by th' hand,
             And with his arms outstretch'd, as he would fly,
             Grasps in the comer. The welcome ever smiles,
             And [farewell] goes out sighing. O, let not virtue seek
                                                                 25

Remuneration for the thing it was;
For beauty, wit,
High birth, vigor of bone, desert in service,
Love, friendship, charity, are subjects all
To envious and calumniating time.   30
One touch of nature makes the whole world kin:
That all with one consent praise new-born gauds
Though they are made and molded of things past,
And [give] to dust that is a little gilt
More laud than gilt oredusted.   35
The present eye praises the present object.
        Troilus and Cressida, III, 3, 146-180

1.	lines 1-2	Time quickly forgets.
2.	line 3	Ingratitude is the norm.
3.	line 4-6	The impact of good deeds is short-lived.
4.	lines 6-7	Persistence is needed.
5.	lines 7-9	Fashions change and deeds are forgotten.
6.	lines 9-11	There is room for only one at the top.
7.	lines 11-13	There are many competitors to take the hero's place.
8.	lines 13-16	The competitors are ready to pounce on the slightest weakness or hesitation.
9.	lines 17-19	The fallen hero is trampled upon.
10.	lines 19-20	Even if the new deed is less than the old, it's *New*.
11.	lines 21-24	Time is eager to forget the former hero, welcoming the new.
12.	lines 24-25	The new hero is happy; the former, sad.
13.	lines 25-27	Don't look for recognition of past achievement.
14.	lines 27-30	Time ultimately destroys everything.

15.   line 31   People are all alike.
16.   lines 32-36   They praise the new, even if inferior.
                       It's the present that matters.

Not only are the images numerous: they are concise and rich in connotation. In lines 27-29, Shakespeare catalogues all the virtues and desirable qualities and ruthlessly calls them "subjects all to envious and calumniating time." Time has already been called *cruel, monstrous*, and utterly *without a redeeming feature*. Here Shakespeare piles on *envious* and *calumniating*, a wonderful word that suggests *malicious, spiteful, slandering*. In 36 colorful lines, Shakespeare has packed an entire philosophy.

Shakespeare doesn't stop here. Three lines later, Ulysses continues to taunt Achillies with Ajax's rise to leadership. "You must move." He uses a simple image of a moving object to bring home the truth to Achilles: "Things in motion sooner catch the eye than what not stirs."

Figurative Language

Imagery is a broad term to include several kinds of figurative language. Shakespeare employs all kinds, though metaphor is the most popular. Indeed, metaphor is common even in the speech of those who know the term only vaguely.

Figurative language, also known as *figures of speech*, is a basic ingredient in our language. Figurative language says one thing and means another. When computer buffs refer to ordinary mail as "snail mail," they are suggesting the superiority, in speed anyway, of E-mail. There is no snail involved in the ordinary postal system. The speakers have taken a characteristic of the snail, slow movement, and transferred it to the relatively slower postal system. Figurative language tends to use comparison more than any other device.

A simile is a comparision with *like* or *as*. William T. Polk described "a baby waving its arms and legs like a capsized beetle." Metaphor makes the comparison without *like* or *as*. Richard R. Bowker said, "It is all right to have a train of thought, if you have a terminal."

Metaphor peppers our speech…and *pepper* is itself a metaphor. We can scarcely hold a conversation without bringing in all kinds of metaphors, as in these metaphors taken from parts of the body: an *arm* of the sea, a *leg* of a chair, *finger* food, a *toehold*, the *eye* of a storm, *teeth* of the gale.

Metaphor in Shakespeare

Shakespeare's works are filled with metaphor, many of which have already been listed. Here's a sample: Mercy Is "the gentle rain from heaven" (*The Merchant of Venice*); the "fresh lap of the crimson rose" (*A Midsummer Night's Dream*): "Cry 'Havoc,' and let slip the dogs of war:' (*Julius Caesar*).

Simile in Shakespeare

Though not so common as metaphor, colorful similes appear throughout the plays: "pale as ashes" (*Romeo and Juliet*) "pale as thy-smock" (*Othello*) "confounds thy fame as whirlwinds shake fair buds" (*The Taming of the Shrew*).

Personification in Shakespeare

Personification is the act of giving to things not human some of the attributes of human beings: "liberty plucks justice by the nose" *(Measure for Measure)*. In the *Troilus and Cressida* selection above, Time is personified in several different ways; for example, as a man with a wallet, a fickle host, and a cruel ruler.

Metonymy in Shakespeare

Metonymy substitutes for the name of one thing the name of another that is associated with it. When King Claudius tries to pray in *Hamlet* he says,

> "Forgive me my foul murder?"
> That cannot be, since I am still possessed
> Of those effects for which I did the murder:
> My crown, mine own ambition, and my queen.

Hamlet, III, 3, 52-55

When Claudius mentions the *crown*, he's not referring to the object; he means the power that comes with being king. Here's another

> The April's in her eyes: it is love's spring
> And these the showers to bring it on.
> *Antony and Cleopatra*, III, 2, 43-44

This selection includes both metonymy and metaphor. April is associated with "April showers." Here Antony, about to leave his new bride Octavia for Egypt (p261), is using the associations with the month to mean *tears*. He continues with the metaphor, a comparison of tears as the spring of love. This brief selection shows Shakespeare's use of imagery to make a point concisely.

Metonymy occurs in common speech. "The pen (writing) is mightier than the sword (force)." "A watched pot (water in the pot) never boils."

Synecdoche in Shakespeare

Synecdoche and metonymy are two unfamiliar names for familiar processes in language. Like metonymy, synecdoche relies upon association rather than comparison. In synecdoche a part is used for the whole or the whole used for a part. "We have a hundred *head* of cattle, three hired *hands*, and a supervisor to count *noses*." All three italicized words are examples of synecdoche.

> Uneasy lies the head that wears a crown.
> *Henry IV, Part Two*, III, 1, 13

Henry IV, formerly Bolinbroke (p236), has successfully wrested the kingship from Richard II, but he is finding out that being king has drawbacks unknown to the common man. During a sleepless night he considers the negatives. *Head* is an example of synecdoche. The entire person is uneasy, not just the head.

> Awake, dear heart, awake! Thou has slept well.
> *The Tempest*, I, 2, 307

Prospero (page) is waking his daughter Miranda after a long conversation with Ariel. Prospero isn't trying to awaken Miranda's heart. Here the word is used for the person.

Irony in Shakespeare

Irony may be divided into verbal and nonverbal irony. In nonverbal irony a situation has implications far beyond the obvious. A man nearly dies of thirst only a few yards from a hidden water hole. "How ironic;" we say of any situation that involves such contrasts.

Verbal irony implies something quite different from what is said. Either the speaker or the listeners may not know the full meaning of the message. Irony is an awareness of the difference between what *seems to be* (appearances) and what *is* (reality).

In *Julius Caesar* (III, 2, 75-119) Antony speaks over the slain body of Caesar. At first he is respectful of the conspirators who slew his friend:

> For Brutus is an honorable man,
> So are they all, all honorable men.

As he speaks he uses the word *honorable* three more times, but the meaning and inflection change until

> You all did see that on the Lupercal
> I thrice presented him a kingly crown,
> Which he did thrice refuse. Was this ambition?
> But Brutus says he was ambitious,
> And sure he is an honorable man.

The last use of *honorable* is ironic, full of scorn. The apparent meaning of *honorable* here is quite the opposite of the surface meaning: Brutus is not honorable: a good example of irony.

Shakespeare's Original Imagery

Ordinary conversation is larded with images used so often that they have become clichés. *Iron man, cold as ice, the heart of the matter, fall down in math* are all commonplace, without the power to stir. Shakespeare's images, as sampled in this chapter, are so vivid and so rich that they sparkle after four centuries.

Because Shakespeare was so good, many of his best images have been adopted and sometimes overused. A sample: *crack of doom, full circle, green-eyed monster, itchy palm, mind's eye, primrose path, sorry sight, tower of strength, vale of tears, honey-tongued.* This list goes on.

Shakespeare shows his genius in many areas. Imagery is one of them.

15

Shakespeare's Allusions

Turn him to any cause of policy,
The Gordian knot of it he will unloose.

Henry V, I, 1, 45-46

In this speech from the beginning of *Henry V*, the Archbishop of Canterbury is praising the new king. When he was a youth, the future Henry V was a wild and reckless wastrel, but the kingship has changed him. The new king is so brilliant that he can cut the Gordian knot in matters of state.

Why does Shakespeare mention the Gordian knot? What does this have to do with the play? The Gordian knot is an allusion, a reference to an old legend. Gordius, king of Phrygia, tied a knot which no one was able to untie. The oracle had said that whoever untied the knot would become ruler of Asia. When Alexander the Great failed to untie the knot, he cut the knot with one blow of his sword and fulfilled the prophecy. Thus, to cut the Gordian knot is to find a quick and bold solution to a perplexing problem. Notice how a knowledge of the allusion enriches the Archbishop's tribute to the new King Henry.

Perhaps you are thinking that allusions are musty old references that have little to do with the modern world, but allusions abound in everyday life, even though the current subjects are quite different from those used by Shakespeare. Popular culture has provided many examples.

A beautiful woman was once called a *Venus de Milo* or a *Helen of Troy*. Nowadays, a beautiful woman may be called a *Marilyn Monroe*, a person in living memory who has achieved a kind of immortality. Similarly a handsome young man may be called another *Clark Gable*. Few people of today would fail to recognize these allusions. Cultured members of Shakespeare's audiences would relish the allusions *he* used. The appropriate references may have been lost on some of the groundlings, but they were a kind of extra spice for the educated.

Try These Current Allusions

I. Refresh your memory by matching the allusions in column A with the appropriate identifications in column B.

	A		B
1.	Annie Oakley	A.	classic comic actor
2.	Paul Bunyan	B.	unquenchable optimist
3.	Vince Lombardi	C.	frontier hero
4.	Jesse James	D.	designer of wild inventions
5.	Adolf Hitler	E.	outstanding football coach
6.	Pollyanna	F.	sharpshooter
7.	John Hancock	G.	evil leader
8.	Rube Goldberg	H.	colorful bandit
9.	Charlie Chaplin	I.	giant lumberman
10.	Davy Crockett	J.	famed signature

Answers on 162.

Try These Allusions from the Bible.

II. Allusions from the Bible have provided us with dozens of colorful stories associated with them. Match the allusions and the appropriate adjective.

	A		B
1.	Samson	A.	evil
2.	Solomon	B.	treacherous
3.	Leviathan	C.	materialistic
4.	Judas	D.	aged
5.	Satan	E.	warring
6.	Jeremiah	F.	strong
7.	Armageddon	G.	joyously happy
8.	Philistine	H.	huge
9.	Eden	I.	prophetically pessimistic
10.	Methusaleh	J.	wise

Answers on 162.

Chained Allusions

Browsing through a dictionary can be rewarding, as one definition leads to another. Allusions are equally challenging. The legend of Althaea is intertwined with the story of Meleager. Meleager's story is linked with the Argonauts. The Argonauts were led by Jason, who is linked with the greatest heroes of myth: Alalanta, Castor and Pollux, and Hercules, among a great many others. Jason is also a major player in the story of Medea, a favorite heroine in Greek tragedy.

A popular amusement, called the "Six Degrees of Kevin-Bacon Game," seeks to prove that every movie star can be connected to Kevin Bacon, or any other actor. Kevin Bacon played in a movie with actor A, who in turn played in a movie with actor B, and so on. Presumably, in six steps any two actors can be linked together in this way. Similarly, it doesn't take many steps to link two seemingly unconnected names in our common experiences. The same is true of mythology.

A Sample of Shakespearean Allusions

Shakespeare's allusions are not for show, not to display Shakespeare's familiarity with traditional proverbs, classical mythology, or ancient history. They are always appropriate, adding a dimension to the dialogue. In *Twelfth Night*, the carousing Sir Toby Belch and his partners in mischief set up a duel between the cowardly Sir Andrew Aguecheek and the messenger from Duke Orsino, Cesario: actually Viola in disguise. The conspirators expect the duel to be a farce. Sir Toby predicts that the two will be so frightened"that they will kill one another by the look, like cockatrices." A cockatrice was a legendary monster that could kill by just a glance. In this way, Sir Toby predicts that the duel will not develop into actual physical violence. The reference adds color to Sir Toby's prediction.

The following samples of Shakespeare's allusions demonstrate again how appropriate they are.

The Burning Brand

> Methinks the realms of England, France, and Ireland
> Bear that proportion to my flesh and blood
> As did the fatal brand Althaea burned
> Unto the Prince's heart of Calydon.
> Anjou and Maine both given to the French!
> *Henry VI, Part Two*, I, 1, 234

Fatal brand burned? What's going on here? Answering that question takes us to the heart of Shakespeare's strength: his ability to use allusions with skill and relevance. He doesn't introduce these references just for show. They are chosen to comment upon or further the plot. Taken from *Henry VI, Part Two*, the quotation above is spoken by the Duke of York. It laments the loss of former English lands taken by France. The speaker is comparing that loss to an episode from legend.

Althaea was the mother of the young Meleager, whose destiny it was to live only as long as a brand then burning on the hearth. Althaea courageously caught up the brand and extinguished it, thus saving her son's life. Meleager grew to manhood and distinguished himself by many brave exploits. He was a member of the famed Argonauts. He helped repel an invasion of his native Aetolia. When a wild boar ravaged the country, Meleager gave it the deathblow. The skin and head were presented to the beautiful Atalanta. When Meleager's two uncles tried to wrest these prizes from Atalanta, Meleager slew them.

In ancient legends, fate always catches up with the heroes, no matter how strong. When Althaea discovered that her son had slain her brothers, she picked up the fatal brand and threw it into the fire. When it was consumed, Melaeger fell dead. The legend seems to say, "Try as we will, we cannot escape our destiny." Modern people tend not to take so fatalistic a view.

In the quotation, the Duke of York compares his fortunes to those of Althaea's son, the prince of Calydon. Why did Shakespeare not just say, "The loss of all my lands is destroying me"? The allusion provides a grace note, an extra satisfying touch for those who know the reference, a tantalizing invitation to learn more about the allusion.

The Anthropophagi

> It was my hint to speak-such was the process;
> And of the Cannibals that each other eat,
> The Anthropophagi, and men whose heads
> Do grow beneath their shoulders. This to hear
> Would Desdemona seriously incline.
> *Othello*, I, 3, 142-146

In this scene, Othello is explaining to the leaders of Venice how the beautiful Desdemona fell in love with him. Two amazing groups of creatures especially enthralled Desdemona: the Cannibals and "men whose heads do grow beneath their shoulders." *Anthropophagi* is another name for *Cannibals*, using the root *anthropos*, "man," and *phag*, "eat." Both cannibals and men with strangely situated heads were common in travelers' tales of the period. *The Travels of Sir John Mandeville*, a fanciful tale of exotic journeys, was translated into English in 1377. It became extremely popular, enjoying many editions. Among the marvels (supposedly true) recounted by the imaginative author are men who ate only serpents and hissed like them, dog-headed men, and men with feet so large they used them for sunshades.

Undoubtedly Shakespeare was familiar with these fantastic travelers' yarns and used them to brighten Othello's descriptions of *his* voyages.

Argus and Briareus

He is a gouty Briareus, or a purblind Argus, all eyes and no sight.
Troilus and Cressida, I, 2, 28-30

In this scene from the Trojan War play, *Troilus and Cressida*, Cressida's servant Alexander is describing the great Greek hero Ajax. Alexander describes him as a contradictory, unpredictable giant of a man. When he calls Ajax *Briareus* and *Argus*, he is choosing two appropriate characters from Greek mythology. Briareus was a giant with fifty heads and a hundred hands. Argus had a hundred eyes, only two of which were asleep at one time. Shakespeare uses the two examples to show the contradictions of Ajax. It's as if Briareus, with all his hands, couldn't use them; as if Argus, with all his eyes, couldn't see.

The story of Argus has a fascinating ending. Because of his ever-wakefulness, the goddess Hera set Argus to spy on her husband Zeus. Zeus was too clever for Hera. He set Hermes to lull Argus to sleep with his music and then slay him. Hera honored the memory of Argus by putting the hundred eyes on the tail of a peacock.

The word *purblind* demonstrates the unpredictability of language. The word once meant *wholly blind*-"pure/blind," but it has now come to mean "partly blind." It may also mean "insensitive," "obtuse," "slow to understand."

Hyperion, Jove, Mars and Mercury

> See what a grace was seated on this brow-
> Hyperion's curls, the front of Jove himself,
> An eye like Mars to threaten and command,
> A station like the herald Mercury,
> New-lighted on a heaven-kissing hill
>   *Hamlet*, III 4, 55-59

In the confrontation between Hamlet and his mother, Hamlet hammers home the differences between her former husband, Hamlet's father, and Claudius, the usurper. He forces her to compare two pictures. In some productions, there are portraits on the wall. In other productions, Hamlet has a locket with his father's picture. Queen Gertrude has a locket with the picture of Claudius.

Hamlet calls the king, his uncle, "a mildewed ear blasting his wholesome brother." For King Hamlet, he draws upon four powerful figures from classical mythology. There were three major generations of deities. Gaea (earth) and Uranus (heavens) were the parents of the Titans. Among the Titans was Hyperion, god of the sun. His brother Cronus, or Saturn, was the father of the great Olympian gods, including Mars and Mercury. Thus, the godlike King Hamlet is contrasted with the depraved usurper, his brother Claudius.

St. Martin's Summer

> Assigned am I to be the English scourge.
> This night the siege assuredly I'll raise:

Expect Saint Martin's summer, halcyon days
Since I have entered into these wars.
                    Henry VI, Part One, I, 2,129-133

Here Joan La Pucelle, usually called *Joan of Arc*, is exhorting her comrades to take heart, to trust her, to have faith in her. To emphasize her confidence, she tells the soldiers to expect St. Martin's summer. St. Martin, the patron saint of France, has given his name to the expression *St. Martin's summer*, a European term for the warm spell we call *Indian summer*.

St Martin's feast day is November 11, a time frequently blessed with good weather before the blasts of winter arrive. Joan is promising good weather ahead. Unfortunately, Joan was ultimately betrayed after a succession of great victories and burned at the stake as a witch. For the English, Joan was the enemy, so she is not too sympathetically portrayed, in the play, but Shakespeare is merely following the English prejudices of his time.

Halcyon is another interesting allusion. Because of the death of her husband, the goddess Alcyone killed herself. The angry gods turned Alcyone and her husband into kingfishers. Alcyone's father was Aeolus, God of the Winds. He took pity on his daughter and decreed that the seas would be calm during the birds' breeding season. Thus seven days before the shortest day of the year and seven days after were always calm and peaceful. These two weeks at the time of the winter solstice kept that positive connotation into the 15th century. Even today, *halcyon days* are reputedly days of peace, calm, serenity, though no longer linked with the solstice.

The Colossus

Why, man, he doth bestride the narrow world
Like a Colossus, and we petty men
Walk under his huge legs and peep about

> To find ourselves dishonorable graves
>> *Julius Caesar*, I, 2, 135-138

In this scene, Cassius is attempting to induce Brutus to join the conspiracy against Caesar. In this vivid image, other Romans are insignificant, overshadowed by the towering Caesar. The Colossus, one of the Seven Wonders of the Ancient World, was said to straddle the harbor of Rhodes. According to legend, ships passed between the legs. This colorful myth has been largely discounted, but the existence of a huge brass statue has been generally accepted. According to some tales, the Colossus was 126 feet high. The Statue of Liberty, 151 feet from base to torch, provides a suitable comparison. When Emma Lazarus wrote her famous poem, now graven on a tablet at the base, she called the Statue the "New Colossus."

In describing Caesar's power, Cassius accepts the old legend of a statue so tall, petty men could walk beneath his legs. So Caesar dominated his fellow Romans.

Phaeton

> Gallop apace, you fiery-footed steeds,
> Towards Phoebus' lodging! Such a waggoner
> As Phaeton would whip you to the west
> And bring in cloudy night immediately.
>> *Romeo and Juliet*, III, 2, 1-4

Juliet, having fallen in love with Romeo, impatiently awaits the arrival of night, so that the lovers can be together again. In making her wish, Juliet calls upon one of the most vivid Greek myths.

Phoebus Apollo, god of the sun, drove the chariot of the sun across the sky bringing day to the earth. Like many fathers, Apollo, also called *Phoebus*, had a son impatient to drive the family chariot. Apollo was reluctant to let an inexperienced youth manage the spirited horses that drove the chariot across the skies.

At last Phaeton was given the reins, but the horses sensed that an unfamiliar and inexperienced hand was guiding the chariot. Off they plunged, out of control. When Zeus saw that the chariot's careening path was a threat to mankind, he hurled a thunderbolt that struck Phaeton, throwing him into the sea. Phoebus Apollo regained control, but much damage had been done. African deserts were created by this ill-fated adventure.

Interestingly here, Juliet isn't thinking about the damage Phaeton did. Perhaps, she fantasizes this reckless youth could speed things up and bring night closer! Again Shakespeare uses an appropriate allusion with a touch of humor.

Charles's Wain

> Heigh-ho! An it be not four by the day, I'll be hanged. Charles's Wain is over the new chimney, and yet our horse not packed!
>
> *Henry IV, Part One*, II, 1, 1-3

A carrier is eager to have his horse saddled, so that he can move out with his merchandise at daybreak. The sleepy innkeeper hasn't done his duty, and the carrier complains. He looks at the stars and sees that the constellation *Charles's Wain* is just over the chimney, a way to tell the time. *Wain* is another word for *wagon*.

Charles's Wain, supposedly named for Charlemagne, is one of the most prominent constellations in the northern hemisphere. Though to modern eyes, the star group looks like a dipper with a handle (the Big Dipper), to other people it suggested something else. Another name for the constellation is *Ursa Major*, or *Great Bear*. Most constellations require a stretch of the imagination to associate the legendary names with the visible stars. Whether it's a wagon or a dipper, the constellation that circles around the polestar, has a fairly close resemblance to the wagon or dipper label.

Pantaloon

> The sixth age shifts
> Into the lean and slippered pantaloon,
> With spectacles on nose and pouch on side;
> His youthful hose, well saved, a world too wide
> For his shrunk shank, and his big manly voice,
> Turning again toward childish treble, pipes
> And whistles in his sound.
>
> *As You Like It*, II, 7, 157-163

This is the famous scene in which Shakespeare, through the character Jaques, declares, "All the world's a stage and all the men and women merely players." He describes the seven stages of life: the infant, child, lover, soldier, justice, old man, person in second childhood. The sixth stage is described here, the old man.

In medieval Italy, the commedia dell' arte developed certain stock characters, or stereotypes. Modern television sitcoms also feature stock characters, like the wisecracking secretary, the accident-prone lead, the meddling mother-in-law. Italian comedy stock types included the old Pantaloon, the clownish Harlequin, and his saucy sweetheart Columbine. Shakespeare accurately describes the character of Pantaloon in these comedies. Other plays, like *The Taming of the Shrew*, include characters perhaps inspired by Pantaloon, like Kate's father Baptista, in *The Taming of the Shrew*, or Justice Shallow in *Henry IV, Part Two*.

Niobe

> Let me not think on't...frailty thy name is woman!
> A little month or ere these shoes were old
> With which she followed my poor father's body
> Like Niobe all tears...
>
> *Hamlet*, I, 2, 146-149

Hamlet here is lamenting the death of his father and the rapidity with which his mother married his uncle. He contrasts that speed with the excessive grief his mother showed at his father's funeral, a grief that seems insincere to Hamlet.

For a woman in myth who showed excessive grief, Shakespeare turns to Niobe, who wept herself to death over the deaths of her twelve children. Niobe had the poor judgment to boast to Latona, mother of Diana and Apollo, about her large family. Latona was enraged and requested her own children to take revenge. All twelve children of Niobe were lost. Superficially Hamlet's mother wept like Niobe, but her grief was short-lived.

Xanthippe

> Be she as foul as was Florentius' love,
> As old as Sibyl, and as curst and shrewd
> As Socrates' Xanthippe, or a worse,
> She moves me not.
> *The Taming of the Shrew*, I, 2, 68-71

Our hero, Petruchio, has come to Padua to find a wealthy bride. To achieve his financial goal, he's willing to overlook bad qualities in a prospective wife. Shakespeare lists three undesirable bride types, all acceptable to Petruchio,...if she has sufficient money.

The first negative was "foul and ugly." Florentius vowed to marry a deformed witch if she would give him the answer to a riddle on which his life depended. The second negative was old age. The Sibyls were aged women who possessed the gift of prophecy. The third negative was nagging. Xanthippe, the wife of the philosopher Socrates, was famous for her bad temper.

Thus Petruchio prepared himself in advance for the worst possible combination of traits. He does better than expected. His eventual bride, Katharina, is neither old nor ugly, but she is indeed ill natured and perpetually scolding. Petruchio vows to tame this "shrew."

Prester John's Foot

> I will fetch you a toothpicker now from the
> furthest inch of Asia: bring you the length of Prester
> John's foot: fetch you a hair of the great Cham's beard: do
> you any embassage to the Pygmies-rather than hold three
> words conference with this harpy.
>
> *Much Ado about Nothing*, II, 1, 247-252

The speaker is Benedick, gallant soldier but disparager of the lady Beatrice. The bickering of Benedick and Beatrice provides much of the humor in this tale of deception and forgiveness. We know that somehow these two will realize their love for each other, despite outward appearances.

At this point, Benedick is expressing to his leader his objections to speaking with this harpy (Beatrice). Since the harpies were loathsome mythical women, Benedick is expressing his disdain for Beatrice in rather strong terms. He'd rather tackle impossible tasks like measuring the foot of the legendary Prester John, monarch of a large Christian kingdom in Asia. Or he'd get a hair of the Mongol Khan's (Cham's) beard. The Pygmies were also symbolic of a distant challenge. Needless to say, Benedick later eats his words.

Deborah

> Stay, stay thy hands! thou art an Amazon
> And fightest with the sword of Deborah.
>
> *Henry VI, Part One*, I, 2, 104-106

This is another scene involving Joan of Arc-La Pucelle. As we have seen on page 155. Joan is exhorting her men to trust her leadership. To prove her strength and determination, she has a sword fight with the Dauphin, seeker of the French crown. She defeats him, and the Dauphin utters the words above. *Amazon*, the label for legendary warrior women, has passed into the language as a common noun. Deborah was also a famous warrior woman, leading her nation of Israel against the oppressor of her people.

For the person interested in mythology, history, or legends, the plays of Shakespeare are a rich storehouse. Shakespeare's allusions are never irrelevant. They always somehow seem to fit the sense of the play, enriching the meaning the speaker intends.

Answers to "Allusions"–Page

===

I. 1F   2I   3E   4H   5G   6B   7J   8D   9A   10C

II. 1F   2J   3H   4B   5A   6I   7E   8C   9G   10D

16

Shakespeare's Humor

> Now could thou and I rob the thieves, and go merrily to London,
> it would be argument for a week, laughter for a month, and a
> good jest forever.
>
> *Henry IV, Part One*, II, 2, 91-94

Falstaff and his band of rogues have robbed and bound travelers and have taken their money (p234). Prince Hal and his buddy Poins prepare to turn the tables on the hapless band of robbers. They do so, and indeed use the episode to taunt Falstaff afterwards. It brings "laughter for a month" and, through the immortality of Shakespeare's plays, it brings "a good jest forever." For comedy in Shakespeare, nothing tops the Falstaff scenes, beloved of audiences for four centuries.

A writer once observed that most people will freely admit to minor faults but not to a lack of humor. They secretly feel that if they are told a joke, any joke, they'll "get it." There is pride in having a "sense of humor," but the situation is complex. *The Encyclopedia Britannica* flatly states: Humor is "a term which not only refuses to be identified, but in a sense boasts of being indefinable; and it would commonly be regarded as a deficiency in humor to search for a definition of humor." This book will not attempt a definition of humor, but point out some Shakespearean ingredients commonly regarded as humorous! Perhaps the point can be made by example rather than by definition.

Comedy and Tragedy

Critics have observed that tragedy never goes out of style, but comedy is often topical and fleeting. The basic human emotions that fuel tragedy change little with the times. One appeal of comedy is often a topical reference, a thrust at contemporary follies, which change. The humor of Jay Leno, David Letterman, and *Saturday Night Live*, for example, is essentially topical and thus dated. A selection of "the best of Leno" will eliminate most topical and dated materials and concentrate on characterization, wit, absurdity, and humorous contrast.

Great American humorists of the nineteenth century include Josh Billings, Charles Brown, Finley Peter Dunne, Bill Nye, Mark Twain, and Artemus Ward. Except for Mark Twain, the list is of interest mainly to scholars. Humor is a fragile substance.

Somehow Shakespeare, in the main, overcame the humor jinx. Though a few Shakespearean situations might be funnier to his audience than to a modern audience, Shakespeare's humor is still fresh. Why? How?

Characterization

Shakespeare introduces many characters who arouse laughter in the theater. Foremost is Falstaff, conceded to be among the funniest of all literary creations. He is a mess of contradictions: cowardly-brave, shrewd-open hearted, greedy-generous, impractical-sensible, unfaithful-true. His relationship with Prince Hal contains some of the happiest lines in the play *Henry IV, Part One*. At one point Falstaff decides to play-act as King Henry, Prince Hal's father, in a mock interview. As the King, Falstaff describes that wonderful old man John Falstaff.

> PRINCE.   What manner of man, an it like your majesty?
> FALSTAFF.   A goodly portly man, i'faith, and a corpulent, of a cheerful
>   look, a pleasing eye, and a most noble carriage, and as I

think his age some fifty, or by'r lady inclining to three-score. And now I remember me, his name is Falstaff. If that man should be lewdly given, he deceiveth me; for, Harry, I see virtue in his looks...If then the tree may be known by the fruit, as the fruit by the tree, then, peremptorily I speak it, there is virtue in that Falstaff-him keep with, the rest banish. And tell me now, thou naughty varlet, tell me, where hast thou been this month?

Henry IV, Part One, II, 4, 413-424

Actually, Prince Hal has been hanging out with Falstaff! Those golden days for Falstaff end when Prince Hal rejects his former unsavory companions and readies himself to take over the role of king.

There are many other figures of fun throughout the plays: Bottom the Weaver in *A Midsummer Night's Dream*, Sir Andrew Aguecheek in *Twelfth Night*, Launce and his dog Crab in *Two Gentlemen of Verona*. The thorny relationship of Benedick and Beatrice in *Much Ado about Nothing* is a source of merriment.

Sometimes, Shakespeare introduces comic elements and characters into the tragedies, perhaps to relieve the tension. The Porter in *Macbeth* has a long comic monologue as he stirs himself to open the castle gates after a night of carousal...and the as-yet-undiscovered murder of Duncan.

Situation

Shakespeare knows how to manipulate incident to generate laughter. In *Twelfth Night* (p281), Sir Toby and his cronies arrange a duel between timid Viola, dressed as the boy Cesario, and Sir Andrew Aguecheek, a cowardly suitor for the hand of Olivia. Viola doesn't want a fight, and Sir Andrew is faint-hearted, though he thinks he can at least manage Cesario. Alas for the plot: Shakespeare brings Viola's brother Sebastian onto the scene.

After an introduction, Sir Andrew enters the scene with drawn sword, expecting to fight the mild Cesario, but instead, unbeknownst to the plotters, his opponent is Sebastian.

SIR ANDREW.   Now, sir, have I met you again? there's for
                   you. (he strikes wide)
SEBASTIAN.   (replies with his fists) Why, there's for thee., and
                   there, and there! (he knocks him down) Are all
                   the people mad? (his hand upon his dagger)
SIR TOBY.   (seizing him from behind) Hold, sir, or I'll throw
                   your dagger o'er the house.
                                   Twelfth Night, IV, 1, 23-27

They struggle. Sir Toby draws his sword and they begin to fight in earnest, only to be interrupted by Olivia, who has mistaken Sebastian for Cesario.

The scene is a classic of comic invention. Though the fight is interrupted by Olivia, we learn later that both Sir Toby and Sir Andrew have fared badly at the hands of Sebastian.

Though Shakespeare is not above creative slapsticks, many comic episodes are more physically restrained. In *Measure for Measure*, for example, the dissolute murderer Barnardine has been in jail nine years and has enjoyed a succession of reprieves. He rather likes the confinement, for somehow or other he manages to stay drunk most of the time. Finally, the Duke orders Barnardine executed and comes to pray with the condemned prisoner.

DUKE.   Sir, induced by my charity, and hearing how
                   hastily you are to depart, I am come to advise
                   you, comfort you, and pray with you.
BARNARDINE.   Friar, not I: I have been drinking hard all night,
                   and I will not consent to die this day, that's certain.
DUKE.   O, sir, you must: and therefor I beseech you.
                   Look forward on the journey you shall go.
BARNARDINE.   I swear I will not die today for any man's persuasion.
DUKE.   But hear you...

BARNARDINE.   Not a word: if you have anything to say to me,
come to my ward: for thence will not I today.
Measure for Measure, IV, 3, 48-61

The picture of a criminal refusing to be executed because it's inconvenient always brings chuckles from the audience.

Wit

Wit is as difficult to pin down as humor. It is narrower than humor, relying on words. Wit may take many forms: repartee, irony, sarcasm, parody, and satire, all practiced by Shakespeare. Shakespeare loved a good pun, a clever insult, a practical joke, malapropisms, and eccentricities of all kinds. Shakespeare is sharply aware of contrasts, of the differences between what is and what, in an ideal world, should be. He loves both exaggeration and understatement. He is not above bawdiness, a device greatly appreciated by Shakespeare's audiences.

Repartee

Repartee, defined as "a quick and witty reply." is a special Shakespearean talent. An excellent example occurs in *Henry IV, Part One*. A strategy counsel by the rebel forces attempting to overthrow King Henry includes, among others, the Welsh Glendower and Henry Percy, nicknamed *Hotspur* because of his fearlessness and impetuosity. Long-winded Glendower irritates the forthright Hotspur. He has just been boasting of his almost-supernatural birth: "I say the earth did shake, when I was born." Hotspur is impatient with this pretentiousness and manages to utter the perfect put-down.

GLENDOWER.   I can call spirits from the vasty deep.
HOTSPUR.   Why, so can I, or so can any man,
But will they come when you do call for them?
Henry IV, Part One, III, 1, 52-54

Irony

Irony, though sometimes classed with wit and humor, often has a bittersweet quality. Irony marches through *Macbeth*. One of the most famous examples is the ironic prophecy by an Apparition called up by the witches.

APPARITION. Be lion-mettled, proud, and take no care
                     Who chafes, who frets, or where conspirers are:
                     Macbeth shall never vanquished be until
                     Great Birnam wood to high Dunsinane hill
                     Shall come against him.
MACBETH.   That will never be;
                     Who can impress the forest, bid the tree
                     Unfix his earth-bound root?
                                        Macbeth, IV, 1, 90-97

Ironically the assurance that gives Macbeth most comfort destroys him in the end when the enemy army advances on Dunsinane with branches as camouflage.

There are other examples in this most ironic of plays. In Act I after the execution of the traitorous Thane of Cawdor, King Duncan speaks about Cawdor.

DUNCAN.   There's no art
                     To find the mind's construction in the face:
                     He was a gentleman on whom I built
                     An absolute trust.
                                        Macbeth, I, 4, 12-15

Clever Shakespeare follows this speech with the stage direction "Enter Macbeth." Duncan also places "absolute trust" in Macbeth!

A bit later, as Duncan approaches Macbeth's castle, the scene of his death, he comments happily on the peace and serenity he feels in this quiet place.

DUNCAN.   This castle hath a pleasant seat: the air
           Nimbly and sweetly recommends itself
           Unto our gentle senses.
                                    Macbeth, I, 6, 1-3

Sometimes the irony is just funny. In *Much Ado about Nothing* (p275), the villain Don Juan and his unsavory crew have succeeded in besmirching the honor of Hero and destroying the love of Hero and Claudio. The villains seem to be getting away with their evildoing.

Then in a supremely ironic twist, the villains are uncovered-not by Don Pedro, Leonato, Claudio, or Benedick, but by a pair of inept constables. Two watchmen overhear Don Juan's followers, Conrade and Borachio, talking over the plot. The watchmen take the rogues to the incompetent constables Dogberry and Verges. They, in turn, approach Leonato, father of Hero, and try to tell about their arrests. Unfortunately, their language is so obscure that Leonato says, in effect, "Later." Ironically, if Leonato had followed up their perplexing thought processes and examined the men, the plot would have been discovered before the damage was done.

Left to their own devices, Dogberry and Verges examine their prisoners in a hilarious scene affectionately revealing the complete incompetence of the two constables. At one point, Conrade can't stand the stupidity of Dogberry and speaks.

CONRADE.   Away! you are an ass, you are an ass.
DOGBERRY. Dost thou not suspect my place? Dost thou not suspect
           my years? O that he were here to write me down an ass!
           but, masters, remember that I am an ass-though it be not
           written down, yet forget not that I am an ass. No, thou

> villain, thou art full of piety, as shall be proved upon thee
> by good witness.
>
> *Much Ado about Nothing*, IV, 2, 72-78

Dogberry is a master of language misuse. He confuses *suspect* with *respect* and considers the word *piety* to mean some sort of villainy and the label *ass* a compliment. Using *suspect* for *respect* is a malapropism (p174).

They finally bring the prisoners to Leonato, Claudio, and the others. The men confess their crimes. Had it not been for the presentation of the two prisoners by Dogberry and Verges, the crime could not have been uncovered. A good example of an extended irony.

Sarcasm

Sarcasm is repartee with intent to hurt. It may be ironic (p146) or satirical. It uses ridicule to wound an individual. It is often bitter in tone. Shakespeare occasionally uses sarcasm. A good example is Hamlet's taunting of Polonius. At the beginning of the play-within-a-play, Hamlet addresses Polonius.

HAMLET.   My lord, you played once i'th'university, you say?
POLONIUS. That did I, my lord, and was accounted a good actor.
HAMLET.   What did you enact?
POLONIUS. I did enact Julius Caesar. I was killed i'th' Capitol, Brutus killed me.
HAMLET.   It was a brute part of him to kill so capital a calf there.

> *Hamlet*, III, 2, 95-103

Also note the double pun (p173) in Hamlet's reply.

Satire

Satire may have elements of sarcasm, but it is usually more extended. Satire holds up human vices to ridicule. In *Gulliver's Travels*, Jonathan Swift devotes almost the entire narrative to human folly. In *Volpone*, Ben

Jonson satirizes greed. Shakespeare's own *Timon and Athens* bitterly condemns ingratitude and the excessive love of money.

Satire need not be biting and savage. Gentle, often good-humored satire appears throughout the plays. *Love's Labour's Lost* pokes fun at verbal affectation and the perils of courtship. Shakespeare points out some of the problems of pastoral utopias in *As You Like It*. His great creation, Falstaff, satirizes exaggerated honor and pride.

Insult

Sometimes the thrust is more direct. Shakespeare is a master of the *insult*. It took a 300-page book to list them play by play. A sample suggests the richness and diversity of Shakespeare's put-downs.

> His brain is as dry as the remainder biscuit after a voyage.
> *As You Like It*, II, 7, 38-40

> I had rather be married to a death's-head with a bone in its mouth.
> *The Merchant of Venice*, I, 2, 49-50

> He's a most notable coward, an infinite and endless liar, an hourly promise-breaker, the owner of no one good quality.
> *All's Well That Ends Well*. III, 6, 9-11

> A hungry lean-face'd villain,
> A mere anatomy, a mountebank,
> A threadbare juggler and a fortune-teller,
> A needy-hollow-ey'd-sharp-looking wretch,
> A living dead man.
> *The Comedy of Errors*, V, 1, 238-242

> All the infections that the sun sucks up
> From bogs, fens, flats on (him) fall, and make him

By inch-meal a disease.
The Tempest, II, 2, 1-3

And that's just a sample! Of course, the language need not be strong for an effective insult.

JAQUES.   Let's meet as little as we can.
ORLANDO.   I do desire we may be better strangers.
As You Like It, III. 2, 255-256

Wordplay

Shakespeare was intoxicated with words. He sometimes wrote for the sheer joy of playing with them. In *Hamlet*, Polunius introduces the players, but he cannot refrain from glorying in the resonant words he loves.

POLONIUS. The best actors in the world, either for tragedy, comedy, history, pastoral, pastoral-comical, historical-pastoral, tragical-historical, tragical-comical-historical-pastoral, scene individable, or poem unlimited. Seneca cannot be too heavy, nor Plautus too light for the law of writ and the liberty, these are the only men.
Hamlet, II, 2, 401-407

This doesn't advance the plot of *Hamlet* one bit, but what a glorious display of word manipulation.

Sometimes Shakespeare toys with pretentious jargon. In *Love's Labour's Lost*, the schoolmaster Holofernes shows off by ridiculing the comment of the constable, the appropriately named *Dull*.

HOLOFERNES. Most barbarous intimation! yet a kind of insinuation, as it were in via, in way, of explication; facere as it were replication, or rather ostentare, to show as it were his inclination-after his undressed, unpolished, uneducated, unpruned, untrained, or rather unlettered or ratherest, unconfirmed fashion-to insert again my haut credo for a deer.

Love's Labour's Lost, IV, 2, 13-19

All the scholarly Latin and convoluted sentence structure doesn't conceal the fact that this is nonsense masquerading as profundity.

Puns

Of all forms of wordplay, puns occupy a strange position, beloved by their creators, often sneered at by listeners! In Shakespeare's day, puns were popular, perhaps a tribute to the exuberance of English writers as they exploited the increasingly rich English language. Shakespearean scholar F. A. Bather has actually counted the puns in Shakespeare's plays and come to some interesting conclusions. He computed frequencies on the basis of hundred-line counts. The percentage of puns in the early plays was 2.12-about two puns for each hundred lines. The percentage drops to .48 in the last plays-about one for each two hundred lines. The author theorizes that the greater number in the early years is a mark of youthful exuberance. The number decreased in later years "to restrict the wordplay to situations of forcible dramatic effect."

One of the most famous puns is delivered by Mercutio as he lies mortally wounded from a thrust by the Capulet Tybalt. Romeo tries to cheer him.

ROMEO. Courage, man; the hurt cannot be much.
MERCUTIO. No, 'tis not so deep as a well, nor so wide as a church door, but 'tis enough, 'twill serve. Ask for me tomorrow and you shall find me a grave man.

Romeo and Juliet, III, 1, 93-96

This pun in a "grave" situation is matched by a famous pun in *Macbeth*. Macbeth has murdered Duncan but has taken away the daggers. Lady

Macbeth sees the fatal flaw in their plot and declares her intention to smear the sleepy grooms of the bedchamber with blood.

LADY MACBETH. Give me the daggers: the sleeping and the dead
      Are but as pictures; 'tis the eye of childhood
      That fears a painted devil. If he do bleed,
      I'll gild the faces of the grooms withal,
      For it must seem their guilt.
             Macbeth, II, 2, 54-59

The pun on *gilt-guilt* has stunned many critics, delighted others. Of course, not all punning occurs in serious contexts. In *As You Like It*, Rosalind and Celia spar back and forth about the verses Orlando has been writing and placing everywhere. All written about Rosalind, they are more flattering than competent. Though Rosalind is secretly pleased, she pretends to criticize these verses. (Keep in mind those poetic "feet"–p110).

CELIA.   Didst thou hear these verses?
ROSALIND.   Ay, but the feet were lame, and could not hear
        themselves without the verse, and therefore stood
        lamely in the verse.

            As You Like It, III, 2, 164-171

Malapropisms

Malapropism is named for Mrs. Malaprop, a character in Richard Brinsley Sheridan's play *The Rivals* (1775). She uses impressive words...incorrectly; *reprehend* for *apprehend*; *allegory* for *alligator*. Constable Dogberry has already been singled out for his speech (p169) and the malapropism *suspect* for *respect*. But the quoted passage is the tip of the iceberg. Dogberry, a superb comic creation, is the master of the malapropism. He can scarcely utter a sentence without misusing words.

His assured self-importance adds humor to everything he does or says. The scenes in which he appears sparkle after four centuries. His rules for enforcing the law are as topsy-turvy as his language. Following his thought processes is a challenge. Here's an example; when he addresses the arrested villains, he says, "O villain! thou wilt be condemned into everlasting redemption for this."

Malapropisms gush forth in torrents, a selection includes these: *senseless* for *sensible*; *comprehend* for *apprehend*; *tolerable* for *intolerable*; *odorous* for *odious*; *auspicious* for *suspicious*; *vigitant* for *vigilant*; *dissembly* for *assembly*; and *opinioned* for *pinioned*.

Dogberry may be the acknowledged monarch of the malaprop, but there are others. Mistress Quickly in *The Merry Wives of Windsor* declares that George Page has "a marvellous infection to the little page." Constable Elbow in *Measure for Measure* arrests "two notorious benefactors" and "detests" that his wife is honorable. The malapropism is not dead but still the source of occasional humor in modern comedy.

Practical Joke

With its aim to embarrass or discomfit someone, the practical joke doesn't rank high in the list of humorous achievements. Yet it survives. Television shows like *Candid Camera* thrive on the good-natured embarrassment of the subjects. Home videos often feature humorous pranks that make the subjects look silly.

Shakespeare is not above the practical joke. An extended practical joke is the central motivation in a subplot of *Twelfth Night* (p281). Malvolio, the haughty steward to Olivia, has earned the undying enmity of Sir Toby, the clown Feste, Sir Andrew, and the Servants. They plot his downfall. The plotters know that Malvolio has aspirations above them, even for the hand of Olivia. They plant an unsigned letter, written by the servant Maria, who can imitate her mistress's handwriting.

The self-deluded Malvolio, thinking the letter is addressed to him, follows the hints in the letter. He dresses strangely and makes himself obnoxious in

Olivia's presence. She thinks him mad and asks her servants to "look to" Malvolio. They look to him. They continue the practical joke by locking Malvolio in a dark room and sending the clown Feste, as Sir Topas, to "comfort" him. After a while, they realize they may have gone too far and allow Malvolio to write a letter to Olivia. He is freed, vows "to be revenged on the whole pack of you."

How shall we consider this prank? It is somewhat cruel by modern standards. There are three considerations. (1) In Shakespeare's time, the prank was considered very funny and quite appropriate. (2) The part of Malvolio is often the most sought after by actors. (3) Olivia expresses the point of view of compassionate audiences: "He hath been most notoriously abused." The Duke follows with "pursue him, and entreat him to a peace." Is Shakespeare finally saying that practical jokes may be fun but also cruel? Again, Shakespeare leaves the matter dangling, ambiguous.

There are practical jokes elsewhere in Shakespeare. In a *Midsummer Night's Dream*, Bottom acquires the ass's head to play a practical joke on Titania. In *The Taming of the Shrew*, Petruchio's handling of Katharina may be considered one long practical joke. Poor Falstaff is made the butt of a practical joke in *The Merry Wives of Windsor*. In *Much Ado about Nothing*, Benedick and Beatrice are also brought together by a practical joke. There are others, but none are better handled than the downfall of the unfortunate Malvolio.

A Final Word

Shakespeare knows what makes us laugh. He revels in eccentrics: Jaques in *As You Like It*, the nurse in *Romeo and Juliet*, Fluellen in *Henry V*, and Justice Shallow in *Henry IV, Part Two*, and *The Merry Wives of Windsor*.

He understands the humorous value of appropriate contrasts: Titania's doting on the grotesque Bottom in *A Midsummer Night's Dream*; Katherina's ranting and Petruchio's unshakable, maddening calm in *The Taming of the Shrew*; and Falstaff's boasts and the reality in the *Henry IV* plays.

He knows how to use exaggeration and understatement where each can be effective. The bitter repartee between Benedick and Beatrice at the beginning of *Much Ado about Nothing* is exaggerated to make the final capitulation more humorous. In *Romeo and Juliet*, Mercutio's understated comment on his mortal wound accentuates the grim humor he often employs.

In Shakespeare, humor can crop up anywhere, in the darkest moments as in the Porter scene in *Macbeth*, but wherever it appears, it rings true.

17

Shakespeare's Sources

> By the lord, our plot is a good plot, as ever was laid, our friends
> true and constant: a good plot, good friends, and full of expecta-
> tion: an excellent plot, very good friends.
>
> *Henry IV, Part One*, **II, 3, 18-21**

Although these lines are spoken by Hotspur (p234), of another kind of
plot, they may humorously echo Shakespeare's satisfaction when he found
a particularly good source for one of his plays. Good plots were much in
demand by the acting companies, and playwrights borrowed freely, often
from each other. The ultimate test was what the playwright did with the
plot that he borrowed.

As every broadcaster knows, television devours material at an alarming
rate. In the struggle for the available viewers, networks compete strenuously. Imitation and repetition are commonplace, and good material is at
a premium. Companies of players during Shakespeare's time shared the
same anxieties.

Though plots were everywhere, some plots were more popular than
others. Classical history, English history, collections of tales-all provided a
convenient source. The demand was acute, and originality was scarce.
Stock characters, like the villain, the boastful soldier, the clown, and the
absent-minded old man, came from classical drama and were welcomed

by the viewers. Similarly, modern television viewers accept stereotyped characters like the wisecracking teenager, the henpecked husband, and the all-wise competent mother.

The Elizabethan playwright, usually a poet, sold his play to a company, which proceeded to do with it as it wished. It was the company's play, not the poet's. In this situation, Shakespeare had an enormous advantage over most of the other playwrights. He was also an actor, who had a hand in the production of his own plays. The combination of actor and playwright accounts for the adaptability of his plays for all those stages since his time.

The story of King Lear, for example, was well known in Shakespeare's day. At least forty versions have been discovered. There is also an earlier play, *King Leir*, but a comparison of Lear and Leir shows the creative genius of Shakespeare. Changes in the basic plot line and a deeper exploration of character make *King Lear* Shakespeare's own.

The plot of *Love's Labour's Lost* may be the most original of all the plays. Shakespeare probably invented his own story. True, the King of Navarre was an actual person. The names of the King's courtiers correspond to prominent political figures in the King's world. The King had actually received a delegation from France headed by a princess, but the situation bore no resemblance to Shakespeare's handling of his own plot lines in the play.

Holinshed's Chronicles

Raphael Holinshed was a historian whose work played a major role in the shaping of Shakespeare's history plays. Holinshed's *Chronicles of England, Scotland, and Ireland* provided many dramatists with source material for their own writings. Shakespeare shared in that bounty. Even *Cymbeline* and *King Lear* owe something to that landmark publication.

With its three and a half million words, *Chronicles* was the most authoritative history of Britain published during the Elizabethan era. Holinshed himself contributed the section on English history. William Harrison and Edmund Campion contributed sections on the histories of Scotland and Ireland. Interestingly, *Chronicles* was part of a much larger, ambitious project: histories of every known nation.

Of Shakespeare's history plays, four deal with The Wars of the Roses (p242). Holinshed contributed a great deal to Shakespeare's treatment, as did Edward Hall's *The Union of the Two Noble and Illustrious Families of Lancaster and York*. These history plays demonstrate the unique strengths of Shakespeare.

The Elizabethan Age, in retrospect, seems to have been a time of great confidence, national glory, and stability after the events of the fairly recent past. The death of Richard III, marking the end of the Wars of the Roses, was closer to the Elizabethans than the Civil War is to our own day. Histories about the period were popular, as the English people tried to find themselves.

At the time, that stability and security were elusive. Protestant England found itself surrounded by the great Catholic powers of Europe. The traditional enemy, France, was joined by a new foe, Spain. Elizabeth's reign, especially in the early years (p 7), was vulnerable. Through the years, confidence grew. The defeat of the Spanish Armada in 1588 gave the English a new sense of pride, increasing the popularity of all plays dealing with English history.

For obvious reasons, the English feared civil war and sought an orderly society, led by a strong monarch. The history plays addressed this attitude by exploring the reasons for anarchy and suggesting those qualities in a monarch most likely to provide stability. The weaknesses of Richard II were deplored, but the usurpation of the throne by Bolingbroke (p 32) was not without taint. As always, Shakespeare explored the apparent contradictions revealed by some leaders, while applauding those qualities that bring peace and continuity. His plays were history lessons, tailored a bit for his purposes, but essentially true to the events he described.

For other history plays, *King John* and *Henry VIII*, Shakespeare used materials from Holinshed and from John Foxe. *Chronicles* also contributed to *Macbeth*. Again, Shakespeare's productive transformation of the Holinshed material is apparent to any reader of both treatments.

Plutarch's Lives

Plutarch, born in the first century, C.E., was a Greek philosopher and biographer. He had an ingenious idea: why not provide parallel biographies, Greek and Roman, to contrast and compare personalities and achievements? One of his famous comparisons is that of Alexander the Great with Julius Caesar, both conquerors dead at the height of their power. Though Plutarch based his *Lives* on historical events, he insisted that he was more interested in their lives than in the history of the times. Not all of his subjects were political leaders. He compared Demosthenes, Greek orator and statesman, with Cicero, Roman orator and statesman. Plutarch always sought the defining moments that developed their personalities. These moments might seem trivial, but Plutarch pointed up their importance.

Plutarch's Lives was a gold mine for Elizabethan dramatists. As translated by Thomas North, the comparative biographies were Shakespeare's primary source for *Antony and Cleopatra, Julius Caesar, Coriolanus*, and *Timon of Athens*. Minor elements in other plays show the influence of Plutarch. Shakespeare's *Julius Caesar* is fairly close to Plutarch. Caesar is given a more enigmatic character than that provided by Plutarch, but Brutus, Portia, and Cassius are fairly close to Plutarch's characterizations. For *Antony and Cleopatra*, Shakespeare starts the play with Antony already captured by Cleopatra's charms. To provide a salty commentator about Antony's infatuation, Shakespeare supplies Enobarbus (page 81), barely a name in Plutarch. In *Coriolanus*, Menenius becomes a better developed, more complex character than his namesake in the *Lives*.

The Italian Novel

Shakespeare had a great deal of romantic material from which to develop his plays. The Italian novel, romantic poems and collections of tales-all provided characters and situations that Shakespeare could alter at will. The device of girls disguised as boys was a common device, a favorite of

Shakespeare's. Viola in *Twelfth Night*, Julia in *The Two Gentlemen of Verona*, Portia in *The Merchant of Venice*, and Rosalind in *As You Like It* are examples of Shakespeare's strategic use of a device guaranteed to arouse interest.

He enriched any plots he used by creating great comic characters like Dogberry in *Much Ado About Nothing*, Touchstone in *As You Like It*, and Sir Andrew Aguecheek in *Twelfth Night*. He invented the quarreling lovers Benedick and Beatrice in *Much Ado about Nothing*. The dazzling and witty Mercutio in *Romeo and Juliet* is entirely Shakespeare's own.

He made other adjustments as needed. He compressed the story of *Romeo and Juliet* to a few days, disregarding the several months suggested in his source. He rearranged episodes in the *Troilus and Cressida* story to heighten the dramatic tension and make more understandable the inaction of Achilles. He even wove together plot strands from different sources. For Shakespeare, "The play's the thing."

Although Italian sources were used, especially in the early comedies, one of the great tragedies had an Italian source also: *Othello*. Based one a novella by the Italian author, Cinthio, *Othello* retains the major plot elements but accelerates the course of events, making for a tighter play. Shakespeare makes Othello and Desdemona more noble and Iago more evil. He adds a number of minor characters, like Roderigo and Brabantio.

The English Novel

For two plays, Shakespeare used English novels, both with pastoral themes. Thomas Lodge's *Rosalynde* was mined for *As You Like It*; Robert Greene's Pandosto, for *The Winter's Tale*. Comparing *Rosalynde* with *As You Like It* (p 278) emphasizes the extent of the changes. Shakespeare follows Lodge's plot closely but the changes are significant. The principal characters have been retained in *As You Like It*, though with different names. The basic motivations of the characters are similar. The resolution of the plot in both works is reasonably similar. Yet Lodge's novel is read only by scholars. Shakespeare's play has been a dramatic favorite for four centuries. Why?

Rosalynde and As You Like It

Shakespeare has added ingredients beyond Lodge's intentions or capacities. He has introduced new characters, among them the melancholy Jaques, a dour philosopher who cannot resist commenting sourly on the actions of the other characters. Jaques provides a negative counterpoint to the optimism of the play. Although his weighty, downbeat pronouncements are often challenged and refuted by the retorts of other characters, Jaques remains an important element in Shakespeare's plans.

It is Jaques who delivers the famous "seven ages of man" speech, but even here his negative philosophy is punctured. He concludes with the depressing picture of old age: "second childhood, and mere oblivion." No sooner has he finished than Orlando enters, carrying Adam, the faithful old servant. Adam, though feeble, is not in his second childhood. He is alert and responsive.

The philosophical underpinnings of the two works are quite different. Lodge's story leads his readers to make discriminations and moral judgments. Shakespeare's introduction of Jaques provides a "counter-voice" that balances other elements in the play and discourages convenient, easy interpretations. As is often true, Shakespeare avoids closure, preferring to leave his audience with a sense of the paradoxes and ambiguities of life (p 92).

Shakespeare has also introduced into As You Like It Touchstone, the clown, somewhat like Jaques in his witty cynicism, but different in his intentions. As a professional jester, Touchstone wants to be funny. The ways of the world amuse and delight him, a reaction quite different from the negativism of Jaques. Touchstone jests; he mimics; he mocks; all with kindly intent. Touchstone's wit, in turn, is refuted by the simple dignity of the shepherd Corin. Shakespeare again seeks a balance, a leveling, an elimination of the artificial distinctions that separate people.

Shakespeare makes other changes. He introduces the country pair, William and Audrey. William is a simple-minded peasant who fancies he has "a pretty wit," but utters no speech longer than seven words. Audrey is an uneducated, unsophisticated peasant with a certain charm. Touchstone weds

Audrey at the end of the play, providing an interesting contrast to the courtly lovers. Rosalind grows more interesting in Shakespeare's version. Lodge's love between Rosalynde and Rosader (Orlando) is conventional and traditional. By contrast, Shakespeare's dialogues between Rosalind and Orlando go far beyond conventions in the exploration of love without the conventional trappings.

At one point, Rosalind, disguised as the boy Ganymede, addresses the lovesick Orlando.

ROSALIND.	Now tell me how long you would have her after you have possessed her.
ORLANDO.	For ever and a day.
ROSALIND.	Say a day without the ever. No, no, Orlando; men are April when they woo, December when they wed. Maids are May when they are maids, but the sky changes when they are wives.

As You Like It, IV, 1, 138-144

There is nothing quite so bittersweet as this in Lodge's novel. Shakespeare introduces still other changes within the framework of the plot. Of course, the language sparkles.

No Obvious Motivation

Beyond the introduction of new characters and the introduction of beautiful language, can a generalization be made about Shakespeare's treatment of his sources? In *The Genius of Shakespeare*, Jonathan Bate declares, "One of the major characteristics of Shakespeare's handling of his sources is a removal of obvious motivation." This technique was considered a fault by many of those who staged Shakespeare's plays in other ages (p 37).

The source for *Othello* (p289), for example, provides a reasonable motivation for the Iago-figure: love for Desdemona. Shakespeare removes that motivation, provides an unconvincing substitute: Othello's passing Iago over for promotion. As a result, the motivation of Iago has been the subject of many essays and books. The poet Samual Taylor Coleridge called it "motiveless malignity."

In *The Winter's Tale*, King Leontes tries to persuade his friend Polixenes (p313) to extend his visit. He fails. He urges his wife Hermione to persuade Polixenes. She succeeds. He becomes insanely jealous and sets in motion the actions that carry the plot. The jealousy is better motivated in his source, Greene's novel *Pandosto*. Again, Shakespeare has essentially removed rational motivation and has left the threads hanging.

The great Russian novelist Leo Tolstoy was bothered and perplexed by Shakespeare's lack of sufficient motivation. He especially attacked *King Lear*, insisting that Lear (p293) had insufficient motivation for his treatment of Cordelia and her sisters. He went on to mention all the great characters from the old plays, romances, and chronicles: Lear, Cordelia, Othello, Desdemona, Falstaff, Hamlet. He felt that Shakespeare "weakened and spoiled" them all!

The characters in Shakespeare's sources tend to be fixed, one-dimensional, understandable. Shakespeare takes the same characters and makes them fluid, flexible, unclassifiable. A manageable Iago in the source becomes the maddeningly complicated Iago in Shakespeare's play. This quality has kept Shakespeare's plays alive while his sources remain unread.

The Human Touches

Shakespeare shows his genius in the human touches that make extensive philosophizing unnecessary. While Lear is agonizing over the body of Cordelia, he speaks.

> Why should a dog, a horse, a rat have life,
> And thou no breath at all? Thou'lt come no more,
> Never, never, never, never, never!
> Pray you, undo this button. Thank you, sir,
>
> Do you see this? Look on her! Look-her lips!
> Look there, look there!
>
> *King Lear*, V, 3, 306-311

At this moment, Lear faints, never to speak again. His last words, a cry of despairing hope, are all effective but the line singled out as a stroke of genius on Shakespeare's part is the simple, "Pray you, undo this button." It's a homely reminder that this is a real situation, a human situation, not just a situation with cardboard characters in an evening's entertainment. Such a line did not appear in the source.

Some critics have considered Shakespeare's lack of original plotting a weakness. Others say that "not being original at all" may be the greater skill. Shakespeare was receptive to everything: in his reading, in his life, in his theatrical experiences. His reading didn't close his mind. It opened it. The range and extent of his borrowing, when filtered through his genius, was a source of his greatness.

Part Three

The Plays and the Poems

18

Dating the Plays

Beyond all date, even to eternity.

Sonnet 122, Line 4

This phrase, written in a sonnet about a personage unknown (p319), is aptly suited to a consideration of Shakespeare's genius. Scholars are rightly concerned with the context, with Shakespeare's world, his actors, his theater, but the plays seem destined to outlive that context for generations to come. Still the challenge and the search go on.

An enduring problem for Shakespeare scholars is the order and dating of the plays. By the absence of firm and recorded publication information, the exact date of many plays is impossible to determine. There are, however, clues that suggest the approximate order in which the plays were written.

A general approach is to establish a date before which the play could not have been written and a date after which the play could not have been written. Scholars rely on both internal and external evidence.

External Evidence

External evidence derives from allusions to the plays in the books, records, travelers' journals, and even letters of the period. The *Henry* plays, for example, are universally accepted as among the earliest of the plays, with good reason. In 1592, Thomas Nash, colorful satirist, novelist and playwright, provided the earliest surviving literary remark about a Shakespearean play, though he doesn't mention the title of the play or its author.

"How would it have joyed brave Talbot (the terror of the French) to think that after he had lain two hundred years in his tomb, he would triumph again on the stage, and have his bones now embalmed with the tears of ten thousand spectators at least."

Lord John Talbot, English military hero of the Hundred Years War, dominates Shakespeare's *Henry VI, Part One*. Brave, virtuous, gallant, Talbot exemplified the best elements in the English character. The English people, yearning for a hero and role model, loved this character from one of Shakespeare's earliest plays. The popularity of the Talbot character has providentially supplied scholars with a fairly firm date for the production of this play.

The dating of the *Henry VI* plays is possible because of another reference. Robert Greene, already mentioned as a rival to Shakespeare (p 48), provided a critical comment useful because of its date. Entered in the Stationer's Register in 1592, three weeks after Greene's early death, *Groatsworth of Wit* had this to say about Shakespeare.

> There is an upstart crow, beautified with our feathers, that with his Tygers hart wrapt in a Players hyde, supposes he is as well able to bombast out a blanke verse as the best of you: and being an absolute *Johnannes Factotum* is in his owne conceit the onely Shake-scene in a country.

This envious, embittered criticism by a University Wit (p 49), about a would be "Jack-of-All Trades" also helps in dating. That reference to a tiger's heart is a parody of a line in *Henry VI, Part Three*: "O tiger's heart wrapt in a woman's hide."

Unfortunately, fairly firm evidence of a similar sort is often lacking for other plays. It is tempting to jump to conclusions, but reflection urges caution, as in the following example. Thomas Platter, a Swiss traveler in England, describes a performance of *Julius Caesar* in 1599.

"On September 21, after dinner, at about two o'clock, I went over the water with my companions and saw in the strewn roof-house the tragedy of the first Emperor Julius Caesar, with about fifteen characters very well acted."

There, that should settle it. It must be a production date for Shakespeare's *Julius Caesar*. Probably, but not certainly. Shakespeare's contemporaries were producing plays in a frenzy of creativity. Was this *Julius Caesar* Shakespeare's?

Francis Meres, author and critic, provided the best help in dating Shakespeare's early plays. In 1598, he published *Palladis Tamia: Wit's Treasury*, an anthology of philosophical and literary maxims. Meres compares contemporary writers with classical models and pays homage to Shakespeare. He mentions *Venus and Adonis* and *The Rape of Lucrece*, along with some of the sonnets. He calls Shakespeare the equal of the Roman Plautus in comedy and Seneca in tragedy. At this point in Shakespeare's career, the greatest of his comedies and tragedies lay ahead, but he had already won an audience with plays like *A Midsummer Night's Dream* and *Richard II*. Besides these, Meres lists *Two Gentlemen of Verona, A Comedy of Errors, Love's Labour's Lost, The Merchant of Venice, Richard III, Henry IV, King John, Titus Andronicus*, and *Romeo and Juliet*. *Love's Labor's Won* may be *The Taming of the Shrew*. The list demonstrates Shakespeare's popularity and versatility.

Other helps in dating the plays derive from mention of contemporary events in the plays. In June 1609, a fleet of nine ships sailed for Virginia to bolster John Smith's colony there. One of the vessels, the *Sea-Venture*, was separated from the rest of the fleet and wrecked on the coast of Bermuda. Pamphlets about the disaster furnished Shakespeare with details of the storm in *The Tempest*, which thus had to be written after 1609. For this play, we have additional help in dating, a record of a court presentation on November 1, 1611.

In *Twelfth Night*, Maria makes reference to a "new map, with the augmentation of the Indies." Although all maps of the Elizabethan period showed the Indies (America), the new map of 1600 was much more detailed, devoting a larger space to America than ever before. This reference dates *Twelfth Night* after this publication. And so it goes.

The Quartos and Dating

Shakespeare's popularity generated many quarto (p 16) versions of his plays. These booklets, one-fourth the size of a folio, or page, are priceless in helping to date the plays. Most of Shakespeare's early plays appeared in quartos. Some were called *Good Quartos*, authoritative publications of the plays. Others, called *Bad Quartos*, were haphazard, often dubious in origin.

Of the 38 plays usually considered part of the Shakespearean canon, 36 appeared in the First Folio (p 3). *Pericles* and *The Two Noble Kinsmen* were omitted from the Folio and are available only through the quartos. *The Two Noble Kinsmen* is accepted into the canon under the protest of some scholars. Most agree that John Fletcher (p 56) wrote part or most of the plays, determined by the scholar's evaluation of lines and speeches. Even *Pericles* is generally considered a collaboration, but with Shakespeare as the major contributor.

Determining the Text

There is no definitive text of the works of Shakespeare. One obvious reason is the disparity between the quartos and the First Folio. Even the quartos sometimes differ from each other. Comparing two quartos of *Hamlet* reveals some of the difficulties.

The First Quarto of 1603, often called the Bad Quarto, differs substantially from the Second Quarto, the Good Quarto. For one thing, it is 1600 lines shorter. Some characters' names have been changed. Polonius is Corambis and Reynaldo is Montano. Differences appear at the very beginning. The First Quarto begins in this way.

FIRST SENTINEL.   Stand! Who is that?
SECOND SENTINEL.   'Tis I.

FIRST SENTINEL.   O, you come most carefully upon your
                         watch.

The Second Quarto begins in this way:

BERNARDO.   Who's there?
FRANCISCO.   Nay answere me. Stand and unfold your selfe.
BERNARDO.   Long live the King
FRANCISCO.   Bernardo.
BERNARDO.   You come most carefully upon your hour,

The opening of the Second Quarto is fuller, richer. In the First Quarto, the soliloquy "To be or not to be" is recognizable but strangely different in tone and emphasis.

HAMLET.   To be, nor not to be-ay, there's the point:
                 To die, to sleep-is that all? ay, all, No;
                 To sleep, to dream-ay, marry, there it goes.

Close but strangely lacking.

Occasionally, the First Quarto provides a line adapted by later scholars in place of the same line in the Second Quarto and the First Folio. When Horatio described the Ghost to Hamlet, he tells how the Ghost appeared "in the dead vast and middle of the night." Both the Second Quarto and the First Folio have *wast* (waste) in place of the more striking *vast*.

How do scholars explain the existence of the so-called Bad Quarto? Was it pirated and published without authorization? Was it an actor's imperfect recollection based upon his acting experience in the play? Was it an early abridged version prepared for touring companies?

Albert B. Weiner makes an interesting case for the last possibility. The text of the Bad Quarto can be played with only 12 actors. Hamlet, the King, and Horatio speak 70% of the lines in the play. The remaining characters are little more than walk-ons. Players can double, triple or even quadruple their roles. Bernardo, for example, can also play the Third

Player, Fortinbras, and the Priest. Even the murdered Corambis can come back as the First Gravedigger, a fascinating challenge for an actor even in the complete quarto.

Is it any wonder that with so many versions to choose from, the available texts vary in small details and even in the numbering of the lines? The Variorum Edition of Shakespeare, edited by H.H. Furness, addresses itself to evaluating the many versions.

A typical analysis in the Variorum involves a line from Horatio's description of the Ghost in Act One.

HORATIO.   So frown'd he once, when, in an angry parle,
                  He smote the sledded Polacks on the ice.

On the face of it, this seems unquestionable. The first King Hamlet, in a warlike mood, struck his enemy, the Poles, who were traveling across the frozen terrain on sleds. But there are alternative readings. Instead of *Polacks*, one version has *poleaxe*, (or battle-axe). Then the interpretation of *sledded* is taken to be *leaded*. This provides an entirely different image, of an angry warrior, annoyed at the failure of the parley, forcefully striking his axe on the ice.

The *Variorum Edition* relishes problems like this, providing two pages of small type for this alternative reading alone. Of course, it's not necessary to sift every line to enjoy Shakespeare, but it's interesting to know that such exhaustive studies exist.

Internal Evidence

Back to dating. In addition to the external evidence, scholars turn to the internal evidence, like the maturing of Shakespeare's style in later plays and the growing subtleties of characterization. Of course, this is often subjective. Shakespeare's Imagery (p135) does, however, provide a believable insight into Shakespeare's mind and method.

The Order of the Plays

Although there is no definitive list of Shakespeare's plays in the order of composition, some reasonable guesses can be made. The following list is conjectural, but when lined up with the life of Shakespeare (Chapter One), it enriches both plays and biography.

The usual chronology assigns a possible date for each play. A less constricting approach provides a grouping of plays probably written during a specific period. Peter Alexander has suggested such a grouping. He theorizes that the earliest plays were written in the 80s and revised later. Thus, he begins his grouping with 1584, though the first known productions of the Henry VI plays were around 1590.

1584-Shakespeare probably arrived in London.
    Comedies

> *A Comedy of Errors*
> *The Taming of the Shrew*
> *Love's Labour's Lost*
> *Two Gentlemen of Verona*

    Histories

> *Henry VI, Parts One-Three*
> *Richard III*
> *King John*

    Tragedy

> *Titus Andronicus*

1590-Shakespeare joins the Lord Chamberlain's Men.
    Comedies

> *A Midsummer Night's Dream*
> *The Merchant of Venice*
> *The Merry Wives of Windsor*

Much Ado about Nothing
As You Like It

Histories

Richard II
Henry IV, Parts One, Two
Henry V

Tragedy

Romeo and Juliet

1599-The Globe Theater is opened. The Chamberlain's Company becomes The King's Men in 1603.
Comedies

Twelfth Night
Troilus and Cressida
Measure for Measure
All's Well That Ends Well

Tragedies

Julius Caesar, Hamlet, Othello
Timon of Athens
King Lear
Macbeth
Antony and Cleopatra
Coriolanus

1608-The King's Men take over Blackfriars
Comedies

Pericles
Cymbeline
The Winter's Tale
The Tempest

History

Henry VIII

The *Two Noble Kinsmen* (p307) is not on Alexander's list. It is dated last, possibly 1613.

In the chapters that follow, the plays are not organized in strict chronological order but in groups inviting discussion and commentary. The major plot of each play is given, with some reference to minor plots and characters. The place of each play in the canon is suggested, with some critical commentary. A scene by scene summary can be counterproductive but a less-detailed critical retelling is more readable, helpful and memorable.

19

The Early Comedies

Your honor's players, hearing your amendment,
Are come to play a pleasant comedy;

The Taming of the Shrew, Induction, 2, 125-126

The Elizabethan theater, like modern television, was voracious, devouring material as soon as it came from the pens of the many competing dramatists, Shakespeare found himself in this highly competitive market, with nothing but his own genius to carry him along, If the market called for a bloody tragedy, he provided *Titus Andronicus*. If the people yearned for a history play, he wrote the *Henry VI* series. If comedy, he had a treasure house of plays to offer. Variety, then as now, motivated the producers in their search for new plays, new materials, new playwrights.

The plays in this section are considered his early comedies, but variety is the spice of life here, too. *The Comedy of Errors* is a joyous farce. *A Midsummer Night's Dream* is an extended fairy tale. *The Merchant of Venice* is a comedy set against the tragedy of Shylock. *The Merry Wives of Windsor* may have been created at the request of Queen Elizabeth herself.

Love is the theme throughout, from the adolescent love of the courtiers in *Love's Labour's Lost* to the more mature love of Portia in *The Merchant of Venice*. The battle of the sexes is a popular theme, from the struggles of

Petruchio and Katharina in *The Taming of the Shrew* to the hapless efforts of Falstaff in *The Merry Wives of Windsor*, as he deals with those merry wives.

Friendship is a recurring theme. Proteus can test the strength of friendship in *Two Gentlemen of Verona*. Antonio can risk his life and fortune for Bassanio in *The Merchant of Venice*.

True to the traditional definition of comedy, the plays all end happily for the principals, though gratification is postponed for those courtiers in *Love's Labour's Lost*. Shylock slinks off in despair.

Modern films often have test tryouts that may affect the final version. Television pilots are tested with real audiences. In this frantic context of writing and producing plays for Elizabethan audiences, Shakespeare learned what worked and what didn't work. The groundlings were vocal in their reactions to the plays being presented. They provided instant feedback for the playwrights. Perhaps Shakespeare modified some plays immediately on the basis of the audience reaction. Certainly, the audience's reaction to *The Comedy of Errors* influenced his treatment in *The Taming of the Shrew*.

Dating the plays is a tricky business. Performance dates are sometimes removed from the dates of composition, but all evidence points to these plays as products of Shakespeare's young manhood. They are sunny crowd-pleasers, untinged with the philosophical problems of a later play like *Measure for Measure*.

The Comedy of Errors

Perhaps there are, as some critics maintain, only a few basic plots, most stemming from the classic "Boy meets girl. Boy loses girl. Boy wins girl." Of course, it isn't the basic plot line that distinguishes one work from another: the embellishments and innovations make a work "new." *The Comedy of Errors* is a perfect illustration. Shakespeare borrowed the central plot idea from the Roman comic dramatist Plautus—who may have borrowed it from a Greek predecessor, (A play by Plautus became the inspiration for the musical *A Funny Thing Happened on the Way to the Forum*.)

In his Roman comedy, *The Menaechmi*, Plautus introduces a set of separated twins. When they come together, they are so alike that one is confused with the other. The resulting confusions and misunderstandings power the play. This is still an attractive idea for a farce. Shakespeare liked the idea so much that he added a second set of twins, thus doubling the potential confusions. He also added the plot of Egeon, father of the twins. He replaced the sexual attractions of *The Menaechmi* with real love. He thus introduced elements of romantic comedy into what could have been simply a farce.

The Comedy of Errors has the distinction of being the shortest of Shakespeare's plays. The brevity requires compression and rapidity of action. Like its classical forerunners, the play enfolds in a single day. As in bedroom farces, with doors opening and closing to provide plot complications, *The Comedy of Errors* has characters wandering in and out, back and forth. Split-second timing is essential. The audience must never be given time enough to contemplate all the coincidences, absurdities, and exaggerations. The play engenders "that willing suspension of disbelief" at the heart of all drama.

The play is set entirely in Ephesus, for two possible reasons. First, strange things reputedly happen in Ephesus. It has the reputation as a place of sorcery. Secondly, it may suggest St. Paul's Epistle to the Ephesians, in which Paul sets forth the duties of wives to husbands. In the play, Luciana expresses the same philosophy in urging her sister to accept the special role of the husband, Her sister Adriana, is more of a free thinker. Of course, playgoers recognized in the seaport Ephesus many of the qualities of their contemporary London. The play opens on a tragic note. Egeon, a merchant of Syracuse, has been arrested in Ephesus as an enemy of the state. The Duke tells him that he must die unless he pays a ransom of 100 marks. Poor Egeon has no such sum. The Duke, pitying him but bound by the law, gives Egeon a day of grace to try to raise the ransom money, a hopeless quest in a strange land.

Shakespeare uses the first scene to inform the audience of the play's background. Egeon explains at length how a shipwreck 23 years ago had divided his family. His wife and one of their twin sons had been separated from him, along with a servant, also a single twin. The other twin and servant survived with him. At the age of 18, the remaining son, accompanied by his servant Dromio, set out to search for his lost twin. Then Egeon went on a quest to learn the fate of either son. His quest had taken him to Ephesus, unfortunately for him; but fortunate for the plot, since both sons happen to be there, too.

Unbeknownst to Egeon, Antipholus of Syracuse is in Ephesus, along with his servant Dromio. A friendly merchant tells this Antipholus to say he's from Epidamnum, not Syracuse, since Syracusans are considered enemies of Ephesus. When he hears this advice, Antipholus bids Dromio return to their inn to guard their money. The separation sets the identity problems in motion. Dromio of Ephesus arrives and assumes that this Antipholus is his master. Improbably, both sons are named *Antipholus*, both servants are named *Dromio*, and both sets are dressed alike, but who cares!

The scenes that follow pile confusion upon confusion. All kinds of identity mix-ups occur, all cleverly choreographed. At one point, Antipholus of Syracuse is taken home with Adriana, wife of Antipholus of Ephesus. While Adriana tries to reawaken her "husband's" love and ardor, this Antipholus has eyes only for Luciana, Adriana's sister. A ring and a gold chain go astray, helping to bring events to a dramatic climax.

In the final scene not only are the sets of twins reunited, but Egeon is re-united with his wife, who has become the abbess of a Priory. Of course, the Abbess has been in Ephesus all these years without realizing that the Ephesus Antipholus is her son, but again Shakespeare is not too concerned with rational explanations. As always, he is interested in character, not just plot.

Though the Antipholus twins are indistinguishable in appearance, they are different in personalities. Antipholus of Syracuse has a pleasing manner. He is bemused by the good fortune that surrounds him when he is mistaken for his twin. He falls in love with Luciana in a charming scene in which he expresses his love as she frantically attempts to deflect that love toward Adriana. Even this mild Antipholus occasionally strikes the available

Dromio, but that ritual beating, intended as humor, was characteristic of classical comedy. Antipholus of Ephesus is a more prickly character, prone to angry outbursts, hotheaded and quick-tempered. At the end, this Antipholus is reconciled with his wife Adriana, and his twin wins the sister, Luciana.

Adriana is a precursor of Shakespeare's attractive heroines, but her counterpart in Plautus is not appealing. *She* is a complaining, nagging, obnoxious creature. By contrast, Adriana is an independent thinker, a superficially forbidding woman but with a soft and loving heart. As always, Shakespeare creates complex characters with conflicted emotions and complex motivations.

The appeal of farce is universal and enduring. In 1938, Rodgers and Hart created the musical comedy *The Boys from Syracuse*. In 1983, the BBC television production was able to cast a single actor as Antipholus of Syracuse and Antipholus of Ephesus. A single actor also played both Dromios. Without the magic of film or video, usually all four parts are played by four actors. *The Comedy of Errors* is so playable that even amateur groups enjoy presenting it.

The Taming of the Shrew

Though rooted in the traditions of the playwright's time, *The Taming of the Shrew* is one of Shakespeare's most enduringly popular plays. The "battle of the sexes" is a literary theme traceable to classical days. Shakespeare also uses the conventions of Italian comedy (p182) to mix traditional stereotypes like the bewildered father and comical servant with the highly individualized Katharina and Petruchio.

Though this is an early comedy, possibly written around 1593-1594, it already shows the insight that will later create a Beatrice in *Much Ado about Nothing*. There are elements of Kate in Beatrice, but other dimensions have been added to that later mistress of barbed wit.

The play opens with a framework involving a drunken beggar (p 67) and a trick played upon him, but that device is soon forgotten. The actual plot begins with the arrival in Padua of Lucentio and his servant Tranio. Lucentio is soon smitten with love for Bianca, daughter of a wealthy gentleman. Bianca already has two suitors, the colorless Hortensio and the elderly Gremio. There is another obstacle: the violent, fiery, untamed, older sister, Katharina. Baptista will not allow Bianca to marry until Katharina is wed, an almost impossible condition.

The two suitors agree to find tutors for Bianca, thus hoping to ingratiate themselves with Bianca and her father. Hortensio does point out that they'd better find a husband for Katharina first.

Enter Petruchio. He seeks out his old friend Hortensio, learns of this wealthy young woman, Katharina, and vows to woo her despite the major obstacle: her shrewishness. Hortensio seeks, with Petruchio's help, to introduce himself to Baptista as a music teacher for Bianca.

Old Gremio also finds a tutor for Bianca: the smitten Lucentio. To conceal his true identity, Lucentio has changed places and clothes with his servant Tranio, who then becomes "Lucentio," ostensibly another suitor for Bianca. Both Hortensio (as Lucio) and Lucentio (as Cambio) are thus given free access to the house and to the lovely Blanca. The way in which each subtly plies his suit provides a minor strand of comedy.

The major plot concerns Petruchio's wooing of Katherina and her ultimate submission. Their first meeting is, as expected, filled with verbal fireworks, punctuated, at one moment, by a slap. Not raising his voice, Petruchio says, "I swear I'll cuff you, if you strike me again." That immediately removes one of Katharina's favorite weapons: physical intimidation. Throughout the encounter, though Katharine rages, Petruchio is the soul of courtesy, commending her charm and flattering her beauty. Katharina is obviously bewildered by this strange wooing as well as upset. No person has ever stood up to her before. Petruchio announces that he'll marry her the following Sunday. The father, Baptista, is glad to get Katharina off his hands.

Sunday arrives. The wedding and accompanying festivities are about to begin, without a groom. Petruchio finally arrives, late, absurdly dressed, but ready for the ceremony. After the wedding, Petruchio announces that he will depart with his bride. Despite the protests of the guests and the entreaties of Katharina not to leave before the feast, Petruchio takes Kate off, supposedly to "save" her from the guests.

Then follow a number of psychological battles between the undisciplined Kate and the imperturbable Petruchio. Petruchio's strategy is to break the will of his fiery bride by using the kind of "behavior modification" familiar to modern psychology. Through devious starvation and sleep derivation, he does essentially break her will. At last, he promises to take her back to her father's house for a visit, but each time he cancels the trip because of some show of will or contradiction by Katharina. If Petruchio comments how bright the moon is, Katherina at first says, "The moon! the sun-it is not moonlight now." When he corrects her, she finally says, in effect, "Whatever you say."

What's going on here? Isn't this the worst kind of male chauvinism, an assault on the basic tenets of feminism? Why isn't this play mothballed and forgotten? Audiences find it hard to dislike the courteous, seemingly affectionate Petruchio Few object strenuously to the taming of an unpleasant woman.

Finally back at the father's house, Petruchio demonstrates at a banquet how sweet, docile, and obedient Kate is. She not only outshines her sister and a widow; she also delivers a speech on the duties of a wife toward a husband. Perhaps Petruchio is also tamed when he says in admiration, "Come on, and kiss me, Kate."

The questions raised in a paragraph above are best answered by a brief description of a free performance in Central Park, New York. Meryl Streep played Kate and Raul Julia played Petruchio, before a sophisticated audience, a cross-section of modern theatergoers. One might expect cool reaction to this play, but the audience was enchanted. Despite their misgivings at some of the implications, the playgoers realized that the play is a farce after all; that it was written when wives were supposed to be submissive; and especially that Kate got what she deserved, as even she realized at last.

Petruchio is a master psychologist. Though he is loud and theatrically overbearing in his dealings with the servants, he is always courteous toward Kate, "concerned" only for her safety and well-being. He affords little opportunity for Kate to play her old shrewish role. He is showing Kate what she was like before he met her.

Meryl Streep and Raul Julia played up the incipient love affair between the antagonists. From their first meeting, Kate/Meryl looked at Petruchio/Raul with hatred...and a tinge of admiration. Their love at the end was real. Shakespeare's genius has taken a well-worn tale and given it psychological depths that resonate with modern audiences.

Love's Labour's Lost

Shakespearean scholar Harold Bloom wrote, "I take more unmixed pleasure from *Love's Labour's Lost* than from any other Shakespearean play." Why does Bloom favor a play that has never been ranked as high as the great comedies, never held the stage as frequently as the great tragedies? He feels that Shakespeare "enjoyed a particular and unique zest in composing it. "*Love's Labour's Lost* is a festival of language, an exuberant fireworks display in which Shakespeare seems to seek the limits of his verbal resources, and discovers that there are none."

Shakespeare is a lover of language (p117), an experimenter and iconoclast. Every play exhibits some of that verbal brilliance. In *Love's Labour's Lost*, however, language play is not merely decoration but a central element.

The exact dating of the play is uncertain. Dates as early as 1590-1592 have been suggested, but some scholars feel that the play shows a sophistication likely associated with a more mature Shakespeare. There are *in* jokes incomprehensible to modern audiences and many contemporary references meaningless to us today. Still there is much recognizable humor and easily appreciated word play.

The entire play is a satire (p170). Affectation and pretension are revealed for their hollowness. Two elements come in especially for Shakespeare's scorn: unnatural vows doomed to be broken and pompous language meant to impress. The noble lords begin the play with high-flown tributes to the values of study as opposed to the more mature delights of feminine companionship. They end with a maturer realization of values and an acceptance of their self-deception.

Shakespeare created many memorable women. In this play, the Princess of France and her handmaidens are more sensible than the men, more perceptive, more aware of insincerity and posturing. They help the men to a greater maturity.

The play opens with a proposal by the King of Navarre to forego revelry, banqueting, and the company of women for three years. Longaville and Dumaine, two of the courtiers, agree to sign at once. Berowne isn't so sure, especially since the Princess of France is visiting with her court. He agrees to sign despite his misgivings.

As the Princess approaches, the ladies talk over the nobles whom they have met earlier. Maria praises Longaville. Katharine admires Dumaine. Rosaline remembers Berowne. Rosaline especially seems to foreshadow later attractive young women: Beatrice, Portia, and her near-namesake Rosalind.

The ladies have heard of the King's unnatural vows. The Princess scolds the King for requiring her retinue to stay in a pavilion outside the royal park. Colorful minor characters move in and out of the mainstream: Costard, a comical rustic; Don De Armado, a ludicrous Spaniard and his page Moth; Holofernes, a pedantic schoolmaster; Sir Nathaniel, a curate, admirer of Holofernes; Dull, a constable; and Jaquenetta, a "country wench." Both Costard and Armado are in love with Jaquenetta.

Armado writes a love letter to Jaquenetta and entrusts it to Costard as messenger. Berowne writes a love letter to Rosaline, and also entrusts the letter to Costard. Costard gets the letters mixed up and delivers Armado's letter to Rosaline. When the letter is read aloud, with its overloaded phrasing, the ladies are overcome with laughter.

Berowne's letter is delivered to Jaquenetta. She asks Nathaniel to read it to her. Nathaniel, recognizing that an error has been made, sends the letter to the King.

In an amusing scene, all four men reveal their love for the Princess and her ladies. Berowne at first plays a smug superior role, but when his letter to Rosaline reaches the King and is read aloud, he also capitulates. The men decide to approach the ladies dressed as a delegation of Russians. The ladies get wind of this plan, don masks, and exchange identifying favors. The "Russians" thus make love to the wrong women. Outmaneuvered, the men retreat and return as themselves. At last, they realize that they have made love to the wrong women and made fools of themselves.

At this point, the lesser characters put on the pageant of the Nine Worthies. The presentation is hopelessly botched to the amusement of the onlookers, somewhat like the play of Pyramus and Thisbe in *A Midsummer Night's Dream.*

The merriment is interrupted by a messenger with news that the Princess's father has died. The ladies must leave, promising their love if the men adopt a severely restricted life for a year. Rosaline directs Berowne to spend the year visiting dying patients in hospitals to teach him the seriousness of life. Thus the tables are turned, and the men are back to a life of asceticism and service.

Much of the play is written in rhymed couplets (p112), a device sparingly used elsewhere, usually only for scene endings. Berowne's love letter to Rosaline is a sonnet. Shakespeare is indeed trying his language skill, playing with rhymes: *society-simplicity, move-love, prose-hose.* As Bloom says, he must have enjoyed writing this play.

In 2000, Kenneth Branagh, presented a version of the play as a musical of the 1930s, with vintage songs and Busby-Berkely-type numbers. It was set in the period just before and after World War I. Unlike the original play, this version finds the suitors joyously reunited with their ladies after surviving the war.

Two Gentlemen of Verona

Sometimes called "an experimental comedy," *The Two Gentlemen of Verona* shows Shakespeare at the beginning of his career. Never very popular, it is sometimes played more as farce than as a traditional comedy. It uses some of the devices exploited later in more polished plays: like the pairs of lovers with confused affections (*A Midsummer Night's Dream*); and the girl disguised as a boy (*Twelfth Night, As You Like It, A Merchant of Venice*). There are comical minor characters in *Two Gentlemen of Verona,* principally

Launce and his dog Crab, but these are adornments, only slightly involved in the plot. In *Much Ado about Nothing*, by contrast, the comical figures, Dogberry and Verges, are crucial to the plot.

The play opens with a dialogue between Valentine and Proteus, the "two gentlemen of Verona." Valentine announces his coming departure for Milan, even as he teases Proteus about Proteus's love for Julia.

Proteus's father decides that his son shall also go to the Duke of Milan to be with his friend Valentine. Since Proteus is so infatuated with Julia, he expresses his sadness at leaving. Before he goes, he and Julia exchange rings and vows of faithfulness.

Meanwhile at the Duke's court, Valentine himself has fallen madly in love—with the Duke's daughter Silvia. Silvia returns his passion. Since the Duke is insistent that Silvia marry a colorless nobleman, Thurio, Valentine and Silvia plan to elope. Into this volatile situation comes Proteus, newly arrived from Verona. Unwisely, Valentine tells Proteus of his plans to escape.

Proteus's arrival sets the plot's major complication in motion. Valentine tells Silvia of his friendship for Proteus and of Proteus's great love for Julia. That love vanishes in an instant when Proteus sees Silvia. Love, friendship, honesty, fidelity, decency-all melt away.

In a soliloquy at the end of the scene, Proteus throws over his love for Valentine, now a competing suitor:

> O! but I love his lady too-too much;
> And that's the reason I love him so little.
> *The Two Gentlemen of Verona*, II, 4, 203-204

Hoping to win Silvia for himself, Proteus plots to break up the Valentine-Silvia relationship. He tells the Duke about the projected elopement so that he'll gain favor with the Duke and wreck his friend's love affair.

Back in Verona, Julia decides to go to her lover Proteus. For safety's sake, she travels as a boy, a page. Her perceptive maid Lucetta warns her that Proteus's love may have diminished, but Julia is confident... she pays an undeserved tribute to her absent lover:

> His words are bonds, his oaths are oracles,
> His love sincere, his thoughts immaculate.
> *The Two Gentlemen of Verona*, II, 7, 75-76

Shakespeare loved irony: Armed with the knowledge provided by Proteus, the Duke exposes the elopement plans and banishes Valentine. For his own purposes, Proteus helps Valentine flee. Returning, he seems to help the rival Thurio's cause by damning Valentine, such condemnation stronger for coming from a close friend. Silvia is disgusted by Proteus's faithlessness to Valentine and to Julia. With the help of a friend, Sir Eglamour, Silvia leaves the court in search of her beloved Valentine. The Duke, Thurio, and Proteus follow in pursuit.

In the forest, in a scenario often ridiculed, Valentine has been captured by outlaws who have been so impressed with him that they have chosen him captain. In her search for Valentine, Silvia is captured by these outlaws, to be taken to their captain. En route, however, Silvia is "rescued" by Proteus, who demands her love as his reward for taking her from the outlaws. When she refuses, he tries to rape her, but Valentine arrives, cursing his friend's treachery. Incredibly, when Proteus expresses remorse, Valentine forgives him and adds, "All that was mine in Silvia I give thee."

Julia, in her disguise as a page, has been looking on. Valentine's latest comment is too much for her: she faints. She reveals her true identity as Julia, and Proteus instantly renews his old love. The friends are reconciled. Julia is happy. Silvia has not said a word since Valentine's offer, nor does she say anything for the rest of the play!

The outlaws bring in the captured Duke and Thurio. Valentine threatens Thurio with death if he fails to relinquish his claims to Silvia. Thurio backs down immediately, saying "Only a fool will endanger his body for a girl who loves him not." The Duke, recognizing the superiority of Valentine over Thurio, gives Valentine his blessing to take Silvia. As an added grace note, the Duke forgives all the outlaws, who are really kind-hearted gentlemen. The play ends with the promise of two marriages.

In so many ways, this is a strange play. Sudden changes of heart occur with small motivation. Proteus is well named, for Proteus was a mythological figure who could change shape at will. The election of Valentine as captain of the outlaws may be a spoof of romances. Perhaps Shakespeare is saying, "Let's have fun and forget any improbabilities."

The play is blessed with several excellent scenes. When the Duke accosts Valentine carrying the elopement ladder under his cloak, he toys with the poor lover, until he finally opens Valentine's cloak. Perhaps the best scenes, however, involve Launce, the servant of Proteus, and his dog Crab. His two long monologues with the dog show the kind of comic ability that will accompany Shakespeare through all the great comedies to come. Without a speaking line, Crab nevertheless becomes a wonderful comic character! Always presented with a real dog, on stage, those scenes fascinate audiences. Any animal on the stage captures the audience's attention. Crab seldom listens to his master's funny comments about Crab's misdeeds and lack of sympathy for his master's problems. Whatever the dog does during those scenes is funny.

Is Shakespeare exploring the limits of friendship and love? Is he poking fun at empty protestations without real substance? Is he asking, "What if two friends loved the same woman, both with a different motive?" Is he biding time until he can provide the magical monologues that have made Launce and Crab immortal? Perhaps all of these. The great comedies lay ahead.

A Midsummer Night's Dream

Some time before 1600, Shakespeare worked on this, one of his most popular plays. The play was registered in 1600, and a quarto appeared in that same year. Publication of the quarto suggests its popularity at the time, a popularity that has survived many different settings and societies.

Shakespeare somehow manages to weave together four different plot strands and bring all together at the end of the play. In most plays a principal plot captures most of the audience's attention. In *Macbeth*, for example, the tragedy of Macbeth dominates the action. In *A Midsummer Night's Dream*, the plot strand of the four lovers adds charm and humor, but it is rivaled by the captivating antics of the townspeople as they prepare a performance for the Duke's wedding. Bottom, the weaver, in all his self-important glory is remembered long after Lysander, Demetrius, Hermia, and Helen are lost in confusion.

A third strand provides the framework of the play, as Duke Theseus, Duke of Athens, prepares to marry Hippolyta, Queen of the Amazons. A fourth strand is concerned with Oberon, King of the Fairies, and his quarrel with Titania, Queen of the Fairies. All four plots interact in ingenious ways, advancing the action and delighting the audience.

Theseus opens the play by expressing his love for Hippolyta and urging the Master of the Revels to stir things up for a happy ceremony. The harmony doesn't last. An Athenian citizen, Egeus, enters with a complaint. His daughter, Hermia, loves Lysander, but Egeus wants her to marry Demetrius. Egeus calls upon Theseus to enforce the ancient privilege of Athens: unless Hermia obeys her father, she must enter a convent or die. Reluctantly, Theseus says he must enforce the rule, but Hermia and Lysander have other plans, Lysander has an aunt at a distance from Athens. They plan to run away to be together.

In true girlish fashion, before leaving, Hermia reveals her plans to her best friend, Helena. Demetrius had once loved Helena, but rejected her when he met Hermia. Thinking to score points with Demetrius and perhaps win him back, Helena tells Demetrius of the lovers' plans. As a result, all four lovers wander off into the woods outside Athens.

The scenes shift as two other plots come into play. A group of townspeople assemble to plan an entertainment for the coming wedding. Among these artisans, Bottom, the weaver, stands out for his unshakable self-confidence and comical ignorance. They plan to meet in that same woods outside the city.

In another scene, Oberon and Titania quarrel over an Indian boy whom both wish for their retinues. Seeking to humiliate Titania and thus win the argument, Oberon sends Puck on a quest for a flower that has the power to create love in the first object seen by anyone who has had the eyes anointed by the juice. Titania is chosen as the victim for this magical trick.

In the forest, Lysander and Hermia lie down to rest near Titania's flowery bed. Demetrius in pursuit of the lovers is himself pursued by the lovelorn Helena. Demetrius loses Helena. Oberon intervenes. He seeks to solve the lovers' problems by having Demetrius's eyes anointed, so that when he awakes, he'll find Helena and love her. Unfortunately, Puck mistakes the lovers and anoints the eyes of Lysander. When he awakens, he first sees Helena and declares his ardent love for her. Helena thinks he's mocking her.

The scene changes to the artisans and their preparations to play "Pyramus and Thisbe" for the wedding. Puck chases the rest away and puts an ass's head on Bottom to further the Titania plot. When she awakens and finds Bottom, ass's head and all, she falls madly in love with him, doting on his every word and action.

Oberon discovers that Puck has got the Athenians mixed up and arranges to have the original victim, Demetrius, charmed by the juice. When he awakens and finds Helena, he falls in love with her. Now Helena, once beloved of neither, is now beloved of both, and Hermia takes it badly! Oberon sends Puck to find the antidote, to relieve Lysander of the charm but keep Demetrius bewitched with Helena.

Having won the boy, Oberon releases Titania from her spell. They are reconciled. Bottom is released to become just plain Bottom again. The four lovers, now conveniently paired, are met by the Athenian nobles. The four, uncertain about recent events, ask that they be forgiven for running away. In the spirit of reconciliation, Theseus forgives them, accepts the new pairings, and overrides the still adamant Egeus. The lovers will be married and join Theseus and Hippolyta for the ceremonies.

The artisans have been rehearsing desperately and finally have the opportunity to display their talents. The results are hilarious. The production is a comical disaster, though the artisans feel that they've done pretty well. The wedding audience has a wonderful time commenting about the lines and the action. Afterward, Puck, Oberon, and Titania provide a kind of happy epilogue, and all the plot strands are tied neatly together.

Modern scholarship suggests that the play was originally intended for an aristocratic wedding. Everything is related to the theme of marriage. Love conquers all, with a little help from the unseen world.

The play runs the gamut of character, from the top ladder of society to the lowest. The earthy artisans also provide a balance to the otherworldliness of the fairies. Lysander and Demetrius have sometimes been labeled copies of each other, but the women, Hermia and Helena, are' individualized. The play has some of Shakespeare's most lyrical poetry, often quoted in anthologies. For modern audiences, the play still works!

The Merchant of Venice

To be classified as a comedy, a play must see the principal characters through to a happy ending. In *The Merchant of Venice* all the principal characters, save one, enjoy happy festivities at the end of the play. That "one" disturbs many modern readers and audiences. Shylock (p 94) appears in only five scenes, but his presence is felt throughout the play.

Some readers condemn *The Merchant of Venice* as being anti-Semitic, a rational worry in this post-Hitler world. Others freely admit that there are anti-Semitic elements in the play, though the play itself is not anti-Semitic. The genius of Shakespeare avoids so simplistic a label.

Almost certainly, most of Shakespeare's audiences considered Shylock an evil character, grotesque, and somewhat comic. He is an alien. He is different. His obsession with money is deplorable. To balance the score, as he always does, Shakespeare provides understandable motivation for Shylock's character. What Shylock attempts to do is monstrous, but that hatred had a source in Shylock's experiences with the Christians.

A comparison of Christopher Marlowe's *The Jew of Malta* (p 51) with *The Merchant of Venice* is revealing. In Marlowe's play, the protagonist is the embodiment of pure evil. In his revenge on so many others during the play, he stirs no sympathetic responses in the audience. In contrast,

Shylock begins to evoke our sympathy when we hear the Christians' comments about him. We respond to a common humanity with Shylock.

The theme has sometimes been presented as the opposition of the Old Testament, with its emphasis on law, and the New Testament, with its emphasis on love and mercy. The fact is that the Christians in the play are as bad as Shylock.

The central theme of the play is Shylock's bond and its consequences. Antonio, the Merchant of Venice, has borrowed 3,000 ducats from Shylock to help his friend Bassanio court Portia, a wealthy heiress. Antonio seeks out Shylock for a loan. Shylock reminds Antonio of Antonio's many insults toward himself, but agrees to lend the money anyway. There is a proviso: if the bond is not repaid on time, Shylock may take a pound of Antonio's flesh from any part of the body he chooses. Both men consider this a humorous provision, since Antonio's ships at sea will return in two months.

The second plot involves Bassanio's courting of Portia. Portia's father has left a strange legacy: three caskets, of gold, silver, and lead. The suitor who chooses the right casket wins Portia—and a share in all that wealth. Two suitors fail, but Bassanio chooses lead, the correct one, and wins Portia as his wife.

Later, Shylock's daughter Jessica runs off with Lorenzo, a Christian, and steals money from Shylock. To many modern readers, Jessica is a contemptible woman, a mockery of a daughter. To Shakespeare's audiences, however, Jessica was escaping from a miser into a love with Lorenzo that helped make this a romantic comedy.

As the time approaches for repayment of the loan, rumors abound that Antonio's ships have sunk, that he is a ruined man. Although Portia offers to repay the bond many times over, the now-embittered Shylock demands his pound of flesh.

Bassanio is called back from the country estate, to help his friend Antonio at the trial. Portia also attends the trial, dressed as a lawyer to prosecute the case against Shylock. Nerissa, Portia's waiting maid, accompanies Portia as her clerk. Portia attempts to dissuade Shylock from his unholy purpose. She points out that he'll be repaid more than he loaned.

She glorifies the quality of mercy, but Shylock is adamant. Then in a swift turnabout, she foils the malevolence of Shylock.

As Shylock is about to make a cut, Portia stops him, requiring him to shed not a drop of blood since blood wasn't mentioned in the bond. Nor can he take an ounce more than a pound. Shylock realizes his defeat, and offers to take the money, but Portia now shows the kind of intransigence that Shylock has just been showing. Ultimately, through Antonio's intercession, Shylock's life is spared, but he must give half his goods to Lorenzo and Jessica. He may retain half, but he must become a Christian. Shylock is broken by this ruling and departs in sorrow.

For her efforts on Antonio's behalf, Portia requests the ring that she had given Bassanio earlier. He at first refuses but ultimately agrees. Nerissa also extracts a ring from her husband, Gratiano.

In a bright Fifth Act, all is harmony until Portia and Nerissa "discover" that their husbands no longer have the rings. After much mock scolding, the women reveal the truths and all ends happily.

The play encourages dissenting views. Can Shylock be treated too generously in production, in opposition to Shakespeare's intent? Is Shylock actually a hero, a proponent of fairness and humanity and an opponent of racism? Is the brightly lighted Act V a cruel reflection on the indignities just visited upon Shylock? Despite her protestations of mercy, is Portia just as cruel toward Shylock as he intended to be toward Antonio? Is Bassanio a less-than-admirable fortune hunter who courts Portia for her wealth and who imposes upon his friend Antonio to get the money for the courtship?

As always with Shakespeare, the play is open-ended. Each age will interpret it in its own special way. The central situation may be of a particular time, but the play itself is timeless.

The Merry Wives of Windsor

Any claim that the Earl of Oxford wrote Shakespeare's plays (p 81) becomes meaningless with the creation of this play. This is unlike the rest of Shakespeare's plays. It is a romp, a depiction of rural customs, a tribute to the vitality of rustic values. The characters are country folk, but they are imbued with the same virtues and faults as those of the nobility. Shakespeare knew the scene intimately and met many of the character types during his days in Stratford.

The tradition is that Queen Elizabeth requested another play with Falstaff in it, showing him in love. She had been enchanted by the brilliant depiction of Sir John Falstaff in the *Henry IV* plays. *The Merry Wives* may have been written as early as 1597, possibly April. The date follows quickly the dates for the completion of those *Henry IV* plays. There is some speculation that Shakespeare wrote the play hastily. This conjecture supports the judgment of those who consider it a hurried work, a minor work. More recent scholarship has recognized its deserved popularity, including its inspiration for Verdi's popular opera *Falstaff*.

Those who expect to meet good Sir John as he was in the *Henry* plays are disappointed. In this play, Falstaff still has verbal facility, "brassy, zestful, and humorously rhetorical as ever." The other Falstaff, the *Henry IV* Falstaff, used his language to confuse his foes and advance his own rascality. Here, nothing works. Falstaff's attempted knavery is thwarted at every turn…and by women! The critic Harold Bloom calls the hero-villain of this play "a nameless impostor masquerading as the great Sir John Falstaff."

The play tells us something about Shakespeare's company (p 26). He obviously had boys who could play strong, no-nonsense women, a foreshadowing of Rosalind, Beatrice, and Viola to come. He apparently had a Welsh actor or two. He features the character Evans in this play, Glendower in *Henry IV, Part One*, and Fluellen in *Henry V*.

The major plot is concerned with the thwarted plans of Falstaff and his eventual discomfiture. An important subplot is the love affair between Ann Page and Fenton. Other ingredients involve a jealous husband, an aborted, comical duel, and various activities involving colorful minor characters.

Ever a fortune-seeker, Falstaff seeks to make advances to two ladies, Mrs. Page and Mrs. Ford, hoping to benefit financially by his charm. He writes identical love letters to the two women. The ladies compare notes and decide to teach Sir John a lesson. Complications ensue. Master Page completely trusts his wife, but Master Ford is an unreasonably jealous husband.

As Falstaff begins his wooing of Mrs. Ford, Page bursts in with the news that the raging Mr. Ford is coming to catch his wife in a tryst. John is obliged to hide in a clothes basket under a pile of soiled linen. Mrs. Ford's servants deposit the contents of the basket into a muddy ditch near the Thames.

Falstaff amorously tries again with Mrs. Ford and again has to take safety measures against the jealous Ford. This time he is disguised in a gown belonging to the local witch. He is driven from the house with Ford's blows.

Master Ford is finally convinced of his wife's fidelity. The Fords and the Pages plan a final embarrassment for Falstaff. They persuade him to play the role of Herne the hunter in an old superstition. Falstaff goes to the forest so dressed and is put upon by a satyr, fairies and hobgoblins, most of them disguised children. A summary does little justice to a chaotic and joyful scene. Shakespeare's audiences loved the foolery. The deception is revealed, and Falstaff is good-naturedly invited home "to laugh this sport o'er a country fire," along with the others at the scene.

The subplot of Ann Page and Fenton is almost thwarted by the presence of two other suitors, each with his own champions. At the end, however, during the forest scene with "Herne the hunter," Anne and Fenton steal away to be married. They, too, are forgiven, and the play ends on a note of forgiveness all around.

Critics have identified some of the characters with stock characters in Italian popular comedy, but Shakespeare is never satisfied merely to copy.

20

The Early Tragedies

O heavens, can you hear a good man groan
And not relent, or not compassion him?

Titus Andronicus, IV, 1, 125-126

Early tragedies *Titus Andronicus* and *Romeo and Juliet* are a study in contrasts. *Titus Andronicus* is a very early play, some say the first Shakespeare wrote, *Romeo and Juliet* came only a few years later, probably between 1593 and 1596. The differences suggest a growth and maturing on the part of Shakespeare, a skill that would come to fruition in a tragedy like *Hamlet* and a comedy like *As You Like It*.

Titus Andronicus is an out-and-out revenge tragedy. *Romeo and Juliet* is a nuanced tragedy, with complex characters and dramatic situations. In *Titus Andronicus*, the bent of the tragedy is set forth in the opening scene, when Titus has the son of Tamora sacrificed.

In *Romeo and Juliet*, the course of true love seems to be proceeding well. The young lovers have a plan that will allow them to be married, despite their warring relatives. All might have worked except for a delayed message. The tragedy arises from chance, not a fatal flaw in their characters. In a sense, Lear brings the tragedy upon himself. Romeo and Juliet are guilty only of young love and a desire to be happy together.

Shakespeare delves even more deeply into character in the tragedies to come, but even here, he shows a mastery of human motivation. The characters in *Titus Andronicus* move almost like automata. In *Romeo and Juliet*, the characters involve the audience in a way that even Lavinia cannot do in *Titus Andronicus*.

Romeo and Juliet was featured in the Academy Award-winning *Shakespeare in Love*.

Titus Andronicus

"But consider young Shakespeare near the beginning of his career, trying to upstage the star dramatists and attract attention to himself. Imagine him sitting down to write the equivalent of today's horror films." Roger Ebert, in a review of the Anthony Hopkins film *Titus*, thus suggests a reason for the overwhelming gore and violence of this very early play. Just as the slasher movies do, "so does *Titus Andronicus* heap up the gore and then wink to show the playwright is in on the joke."

At the time he wrote *Titus Andronicus*, Shakespeare faced stiff competition. Cruel sports like bearbaiting and bullbaiting drew crowds. The theater produced bloody revenge plays to satisfy this audience. *Titus Andronicus* rises to the occasion and includes every kind of brutality and treachery: kidnaping, rape, dismemberment, decapitation, and even cannibalism. His audiences, conditioned by the Roman tragedies of Seneca, expected sensationalism...and Shakespeare provided it.

The Anthony Hopkins film presented the play using the tricks of modern technology. The director, Julie Taymor, brought in modern parallels by suggesting the actions of two renegade nations of our day: Nazi Germany and Fascist Italy. Roger Ebert joyfully called it an *absurd film*. In his book, Harold Bloom called the play a *parody*. But Shakespeare, even at his most immature, puts on a good show.

There are plots and counterplots, with death and revenge throughout. The protagonist, Titus Andronicus, a Roman general with an overdeveloped sense of honor, is responsible for part of the tragedy. It is his decision at the beginning of the play to support Saturninus as the emperor of

Rome. That sets the tragic events in motion. When Saturninus assumes the throne, matters deteriorate.

Titus is returning to Rome from a successful campaign against the Goths. He has brought captives, including the beautiful Tamora, Queen of the Goths. Since Titus has lost several sons in the war, another son, Lucius, calls for the sacrifice of Tamora's son Alarbus. Tamara pleads with Titus for mercy, but Titus is adamant. Tamora determines to avenge her son's death.

The Roman emperor has died, and there are two sons who claim the throne: Bassianus and the oldest son Saturninus. When Titus supports Saturninus's claim, the new emperor declares in supposed gratitude that he will marry Lavinia, Titus's daughter. Titus turns his prisoners over to Saturninus, who is immediately smitten with Tamora's beauty. At this point, Bassianus claims Lavinia, to whom he had been betrothed.

Stubborn Titus, always shackled to a rigid course of honor, calls Bassianus and his own sons "traitors." When a son, Mutius, blocks Titus's pursuit of Bassianus and his group, Titus kills him. In his rigidity of mind and action, Titus tries at first to keep the other sons from giving Mutius decent burial. Saturninus, who fears Titus's popularity with the common people, takes the opportunity to renounce Titus and his sons. He declares his intention to marry Tamora, the beautiful captive who has captivated him.

Though Saturninus vows to act harshly, Tamora counsels reconciliation, promising in an aside to wreak vengeance later for her son's death. The apparent reconciliation with Bassianus results in the promise of a double wedding: Bassianus and Lavinia, Saturninus and Tamora. Two deaths-Alarbus and Mutius-set the tone for events to come. Revenge becomes the dominant theme of the play.

Another character, Aaron the Moor, is present during Act I, but the opening soliloquy of Act II brings him to life. He is the arch-villain who revels in evil, proudly boasting of his malevolence. He may be a crude forerunner of Iago, but his evil is so one-dimensional as to be grotesque. The many layers of Iago's personality are lacking here, though Shakespeare cannot resist a human touch: Aaron's tenderness when confronted with his infant son later. Aaron demonstrates his malice by proposing that Chiron and Demetrius, sons of Tamora, kidnap Lavinia to indulge their sexual cruelties.

The two couples are married and go forth on a hunt. At Aaron's direction, Tamora's sons kill Bassianus and carry Lavinia off to rape and mutilate her. Aaron devises a forged letter that implicates Martius and Quintus sons of Titus, in the murder. Lavinia, raped, with hands and tongue cut off, is abandoned.

Supposedly guilty of Bassianus's murder, the sons of Titus are carried off to be executed. They will supposedly be liberated if Titus cuts off a hand and sends it to Saturninus. Instead, the heads of the sons are brought in, along with Titus's severed hand. Lavinia is able to name her attackers by holding a staff in her mouth and writing their names in the sand.

Sitting with Chiron and Demetrius, Aaron is shown a baby, his own child, born of Tamora. Tamora's sons, to prevent scandal, want to kill the child, but Aaron proposes to place the child in a foster home and substitute a white child to give to Tamora. To keep the secret, Aaron kills the nurse, who had brought the child.

Meanwhile Titus's son Lucius, with an army of Goths, is threatening Rome.

Aaron with his baby is captured and threatened with death for him and the child. Aaron strikes a bargain. If Lucius promises to spare the child, Aaron will tell all about the terrible deeds and he does. The horrors he describes strengthen anew the resolve of Lucius for revenge.

The final scene is bloody and macabre. A supposed peace parley brings together the surviving principals. Titus has managed to kill Chiron and Demetrius for their assault on Lavinia and has baked them into a pie for the banquet. Before making the awful disclosure, Titus stabs Lavinia to rescue her from shame and misery. Then he announces to the Queen that she has been "Eating the flesh that she herself had bred."

The horrid tempo increases. Titus stabs Tamora. Saturninus kills Titus. Lucius kills Saturninus. Lucius is acclaimed the new emperor, who has the final word to bring order into chaos. Just before Lucius's final words of peace and accommodation, Aaron has a speech of his own, ending thus:

If one good deed in all my life I did,
I do repent it from my very soul.
Titus Andronicus, V, 3, 184-185

Shakespeare clearly labels this a mighty conflict between good and evil, and we all get the point. In later plays, he proved more supple, more flexible, more ambiguous.

Romeo and Juliet

According to the Oscar-winning *Shakespeare in Love*, *Romeo and Juliet* started out as *Romeo and Ethel, the Pirate's Daughter*, but was changed to *Romeo and Juliet* after Shakespeare's tempestuous love affair with a well-born woman. This pleasant fiction still provides many insights into Shakespeare's early life, his rivals, conditions in the Elizabethan theater, and relationships between Queen and players. Again, according to this make-believe scenario, Shakespeare's love affair with the beautiful Viola broke up his writer's block and inspired him to fashion the immortal *Romeo and Juliet* from a mediocre plot idea. Whatever the source of Shakespeare's inspiration, *Romeo and Juliet* is a theatrical blockbuster.

From the beginning, the play has been widely acclaimed for the beauty of its poetry, the tragedy of the young lovers, and the rapidity with which events move toward a climax. At the time Shakespeare wrote the play, play types were clearly defined. Comedies were comedies; they were stories about love and ended in marriage. Tragedies were tragedies, ending in death. Shakespeare takes the courageous initiative of beginning in comedy and ending in death. There is a lighthearted quality in the early scenes: the banter of Romeo's friends; the nurse's acid observations; Romeo and Juliet's love struck conversation. But the audience is warned immediately in the Prologue: "A pair of star-crossed lovers take their life." This warning gives a special poignance to the doomed happiness of the two young lovers. Some adaptations of this play through the centuries have provided happy endings and thus destroyed its special bittersweet quality.

The play itself starts with a street brawl between followers of the Montagues and Capulets. This scene introduces key opposites: Tybalt, the hotheaded Capulet, and Romeo, the lovesick Montague. At this point, Romeo pines for a Rosaline, much to the merriment of his friend Benvolio. The irony is that he quickly forgets Rosaline once he sees Juliet, daughter of the opposing family.

The scene shifts to the Capulet house. Paris, a nobleman, wishes to marry Capulet's daughter Juliet. Capulet hesitates because Juliet is not yet fourteen, but he gives her to Paris if Juliet approves. Capulet invites Paris to a feast, so that he can decide if he truly wishes to marry Juliet. Capulet sends an illiterate servant to invite those persons whose names are on a list. When the servant seeks to find someone to help in reading the names, he comes upon the two friends, Benvolio and Romeo. Since Rosaline is to be among the guests, Romeo agrees to attend the feast.

The next scene introduces us to Juliet, her mother, and the bawdy Nurse. They talk over the possibility of Juliet's becoming Paris's wife. Romeo, Benvolio, and Mercutio, a lighthearted but hotheaded friend of Romeo, manage to crash the party. Events begin to move rapidly, for Romeo has spotted Juliet and lost all thought of his former love, Rosaline. It is love at first sight for both young people, but their families are bitter enemies.

Afterward, Romeo risks danger by hiding near Juliet's bedroom window. She calls out, "Romeo, Romeo, wherefore (why) art thou Romeo?" He makes himself known. They exchange vows of love and plan an immediate marriage.

Romeo approaches Friar Laurence to marry the two. Though the Friar is reluctant, he agrees, hoping that the marriage will bring peace between the two families. Juliet's nurse finds Romeo, and he tells her of the marriage plans. They do meet and are married. Perhaps this union could bring about reconciliation between the two families, but fate intervenes.

Mercutio and Romeo encounter Tybalt on the street. Tybalt insults Romeo, but Romeo, fearful of further strife between the two families, gives Tybalt a soft answer. The two hotheads, Mercutio and Tybalt, raise the temperature with insults and begin to fight. Romeo tries to separate them, thus ending the fight, but Tybalt strikes Mercutio a cowardly blow beneath Romeo's arm. The wound proves to be mortal, and Romeo rages after Tybalt. In the ensuing fight, Tybalt is killed. Although Benvolio tries to explain that Romeo was not the aggressor, the Prince banishes Romeo on pain of death.

When Juliet hears the news, she is grief-stricken for her fallen relative, but relieved that Romeo was not the aggressor. Romeo makes a last visit to Juliet before his banishment. After he leaves, the Nurse arrives to tell Juliet that she is to marry Paris within three days. Juliet protests, but Capulet is adamant. She pretends to acquiesce, but she secretly seeks the help of Friar Laurence. He gives her a drug to take the night before the arranged wedding. The drug will produce the effect of death. She will then be put into the family vault, where Romeo can find her and rescue her. The Nurse enters her room in the morning to wake her, but Juliet is apparently dead.

Friar Laurence has sent Friar John to deliver a letter to Romeo, explaining the plan, but Friar John is unable to reach Romeo. What can go wrong does go wrong. Romeo hears of Juliet's "death" without knowing that her death is a subterfuge to avoid marrying Paris. When Friar Lawrence learns of the undelivered letter he hurries to the tomb to be there when Juliet awakens, not realizing that Romeo will get there first.

Romeo finds the grieving Paris at the Capulet tomb and kills him when he refuses to leave. In despair at finding Juliet "dead", Romeo takes a poison he had obtained from an apothecary and dies. When Juliet revives, Friar Laurence tries to take her away from the tomb, but she will not leave the body of Romeo. The Friar leaves, and Juliet stabs herself with Romeo's dagger.

Too late the Montagues and Capulets and the Prince arrive to find the bodies of the two lovers. Friar Laurence, now returned, explains the circumstances that brought about the suicides of these two young people. When all the facts become apparent, the Prince says,

> Where be these enemies? Capulet! Montague!
> See what a scourge is laid upon your hate.

Thoroughly chastened, Capulet and Montague agree to end their senseless feud. There are wonderfully comic moments in the play, like the wit of Mercutio and the ribald commentary of the Nurse, but the tragedy at the end is painfully poignant. In Shakespeare's source, the action takes place over a period of nine months. Shakespeare compresses the time to less than five days, taking the audience from first love to death at breathless speed.

21

The English History Plays-
The Wars of the Roses

Think, when we talk of horses, that you see them
Printing their proud hoofs i' the receiving earth.
For tis your thoughts that now must deck our kings,
Carry them here and there, jumping o'er times,
Turning the accomplishment of many years
Into an hourglass.

Henry V, **Prologue, 26-31**

Shakespeare's contemporaries were eager to learn more about their history. England had gone through dangerous times. The dynastic wars called The Wars of the Roses had destroyed the feudal culture. Their own queen, Elizabeth I, had survived desperate times: challenges from within and threatened invasions from without. When Shakespeare wrote the *Henry VI* plays, the defeat of the Spanish Armada was but a few years in the past. A general sense of pride and well being pervaded the land.

For his sources, Shakespeare had to rely on contemporary chronicles (p179). Histories are written by the winning side. Henry VII, Elizabeth's grandfather, was a winner. He understood the power of selective or slanted histories. He encouraged scholarly propaganda to justify his seizure of the throne. During his reign, biographies emphasized the faults of earlier rules. Those writings emphasized Henry's accession as the nation's salvation. His official history of England strongly influenced Raphael Holinshed and Edward Hall (p 179), both of whom also strongly influenced Shakespeare.

Major or minor discrepancies didn't bother the playgoers. They relished the color and pageantry of the history plays. If the plays glorified England in the process, so much the better. There are discrepancies and liberties in the history plays, but Shakespeare's genius captures the essence of the times portrayed. Many of his historical figures are not one-dimensional, cardboard figures. They are rich and complex human beings. Even the evil Richard III has a personality that fascinates viewers and lights up the stage whenever he appears.

King John

Though *King John* is not the first of the English history plays written by Shakespeare, the events it describes precede the others by nearly two centuries. Except for *Henry VIII*, the other history plays cover an unbroken 87-year period in English history. Even *Henry VIII* is closely linked to those plays through the triumph of the Tudors. *King John* stands apart; yet Shakespeare is again concerned with the instability caused by dynastic ambitions. In play after play, he strikes a blow for order and continuity. At the end of *King John*, he obviously approves the anointing of Prince Henry as Henry III. As the nobles rally around, stability is promised.

Historically, King John's reign had its share of plots and counterplots, broken agreements, and treachery. John's father was the dynamic Henry II, hero of the classic movie *The Lion in Winter*. His mother was the vigorous Eleanor of Aquitaine, played to perfection by Katherine Hepburn in the movie. It was during the reign of King John that the Magna Carta was signed.

John's claim to the throne was unclear. Henry's third son, Richard I, the Lionheart, had reigned for ten years but had spent only five months in England. He spent most of his time on a crusade and in battles against the French. He died in 1199 during a siege. Before Richard died, he nominated

John as his successor, thus setting aside the rights of Arthur, son of Richard's elder brother Geoffrey. Like his unruly brothers, Geoffrey had been involved in various intrigues, but he died before his father Henry, thus allowing Richard to take the throne and, after him, John. As always, Shakespeare gathered the historical facts and legends and shaped them to suit his purposes.

Though an early play, *King John* shows Shakespeare's potential in his creation of the Bastard, Faulconbridge, illegitimate son of Richard the Lion-heart. Complicated, contradictory, sometimes comical, sometimes serious, the Bastard is the most interesting character in the play. In a famous soliloquy, he deplores commodity (self-interest) and cheerfully pursues his own self-interests. Though he jests and exposes weaknesses that he cheerfully exemplifies himself, he is the strongest proponent of the best English virtues. His speech at the end of the play could have been spoken by Winston Churchill at the Battle of Britain:

> This England never did, nor never shall,
> Lie at the proud foot of a conqueror.
> *King John*, V, 7, 112-118

The play opens with a French challenge to John to step down in favor of Arthur, son of John's elder brother Geoffrey. John vows to fight. At this point, two sons of Sir Robert Faulconbridge appeal to the King for justice. Both claim the inheritance of their father. Elinor (so spelled here), widow of Henry II, notes the strong resemblance of one son, Philip Faulconbridge, to her dead son, Richard the Lionheart. Faulconbridge, labeled the *Bastard* throughout the play, is delighted to have such a genetic birthright and gladly yields his Faulconbridge inheritance to his brother. He agrees to enter Elinor's service, and the King dubs him *Sir Richard Plantagenet*. The Bastard's mother arrives, eager to defend herself against the suggestion of adultery with Richard. After a teasing dialogue, however, Lady Faulconbridge describes her effort to keep Richard away and her ultimate surrender. "King Richard was thy father."

When King Philip and John meet, they strike a truce. Philip's son Lewis will marry the Lady Blanche, niece of King John. This new alliance abandons the cause of Arthur, and his mother Constance is enraged. Pandulph, a papal legate, arrives and destroys the truce by excommunicating John for some highhanded actions against the church. Pandulph threatens to excommunicate Philip also, and Philip yields, breaking off with the English.

The war is on. The Bastard, discovering his talent for warfare, has killed Austria, the ally of Philip. Throughout the play he urges John to fight for England, against France. During the battle, Arthur has been captured by the English. John entrusts Arthur to Sir Hubert de Burgh, with a hint that the boy be put to death. Hubert promises to do so, but at the last moment he is won over by Arthur's pleas. He decides to deceive John, to keep the boy safe.

In France, Philip grieves over his defeat. To add to his woes, Constance, mother of Arthur, rails against him, bitterly and articulately, for the loss of her child. She correctly perceives that, as a rival claimant to the throne, Arthur is in danger.

Back in England, John is planning a second coronation, a decision that his nobles dislike. When news comes that Arthur is dead, for so Hubert has reported, the nobles reject John and defect to the French. A messenger arrives with news that both Elinor and Constance are dead. After the nobles' defection, John criticizes Hubert for killing Arthur, ever though Hubert had acted at the King's suggestion. Hubert confesses that Arthur is alive, and John joyfully sends Hubert to tell the lords the good news.

Uncertain about his fate, Arthur tries to escape from the castle prison and falls to his death. When the lords find Arthur's broken body, they vow to kill Hubert, but the Bastard protects the unjustly accused noble.

John agrees to yield to the Pope's authority. In return, Pandulph will try to persuade the French to withdraw from a new invasion. John is dispirited, unready to take action. The Bastard urges him to be strong in the face of these new adversities. John gives the Bastard responsibility: "Have thou the ordering of this present time."

The French under the Dauphin, Lewis, refuse Pandulph's offers to end the fray. The dissident English lords are encouraged to return to the English fold by a warning from a dying French lord that Lewis is planning to execute them at the end of the battle. The Bastard is pressing the battle successfully.

To add to Lewis's woes, news reaches him that his reinforcements have been lost in a shipwreck.

The final scene is set in Swinstead's Abbey. John is dying, poisoned by a monk. The nobles have brought young Prince Henry to his father's side. As the Bastard tells of battle victories, the King dies. The French have made overtures of peace. The Bastard proclaims Prince Henry the new King, Henry III, and the play ends with the patriotic sentiment quoted above.

Not played as often as the *Henry IV* and *V* plays, *King John* has had a spotty theatrical history. Because of its patriotic sentiments, however, it is popular in England during periods of stress. It has many positive qualities, looking ahead to the superb productions to come.

Shakespeare has often been commended for his strong women. The plays abound with such comic heroines as Beatrice, Rosalind, Viola, and the Nurse and such tragic heroines as Volumnia, Cleopatra, Margaret of Anjou, and Lady Macbeth. *King John* offers two, worthy additions to the list: Elinor and Constance, passionate women. They are bitter antagonists, supporting the rival claims of John and Arthur.

Shakespeare has sometimes been criticized because his children are not children, but miniature adults. MacDuff's son in *Macbeth* speaks like a mature philosopher. Both Arthur and Prince Henry in this play speak like sensible adults. Perhaps Shakespeare is merely accepting the older conception of children as young adults. The concept of "teenagers" is a fairly modern development.

Richard II

The English monarchs from Richard II to Richard III are all dramatized by Shakespeare in a series of eight plays, the last four of them devoted to the "Wars of the Roses," (p242). The order of composition does not correspond to the historical order. *Richard II*, the first in the series chronologically was written after the *Henry VI* plays and *Richard III*.

The actions of King Richard II bring rumblings that reverberate through the seven plays that follow the historical sequence. Richard became king in a dangerous situation. His father, the Black Prince, died in 1376, a year before *his* father, Edward III. Richard came to the throne at ten. He had six powerful uncles, all sons of Edward III. Two of the uncles played an especially important role in history: John of Gaunt, Duke of Lancaster; Edmund of Woodstock, Duke of Gloucester.

Despite the internal and external threats to his reign, Richard proved a courageous young man, even facing the dissidents personally during the Peasant's Revolt. During those early years, John of Gaunt played an especially important role.

Shakespeare takes up the story at a high point in Richard's power. As the play begins, two noblemen appear before the King, each accusing the other of treason. Bolingbroke, the son of John of Gaunt, challenges Thomas Mowbray to combat to prove the guilt or innocence of the charges. The opponents will not be mollified, insisting on the trial by combat. A time and date are set.

A brief interlude introduces the Duchess of Gloucester. She is upbraiding John of Gaunt for not blaming the King for her husband's murder earlier. Gaunt insists on leaving any punishment to heaven.

As the combatants are about to test each other's mettle in combat, the King stops the proceedings. He banishes Mowbray for life and Hereford (Bolingbroke) for six years. Banishment is part of Richard's strategy. He dislikes Bolingbroke because of Bolingbroke's widespread popularity.

Trouble in Ireland prompts the King to lead an expedition against the rebellion. Because the campaign will be expensive, Richard plans to levy taxes and collect unpopular loans from wealthy noblemen. When he hears that John of Gaunt is dying, he visits the bedside, where he is scolded for his wasteful ways and his part in the murder of Gloucester.

Upon the death of Gaunt, Richard decides to appropriate the wealth of Gaunt to finance his Irish war, a move with fatal consequences. Gaunt's brother, York, criticizes the King for this illegal measure. Richard pays no attention but appoints York to be governor of England in his absence.

The King's prospects begin to go downhill almost immediately. Other nobles, fearing that they may suffer the fate of Gaunt, begin to desert. Bolingbroke invades England, solely, he says, for the purpose of regaining his lost estates. York at first tries to persuade Bolingbroke to stop the attack, but he too is eventually persuaded that Richard has been too cruel, too arbitrary, too dangerous. York resolves to stay neutral, thus removing the last major obstacle to Bolingbroke's invasion.

When Richard returns to England, the cause is soon lost. Some of Richard's henchmen are captured and beheaded. Momentarily cheered by reminders of his divine right to the throne, Richard takes heart but soon gives way to despair as he realizes the hopelessness of his position.

A quiet interlude involves gardeners discussing Richard's plight (p115). This scene brings the situation realistically up to date. The Queen overhears their conversation and erupts in anger. She is told that Richard's cause is indeed hopeless.

Richard accepts his fate with articulate resignation. In a series of brilliant monologues, he muses upon the perils of kingship. Though Bolingbroke at first asserts undying loyalty to the King, he moves events along until the King agrees to abdicate.

Richard is imprisoned. Thinking he is doing what the king really wants, a noble, Sir Piers Exton, with a group of accomplices, murders Richard, When presented with Richard's corpse, Bolingbroke disclaims the deed. He rejects Exton and vows to lead a crusade to the Holy Land to atone for his part in the death.

Richard II is written entirely in verse. It has some of the most beautiful and poetic moments in any of the plays. Richard is a poor monarch but a great poet.

There are links to the plays that follow. We hear about Bolingbroke's son, who wastes his time with a disreputable group of criminals and prostitutes-Falstaff's cronies. This, of course, is a foreshadowing of Prince Hal in the two *Henry IV* plays that follow. Bolingbroke also shows the guilt feeling he displays in the later plays. After all, he has displaced an anointed King and has even been responsible for his murder. Henry eventually makes a pilgrimage to "Jerusalem" by dying in the palace's Jerusalem

Chamber. The usurpation later bolsters the claim of the Yorkists to the crown (*Henry VI, Part Three*, I, 1, 21-27).

Henry IV, Part One

The two *Henry IV* plays and *Henry V* constitute a trilogy presumably featuring Henry V in youth and maturity, but Harold Bloom insists that the two *Henry IV* plays belong first of all to Falstaff. Orson Welles called Falstaff the greatest role Shakespeare ever wrote. In support of these statements, a San Diego production combined the two plays and emphasized all the Falstaff (John Goodman) scenes. Prince Hal was subordinate. However interpreted, Falstaff is here the creation of genius. Six quartos (p 16) printed between 1598 and 1622, just before the publication of the First Folio (p 85), attest to the plays' continuing popularity.

Shakespeare took a step, daring for his time, of shifting the focus between crucial matters of state and the bawdy irreverence of Falstaff and his crew. By alternating serious scenes and comical ones, Shakespeare presents a picture of a whole society, not just a segment.

The play opens with a meeting in which Henry IV expresses his desire to lead a crusade to the Holy Land, partly in penance for usurping the crown of Richard II. His plans are immediately upset by news that Henry Percy, son of the Earl of Northumberland, has refused to relinquish to the King some Scottish prisoners he has taken. The King admires Henry Percy, also called Hotspur, for displaying all the qualities that seem to be lacking in his own son, Prince Hal.

He envies Northumberland for being "the father of so blest a son." We don't have long to meet that disappointing son. In the next scene, Sir John Falstaff and Hal (here called the *Prince of Wales*) enter, bickering good-naturedly. Hal constantly disparages Falstaff's bad habits, many of which Hal is imitating. Their verbal sparring throughout the play is one of its joys. The obvious affection between the two, almost of son and surrogate father, has a warmth that shines through the superficial reproaches. Their lines feed on each other, providing some of the best comic dialogue in

Shakespeare. Modern sitcoms could learn from a study of these lines: Hal's ultimate, necessary rejection of Falstaff later breaks the old man's heart.

During this second scene, Hal and his companion Poins plan a trick on Falstaff. After Falstaff and his gang rob some travelers, Hal and Poins will effortlessly take the booty from the hapless robbers. Later they will enjoy Falstaff's report of the encounter, with much embellishment about Falstaff's nonexistent valor.

The third scene returns to the royal dilemma. A parley between Hotspur and the King over the prisoners fails. Hotspur stalks out of the room promising martial defiance of the King. The King will be facing the combined forces of Hotspur and the Earl of Northumberland, the Welsh Glendower, and the Archbishop of York. This is a formidable threat. Meanwhile, Hal is off with his lowlife companions, frolicking.

Back to the rogues. The projected robbery goes off as planned, as does the subsequent robbery of the booty by the masked Poins and Hal. At the Boar's Head Tavern, Falstaff enters and criticizes Hal and Poins for running off before the robbery was completed. To show his own bravery, he makes up a glorious story, escalating the number of enemies that Falstaff had to fight. Hal lets him embroider his fantasy and then stops him, revealing the trick. Falstaff immediately recovers, saying "I knew ye as well as he that made ye…was it for me to kill the heir-apparent? Should I turn upon the true prince?" The fun is dampened by a message from the King, summoning Hal. Falstaff encourages Hal to practice his response to the King in a mock interview.

In this hilarious interview, Falstaff plays King Henry. He enlarges on the terrible company that Hal has been keeping, but he makes an exception for one man: himself. "There is virtue in that Falstaff. Him keep with, the rest banish." Although Hal has contrasted himself with Hotspur as a person fonder of fun than battle, he looks forward to the campaign against the rebels.

In the following scene, the rebel leaders convene to join forces. Hotspur and the Welsh Glendower disagree, but a tenuous agreement is finally reached. The scene also shows a human side to Hotspur, especially in good-humored banter with his wife. In an earlier scene, Lady Percy had expressed misgivings about her husband's martial propensities. These touches build the picture of Hotspur: valiant, heroic, headstrong, presumably more than a match for the easygoing Hal.

Though the King has misgivings about Hal's military prowess, he accepts Hal's assurances and gives him command of one of the armies. Hal visits the Boar's Head before he leaves. There follows another scene of badinage and witty repartee between Hal and Falstaff. Hal tells Falstaff to meet him the next day for his battle orders. Shakespeare has decided to bring Falstaff into the battle, for there are many opportunities there for Falstaff to show his comic wit and ability to survive.

Just before the battle, Hotspur receives disquieting news about the failure of his allies' troops to arrive, but he urges a fight anyway. Falstaff for his part mopes along the way. He declares that he prefers to arrive at the *beginning* of a feast and the *end* of a fray.

Even at this late date, there is an attempt to negotiate a truce, but the rebel negotiators resolve to keep the news from Hotspur lest he accept the offer. War is inevitable. Price Hal offers to fight Hotspur in single combat to settle the dispute, but Henry refuses. Henry offers the rebels amnesty, but the war goes on. Falstaff drinks his way through the battle, avoiding dangerous contact with the enemy. Hal has proved a courageous warrior, killing a noble who had almost killed the King. Finally, Hal fights Hotspur and kills him. Falstaff comes upon the body of Hotspur, stabs it, and plans to claim a reward for his "valor."

This battle has been won, but the rebellion will continue. Henry divides the command among his sons and Westmoreland. We must wait until the opening of *Henry IV, Part Two*, to see what follows. Hal has proved himself a valiant warrior, foreshadowing his victories as Henry V. Falstaff is still alive, enjoying life, pricking the bubbles of pretense, ready to take up with Hal where they had left off. But Hal is already a changed man.

Henry IV, Part Two

Although Falstaff plays a greater role in *Part Two*, his repartee with Prince Hal is diminished. Hal has other matters on his mind, leaving little time for the madcap adventures of *Part One*. Until their final scene, they appear together only once, in the Boar's Head Tavern scene, where the tone is less jolly and the farewell more icy than the badinage in *Part One*. Shakespeare doesn't minimize Falstaff's role, however. In his picture of the life of the common people, Shakespeare shines. He knew and understood that life far better than any other claimant to the authorship of the plays (p 80).

Irreverent as ever and wittily perceptive, the Falstaff of *Part Two* is, however, also a changed man. He is ill and old, but he still enjoys the companionship of a host of colorful characters created by Shakespeare, including the loving and sentimental Doll Tearsheet. When Falstaff admits, "I am old, I am old," she replies, "I love thee better than I love e'er a scurvy young boy of them all."

Shakespeare invents a character named *Rumour* to set the stage. A false report has told Northumberland of the success of his son Hotspur and victory over the King's forces. He is soon disabused of this misinformation and accepts his son's death. He vows revenge.

The next scene brings back the beloved Falstaff. Though Shakespeare is concerned to present the political significance of the play's action, the audience probably rejoiced to find their old friend Falstaff back on the stage. Falstaff has a commission to join the forces of Prince John, Hal's younger brother, against the army of Northumberland. His major concern is now to get the needed funds to finance his expedition. Scenes involving the principal nobles on either side of the battle are inserted between scenes involving Falstaff and his merrymakers. The former scenes advance the play's action, but the latter scenes give life and boisterous energy to the play.

The scene involving Prince Hal and Falstaff is set in the Boar's Head Tavern. Hal and his friend Poins conceal themselves, seeking the old fun in Falstaff's comments on life. When Doll asks Falstaff about the Prince, he replies "A good shallow young fellow: a' would have made a good pantler (pantry servant), a' would have chopped bread well." He goes on in unflattering fashion until finally the Prince and Poins come forward. Falstaff tries an insulting reply in the manner of the old jesting, but the Prince is less than amused. Falstaff, as always, thinks on his feet. His explanation: he disparaged the Prince so that he would not be admired by such wicked sorts as those at the Tavern. "No abuse, Hal; none."

Shortly after the exchange, a messenger arrives with news about the war. Hal, conscience-stricken, regrets this foolish encounter at the Tavern while he is needed at the war. He leaves with a curt, "Falstaff, good night." This is his last word to Falstaff before the rejection to come.

In his search for recruits, Falstaff asks the help of Justice Silence and Justice Shallow. Like Charles Dickens, Shakespeare occasionally permits himself to choose a name appropriate for the character. *Doll Tearsheet*, for example, suggests Doll's occupation. Justice *Shallow* is well named: a foolish, garrulous old man who considers himself sophisticated. He is actually gullible, easily fooled, perfect prey for the verbal master manipulator: Falstaff. His friend Justice Silence, as might be expected, speaks very little, except under the influence of wine. During a bout of their reminiscences of good times together, Falstaff says, "We have heard the chimes at midnight, Master Shallow."

The sorry recruits present an unmilitary spectacle, but Falstaff and his assistant Bardolph don't object, making some money from those released from service. Falstaff humorously sets up his standards for choosing soldiers, quite opposed to the traditional ones. He says, "O: give me the spare ones, and spare me the great ones." The scene ends with Falstaff's resolve to fleece trusting Shallow.

Scenes of the war bring together the serious and the comic. Falstaff actually takes a rebel officer prisoner and delivers him to Prince John, identified also as *Lancaster*. John has proved to be a ruthless warrior, having treacherously persuaded the rebels to lay down their arms, only to be executed. Falstaff cannot make John laugh, as he did Hal, and considers him a sourpuss. Back at Westminster, in the Jerusalem Chapel, the King lies dying. News arrives that the rebels have been defeated, but the King cannot rally, and is taken into a bedroom.

At this point, Hal returns. He watches the King sleeping, contemplates all the burdens of kingship, and thoughtfully puts on the crown. When Henry awakes and discovers that Hal has tried on the crown, he says sadly, "Thy wish, Harry, was father to that thought." Hal persuades the King that his action did not reflect any wish of his to be King. The King forgives him and gives Hal advice for ruling when his time comes. The King also asks to be taken back to the Jerusalem Chamber to die. Though he never got to Jerusalem on a crusade, he then dies in "Jerusalem" as he had hoped.

Falstaff has returned to Shallow's house. Shallow welcomes Falstaff warmly and invites him to spend the night. Ever the rogue, Falstaff talks about deceiving the old man and then reporting the comedy to his old friend, Prince Hal. When the news arrives of the King's death, Falstaff excitedly sets out to meet with Hal, now Henry V, expecting warm and preferential treatment.

Falstaff and his companions attend the coronation parade. When Falstaff accosts him, Hal says, "I know thee not, old man." He says that his days of misdeeds with Falstaff were but a dream. "Presume not that I am the thing I was." Henry rejects his old drinking companions and orders them to stay ten miles away from Henry under pain of death. In a hint of his former affection, he offers Falstaff a modest pension. Falstaff maintains that this renunciation is all a public show. The new King Henry will send for him in private later, but Henry never sees Falstaff again. An epilogue, in the person of a dancer, promises more to come: the introduction of Katherine of France and a continuing story "with Sir John in it." Falstaff never appears in *Henry V* (p239), though he reappears as a buffoon in *The Merry Wives of Windsor* (p215). The profligate Hal has become sober Henry V, one of England's greatest kings.

Henry V

Prince Hal has become *Henry V*. Gone are the old associates, led by Sir John Falstaff. This is a serious, businesslike king whose only suggestion of levity occurs in the last scene, in which he woos Katharine, daughter of the French king. At the end of *Henry IV, Part Two*, Shakespeare had promised to bring Falstaff back (p 31). Two explanations are offered for the loss of Falstaff: (1) Shakespeare's company may not have had the player who could have handled the part after the departure of Will Kempe (p 31); (2) Shakespeare may have felt that Falstaff would overshadow the king dramatically. This was to be Henry's play, no one else's.

Henry asserts his authority almost immediately. A Prologue invites the audience to use their imaginations, accepting the stage as the field of Agincourt. Then the Archbishop of Canterbury and the Bishop of Ely discuss Henry's capacity for leadership and the prospects of a campaign in France. The Archbishop assures Henry that Henry has a legitimate claim to the throne of France and offers him money to pursue that claim.

At precisely the right moment, an ambassador from France arrives. The ambassador insults Henry, giving him a gift of tennis balls with the suggestion that he stay home and play games. Henry threatens the Dauphin, promising to make him regret his insult.

We can imagine Shakespeare's audience, patiently expecting the arrival of their favorite comic character, Falstaff. They are doomed to disappointment. Pistol and Nym, seedy Falstaff associates, argue over the Hostess of the tavern. Nym had been betrothed to her; Pistol had married her. Bardolph attempts to quell the dispute. The Hostess breaks in with sad news: Falstaff's illness has worsened. Heartbroken by his break from Hal, he has lost his will to live.

Falstaff never appears on stage in *Henry V*, but the description of his death is a Shakespearean masterpiece. His dear old friend, the Hostess, is given the immortal lines. When Bardolph says, "would I were with him…either in heaven or hell." the Hostess replies, "Nay, sure, he's not in hell. He's in Arthur's bosom." Just before he died, he "babbled of green fields." The assured, self-possessed, unfazed master of wit and conversation dies with visions of a quieter life long ago. Before dying, he characteristically asks for sack (wine).

Although the lesser characters, former associates of Falstaff, appear in the battle scenes for comic relief, the rest of the play is devoted to Henry. There is an escalation of activity, all leading up to the Battle of Agincourt. Scenes fluctuate between England and France, between English and

French camps. As the play progresses, Henry grows in leadership stature. He ruthlessly orders the execution of three traitors but forgives a man who had criticized him while drinking. The assault on personal vanity is a minor sin, but treason is a capital crime.

In France, Henry storms Harfleur, threatening the town with complete destruction. If the townspeople refuse, war will destroy "pure maidens" and "flow'ring infants," as well as the male inhabitants. The threat has its effect. Harfleur capitulates.

As the tension grows, Shakespeare inserts a scene in the French king's palace. Katherine, daughter of the French king, takes an English lesson from one of her attendants. The scene is charming, funny, a prelude to the wooing scene at the end of the play.

The French make overtures to Henry, but he rejects them, considering them insulting. Henry realizes however, that he is insecure. He is on strange terrain. His forces are greatly outnumbered. The French seem to have every military advantage. Gloucester says nervously, "I hope they will not come upon us now." Henry replies, "We are in God's hand, brother, not in theirs."

In the French camp the night before the battle, the Dauphin and his nobles are in an exultant mood. They expect to rout the English. They jest about the number of prisoners they expect to take. They continue to boast and wonder at the stupidity of the English.

The mood in the English camp is quite different. The soldiers realize their desperate situation and wonder how many will survive the coming slaughter. To test his soldiers' feelings, the King moves among them disguised. He is soon made aware of the soldiers' anxieties. One soldier in particular, Michael Williams, expresses doubts about the value of the English invasion. If the cause is not just, then the King must accept responsibility for his decision. Henry is sufficiently annoyed to arrange for a fight if both survive the battle. They exchange gloves to be worn on their hats as identification.

Several plot twists avert the confrontation, but the incident is instructive. If Henry is a great epic hero, then his encounter with Williams shows his empathy with the common soldier. If the play is taken as a satire on war and politics, Williams grows in stature, his honest doubts sloughed off by a manipulative king. Undoubtedly, Shakespeare's audiences leaned to the former explanation. Still, Shakespeare's genius has again left a question open-ended.

Henry's exhortation to his troops before the Battle of Agincourt is a set piece, beloved of actors (p 70). His martial genius neutralizes the French's overwhelming numerical superiority and wins the day. English losses are minimal compared with the French casualties.

To join the two sides, the victorious Henry woos and wins Katherine, the French King's daughter. An Epilogue in sonnet form (p112) extols the greatness of Henry and bemoans the reign to follow, that of Henry VI, destroyed by his ambitious protectors.

Typically, *Henry V* provides colorful characters from the lower classes: Bardolph, Nym, Pistol, Fluellen, Macmorris. These are individualized, so that an actor playing one of the roles can find distinctive qualities to separate his character from the rest. Pistol, for example, a character in *Henry IV, Part Two*, *Henry V*, and *The Merry Wives of Windsor*, is not just a cardboard imitation of Nym or Bardolph. He is a recognizable individual in his own right, always in character; grandiose in speech and insulting in manner. Critics theorize that some of Falstaff's wit as planned for Falstaff was eventually assigned to Pistol. Shakespeare's characters are individual, not generic.

Quiet, unassuming Katherine played a surprising role in the cavalcade of English kings. When Henry died after only nine years as king, his infant son Henry became Henry VI, with all the catastrophes ahead of him. Katherine herself withdrew from the royal scene-but not from history. Some years after the death of Henry, she married an obscure Welsh nobleman, Owen Tudor. Their eldest son Edmund became the Earl of Richmond. He married Margaret Beaufort, a descendant of John of Gaunt. Their posthumous son Henry assumed the Richmond title and also laid claim to the English throne through his grandmother, wife of Henry V. After defeating Richard III, he established the Tudor reign: Henry VII, Henry VIII, Edward VI, Mary Tudor, and Elizabeth. Katherine was the mother of a king by one husband and the grandmother of a king by another.

The Wars of the Roses

When Shakespeare turned his attention to English history at the beginning of his career, he chose as his subject the period known as the "Wars of the Roses." The years 1455-1485 were marked by dynastic wars, as various ambitious nobles asserted their claims to the throne. The reign of Henry VI subjected England to a seesaw battle between the rival houses of York and Lancaster. The supposed emblems of the rival factions-white rose for York and red rose for Lancaster-gave the name to the tumultuous period.

Scholars generally agree that the wars weakened the nobility, paving the way for the stronger reigns of the Tudors: Henry VII, Henry VIII, and Elizabeth I. The older feudal society disappeared.

The troubles resulted from two unfortunate circumstances: the untimely death of Henry V and the accession to the throne of his infant son, Henry VI. Not yet nine months old, Henry ruled under the protectorate of his uncles John of Lancaster and Humphrey, Duke of Gloucester. They in turn were subject to a council headed by Henry Beaufort. Other nobles exerted authority, often conflicting. It was a volatile situation that was not improved when Henry reached maturity.

Much has been written about Henry VI. He was pious, gentle, interested in the arts, but unstable, politically naive, and utterly unprepared for the power struggles that poisoned his reign. He was easily led, often under the domination of his wife, Margaret of Anjou. Strong-minded where Henry was weak, Margaret set the tone for much of the bloodshed that followed. Fiercely protective of her husband, his rights, and the rights of her son, she marshaled forces for battle and won some victories against the opposing Yorkists. At the battle of Wakefield, her archenemy, the Duke of York, was slain, but his son Edward was ready to take his place.

In and out as sovereign, Henry was finally put in the Tower, where he died in 1471, possibly murdered. Since Henry's own son had been killed in battle, York's son became king as Edward IV. His reign was relatively peaceful, but not without smoldering dissatisfaction. Edward's marriage to Elizabeth Woodville and his favoritism toward her family alienated the ambitious Richard Neville, Earl of Warwick.

Edward had two reigns: from 1461 to 1470 and from 1471 to 1483. In 1470 he was temporarily dispossessed by Henry's forces with the assistance of the disgruntled Warwick and Edward's brother, the Duke of Clarence. Edward returned from exile to defeat the Lancastrian forces. Warwick and Henry's son were killed in battle, and the throne was secured for Edward until his death in 1483.

Unfortunately, Edward's brother Richard of Gloucester had his own plans. In the normal course of events the twelve-year-old son of Edward was proclaimed king as Edward V. Richard was not a normal, loving uncle. He seized custody of the young king from his mother Elizabeth Woodville and became Edward's "protector." Having had Lord Hastings summarily executed, he intimidated the parliament into declaring Edward's children illegitimate. They were placed in the Tower, where they mysteriously disappeared, possibly murdered at the instigation of Richard. The fate of the "Princes in the Tower" has been the subject of histories, romances, and even detective stories. Their fate has been labeled "impenetrably obscure."

Richard had himself crowned Richard III, but his reign was a short one. In his headlong dash for the crown, he alienated former associates. One of them, the Duke of Buckingham, led a revolt to put Henry Tudor, the Earl of Richmond, on the throne. The revolt failed, and Buckingham was executed. Richmond bided his time and invaded England in 1485. Richard was slain at the battle of Bosworth Field. Richmond married Elizabeth, daughter of Edward IV, and thus united the houses of Lancaster and York. As Henry VII, he established the Tudor line.

This has been a historical report, suggesting the materials that Shakespeare had to deal with. The following commentaries repeat some of the given information and also suggest Shakespeare's skill in handling this treasure house of material. He enjoyed reporting on these tumultuous events in his *Henry VI* and *Richard III* plays. He was generally true to his sources, but like any creative artist, he did take some liberties with his material. He compressed the time scale, thus giving greater tension to the events. There were really only four campaigns over 30 years and one strikingly bloody battle: Towton. There was only one example of civil plundering-by

Margaret's army. Thus, the general population was relatively little affected by the Wars of the Roses, but the effects on the nobility were far-reaching.

Shakespeare also overemphasized the Tudor "rescue" of the country. After all, he was writing during the reign of the fifth Tudor sovereign, Elizabeth I. He may have overstressed Richard's evil plans and perhaps made him more villainous than he was in reality. History is written by the winners, and the losers are likely to be demonized. Still, the plays are in general an accurate picture of a segment of English history only a century in Shakespeare's past.

Henry VI, Part One

Written at the beginning of Shakespeare's career, this trilogy foreshadows Shakespeare's greatness. This is English history for the masses of people who relied on theater for explanation, interpretation, and good narrative. The *Henry VI* plays are filled with action, intrigue, betrayal, and heroism. Each of the plays has a cast of over 40 identified characters, some confined to one play, many appearing in two or more plays. A detailed plot summary can also be confusing, as the characters move in and out. Good stage productions, however, minimize he difficulties and present a magnificent pageant of fifteenth-century life.

Running through all three plays is the chaos brought on by the weaknesses of Henry VI, a victim of his own good qualities as well as his defects. Other continuing strands are the wars with France and the dynastic struggles of the English nobility.

Part One opens with the funeral of Henry V, the great warrior king, victor at Agincourt. Darkening the glories of his reign, news reaches the court of disaster in France. The Dauphin has been crowned King Charles VII, violating a treaty made with Henry V. Battle news is equally bad. The great English leader Lord Talbot has been captured by the French. Thus begins the inauspicious reign of the infant Henry VI.

Almost immediately, infighting mars any chance of a fruitful, happy maturity for the young king. Without a strong leader, the country wavers, weakened by the intrigue of the ambitious nobles.

The second scene is set in France. *Dauphin* is the title for the eldest son of the French monarch. The English throughout refer to the recently crowned Charles VII as the *Dauphin*, reinforcing their claim that Charles is not rightfully the king.

Charles has had a military setback. At a critical time, a young woman, Joan La Pucelle (whom we know as *Joan of Arc*), offers help. At first skeptical, Charles is reluctant, but when Joan bests him in single combat, he welcomes her assistance. The saga of the historical Joan of Arc does not quite match Shakespeare's depiction of La Pucelle.

The French had been traditional enemies of the French. English claims to portions of France persisted through centuries. Only in 1801 did the English finally abandon the title of *King of France*. The Hundred Years War between France and England persisted through most of Henry's reign. Shakespeare accepted the English historical point of view that made Joan of Arc a detested enemy. Modern readers and theatergoers are shocked by the obvious distortions, but Shakespeare's contemporaries would have applauded the picture he painted.

La Pucelle is devious and contemptible. Though courageous and successful in battle, she could credit her success to the dissension in the English ranks, the central theme of *Henry VI*. Through the confusing machinations of the Burgundian, English, and French leaders, La Pucelle is sacrificed. She is captured, put on trial, and sentenced to death. Her actions in this play, in contrast to the historical record, are ultimately cowardly. Yet Harold Bloom insists that Joan is the most colorful and pivotal character in the play. "It remains her play, not Talbot's." Shakespeare took this "demonic" enemy of the English and made her exciting to watch on the stage.

In contrast to the wicked La Pucelle is the virtuous Talbot. Captured and then ransomed, Talbot takes up the military leadership of the English forces in France. In an alternating series of victories and defeats, Lord John Talbot exemplifies the best qualities of manhood: bravery, selflessness, virtue. When he finally falls in battle, along with his son, the jealous rivalry of York and Somerset contributes directly to the tragedy. Their dispute prevents reinforcements from reaching him.

The play moves with dizzying speed from Westminster Abbey to Orleans, Auvergne, the Tower of London, Gascony, Bordeaux, Anjou, Angers, the royal palace in London. Plots and counterplots, intrigues involving many noblemen-all threaten the stability of the monarchy and the nation.

The play ends with the momentous decision by Henry to marry Margaret of Anjou, despite previous agreements for his marriage to the daughter of the Earl of Armignac. The Earl of Suffolk, who has furthered the marriage with Margaret, hopes to control King Henry through his influence.

Margaret appears in a very minor role near the end of *Henry VI, Part One* and she appears in the remaining *Henry VI* plays as well as in *Richard III*. Her role has been called "the greatest female part in Shakespeare." A modest maiden in *Part One*, she becomes a dominant figure in the remaining plays, the unrelenting leader of the Lancastrian faction. Poor Henry is but her shadow.

Margaret makes a wonderful but brief appearance in *Richard III*, her spirit still unbroken. She stands up to Richard as no one else dares to and warns others of their doom under the evil King. She warns the current Queen, Elizabeth, not to be deceived by Richard.

> Poor painted queen, vain flourish of my fortune
> Why strew'st thou sugar on that bottled spider,
> Whose deadly web ensnareth thee about?
> Fool, fool: thou whet'st a knife to kill thyself.
> The day will come that thou shalt wish for me
> To help thee curse this poisonous bunch-back'd toad.
> *Richard III*, 1, 3, 241-246

This is really a postscript to the *Henry VI* plays, but it does provide a keen insight into the heart and mind of this remarkable woman.

Henry VI, Part Two

The second of the *Henry VI* plays chronicles England's descent into near-anarchy. Henry is ineffectual, allowing the conniving nobles to ruin the country for their selfish ends. Even his new wife, Margaret, contributes to the disasters that ensue.

The play opens with the King's delighted acceptance of his new Queen, Margaret of Anjou. When Henry chose her over the daughter of the Earl of Armignac, he cast aside a valuable dowry. Henry, however, rejoices at getting, with Suffolk's help, the hand of this beautiful woman. What Henry doesn't realize is that he has taken to wife a schemer for her own purposes. Margaret has a lust for power that propels her through the Wars of the Roses. Henry is naive. A tigress and a lamb make strange bedfellows.

Despite the threat of anarchy, for a while Humphrey, the Duke of Gloucester, provides the kind of honest leadership that could preserve the peace, but he is arrested and murdered, through the connivance of Margaret and Suffolk. Before he leaves under guard, he makes a prophetic pronouncement that encapsulates later events.

> Ah! thus King Henry throws away his crutch
> Before his legs be firm to bear his body:
> Thus is the shepherd beaten from thy side,
> And wolves are gnarling who shall gnaw thee first.
> Ah! that my fears were false, ah! that it were;
> For, good King Henry, thy decay I fear.
> *Henry VI, Part Two*, III 1, 189-194

Jealous of Humphrey's influence over Henry, Margaret has had a hand in Humphrey's destruction. Poor deluded Henry does nothing to save his virtuous uncle, though he later expresses his grief.

Throughout the histories, readers and theatergoers must realize that titles pass from generation to generation. In *Henry VI*, Gloucester is Humphrey, the youngest son of Henry IV and brother of Henry V, uncle of Henry VI. In *Richard II*, Gloucester is another person, Thomas of

Woodstock, uncle of Richard II. His murder, which took place six months before the opening of *Richard II*, initiates the events that ultimately lead to Richard's deposition in *Richard II*. Gloucester is also Richard Plantagenet, later King of England. So is it with other titles: York, Suffolk, Warwick, Somerset Buckingham. It is sometimes difficult to keep all these personalities apart, as they weave in and out of the action. Charges and countercharges, arrests and executions, fortunes rise and fall. It may sometimes be impossible to follow every political nuance, but it is always possible to sit back and enjoy the poetry and the pageantry.

A major thread in Act IV is the rebellion of Jack Cade. A supposed pretender to the throne of England, Cade leads a mob into the heart of London, threatening the monarchy and the stability of the realm. Cade provides grim comic relief for a while, but his actions turn more and more unreasonable and bloody. In a preview of the Cultural Revolution in China, Cade has a man executed simply because he is literate. He utters the famous phrase, beloved of all defendants: "The first thing we do, let's kill all the lawyers." He sends forth weird pronouncements. Having declared himself Lord of London, he orders that the water fountain be made to flow claret for a year. He declares that it will be treason for anyone to call him anything but *Lord Mortimer*. The vicious side of Cade is shown when a soldier, unaware of the new regulations, calls out, "Jack Cade, Jack Cade." Cade orders him killed. Cade is himself eventually killed in a single sword fight by Iden, a wealthy landowner.

Shakespeare suggests that York had a hand in the uprising, to further his own political ends. Here, as elsewhere in the play, Shakespeare takes liberties with the truth to further dramatic ends.

In the seesaw events throughout the play, power flows from one side to another. Instigator of many plots, Suffolk is beheaded. The lines between Lancastrians and Yorkists begin to be even more sharply drawn. The rivalry between the Lancastrian Duke of Somerset and the Duke of York was a central feature in *Part One*. In *Part Two*, the division becomes more ominous, with maneuverings by the King's party and a rebellion led by York. In the first battle of the Wars of the Roses, at St. Albans, the Yorkists prevail. The King and his retinue flee the city. Somerset and York meet in a duel. Somerset is killed.

With such a victory, the Yorkists seem to be in full control, with the King's party in disorder. The bloody chapters ahead prove otherwise.

Henry VI, Part Three

Critics have pointed out that in this play, Shakespeare seems more interested in character analysis and contrast than in the earlier plays. From the villains of the *Henry VI* plays to Iago is a quantum leap, but Shakespeare's ever-increasing maturity had its beginnings in these early successes.

Part Three covers the period from 1460-1471. *Part Two* ended with the Battle of St. Albans. This play takes events to the death of Henry VI.. With St. Albans in the past, the victorious Yorkists talk over events, glorying in their victory. The head of the slain Somerset is brought in, as York claims the throne of England. At this point, Henry and his party enter. Henry and York present rival claims. York declares that Henry is descended from the usurper, Henry IV. York, however, is descended from the anointed, displaced king, Richard II, and should therefore be king. As violence threatens, Henry agrees to name York as his heir if he, Henry, can retain the throne till his death.

While this agreement seems reasonable enough, Henry had not taken his wife Margaret into account. She upbraids Henry for disinheriting his own son, the Prince of Wales. She declares herself divorced from him and stalks out to lead the northern loyal lords against York.

Margaret rallies her support and approaches York's castle with 20,000 men. Though outnumbered four to one, the Yorkists are confident against an army led by "a woman's general." At the ensuing battle of Wakefield, York loses his own son, Rutland, slaughtered by Clifford, who is acting in revenge for the death of *his* father at York's hands. Thus, the slaughter goes on. Ultimately, York is captured and stabbed to death.

When Margaret displays York's head mounted outside his castle, Henry exhibits the good qualities that have affected his reign disastrously. He is dismayed by the sight and gets a lecture from Clifford about his responsibilities as king. Henry responds as the gentle soul he is: Evil cannot produce success. Though prodded by his nobles, his wife, and his son, Henry cannot strike a warlike pose. He is in the wrong place at the wrong time.

Word comes that a powerful Yorkist army, headed by the Earl of Warwick, is approaching. Displaying the lack of respect shown Henry by his nobles, Clifford bluntly says,

> I would your highness would depart the field:
> The queen hath best success when you are absent.
> *Henry VI, Part Three*, II, 2, 73-74

When Edward, heir to his father York, arrives, he claims the kingship and demands that Henry kneel to him. The King has no chance to speak, but his wife Margaret calls Edward a "proud, insulting boy." There is bickering back and forth, while Henry tries to get in a word. The parley breaks up and Edward promises ten thousand deaths for the intransigence of Henry's party.

The Battle of Towton favors first one side and then the other. During the fighting, Henry withdraws, wishing that he had been born a lowly shepherd. He is horror stricken as he observes a son slaying his father and a father slaying his son. This bloodiest battle of the war favors the Yorkists. As Margaret and her son the Prince retreat, they take Henry with them. Henry hides and is captured. Margaret goes abroad.

Margaret seeks help from France. Happily for her, King Edward has changed his marital plans and aroused the anger of Warwick. He mounts an army for the invasion of England in the name of Henry VI. Edward is captured, but rescued not long afterward by Edward's brother Richard, later Richard III. Richard knows his own road to the crown runs through Edward's reign. Richard is patient.

Henry is not overjoyed by kingship. He would like to retire, leaving Warwick to run the country. During the battle of Barnet, Warwick is mortally wounded. The fate of Henry lies solely with Margaret's army.

Three weeks later, just before the battle of Tewkesbury, Margaret gives a stirring speech, but in the following scene, she is a captive, Her son the

Prince is defiant, but his railing has him killed. Henry has had too little mettle; the Prince, too much. In her agony, the Queen asks for death, but the Yorkists refuse to give her such peace. Unrepentant to the end, the Queen is led away, still cursing the Yorkists. She reappears briefly in *Richard III* (p252).

The Yorkists have won. Richard kills Henry in the tower. Edward is happy at the birth of his son, the new Prince of Wales. This infant, later to become king for two months, is ultimately put in the tower by his malevolent uncle, Richard. Despite Shakespeare's "adjustment" of timelines, again for dramatic purposes, Edward's reign was fairly peaceful. His successor's was not.

Before the play ends, Richard of Gloucester gives the audience some hints of his malefactions to come. As early as act III, scene 2, he had revealed his plans for "the golden time I long for," the kingship. He lists the names of those who might stand in the way of his becoming king. He accepts all the hypocrisies and deceits that lie ahead, but at last he says of the crown, "I'll pluck it down." In the last scene of this play, he compares his behavior with that of Judas. We can imagine the audience's impatience to meet this unlovely, slimy, fascinating villain. They had their wish in the next play, *Richard III*.

The theatrical history of the *Henry VI* plays is brief. Popular in Shakespeare's time, the plays largely disappeared for almost three centuries. The plays *have* appeared in the 20th century, usually in cycles (p 74), heavily abridged. The three plays are sometimes combined into two, the first called *Lancaster* and the second *York*, reflecting the changing fortunes of the two parties. One version available on video substitutes World War I for the struggles of 15th century England. It seems odd to have Joan of Arc on a 20th century French battlefield.

Richard III

Richard III concludes the plays about the Wars of the Roses. Though it was written before the *Henry IV*, *Henry V*, and *Richard II* plays, it covers a historical period after the reigns of those monarchs. Presented during the reign of a Tudor monarch, Elizabeth I, it chronicles the horrors of the last Yorkist king before 'the redemption of English public life through the efforts of Henry Tudor, later Henry VII, and grandfather of Elizabeth.

Often called a melodrama, *Richard III* traces the infamous career of Richard, Duke of Gloucester, from betrayal to betrayal, and ultimately to the crown. The play opens with a self-revealing soliloquy, filled with villainous plots to eliminate all barriers to Richard's becoming King. At the time, his brother Edward IV is still the ruler of England, but Richard looks ahead. He manages to dispose of his brother, the Duke of Clarence, pretending all the time to be protecting him.

The second scene is a tour de force. Lady Anne, widow of Edward, Prince of Wales, enters with the corpse of Henry VI on the way to the monastery of Chertsey. She curses Richard for the murders of her husband, Edward, and her father-in-law Henry VI. There could never be a more inauspicious time for the presence of Richard, but he appears and in one of the most incredible scenes in Shakespeare, woos the grieving widow.

He orders the bearers to put down the coffin. Anne calls Richard the "dreadful minister of hell." He answers mildly, "Sweet saint, for charity, be not so curst." No summary can do justice to the magic that follows. Gradually, she falls under the spell of this master hypnotist and even accepts a ring from him. When he asks her to kill him, she pulls back. What he did, he tells her, he did for love of her. Anne says she is happy to see Richard so penitent. She does become the unhappy wife of Richard, possibly murdered by him later.

In this scene, Shakespeare challenged himself to show a complete about-face manipulated by a resourceful villain. From rage and anger, Anne is gradually mollified and won over in a scene that might not be realistic but is a theatrical triumph, a challenge to the two actors who play the roles. For dramatic reasons, Shakespeare takes liberties with the facts; Anne did not actually attend the funeral of Henry VI and may have died a peaceful death. This magnificent scene is entirely fictitious, the creation of a genius who dared the impossible. Watching the scene on the stage is a memorable experience.

The scene serves an important dramatic purpose. It shows the hypocrisy of Richard along with his irresistible appeal. Shakespeare makes much of Richard's physical deformity, though historians are uncertain about this flaw. No matter. Richard's ungainly appearance doesn't hinder him in his conquest of women or his manipulation of men.

Richard dominates the play. Upon the death of Edward IV, he manages to get control of the princes, sons of Edward IV. The eldest son, the Prince of Wales, becomes Edward V on his father's death, but his reign lasts only two months. The two Princes are sent to the Tower and never seen again. Their fate has been debated ever since, though Shakespeare suggests that Richard was the cause of their death. Through Richard's devious arguments, the children are declared illegitimate, and Richard becomes king.

His reign is marked by intrigue and bloodshed. Executions of former accomplices eventually make the remaining nobles nervous, and they join the revolt against him. The end comes at Bosworth field, where Richard is finally slain by his enemy, Richmond, who becomes Henry VII. He announces his intention to marry the daughter of Elizabeth Woodville, wife of Edward IV, thus joining the old warring factions and bringing peace to England.

Earlier, Richard had tried to marry that same daughter, but at this point in the play, Richard has lost his charm. Elizabeth puts him off, finally rejecting his offer of marriage. Richard's charm, bluster, and self-assurance desert him at the end.

The victors write the histories (p254). Though Henry VII is glorified as a peacemaker, he was also ruthless in pursuit of his objectives. Some of the crimes ascribed to Richard, were actually traceable to Henry VII, like the execution of Edward of Warwick. It was risky to have royal blood. Potential claimants for the throne were routinely executed…and not just by Richard.

In the main, Shakespeare has accepted the Tudor interpretation of historical events and has created a colorful, wicked character beloved by actors.

Henry VIII

All Shakespeare's? None of it Shakespeare's? Part Shakespeare's and part John Fletcher's (p 56)? All three points of view have had their proponents, though the first is becoming increasingly popular. After all, the editors of the First Folio (p 85) accepted *Henry VIII* while rejecting other plays assumed to be of joint authorship. No matter. Though written at the close of Shakespeare's career, it shows touches of brilliance, especially in characterization and language.

It is a long, episodic play with at least 26 named characters in the cast and a number of other unnamed characters, like gentlemen, secretaries, a page, a porter, a gatekeeper, a surveyor, and an old lady, friend to Anne Bullen (usually known as Anne Boleyn). Some of these unnamed characters have important lines. Two Gentlemen impart news about the trial and execution of Buckingham and provide a glimpse into the character of Wolsey. They also reappear at the coronation of Queen Anne. They tell the audience about Queen Katherine's fate and then remark on Wolsey's fall. Though superficially minor, unnamed roles, the Two Gentlemen have lines that good actors relish.

The play is a glorification of the Tudor dynasty, with some words of praise for the reigning monarch, the Stuart King James I. Actually James himself was partially a Tudor. His great grandfather was Henry VII, who was also the grandfather of Elizabeth. Reality presented Shakespeare with a problem, Henry VIII, a potentially fine monarch at his coronation, degenerated into a tyrant. His treatment of his loyal first wife was cruel. The execution of his second wife, Anne Boleyn, on probably trumped-up charges of adultery, revealed his disintegrating personality. That same Anne, who died in disgrace, was the mother of Elizabeth, the monarch during most of Shakespeare's life. Elizabeth herself came to the throne through a series of complex events and fortunate circumstances. How could Shakespeare glorify this dynasty? What could Shakespeare do with this daunting material: a merciless king, a disgraced queen, and a "tainted child" of the Henry-Anne union? Shakespeare took some liberties, as he often did, made changes for dramatic reasons, toyed with dates, even listed Brandon and the Duke of

Suffolk as separate characters, though they are probably the same. The result is a colorful play, with much pageantry, a study in contrasting personalities, and a feast of language when Katherine pleads her case before the Council or when Wolsey reflects upon his fall.

As for those problems mentioned above, Shakespeare made Henry sympathetic, Anne gloriously virtuous, and that "tainted child" the harbinger of greatness to come: Elizabeth I.

After a brief prologue, the play opens with essential information, foreshadowing events to come. Norfolk and Buckingham talk over a recent meeting of Henry and the French ruler, commenting on its pointlessness. They then plunge immediately into the heart of the play: the plotting of Cardinal Wolsey, the power behind the throne. Norfolk warns Buckingham, who hates Wolsey, to be careful. Wolsey himself passes by, casting a baleful eye on the lords. Soon an officer enters to arrest Buckingham for treason, a charge manipulated by Wolsey.

The opening scene sets the stage for the events that follow. The audience learns that Wolsey is a villainous schemer, who destroys good men to further his own ambition. The second scene demonstrates clearly that Henry is under the sway of Wolsey. The development of the play, however, shows how Henry matures, gradually seeing through Wolsey's duplicity, and becoming his own man.

The political and religious ramifications power the play. Henry wishes to divorce Katherine because she hasn't borne him a son and heir. He puts Katherine aside and marries Anne Bullen. The rise of Protestantism is a direct offshoot of his inability to get church sanction for the divorce.

The rest of the play is devoted to the machinations of rival factions, Protestant-leaning prelates like Cranmer find increasing favor, while those who favor the old religion find themselves increasingly isolated from the King. Wolsey, once so arrogant and brutal, is bereft of power and wealth, and dies a broken man.

As always, Shakespeare shows his characters as complex human beings. Katherine is a virtuous woman, true to Henry till her death. Henry shows pangs of conscience in his dealings with her. Anne Bullen, far from being a marriage-wrecker, doesn't seek the King's favor and herself becomes the victim of circumstance. Even the treacherous Wolsey is praised for his good qualities by Griffith, an attendant to Queen Katherine.

All the events lead up to the birth of Elizabeth, the baptism, and the predictions of greatness to come.

CRANMER.   This royal infant-heaven still move about her!-
             Though in her cradle, yet now promises
             Upon this land a thousand thousand blessings,
             Which time shall bring to ripeness.
                                        Henry VIII, V, 5, 17-20

Thus Cranmer supposedly gave this blessing, little realizing that he, the favorite of Henry, would be put to death during the following brief reign, of Mary Tudor, Henry's daughter by Katherine. She tried to restore Catholicism (p   7), was thwarted, and died an unhappy woman. Elizabeth, that "royal infant," succeeded her, and changed the course of English history.

Nine Days a Queen

Charles Brandon played a role on the fringe of history. Henry VIII's sister Mary had been married off to the ailing 52-year-old Louis XII of France. After several months of failing health, Louis died, and Mary was widowed. Despite Henry's opposition, Mary later married Brandon, a love match celebrated in Charles Major's novel *When Knighthood Was in Flower*.

The marriage was happy but dangerous for a descendant of that union. The couple's daughter, Frances Brandon, married Henry Grey, producing in turn a daughter, Lady Jane Grey. The young Edward VI, son of Henry VIII, had been induced to declare Lady Jane his successor, if he should die. At his untimely death, she was proclaimed queen. Her reign lasted nine days. The forces of Mary Tudor prevailed, and Lady Jane, only 15, was beheaded. In this troubling period, Elizabeth supported her half-sister against the forces of Lady Jane Grey. This support may have saved her life later (p 7).

These turbulent events occurred only ten years before the birth of Shakespeare, a reminder to Englishmen of the perils of political unrest.

22

The Greek and Roman Plays

Cry "Havoc!" and let slip the dogs of war.

Julius Caesar, **III, 1, 275**

Histories of Greece and Rome provided fruitful sources for Shakespeare and his contemporaries. When Sir Thomas North translated Plutarch's *Lives* (p181), vast areas opened up for dramatic treatment. North's efforts helped generate *Julius Caesar*, *Antony and Cleopatra*, and *Coriolanus*. Lovers of Shakespeare owe North a vote of thanks.

The Greek plays had different origins. Scholars are uncertain about *Timon*, but most agree that *Troilus and Cressida* had two main sources: George Chapman's translation of Homer's *Iliad* (p57), and a medieval legend of the two lovers.

All five plays have tragic components: the deaths of Julius Caesar and Brutus; the suicides of Antony and Cleopatra; the destruction of Coriolanus; the death of Hector and the disillusionment of Troilus; and the bitter death of Timon. There are comic moments in both *Troilus and Cressida* and *Timon*, but the overall hue is somber.

A Midsummer Night's Dream is supposedly set in and around Athens, but the real setting is fairyland. Though one of the characters is the Greek hero Theseus, his role is not as a Greek mythic hero.

Whether writing a tragedy, comedy, or history, Shakespeare has the ability to make a specific scene universal. These five plays, different as they are, were not written in sequence as a group, but were interspersed with other plays in composition and presentation.

Julius Caesar

Because of its popularity in high school classrooms, *Julius Caesar* is one of the best known of Shakespeare's plays. Probably written soon after *Henry V*, *Julius Caesar* is a dramatic hybrid, with the episodic quality of the history plays and the emphasis upon character of the tragedies. Brutus, the protagonist, is a flawed hero, like the heroes of the great tragedies. He aspires to heroism, but his personal failings eventually destroy him.

In the histories, Shakespeare has been pointing out the dangers of civil disorder. At the end of *King John*, the selection of King John's son as Henry III promised peace and order. The reign of Henry V was a time of national unity and internal peace under the leadership of a strong king. Henry VII promised a strong reign after the tragic Wars of the Roses. Shakespeare often preached the dangers of anarchy, loss of firm leadership. *Julius Caesar* explores those perils, too.

The opening scene tells the audience that something is amiss. There are factions within Rome, one favoring Caesar and the other his rival, Pompey. (Not a factor in this play, Pompey plays a role in *Antony and Cleopatra*.) Flavius and Marullus, two tribunes, are obviously not on the side of Caesar. Their discontent foreshadows troubles to come.

In the second scene, Caesar is advised by a soothsayer to beware the Ides (15th day) of March, when Caesar is to proceed to the feast of Lupercalia. Associates stay behind, notably Cassius and Brutus. Cassius emphasizes that Caesar is becoming too powerful, endangering their republican form of government. Casca enters and reports that Mark Antony has actually offered the crown to Caesar three times, to great acclamation by the crowd. Though Caesar had refused the crown three times, his manner seemed to indicate his yearning for power. Brutus, who has been a close friend of Caesar's, is deeply troubled by Cassius' urgings and vows to think about the problem.

Conspirators gather and make plans to add the reluctant Brutus to their band. They plant messages around where Brutus can find them. Then they decide to call upon Brutus to seek his support. Brutus has a sleepless night, but he finally decides that the ambitious Caesar must die. When the conspirators arrive, they settle on the murderous details. They seek to kill Antony also, as a danger to their cause, but Brutus forbids this extra slaying. They'll kill only Caesar, in the Capitol.

Calpurnia, Caesar's wife, tries to dissuade Caesar from going to the Capitol. In addition to the soothsayer's foreboding warning, there have been many ill omens usually associated with civil unrest. At first, Caesar agrees to humor his wife, but when a messenger arrives to escort Caesar to the Capitol, he declares that superstitions will not rule his actions, and he departs for the Capitol.

On the way, Artemidorus presses a letter upon Caesar, warning him of the conspiracy, but Caesar brushes him aside. Caesar is stabbed to death, with Brutus giving the last wound. Caesar cries out, "Et tu, Brute? Then fall, Caesar!" Having been overridden by Brutus, the conspirators let Antony live and even allow him to speak at the funeral, despite their misgivings. Brutus speaks to the crowd and gains respectful attention. Antony speaks, first commenting mildly on the death of Caesar and then building to a towering rage at the violence. The crowd completely reverses its position and joins Antony in a riotous denunciation of the conspirators. Here Shakespeare indulges his deep hatred of mob rule and heedless anarchy.

Three men are left to rule Rome: Antony, Octavius and Lepidus. A triumvirate is a shaky arrangement. Lepidus, the weakest of the three, was doomed to see his power evaporate until at last Octavius was in control. Shakespeare dramatizes the dissolution of the partnership of Octavius and Antony in *Antony and Cleopatra*.

The fate of the conspirators deteriorates. Cassius and Brutus squabble, exchanging bitter recriminations. Caesar's Ghost appears to Brutus, warning him of the defeat to come. In despair, Cassius orders his servant to kill his master. Brutus too commits suicide. The victors promise honorable rites for their dead enemies. At the end, Antony pays Brutus the famous tribute: "This was the noblest Roman of them all."

What are we to think of "the noblest Roman"? Is Antony's tribute justi-fied? As always with Shakespeare, the question is not easily answered. Just what were Brutus's motives? Patriotism? Envy? A neurotic failure to antic-ipate the results of his actions? Shakespeare provides lines that support any of these answers.

Perhaps the times determine the interpretation. During the rise of fas-cism in Europe, in the 1920s and 1930s, Caesar was viewed as a potential dictator. Brutus was played in those days as a great hero, with a few minor failings. Recently, however, some productions have seen Caesar as a force for order and Brutus as a threat to the stability of the state. He does dete-riorate morally in the second half of the play, ironically resembling Caesar.

Shakespeare cannot resist the immediate ironic outcome of the assassi-nation. Brutus has done his horrible deed to save the republic from tyranny. After he finishes speaking, at the funeral, a plebeian cries out. "Let him be Caesar!"

The play is episodic, like some of the battle scenes in the history plays. The enemy camps appear in alternating scenes, until the adversaries come together at last. Shakespeare's narrative gift is intact, but his gift for char-acterization has been enriched. The gallery of fascinating playable charac-ters is a director's dream: Cassius, Antony, Caesar, Casca, and those two realistically portrayed women, Portia and Calpurnia.

The conflict at the heart of *Julius Caesar* is with us still: the uneasy mar-riage between the ideal and the real. Shakespeare seems to be saying, "Let's do all we can to make this a perfect world, but let's also keep our feet on the ground."

Antony and Cleopatra

Antony and Octavius have won. They have divided the Roman world into two parts. Octavius (called *Caesar* in this play) rules the West; Antony, the East. Both men are ambitious, power hungry, ruthless leaders. As potential adversaries, both command Roman armies devoted to their leaders.

The opening scene immediately suggests the coming conflict. Antony has begun to lose the drive that had propelled him to the leadership of half the world. He has become infatuated with the Egyptian queen Cleopatra.

In the midst of their conversation, an envoy arrives from Rome, but Antony refuses to hear the messages. "Let Rome in Tiber melt."

Later, a second message turns his reluctant thoughts toward Rome. His faithful wife Fulvia has died while on a campaign for him. Pompey's son and allies have risen against Caesar, raising a challenge that will ultimately impact Antony's role in the empire. Cleopatra tries to lure him to stay, but Antony is adamant. Cleopatra wishes him well as he departs for Rome.

The scene shifts to the camp of Pompey, as the rebellious generals consider their chances against Caesar. When a messenger brings news that Antony is back in Rome, Pompey is less certain of his success but still hopeful. There is always the possibility that Antony and Caesar will split.

The play returns to Rome and Antony's meeting with Caesar. Antony apologizes for his indolent behavior and promises to fight with Caesar against the enemy forces. To cement their relationship, Antony agrees to marry Caesar's sister Octavia. All seems well, but one grizzled old soldier knows the truth. In describing Cleopatra to two friends, Enobarbus explains why Antony will never leave Cleopatra for good. That speech (p104) is one of the poetic gems of the play.

When she hears the news of Antony's marriage to Octavia, Cleopatra rages. When she learns later that Octavia is modest, unassuming, and unattractive, she calms down and rejoices! She appraises the situation and declares, "All will be well enough." Octavia is no match for Cleopatra.

The compact between Antony and Caesar doesn't last. Octavia leaves Athens to intercede with her brother. When she pleads for Antony, Caesar asks, "Where is he now?" When Octavia answers, "My lord, in Athens," Caesar disabuses her of this fantasy.

> No, my most wronged sister. Cleopatra
> Hath nodded him to her. He hath given his empire
> Up to a whore.
>
> *Antony and Cleopatra*, III, 6, 67-68

The central theme could not be stated better, though Caesar's label for Cleopatra is simplistic. This complicated woman resists all labels.

The play takes on a newsreel quality. Scenes jump back and forth with dizzying speed, as the opposing armies approach a decisive battle. Act 4 alone has fifteen different scenes. Throughout, the passion between Antony and Cleopatra is cleverly suggested. The audience begins to understand their ruinous obsession.

The climactic sea battle is a disaster for the forces of Cleopatra and Antony. At a crucial moment, Cleopatra's ships turn about and leave the battle. Antony rails against Cleopatra and strides angrily away. Fearing that he may kill her in his rage, Cleopatra sends out a message that she has killed herself. Antony decides to kill himself, too, and succeeds in wounding himself. He learns that Cleopatra gave out the false report of her death to protect herself. Dying, Antony asks to be taken to her. Their final meeting is an actor's dream. Antony's self-appraisal is keen.

> Not Caesar's valor hath o'erthrown Antony,
> But Antony's hath triumphed on itself,
> *Antony and Cleopatra*, IV, 15, 16-17

Antony has little to say, but Cleopatra pours out her love. Antony offers a few words of solace and dies in her arms. Realizing that she will be the captive of Caesar, Cleopatra vows to die rather than suffer ignominy. A Roman messenger promises that Cleopatra will be treated kindly by the "princely hand" of Caesar. At this point, guards surprise Cleopatra and capture her. She tries to stab herself but is prevented. Cleopatra defiantly vows not to be disgraced and makes a perceptive comment: "I will not be chastised...with the sober eye of dull Octavia."

Caesar enters with all the pomp of Rome, and Cleopatra kneels. She seems to surrender, recognizing that she is powerless. In a neat Shakespearean twist, Cleopatra supposedly yields to Caesar all her wealth, counting on her treasurer Seleucus to back up her story, but he blurts out that she has held back as much as she has acknowledged, She is the "Serpent of the Nile" to the end. Caesar doesn't blame her for this last deception. He speaks gently, promising her courteous treatment, but both know that Cleopatra is destined for a Roman triumph. Shakespeare uses language here especially creatively. After Caesar has left, Cleopatra says, "He words me, girls, he words me."

Cleopatra arranges to have a poisonous asp brought in. Dying, she cheats Caesar of his triumph, but at the end Caesar is magnanimous. He praises both Cleopatra and Antony and promises them burial side by side. Though of a completely different personality, Caesar pays tribute to their great love. The army shall "in solemn show attend this funeral."

The geographic magnitude of *Antony and Cleopatra* makes this a challenging play for a traditional proscenium stage with elaborate stage sets. It was no problem for a Shakespearean stage, with the audience visualizing each scene. Nor is it a problem for modern films, in which frequent breaks are easily managed. The play covers much of the Roman world: Alexandria, Rome, Messina, Athens, and Actium, but it's the central, doomed passion of Antony and Cleopatra that raises this above a history play.

Coriolanus

The *Concordance to Shakespeare* lists the word *alone* 14 times in *Coriolanus*, more than in any other play except *Romeo and Juliet*. The frequency of use is not accidental. The hero, Coriolanus, is a loner, used to acting alone, unable to establish ordinary human relationships. He is an amalgam of conflicting human qualities: courage and arrogance, strength and weakness, angry independence of others and an almost-childish dependency upon his mother, Volumnia.

Volumnia is one of Shakespeare's strongest creations: a Roman matron with an iron will, unyielding values, and a pathological thirst for glory achieved vicariously through her son. She manipulates Coriolanus and ultimately causes his destruction. He is a creature of her own devising. She is not onstage as frequently as many other characters, but when she appears, she dominates. Her philosophy is set forth on many occasions. Early on, she converses with Virgilia, wife of Martius (later called *Coriolanus*). The scene is a study in contrasts. Volumnia is all blood and glory; Virgilia is human, restrained, worried about her husband.

VOLUMNIA. If my son were my husband, I should freelier rejoice in
                that absence wherein he won honour than in the embrace-
                ments of his bed where he would show most love...To a
                cruel war I sent him; from whence he returned, his brows
                bound with oak. I tell, thee, daughter, I sprang not more
                in joy at first hearing he was a man-child then now in first
                seeing he had proved himself a man.
VIRGILIA. But had he died in the business, madam; how then?
VOLUMNIA. Then his good report should have been my son; I therein
                would have found issue.

Coriolanus, I, 3, 2-6, 16-23

In this quiet exchange, Shakespeare says more about Coriolanus and the play than all the battle scenes put together. The plot is fairly simple and direct. The opening scenes introduce Martius through the comments of an angry mob bent on seeking his death. Martius arrives and, by the force of his personality, quiets the mob. He tells of certain concessions by the patricians. News arrives that the Volscians, a neighboring tribe, are threatening. Martius agrees to fight the enemy.

The next scene introduces Aufidius, leader of the Volscians, an oft-defeated rival of Martius. He vows some day to bring Martius down, either by force or guile.

Combat begins before the Volscian city of Corioli. Through the incredible personal bravery of Martius, the Romans take the city. As a reward, Martius is called *Coriolanus* from then on. Aufidius reaffirms his desire to defeat Coriolanus next time by whatever means.

As a reward, the aristocrats seek to make Coriolanus consul, to the dismay of the tribunes and common people. There is a long string attached to the position. Coriolanus must first humble himself before the common people. Volumnia urges him to do so, and Coriolanus against his better judgment accedes, as always, to his mother's wishes. Unfortunately, Coriolanus' pride destroys any chance of success. He explodes in anger, shouting, "You common cry of curs!" The tribunes declare him banished from Rome, and Coriolanus in his rage, declares, "For you, the city, thus I turn my back."

Coriolanus finds his way to Antium and offers to fight against Rome. Though Aufidius welcomes him warmly, he secretly declares his plan to destroy Coriolanus at the end. The Romans are nervous when they hear that the great warrior Coriolanus will be fighting against them, not for them.

Various Romans meet with Coriolanus, begging him not to turn against his native city, but Coriolanus rejects them all. Act V, scene 3, is one of those Shakespearean scenes that hypnotize audiences. Volumnia, Virgilia, Coriolanus' son, and Valeria, another Roman matron, enter. At first, Coriolanus reminds them of the wrongs done to him, but gradually he begins to falter in his resolve to attack Rome. His resistance finally crumbles when Volumnia manipulates him, as she has always done. Coriolanus cries out,

> O, mother, mother!
> What have you done! Behold! the heavens do ope,
> The gods look down, and this unnatural scene
> They laugh at. O my mother! Mother! O!
> You have won a happy victory to Rome;
> But, for your son, believe it, O believe it,
> Most dangerously you have with him prevail'd.
> If not most mortal to him. But let it come.
> *Coriolanus*, V, 3, 182-189

As always, Volumnia has prevailed, and this man-child obeys… fatally for him.

Back to Corioli, Coriolanus presents the Roman treaty as a victory, but Aufidius seizes the opportunity he has been waiting for and charges Coriolanus with treason. Shakespeare again shows his disgust with mob behavior, as the Volseian crowd calls for Coriolanus' death. It is soon achieved, and Aufidius pays a final tribute to his old foe, now safely dead.

Much has been written about Shakespeare's silences. Why does Silvia say nothing in *Two Gentlemen of Verona* when Valentine seems to yield his love for Proteus? How does Isabella react to the Duke's proposal of marriage in *Measure for Measure*? Thomas Carlyle said that Dante's "silence is more eloquent than words." He may have said the same thing about Shakespeare. Is Portia really silent while Bassanio is choosing the right casket in *The Merchant of Venice*? The shrew is silent during Petruchio's statement that she concurs in the proposed wedding. Is she agreeing to this whirlwind romantic courtship (*The Taming of the Shrew*)?

There is a touching example of silence in *Coriolanus*. The hero has returned in triumph from Corioli. He is greeted effusively by a herald, a dignitary, and, of course, proud Volumnia. But his wife, Virgilia, says not a word. He addresses her affectionately: "My gracious silence, hail!" Why is she silent? She has already given us her misgivings about the warrior's role that Coriolanus has undertaken at the prodding of his mother. Coriolanus joshes her about weeping in his moment of triumph, but she knows the price that heroes pay and the anxieties they make their wives endure. Nothing she could have said is more expressive than her silence. Her love doesn't depend on the trumpet's call. Volumnia's does.

Troilus and Cressida

Although *Troilus and Cressida* has humorous characters and situations it is scarcely a comedy in the usual sense. The comedy has a sharp and biting edge. It is usually considered a "problem play," along with *All's Well That Ends Well* and *Measure for Measure*. All three are often puzzling, with ambiguous characters and situations. They are more cynical than the lighthearted comedies that preceded them, like *As You Like It*, and the mature comedies that followed, like *The Winter's Tale*. The poet Samuel Taylor Coleridge called *Troilus and Cressida* the most difficult play of Shakespeare's to characterize. Many modern critics agree. These three plays leave audiences with unanswered questions and an awareness of life's uncertainties and paradoxes.

One label that no one disputes is that of *satire*. In *Troilus and Cressida*, Shakespeare pokes fun at comforting assumptions, legendary heroics, and the tortuous course of true love. Shakespeare's mockery turns the heroics of Homer's *Iliad* upside down. The great champions are shown with all their warts. Thersites, an unpleasant commentator on the events in the play, describes certain key heroes most unflatteringly:

AJAX. He "stalks up and down like a peacock," a "beef-witted lord."

NESTOR. His "wit was moldy ere your grandsires had nails on their toes."

AGAMEMNON. "He has not so much brain as earwax."

ULYSSES. "That same dog fox, Ulysses, is not proved worth a blackberry."

ACHILLES. "A rare engineer: If Troy not be taken till these two [Ajax and Achilles] undermine it, the walls will stand till they fall of themselves.

Though bitter, Thersites' comments are generally accurate in the context of the play. The great heroes show petty jealousy, adolescently hurt feelings, and dishonesty in comments to each other. On the Greek side, Ulysses comes out fairly well. On the Trojan side, Hector is the conventionally heroic figure, but most of the other characters, Greeks and Trojans, are deeply flawed. Achilles loses most stature. In the *Iliad*, he slays Hector in fair and open combat. In *Troilus and Cressida*, Achilles has his men treacherously assassinate an unarmed Hector. While the *Iliad* is often interpreted as an anti-war poem, at least its participants show some courage, even if wrong-headed. In *Troilus and Cressida*, the protagonists are satirized along with war.

There are two major sources of satire in the play: war and love. Both young lovers, Troilus and Cressida, seem destined for a steadfast, lifelong love, but disillusion sets in early. Because of the political background of the play, the lovers are separated.

A prologue sets the stage, outlining the origin and course of the Trojan War. The play itself immediately introduces the audience to lovelorn Troilus, mad for the love of beautiful Cressida. Pandarus, the uncle of

Cressida, promises to help Troilus win her. Procuring the girl for Troilus has given to the English language the word *pander*. The go-between ultimately succeeds in bringing Troilus and Cressida together, and their love is ardent, passionate, and articulate. They promise eternal fidelity.

Scenes inside the palace of Troy and the Greek camp provide insights into the protagonists. In Troy, Hector urges that Helen be returned to the Greeks. The "honor" involved in fighting to the end doesn't justify the slaughter. Hotheaded Troilus takes the opposite position: that Trojan honor must be upheld. Hector agrees to continue the combat.

The Greeks are having their own problems. Their foremost warrior, Achilles, is sulking in his tent. Agamemnon, leader of the Greeks, assigns Ulysses to persuade Achilles to return. In a famous image-laden speech (p141), Ulysses tells Achilles that fame is transitory. It must be won and rewon. Achilles refuses to fight, but when his close friend Patroclus is slain in battle, Achilles vows to seek Hector on the battlefield and kill him. He does so, but in a treacherous manner.

The love of Troilus and Cressida is doomed. Cressida's father, Calchas has gone over to the Greek side. He wants his daughter exchanged, so that she can be with him. The opposing factions agree to exchange the warrior Antenor for Cressida. She is to be awarded to Diomedes. Troilus and Cressida try to make the best of it, promising to meet somehow in secret. Troilus gives Cressida a sleeve to be kept as a symbol of his eternal love for her.

In a painful scene in the Greek camp, Troilus, with the help of Ulysses, spies on Cressida in her coy playfulness with Diomedes. Diomedes can play the game, too. He eventually gets from Cressida the sleeve that Troilus had entrusted to her. As Troilus looks on in a rage, he vows to kill Diomedes on the battlefield if Cressida's new lord dares to wear Troilus's sleeve. Cressida does have some pangs of conscience, but these are suppressed in her new role.

Diomedes does wear the sleeve. He and Troilus meet on the battlefield, but with indeterminate results. The play ends without any clear resolution of love or war, leaving to the procurer Pandarus the last speech. It is filled with self-pity, ribald humor, and a promise to the audience to "bequeath you my diseases."

Historically, Troilus was a son of Priam, a minor character in the Iliad, slain by Achilles before the death of Hector. The story of Troilus and Cressida does not appear in the classics, arising in legends from the Middle Ages. Cressida's name has become a symbol of female faithlessness.

The major English poet of the 14th century, Geoffrey Chaucer, wrote a long poem on the legend: *Troilus and Criseyde*. Chaucer introduces more philosophy and moralizing than Shakespeare but stays close to the story as he had received it from Bocaccio.

Timon of Athens

This is a strange Shakespearean play, a battleground for critics and a headache for aspiring producers. With few records of performances at any time in the past, *Timon of Athens* is certainly one of Shakespeare's least popular plays. Though it found a place in the First Folio (p 85), it may have been inserted at the last moment for reasons of space. The copy used was not a desirable one. It was probably based on a rough copy in Shakespeare's hand, along with transcripts by a professional scribe.

At first, arguments raged over whether Shakespeare had a collaborator on this strange project. Modern criticism accepts Shakespeare as the author, but concedes that the play is unfinished. Possibly Shakespeare tired of it and put it aside, unable to round out the play in a way satisfactory to him. Various reasons are given for Shakespeare's decision to abandon the unfinished play. Some suggest that there was an emotional crisis in his life that soured his outlook on the world. Others believe that Shakespeare was still honing his skill here, on the way to the great final romances, like *The Winter's Tale*. There are fine things in *Timon*, but it lacks a sense of strong structure.

It is the tragic story of a bitter hero; yet the play has many comical lines and situations. The play opens with a dialogue between a poet and a painter, beneficiaries of Timon's generosity. Other feeders at the Timon trough join in the conversation about Timon and his bounty. Timon demonstrates his generosity by freeing his friend Ventidius from prison by paying his debts and by making his servant Lucilius wealthy enough to marry a young woman of high rank. At first, he idealizes friendship, linking it with open-hearted generosity. Unfortunately, Timon's own fortunes are in a precarious state, as his steward Flavius has warned him.

The first scene introduces two other important characters. Apemantus is a surly misanthropic philosopher, unpleasant in manner and speech, but it is he who warns Timon, ineffectually, about the stupidity of wasting his resources on insincere flatterers. The other main character is Alcibiades, a historical figure. Athenian general, and true friend to Timon.

Apemantus insults, rails, criticizes, derides Timon's actions and participates as a gadfly. He acts as a running commentary, often telling Timon the bitter truth. He is distinctly unlikable, but he provides a necessary realistic note in the false situation created by Timon's blind liberality.

Alcibiades is the most realistic character in the play. Though the others sometimes take on allegorical significance, Alcibiades is a flesh-and-blood hero, a sensible actor in a changing world, a person who reacts effectively and quickly in response to adversity. Timon collapses later, turning from a sweet-natured gentleman to a raging misanthrope. By contrast, Alcibiades works through adversity and emerges stronger.

To demonstrate his lavish generosity, Timon invites his friends to a sumptuous banquet. He extols friendship and the reciprocity expected of true friends: "What need we have any friends, if we should ne'er have need of 'em?" It's wonderful to have friends, for they'll be there when needed, ready to be helpful. In this atmosphere of sweetness and admiration of Timon, Apemantus strikes a negative note, scorning the noble sentiments as absurd.

Apemantus's proves to be a prophet. Timon's loans are called in. He faces financial ruin, and so he calls upon all those "friends" who accepted his gifts with flattering admiration. Every person called upon has an excuse, all different, some ingenious, including the refusal by Sempronius, who was "insulted" because Timon had asked others for help before him. Timon is crushed by this ingratitude, but insists on setting up one more feast, to the dismay of Flavius, who says, "There is not so much left to furnish out a moderate table." Timon says, "I'll provide."

The banquet is a raucous, dramatic highlight of the play. Thinking that Timon has somehow recovered his wealth, his false friends flock to his house for another free meal. They apologize for their refusals to help, but Timon brushes off the insincere words. When the dishes are brought in and uncovered, they contain only water and stones. Timon drives off his guests, pelting them with the water and stones.

Timon goes into the woods and survives by digging for roots. While doing so, he finds gold. Timon gives part of his gold to harlots, urging them to give men fatal infections. He gives part to thieves, urging them to increase their crimes. He also gives gold to the deserving Flavius and sends him away.

Word of Timon's gold brings the poet and the painter to him, seeking further generosity. They are rebuffed. Then Alcibiades appears in exile from Athens, having been banished for disagreeing with a senate ruling. Timon rejects Alcibiades' pity. Battered Timon has now become a symbol of the tightly wound, irascible cynic, unrelenting in his hatred of everyone. Since Alcibiades has threatened to defeat Athens for his shabby treatment, two senators come to Timon to urge him to return home to Athens to help defend the city against Alcibiades. Timon provides a solution: a tree upon which the Athenians can hang themselves.

Not long after the senators depart, a soldier comes upon Timon's grave and his epitaph. He takes a wax impression of the inscription to bring to Alcibiades. Meanwhile, Alcibiades has agreed not to sack Athens. He has shown the forgiveness and humanity lacking in Timon. Even in death, the inscription cries out Timon's extreme and unnatural hatred:

> "Here lies a wretched corse, of wretched soul bereft:
> Seek not my name: a plague consume you wicked caitiffs left!
> Here lie I, Timon; who, alive, all living men did hate:
> Pass by, and curse thy fill, but pass and stay not here thy gait.
> *Timon of Athens*, V, 4, 70-73

Like many of the comedies and romances, *Timon of Athens* ends in a spirit of reconciliation, but the human gesture belongs to Alcibiades, not Timon.

23

The Romantic Comedies

If ever—as that ever may be near—
You meet in some fresh cheek the power of fancy,
Then shall you know the wounds invisible
That love's keen arrow makes.

As You Like It, III, 5, 28-31

There is exhilaration in seeing an artist at the top of his or her form. With these three plays, Shakespeare reached a height of comedic genius foreshadowed in his earlier works. Whether in stage presentations, films, television productions, or amateur theatricals, these three plays are surefire. They are romantic, bright, pleasingly plotted, lively, filled with attractive characters. There are gallant heroes, like Benedick in *Much Ado about Nothing*, and the lovelorn Orlando in *As You Like It*, but it's the women who steal the plays.

In *As She Likes It*, Penny Gay studies performances and reviews of the past half-century to see how actors have interpreted their roles, with special attention paid to women. Two of the women studied are from early and late plays: Katharina in *The Taming of the Shrew* and Isabella in *Measure for Measure*. The other three are from the plays in this grouping: Rosalind in *As You Like It*; Viola in *Twelfth Night*; and Beatrice in *Much Ado about Nothing*. Though Shakespeare had to use boys to play women on his stage, he somehow managed to create three-dimensional characters that have challenged actresses since the beginning of the 17th century.

Penny Gay has modified the title of Shakespeare's play to *As She Likes It* and has provided a subtitle: *Shakespeare's Unruly Women*. She traces the characterizations through five decades, emphasizing how the social setting of the time affects the interpretations. She also makes clear that Shakespeare's text provides ample opportunity for these modern "unruly women" to score points against sexism and the patriarchal mindset of the plays. Shakespeare has created dream roles and provided the flexibility to satisfy the most modern bias against gender inequality.

Rosalind, Viola, and Beatrice are certainly different personalities. They are part of a patriarchal society, but they somehow manage to override the controls placed upon them. Beatrice is a firebrand whose wit can sting. Rosalind has a mature sense of humor and a great capacity for love. Viola shows strength in patience and an understanding of love that her fellows lack. All three are real women, models with whom the audience can identify. All three play a major role in solving the complications that the rest of the cast has created.

Throughout the years studied by Penny Gay, interpretations varied widely. Viola, for example, has often been portrayed as a mild, shy person, doleful in her first appearance, but Diana Rigg and Jane Lapotaire developed lively, characters, somewhat aggressive at times. Shakespeare has made those conflicting interpretations possible.

Much Ado about Nothing

How can a subplot overpower the main plot? When Shakespeare created the two sparring lovers, Benedick and Beatrice, he guaranteed that audiences would be most interested in the arguments, antics, and love of this incredible pair. The main plot, involving the threatened romance of Claudio and Hero, would be colorless without the hate/love of Benedick and Beatrice.

In Much Ado about Nothing, Shakespeare displays the maturity of his in-sights. Though classified as a comedy, the play has a central, tragic theme, whose direction is ironically changed by a group of simpletons.

But it is in the dialogue that Shakespeare shows his mastery. The bantering dialogue between Benedick and Beatrice captures the stage and dominates the play.

Don Pedro of Aragon and his company visit Leonato, governor of Messina. In the company are Don John, Don Pedro's malicious half-brother; Claudio, a young lord; and Benedick, another young lord. These three play crucial roles in the plot. In the course of the visit, Claudio falls in love with Leonato's daughter, Hero; Benedick meets Beatrice, Leonato's niece and Benedick's old friend and adversary; and Don John plots against Claudio, who has risen at the expense of Don John.

With Don Pedro's help, Claudio wins the hand of Hero, and a wedding date is set. With the help of Borachio, his lieutenant, Don John sets in motion a trick to prevent the marriage and cause dismay all around. Hero's waiting woman, Margaret, dresses in Hero's clothes and is persuaded to stand at the window. Down below, Borachio is supposedly there for a romantic tryst with Hero. Don Pedro and Claudio are lured to the scene and conclude, too hastily, that Hero is unfaithful. They are both enraged and vow to disgrace Hero publicly.

Later Borachio boasts drunkenly to his friend Conrade of his night's deceit. By a fortunate coincidence, two watchmen overhear the plot and arrest the two men. They bring the men to the constables, the completely inept Dogberry and Verges (p174). The constables try to bring the matter before Leonato, but he is too busy with preparations for the wedding and puts them off till later. The lack of clarity of the constables' language also plays a part in Leonato's impatience. Of course, if Leonato had paid attention to the rambling message, there would have been no play!

The wedding day arrives. During the ceremony, when Leonato gives Hero to Claudio, Claudio cruelly says, "There, Leonato, take her back again." Claudio denounces Hero, and Don Pedro concurs. Hero protests her innocence, to no avail. She falls into a dead faint, later mistaken for death. Even Leonato temporarily turns against her, persuaded by the words of these two irreproachable gentlemen. Benedick doesn't join in the condemnation, though he does defend the actions of the two lords, suggesting that Don John probably played a part in the disaster. At Beatrice's insistence, he agrees to challenge Claudio to a duel to avenge Hero's honor.

The scene shifts to the prison where Borachio and Conrade are both held. The hilarious interlude after the grim tragedy preceding shows Shakespeare's mastery of timing and plot control. Dogberry and Verges question the two villains, without any practical result. Then the Sexton, exasperated by the incompetence of the constables, takes over the questioning. He realizes that the watchmen have uncovered the plot against Hero and Claudio. He also reveals that Don John has stolen away. He tells Dogberry and Verges to bring the two villains to Leonato, while he goes ahead to break the news.

Leonato tells his brother Antonio of his grief at losing his child, presumed dead. When Claudio and Don Pedro enter, the brothers challenge the two lords to a fight, but the lords, thoroughly discomfited and embarrassed, refuse. Then the constables bring in Borachio, who confesses all.

By this time, Leonato has also been informed. He enters and berates Claudio and Don Pedro for their part in the tragedy. Both men are penitent, eager to do anything that might make slight amends. Leonato suggests that Claudio marry his niece, who looks very much like Hero. Claudio agrees. At the church he publicly mourns Hero.

The day of the new wedding arrives. Hero has arrived, masked. During the ceremony, Claudio says, "Give me your hand: before this holy friar, I am your husband, if you like of me."

Hero replies, "And when I liv'd, I was your other wife." She takes off her mask, to the amazement and joy of all present. A messenger arrives to report that Don John has been captured in flight. Even Borachio repents, and the play ends in general happiness.

At first, Beatrice and Benedick are brought together by deception. Each one overhears others saying how much Benedick really loves Beatrice and Beatrice loves Benedick. The mocking tone of their repartee begins to soften, a delightful change for the audience. Once committed, Benedick backs up his love. For Beatrice's sake, he agrees to a duel with Claudio to defend Hero's honor. Throughout the latter half of the play, Benedick shows his devotion to Beatrice in many ways. This acid-tongued warrior is really a softy. Near the close of the play, Don Pedro says, "How dost thou, 'Benedick, the married man'?" Even today, a newly married man, saved from bachelordom, may be called a "benedict."

All the characters have had their critics. Claudio is too easily persuaded. Don Pedro, also, is too readily duped. Don John is a cardboard villain. And so it goes. But there is universal agreement on two points. Benedick and Beatrice are marvelous stage lovers. Dogberrry and Verges are two of the most delightful comic characters in all of Shakespeare.

The repartee of Benedick and Beatrice charms audiences because beneath the banter is a potential love story. Ideally suited in many ways, Benedick and Beatrice have wasted their time in stinging put-downs. But when the doors are opened through the good-natured connivance of others, the two lovers show the affection that has been dormant all that time.

Romeo and Juliet are icons for young lovers. Antony and Cleopatra demonstrate the power of mature passion. Benedick and Beatrice fill another niche: the intelligent lovers whose passion has been repressed by verbal warfare but explosive when released.

As You Like It

Shakespeare's creation of women characters is especially amazing when we realize that boys had to play these roles. The three mature, romantic comedies present three of Shakespeare's most attractive women: Viola, in *Twelfth Night*; Beatrice, in *Much Ado about Nothing*; and Rosalind in *As You Like It*. For many critics, Rosalind is the jewel in the crown, a high-spirited, intelligent, witty example of the best in Shakespeare's comedy.

The opening scenes set the plot in motion with important information. The hero, Orlando, has been mistreated by his older brother, Oliver, who has inherited the father's estate. Devoted cousins, Celia and Rosalind, remain attached to each other even though Celia's father has usurped the dukedom of his brother, Rosalind's father. As the result of a challenge, Orlando engages in a wrestling match and surprisingly overcomes his professional opponent, Charles. Through Charles, Oliver had plotted the death of Orlando. Shakespeare uses Charles as the source of important plot information: that Duke Senior, the banished duke, has set up court in the Forest of Arden. Thus the audience is quickly apprised of the necessary background.

At the wrestling match, Rosalind and Orlando fall in love. That attraction is frustrated when Duke Frederick, Celia's father, suddenly orders Rosalind to leave the court on pain of death. Frederick has been jealous of Rosalind's popularity and mindful of his own ill treatment of Rosalind's father. Celia determines to go with Rosalind. For greater safety, Rosalind dresses as a man, and the two go off into the Forest of Arden to seek Rosalind's father. They take along with them Touchstone, a professional fool and sometime philosopher.

The scene shifts to the forest, where Duke Senior, Rosalind's father, enjoys the simple pleasures of woodland life. One of the Duke's followers, Jaques, provides a contrast to much of the lighthearted fun in ensuing episodes. Pessimistic and cynical, Jaques comments sourly about life in the forest, love, and the dreadful state of humankind. Contradicted by the major characters in the play, Jaques is nevertheless given one of the most famous speeches in Shakespeare: "All the world's a stage."

Back at Oliver's house, Adam, Orlando's old, faithful servant, warns his master that he is in danger, that Oliver has designs on his life. They leave together and seek their fortunes elsewhere.

Events begin to ruffle the serenity of the Forest of Arden. We suspect that the characters will all meet there eventually. First we meet Rosalind, Celia, and Touchstone. They come upon Corin, a shepherd, who tells them that a nearby cottage and pasture are to be sold by his master. Rosalind determines to buy the property. Adam and Orlando appear in another part of the forest. Adam is exhausted by the exertions of the Journey, and Orlando goes off in search of food. He comes upon Duke Senior, who graciously offers him the food he seeks.

Back at the palace, Oliver is threatened by Duke Frederick unless he can produce Orlando, whom the Duke blames for the runaway girls. We know that Oliver will also go into the forest in his search.

Orlando is lovesick for Rosalind. He goes about the forest, decorating trees with verses about Rosalind's beauty. Celia and Rosalind find some of these love notes, and Rosalind resolves to have fun with her devoted admirer. Secure in her disguise as Ganymede, Rosalind pretends to give Orlando advice to cure him of his obsession. She will demonstrate the fickleness of feminine behavior. In this game, Rosalind, now disguised, insists that Orlando call her *Rosalind* during these teaching sessions. So Orlando must call Ganymede *Rosalind*, little knowing that this is indeed his beloved Rosalind.

Shakespeare introduces other characters: Silvius, a shepherd, helplessly in love with the disdainful Phebe; Audrey, a simple country maid, sought after by Touchstone; William, a rustic simpleton, also in love with Audrey. Indignant at Phebe's curt dismissal of the adoring Silvius, Rosalind in effect says, "You're not that great." Instead of being chastened, Phebe falls in love with Ganymede/Rosalind.

Oliver is now in the forest. He comes upon Celia and Rosalind and tells how his brother unselfishly saved him from a lioness, even though Oliver had plotted to kill him earlier. This act of kindness strikes a chord in Oliver, and he reforms, thoroughly ashamed of his previous villainy. When Rosalind learns that Orlando has been wounded calling out the name *Rosalind*, she faints. Oliver considers this faint a sign of weakness for a man. Rosalind recovers and continues to keep up the pretense, though Oliver is unimpressed.

Later Oliver and Orlando enter. Oliver confesses that he and Celia have fallen in love and plan to marry. He offers the whole estate to Orlando. Rosalind enters and gives her blessing to the union. Seeing this happiness, Orlando yearns openly for his missing Rosalind. Rosalind decides to drop the charade. She promises Orlando that she'll produce his Rosalind, so that they can marry, along with Oliver and Celia.

All characters come together. Rosalind gets Phebe to agree to marry Silvius if she realizes she cannot have Ganymede. When Ganymede becomes Rosalind, Phebe gives in. Orlando and Rosalind, Oliver and Celia, Touchstone and Audrey, Silvius and Phebe-all prepare to marry. To heighten the joy, a messenger reports that the evil Duke Frederick has been converted by a holy man and renounces his usurpation, restoring the lands to Duke Senior.

This may seem a bit pat and too contrived. All the loose ends are tied together abruptly and happily. Perhaps the conversions of Oliver and Duke Frederick are insufficiently motivated. No matter. Shakespeare has achieved his aims. He has explored love in many forms and has acclaimed the power of love to overcome evil (Oliver and Duke Fredrick), pessimism (Jaques), and cynicism (Touchstone).

Shakespeare has glorified the ideal rustic life, but he presents some counter arguments from time to time. The Forest of Arden may be an earthly paradise, but there are lions and serpents there, too. He has taken stock figures from typical pastoral comedy and has woven them into a seamless fabric. Above all, he has supplied brilliant dialogue, especially by the witty Rosalind and sarcastic Touchstone. The play is truly "as you like it."

Twelfth Night

Twelfth Night probably followed the mature comedies, *Much Ado about Nothing* and *As You Like It*. *Twelfth Night* itself was probably followed shortly by *Hamlet*. It thus provides a transition between the relatively light-hearted comedies and the subtly complex tragedies to come. Though the mood of *Twelfth Night* is generally merry and romantic, there are anti-romantic elements, as well as ridicule and bitterness.

The title sets the tone of the play. *Twelfth Night* was January 5, the eve of the Twelfth Day after, Christmas. It was a time of revelry and festivities derived from ancient times. Probably Shakespeare's play was written to be performed during the revels.

Like other Shakespearean plays involving a disguise, *Twelfth Night* has a girl disguised as a boy. Since these roles were performed by boys in Shakespeare's time, the main character Viola would have been a boy pretending to be a girl disguised as a boy!

Shipwrecked on the coast of Illyria, Viola is advised by the Captain to disguise herself as a boy to avoid unnecessary advances by men. The Captain assures Viola that her twin brother, Sebastian, has also been saved, though he was cast ashore elsewhere.

The ruler of Illyria, Duke Orsino, is introduced as a hopeless victim of unrequited passion. He is madly in love with the lady Olivia, but she rebuffs his every advance. The Duke may be in love with love rather than with a real-live person, but he pursues his suit with unflagging persistence. It is into this unlikely scenario that Viola enters.

Orsino takes a liking to the "boy," Cesario, and enrolls him/her as a messenger to the hard-hearted Olivia. Viola/Cesario falls in love with Orsino but cannot express her love. As it would happen, Olivia in turn falls in love with Viola as the page Cesario. This seems to be a problem without solution, but Shakespeare cleverly manipulates the plot so that all turns out well for the principal characters.

Not all the characters fare so well. An important subplot includes many colorful characters: Malvolio, Olivia's steward; Sir Toby Belch, Olivia's uncle and hanger-on; Sir Andrew Aguecheek, a dim-witted suitor of Olivia and a dupe of Sir Toby; Maria, a saucy maid to Olivia; Feste, Olivia's jester; and Fabian, a co-conspirator in the plot against Malvolio. By his superior attitude and condescending remarks to Olivia's household, Malvolio has earned the undying hatred of those he considers his inferiors. The aggrieved "inferiors" plan his downfall.

Maria can imitate Olivia's handwriting. She writes a note, supposedly written by a lovesick Olivia, about Olivia's passion for Malvolio. The note is dropped where Malvolio will pick it up. Though never mentioned by name, the conceited Malvolio immediately thinks he's the one Olivia is talking about. He takes hints from the note, dresses in absurd fashion and drops suggestive hints that he knows Olivia's true feelings. Olivia thinks he's gone mad and charges Sir Toby and the rest to look to him. They lock Malvolio up in a dark place, where Feste plays Sir Topas, a curate, and taunts Malvolio as a madman. Malvolio is finally released and brought before Olivia. She regrets the wrongs done him, but he is unforgiving. He exits with the famous line: "I'll be revenged on the whole pack of you."

The minor characters impinge upon the main plot when Viola is challenged to a duel by Sir Andrew. Jealous because Olivia has shown an interest in this messenger, Sir Andrew is urged on to fight a duel with the apparently harmless object of his dislike, Cesario. Meanwhile, Viola's brother Sebastian arrives on the scene.

The duel finally begins, with two shaky adversaries: the cowardly Sir Andrew and the feminine Viola. After an interruption, the fight is resumed, but this time Sebastian has been mistaken for Viola. He proceeds to overwhelm both Sir Andrew and Sir Toby.

Still madly smitten with her messenger, Olivia swoops down upon the startled Sebastian and persuades him to marry her. Though completely baffled by the situation, Sebastian is overcome by Olivia's beauty and agrees to the marriage.

The confusion of identities brings sorrow to Antonio, who has saved Sebastian from the sea. He is so taken with the noble Sebastian that he offers to be his servant, Sebastian refuses, but Antonio stays on in Illyria anyway. Antonio is on unsafe ground since previous experiences have made him an outlaw in that land. When he finds Sebastian on the streets of Orsino's dukedom, he gives Sebastian his purse in case he is captured by Orsino's men. When Viola later is terrified at the very beginning of the duel, Antonio rushes in to save her, thinking she is Sebastian. Antonio is captured by Orsino's men. When he asks Viola for his purse, she is baffled. He accuses her of treachery.

This mix of confusing identities and puzzling incidents is cleared up at the end. When all the principals are on the scene, the twins, Viola and Sebastian, are reunited to their joy. Olivia is happy that she has snagged Sebastian. Orsino remembers Viola's many expressions of love for him and agrees to marry her. Antonio is pardoned. Only Malvolio's treatment adds a sad tinge to the celebrations, but to Shakespeare's audience, Malvolio got what he deserved for trying to break down class barriers. The song ends with a happy song by Feste. Since he was played by Robert Armin (p 32), a good singer, Shakespeare provides opportunities for him to display his talents.

Once again, threatening complications bring a happy ending. The plot strands are woven together. The principal characters are happily taken care of. There are the occasional undertones of disquiet and potential violence, but good will and courtly manners prevail.

24

The Great Tragedies

Then must you speak
Of me that loved not wisely but too well.

Othello, V, 2, 353-354

Here again, Shakespeare is at the top of his form. The four tragedies, often grouped as examples of Shakespeare's skill and maturity, were written within a few years of each other. Did Shakespeare experience a personal tragedy at this time, or is his genius beyond such limitations? His son Hamnet had died in 1596; yet *Hamlet* was probably written three or four years later, certainly not an immediate reaction. A counter argument to the personal tragedy explanation for the great tragedies is the date generally assigned to the sunny comedy *As You Like It*: 1599, about the same time as *Hamlet*.

The four plays are sometimes compared with Greek tragedies. Each hero has some fatal "moral flaw." Hamlet's is indecision. Lear's is vanity. Othello's is jealousy. Macbeth's is ambition. According to this reasoning, each of the tragic heroes brings about his own demise because he has a fatal flaw.

Such interpretations are too simplistic, too flat for these complicated heroes. They are multifaceted individuals, ultimately aware of their own shortcomings, sad that they lacked the wisdom to avoid the blood baths at the end of each tragedy. Ironically, the heroes are victims of their own strengths, their own positive qualities. Hamlet's indecision is that of a sensitive, intelligent man unwilling to do murder without just cause. Lear's vanity has arisen from a love for his daughters and a too-deep love for Cordelia, who cannot play his stupid mind game. Othello's jealousy is an outcome of his great courage and masterful handling of disturbances and foreign wars. He cannot understand hypocrisy. Macbeth's military prowess and leadership lead to his overpowering ambition.

The motivations of these great heroes are mixed. They are torn by conflicting impulses, just as people are in life. It is the internal warfare of these tragic heroes that motivates the plays.

Hamlet

As Oscar Wilde once wrote about *Hamlet*, "Are the critics mad or just pretending to be?" With one sentence, Wilde took a poke at the endless critical attempts to fathom Hamlet's character. "Is Hamlet mad or not?" is but one of the questions debated by commentators. Shakespeare's audiences didn't worry about such things. They saw *Hamlet* as great theater, and audiences have agreed for 400 years. The inescapable truth is that there are no definitive "answers" to Hamlet. Each generation in every kind of society finds in *Hamlet* universal qualities. The critics may interpret, unravel, decipher to their heart's content, but readers and theatergoers interpret *Hamlet* in the context of their own person-alities.

The plot itself is not the source of *Hamlet's* greatness. Simply put, Hamlet is a revenge play. Hamlet's father has been murdered by his uncle, and Hamlet must make his way through uncertainties, intrigues, and setbacks to ultimate revenge. The bleak and chilly opening sets the mood for the play. Guards have seen the ghost of Hamlet's father roaming the battlements. They call upon Horatio, the educated friend of Hamlet, to watch with them. The Ghost appears but refuses to speak. The awed watchers determine to let Hamlet know. Part of the plot has been set in motion.

The next scene introduces another plot element, a contrast. In the King's Council Chamber, the new king, Claudius, is holding court with his newly married wife, Hamlet's mother, Gertrude. Some official business is transacted, and Claudius tries to establish a friendly rapport with Hamlet, but without success. Hamlet is left alone for his first soliloquy. Horatio and the guards enter to tell Hamlet about the apparition they've seen.

Shakespeare shows his mastery of suspense. The audience is eager to get Hamlet on the battlements to meet the Ghost, but the next scene is a domestic scene involving Polonius, respected courtier; Ophelia, his daughter, and son Laertes, who is going off to France. Hamlet has shown Ophelia attentions that Polonius mistrusts. He orders her to break off these connections.

Back to the battlements. Hamlet meets the Ghost, but not right away. Hamlet is lured to a lonely section of the castle, where Hamlet, senior, tells Hamlet of his murder by his brother, Claudius, who has taken his crown and his queen. The Ghost calls for revenge. The rest of the play follows the trail to that resolution.

Why doesn't Hamlet immediately sweep to his revenge? Commentators have discussed this problem for centuries. Certain obvious elements underlie the "answers." Being a civilized man, Hamlet doesn't at this point take murder lightly. In an age when people believed in satanic forces seeking to send the souls to Hell, Hamlet wonders whether the Ghost is perhaps a demon.

Hamlet arranges for a play in which the players will enact a murder very much like the murder of King Hamlet. If the King is upset by the enactment, Hamlet will have a reason for killing his father's murderer. Everything goes as planned. The King is visibly upset at the vision of his own treachery and leaves the chamber in a frenzy. Hamlet now knows that the Ghost's story is true.

Rosencrantz and Guildenstern, two old friends of Hamlet, have been summoned by the King to find out what ails Hamlet. They are typical courtiers and follow the King's wishes, betraying their former friendship with Hamlet. After the play scene, they tell Hamlet that his mother wants to see him in her room. On the way to that room, Hamlet passes Claudius in prayer. The time seems right. Hamlet can achieve his revenge with one blow, but he hesitates. If he kills Claudius in prayer, Claudius will escape deserved punishment in the afterlife. Hamlet doesn't know that Claudius cannot pray. He cannot give up his crown and his queen, no matter what. So Hamlet passes on and arrives to chide his mother.

The "closet scene" is one of the play's highlights and probably the actual climax. After it, the end is inevitable. Gertrude immediately takes the offensive, berating Hamlet for upsetting her new husband. Hamlet turns the tables, chastising Gertrude for her hasty marriage to this vile replacement for her former husband. He becomes so wildly violent that Gertrude cries out in terror. Polonius, who has hidden behind the arras, calls out. Mistaking Polonius for Claudius, Hamlet strikes through the arras and kills the old courtier. The Ghost appears to Hamlet, telling him not to berate his mother but attend to Claudius. Since the Queen cannot see the Ghost, she assumes that Hamlet is truly mad.

The King has realized his mortal danger and has arranged for Rosencrantz and Guildenstern to escort Hamlet to England. Their secret orders require the King of England to put Hamlet to death. After the murder of Polonius, Hamlet is taken and escorted away under guard.

Ophelia has been distracted by her father's death at the hands of the man she loves. When she appears before the King and Queen, they are troubled by her wild ravings. She leaves and her brother Laertes comes storming in, raging to avenge the murder of his father Polonius. The King finally persuades Laertes that he, Claudius, is not to blame. Ophelia reappears, devastating the onlookers by her appearance and rantings, all related to the death of her father and the blasted love affair with Hamlet. The King quiets Laertes and promises to inform him about the death of Polonius. At this moment, the King believes that Hamlet has been executed in England.

The next scene reveals in a letter received by Horatio that Hamlet is alive and returning to Denmark. Captured by pirates and then released, Hamlet has changed Claudius's orders and sent Rosencrantz and Guildenstern to their deaths instead in England.

As Claudius is placating Laertes, the news arrives that Hamlet is alive and on his way back to Denmark. Ever the resourceful villain, the King hits upon another plan to kill Hamlet. He'll arrange a friendly duel between Laertes and Hamlet. He'll provide Laertes with a poisoned rapier.

For a double guarantee, the King will also provide a poisoned drink for Hamlet.

As Hamlet and Horatio pass through the cemetery on their way to the castle, they see a funeral procession approaching. They hide and discover that Ophelia is being buried. Her brother Laertes makes a show of grief by leaping into Ophelia's grave. This action is too much for Hamlet, who leaps in after Laertes. They scuffle and are separated.

In the final scene, Hamlet is challenged to a friendly duel by Laertes. At the onset, Laertes manages to get the poisoned rapier. The duel starts out amicably enough, with supposedly blunted tips to the rapiers. Hamlet more than holds his own. Worried, the King tries his backup plan and offers Hamlet a drink, into which Claudius has put a pearl (poison). Gertrude decides to drink to Hamlet's success, despite the pleas of Claudius not to drink. She has now been poisoned.

Laertes manages to catch Hamlet off guard and pricks him with the poisoned tip. The tempo accelerates. In a scuffle, the duelists exchange rapiers. Hamlet strikes Laertes. The Queen dies, calling out that she has been poisoned. Laertes, also dying, confesses his treachery with the rapiers. The two exchange forgiveness. Realizing the King's treachery, Hamlet stabs him and then insists he drink part of the poisoned cup. The King dies. Hamlet also dies, leaving his friend Horatio to mourn him. Fortinbras, prince of Norway, arrives with his army. Before dying, Hamlet names Fortinbras his successor, who orders a death march for the fallen hero.

Any plot summary fails to do justice to the rich fabric of characterizations, motivations, and sheer poetry of the play. What makes Hamlet tick? Ultimately, what makes any complicated human being tick? Shakespeare has caught the ambivalences and complexities of life perhaps better than any other playwright.

Othello

Does evil exist for its own sake? Can a virtuous, loving, trusting husband be converted almost overnight into a jealous, raging, intractable murderer? How can a flawlessly faithful wife be somehow made to seem like a sensually depraved adulteress? Does the human race contain characters so base that conscience plays not the slightest role in acting out a villainous role?

In his maturity, Shakespeare comes to grips with questions like these. He has created villains before Iago. The scoundrels in *Titus Andronicus* are almost caricatures. In *Richard III*, Shakespeare presents a ruthless evildoer, but his actions are motivated by his lust for the crown. In *Hamlet*, King Claudius is also motivated by seeking the crown and his brother's wife, an understandable motivation, even if unscrupulous. By contrast, Iago displays "motiveless: malignity" (p185) as Samuel Taylor Coleridge put it. The casually suggested motivation, his being passed over for promotion, doesn't begin to explain Iago. Shakespeare is demonstrating that there are matters beyond explanation. As the daily papers remind us, nothing is alien to human nature.

Unlike a complicated play like *A Midsummer Night's Dream*, *Othello* has a stark directness. It moves with deadly precision to its fated conclusion. We meet Iago in the opening scene, conniving with a dupe Roderigo, against Iago's master, Othello. Roderigo would like to seduce Desdemona, daughter of Brabantio, a senator of Venice. Iago expresses his hatred of a fellow soldier, Michael Cassio, supposedly because Cassio has been elevated in rank above Iago. Iago's first thrust against Othello occurs almost immediately. He emboldens Roderigo to awaken Brabantio with the news that Othello has eloped with Brabantio's lovely daughter. Brabantio is incensed and rushes off to accost the pair.

With typical economy, Shakespeare has plunged the audience into the story, with dire hints of what's to come. We learn about Iago's hatred of Othello. In his honest and unflinching appraisal of his own emotions, Iago demonstrates what Othello will be up against. We discover that Othello has already married Desdemona, despite her father's disapproval.

Othello and Desdemona are brought before the Duke of Venice. Othello explains how he won Desdemona and in the telling wins over the Duke and other members of his council. Besides, as a successful military leader, Othello is needed in Cyprus, remote outpost of the Venetian empire. A Turkish attack on Cyprus is imminent, and Othello is ordered to sail at once. Desdemona requests permission to go to Cyprus, too.

Othello sets out, leaving Desdemona in the company of Iago, whom he trusts implicitly. Before the scene is out, Iago plays further upon the gullibility of Roderigo and extracts money from him, supposedly to advance Roderigo's cause with Desdemona.

The poison slowly takes hold. Iago and Desdemona's ship arrives first in Cyprus. Othello is delayed by a storm, providential because it destroys the Turkish invasion fleet. At Cyprus, Iago gets Roderigo aside and deliberately uses Desdemona's courtesy to Cassio as a reason why she would naturally prefer the handsome young soldier to the hardened veteran, Iago presents a plan to destroy Cassio and thus make easier Roderigo's approach to Desdemona, who knows nothing of Roderigo or Iago's plotting.

Othello arrives at Cyprus and calls for a double celebration; of his marriage and the destruction of the Turkish fleet. Iago's devilish cleverness soon manifests itself in action. He gets Cassio drunk and involves him in a brawl. Othello is disgusted with his trusted lieutenant and discharges him. Iago, supposedly a "friend" to Cassio, advises him to get Desdemona to intercede for him. Iago will twist this innocent kindness into a proof of Desdemona's love for Cassio.

Desdemona indeed pleads for Cassio as a loyal friend. Cassio asks to speak to her personally to advance his pardon. Othello notices Cassio's departure followed by Desdemona's pleading for Cassio. Iago picks up on this "suspicious-looking meeting" and says, "Ha! I like not that." Othello catches the brief insinuation and begins a questioning of Iago. In half a dozen lines Iago while pretending to be honest and above board, sows the seeds of distrust. Othello never has an easy moment thereafter.

The play gathers momentum, Iago plays upon the gruff but naive soldier's weaknesses and gradually convinces him that Desdemona has been unfaithful many times with Cassio. With the help of his unsuspecting wife Emilia, Iago obtains a keepsake handkerchief belonging to Desdemona. He plants it where Cassio will find it, not knowing its owner's name.

Upon Iago's urgings and insinuations, Othello demands to see the handkerchief that he had given Desdemona. She is panicked by not being able to find it. She denies that she lost it, but her upset feeds his suspicions. Though seemingly reluctant at first to set a bar between wife and husband, Iago becomes more openly slanderous. Othello questions Emilia, who stoutly defends her mistress's innocence, but Othello refuses to believe these protestations.

Iago prevails upon dim-wltted Roderigo to kill Cassio, so to further his own cause with Desdemona. In the scuffle, Cassio wounds Roderigo. Iago comes up behind Cassio and stabs him, but not fatally, Iago turns the event to his own advantage, slaying Roderigo for his assault on Cassio.

The climax comes quickly. Determined to kill his supposedly unfaithful wife, Othello is almost put off by her innocent beauty as she sleeps. The poisons take their toll, and Othello smothers Desdemona. Emilia knocks at the door and enters. She berates Othello for believing that his wife was an adulteress. When Othello advances the missing handkerchief as proof, Emilia realizes the treachery of her husband. When she confronts him with his wickedness, Iago stabs her fatally. Undeceived at last, Othello tries to kill Iago, but he is restrained. He kills himself and Iago is led off for punishment.

To answer the second question of this section: Othello is converted into a jealous madman because of his inner weaknesses and the brilliant deception of Iago. Despite his military prowess, Othello is unsophisticated in matters of love. He realizes that he has won Desdemona because she misled her father. Perhaps she has deceived him too. Iago, subtly at first and then openly later, plays upon Othello's insecurities, and turns this impressive leader of men into his puppet.

How can Iago deceive Othello? Iago is a master of duplicity. Throughout the play, various characters refer to Iago as "honest." He seems to be the soul of integrity and fairness. What you see is what you get! He is a great stage character. He has some of the finest lines. He captures the audience's attention at once, as the theatergoers are spellbound by his devilish ingenuity.

The theme of the play is Othello's jealousy, but it is Iago's jealousy of Othello, Desdemona, and Cassio that really powers the play.

King Lear

> How sharper than a serpent's tooth it is
> To have a thankless child.
>
> *King Lear*, 1, 4, 294-295

How many parents through the ages have echoed this sentiment, put so brilliantly by Shakespeare? *King Lear* is a play built upon this theme, but it is also a story of moral regeneration through heartbreak and misery.

The opening scene sets the plot in motion. Lear, legendary King of Britain, wishes to retire, dividing his kingdom among his three daughters; Goneril, Regan, and Cordelia. Vain, proud, dictatorial, and unreasonable, Lear asks his daughters to tell which one loves him most. Goneril and Regan, greedy and insincere, express their supposed love in extravagant terms. Cordelia, disgusted by their preposterous, excessive expressions of love, answers, "Nothing" when he urges her to top her sisters' absurdities. Though she loves him most and is true to him, he rages at her refusal to play his game. He cuts off her inheritance and divides his kingdom between the hypocritical Goneril and Regan. The noble Earl of Kent tries to dissuade Lear from his folly, but Lear is adamant.

Disillusionment is not long in coming. The second scene introduces a subplot, to be touched upon later. The third scene foreshadows the tragedy to come. Goneril is the wife of the Duke of Albany, a virtuous but weak man who discovers his wife's villainy too late. Lear visits Goneril's castle. She finds fault with the King's entourage and makes plans to be rid of him.

Also too late, Lear begins to realize the stupidity of his actions. His new insights are strengthened by his jester, the Fool, who has constantly tried to open Lear's eyes to the folly of his actions. At one point, the Fool says,"Thou should'st not have been old till thou hadst been wise."

Regan, a less developed character than her sister Goneril, agrees with her that Lear must dismiss all his followers. Shorn of all power, humiliated, Lear rages into the stormy night, accompanied by the Fool.

The subplot mirrors the main plot. The Earl of Gloucester has two sons, Edgar and Edmund. Like Goneril and Regan, the illegitimate son, Edmund, is a villain seeking to inherit the lands of his father Gloucester. Like Lear, Gloucester is deceived, banishing his good and faithful son Edgar.

Because Gloucester has been faithful to Lear, now an outcast, Edmund turns Gloucester over to his enemy, the Duke of Cornwall, Regan's husband. In collusion with Edmund, Cornwall places the absent Edgar under the sentence of death. Accusing Gloucester of colluding with their enemies, Regan and Cornwall confront him; Cornwall blinds Gloucester and is in turn killed by a shocked servant. Now without a husband, Regan sets her eyes on Edmund, Goneril's lover.

Perhaps the most famous scenes in King Lear occur on the heath in a raging storm. Gloucester, turned out, wanders on the heath, led by an old man. He meets his son Edgar, who has been pretending madness as a disguise. Eyeless, Gloucester does not recognize him. Ultimately, the two old men, Lear and Gloucester, come together on the heath, both victims of the serpent's tooth. Lear is quite mad, but his madness has flashes of brilliant poetry and insight.

The King of France is leading an invading army to right the wrong done to Cordelia and her father. Unfortunately, the King is called away, and Cordelia is left with the army. She sends men out to find Lear on the Heath, but when found, Lear mistrusts the men and runs away. At this point, Oswald, Goneril's evil steward, arrives on the scene and attempts to kill Gloucester. Edgar steps in and kills Oswald. As he lies dying, Oswald gives Edgar a letter to deliver to Edmund. In it, Goneril professes her love for Edmund and seeks the death of her husband Albany.

A gentle scene before the bloody resolution at the end brings Cordelia and Lear together for a touching reconciliation. Lear apologizes profusely for his stupidities and says, "Pray you now, forget and forgive. I am old and foolish." Thus does Lear come to an understanding of his weaknesses and overbearing behavior. Their happiness is short-lived.

As Edmund and Regan prepare for battle, Goneril and Albany appear. Goneril, who loves Edmund, says in an aside that she'd rather lose the battle than lose Edmund to Regan. Edgar, disguised, gives Albany a letter that reveals the villainy of Edmund and Goneril. Edmund weighs the pros and cons of choosing one sister over another. He reveals a plan to get rid of Albany, Goneril's husband, who has vowed to be merciful to Lear and Cordelia.

The following brief scene shows the army of France, with Cordelia holding her father by the hand. The climactic final scene weaves together the threads of the plot in headlong action. Cordelia and Lear are prisoners of the victorious Edmund. He sends them off with hints to a captain to kill them. With the aid of Edgar, Albany is now aware of Edmund's treachery and orders him arrested. In the ensuing action, Regan dies, poisoned by Goneril, and Goneril kills herself. Edgar enters in full armor and mortally wounds Edmund in a fight.

The end comes rapidly. Lear enters, carrying the body of the slain Cordelia. Kent reappears, bur Lear doesn't recognize him. A messenger announces that Edmund is dead. Lear tries to believe that Cordelia is not really dead, but when he realizes the truth, he dies. Albany accepts Edgar and Kent as the rulers of "this realm," but Kent says he has not long to live. The play ends with Edgar's statement that Lear's woes will not be seen again.

A summary cannot do justice to the range and power of King Lear. The theme has been characterized as the spiritual rebirth of a vain and arrogant ruler through adversity and tragedy. Throughout the play, the forces of evil are personified by Goneril, Regan, Cornwall, and Edmund. Though ultimately defeated, these forces destroy Lear and Gloucester, who had brought tragedy on themselves. But blameless Cordelia also suffers, perhaps indicating that justice does not necessarily prevail in this life. As usual, Shakespeare provides many questions, but he doesn't always provide answers.

An interesting postscript: Brian Annesley, a contemporary of Shakespeare, may have been the model for King Lear. Two of his three daughters sought control of his estate, seeking to have him committed as insane. The third daughter fought for her father and made sure that his waning months were spent in the care of a family friend, not the mad-house. Her name was Cordell!

Macbeth

Almost since its creation, *Macbeth* has been enduringly popular on the stage. Although at some periods "improved" by lesser playwrights, Macbeth has risen above inept editors and egocentric actors and has retained a central place in the Shakespeare repertory. Probably written about 1606, it flatters the reigning monarch, James I. Scholars have found references to contemporary events, helping to support the suggested date of composition.

Usually labeled one of the four great tragedies, *Macbeth* is by far the shortest. *Hamlet* is almost twice as long. This brevity increases its dramatic impact. Events occur in rapid succession with scarcely a breath for contemplation. Only one episode, the Porter scene in Act II (p 78), breaks the mood temporarily, as events move toward their inevitable climax.

The play's opening immediately sets the tone of the play. Three mysterious Witches announce a meeting with Macbeth. With headlong haste, the second scene sets the plot in motion. A messenger reports to King Duncan the news of the battle between Duncan's forces on one side and a combination of Norwegian invaders and a local traitor on the other. During this combat, Macbeth has distinguished himself, helping to defeat the Norwegian invaders and actually killing the disloyal Thane of Cawdor. Duncan praises Macbeth and instantly adds the title of Cawdor to Macbeth's own title, Thane of Glamis.

In scene three, Duncan and his friend Banquo come upon the Three Witches, who have previously mentioned Macbeth. They hail Macbeth as Thane of Glamis (his present title), Thane of Cawdor (his new title) and "King hereafter." They prophesy that Banquo will beget kings. After they vanish, the Thanes Ross and Angus arrive with news that Macbeth has just been made Thane of Cawdor. Since one prophecy has come true, Macbeth wonders whether the second prophecy will also. He decides, "If chance will have me king, why, chance will crown me." If Macbeth had followed up on that prophecy, the tragedy would not have occurred.

When Macbeth is reunited with King Duncan, he is praised for his loyal service. Duncan promises further advancement for Macbeth and then announces that he has designated his son Malcolm as the next in line for the throne. Macbeth's hopes for the crown, so recently aroused, are dashed by the news that the younger Malcolm will take the throne prophesied for him by the Three Witches.

Since Duncan is to visit Inverness, Macbeth's castle, Macbeth writes to his wife to tell her of the king's coming visit and of the Witches' prophecy. The possibility of Macbeth's becoming king is a topic that has evidently been in their thoughts. The Witches' prophecy has fueled that ambition, but Duncan's announcement of Malcolm's succession has dashed it.

When Macbeth arrives home, Lady Macbeth incites her husband to murder the coming houseguest. Temporarily willing to put matters off, Macbeth finally yields to his wife's persuasion and murders Duncan in his sleep. In his revulsion at the deed, he fails to smear Duncan's drugged guards with blood and even returns to Lady Macbeth with the bloody daggers in his hands. She is disgusted with him and goes to the bedchamber herself and arranges the scene to throw guilt on the sleeping guards.

Then there is a knocking at the gate (p 78) of the castle. Lennox and Macduff have arrived to call upon King Duncan. Macduff goes to the bedchamber to rouse the king and returns crying, "O, horror, horror, horror." Lennox and Macbeth go to see for themselves. Macbeth kills the groggy guards, thus eliminating any protestations of their innocence but also arousing suspicion in the minds of the guests. Feeling insecure themselves in this house of blood, Malcolm and Donalbain, Duncan's sons, flee for their lives.

Their flight opens the door for Macbeth's accession to the throne, but it is an uneasy reign. Macduff joins Malcolm in exile in England. Banquo, who also had a favorable prophecy from the Witches, has a different reaction. He considers them creatures of evil and fears that Macbeth has "played most foully" for the crown. Macbeth considers Banquo a threat and hires murderers to kill both Banquo and his son Fleance. The murderers kill Banquo, but Fleance escapes, thus leaving the way to the prophecy that Banquo's descendants will be kings. At the banquet after Banquo's murder, his ghost appears but only to Macbeth.

Macbeth sinks deeper into villainy. Not able to reach Macduff, he has Macduff's wife and children slain. As Macbeth becomes stronger in evil, Lady Macbeth becomes weaker. She begins to disintegrate under the weight of the evil she has been part of.

Seeking further help in retaining his kingdom, Macbeth visits the Witches again. They give him seemingly unassailable advice. No man born of woman can conquer Macbeth. He cannot be defeated until Birnam Wood comes to his castle, Dunsinane. The Witches also make clear that Banquo's descendants will indeed become kings. The reigning monarch, James I, was of this line.

In England, Macduff has sought out Malcolm to urge him to depose the monster Macbeth. When news of the massacre of his family reaches Macduff, he is doubly bent on revenge. Lady Macbeth herself dies after suffering the pangs of conscience.

The denouement is rapid, with scene after scene in quick order, jumping back and forth from the forces of Malcolm and Macduff to the castle manned by Macbeth. Malcolm's army chooses camouflage, carrying boughs from Birnam Wood. Thus Birnam Wood does indeed come to Dunsinane.

Though apparently safe in his fortified castle, Macbeth impetuously strides forth to attack the enemy. He feels secure in the prophecy that no man of woman born can harm him, but Macduff was "from his mother's womb untimely ripped." This news unsettles Macbeth and he is himself slain by Macduff.

Macbeth has made a Faustian pact with the forces of evil, but the association ultimately destroys him. The Witches' prophecies have all been double-edged, superficially positive, but ultimately deadly.

25

The Problem Plays

No ceremony that to great ones longs,
Not the king's crown, nor the deputed sword,
The marshall's truncheon, nor the judge's robe,
Became them with one half so good a grace
As mercy does.

Measure for Measure, II, 2, 64-68

The comedies in this section, along with *Troilus and Cressida* (p267), are often labeled "dark comedies" or "problem plays." The latter designation was unknown in Shakespeare's day. The phrase as applied to these plays was first used by Frederick S. Boas, a Shakespearean scholar in 1896. The great contemporary dramatists of Boas's day were Henrik Ibsen and George Bernard Shaw, playwrights whose plays dealt with social problems and moral dilemmas: "problem plays." Boas saw their similarity to these Shakespeare plays.

The plays in this group were not popular in Shakespeare's day, generally overlooked on the stage for a century or more. By the end of the 19th century, however, they were being reappraised and performed. Shaw, a frequent critic of Shakespeare (p 75), found much to appreciate in these "problem plays." He said in 1907 that in these plays Shakespeare "was ready and willing to start at the twentieth century if the seventeenth century would only let him."

Recent productions have demonstrated Shaw's foresight.

All's Well That Ends Well

All's Well That Ends Well is often grouped with *Measure for Measure* and *Troilus and Cressida* as "problem plays." They have a dark tone, sometimes bitterly commenting on human nature. They show the characters' actions cynically. Bertram in *All's Well That Ends Well* and Angelo in *Measure for Measure* are deeply flawed human beings, but there is a difference between the fate of these characters and that of the tragic heroes of *Macbeth* and *Othello*. *All's Well* and *Measure for Measure* are comedies, dark comedies to be sure, but at the end of both plays, happiness and reconciliation prevail.

The conjectured date for the play is 1602-1603. This is the period of the great tragedies: *Hamlet* perhaps a bit earlier; and *Othello*, *Lear*, and *Macbeth* a bit later. Does the somber turn reflect a change in Shakespeare because of his private life? Or did the mood of the audiences favor tragedy at this time? No one knows; perhaps there is truth in both possibilities.

The heroine of the play, Helena, is hopelessly in love with Bertram, the son of the Countess of Roussillon. Since Helena is not of noble birth and is but an attendant on the Countess, she pines for Bertram fruitlessly. A favorite of the Countess, Helena reveals her love and her acceptance of its hopelessness.

Bertram is at the court of the King, who is suffering from a serious illness. Helena's dead father had been a skilled physician, and Helena had learned many of his skills. The Countess gives Helena permission to go to the King's court to see whether she can heal the King.

Helena arrives at the court and is ushered into the King's presence. She vows to cure the King within 24 hours on pain of disgrace, torture, or death. She asks one favor: to be given the husband of her choice. The King is cured. The court is assembled. Helena picks Bertram as her choice of husband. Bertram is furious at the thought of marrying a poor physician's daughter. Embarrassed, Helena says to the King, "That you are well restored my lord, I'm glad; let the rest go." The King has pledged his word, however, and insists that Bertram marry Helena. They marry, but Bertram has other plans.

He claims urgent business, sends Helena back to his mother, the Countess, and departs with an unsavory character, Parolles. Despite his bluster, Bertram is easily led. Parolles is a despicable character, who caters to Bertram's basest instincts. He persuades Bertram to disobey the King and run off to the wars in Italy. He is unmasked later in the play, but by then the damage has been done.

Bertram informs the Countess by letter that he is determined not to live with Helena. In another letter, to Helena, Bertram says, "When thou canst get the ring upon my finger, which never shall come off, and show me a child begotten of thy body that I am father to, then call me husband: but in such a 'then' I write a 'never'." Shakespeare is tapping into two medieval folktales stories.

In one, a devoted and virtuous woman wins the love of a contemptuous man. She overcomes impossible conditions and wins a husband and his respect. In the second story, the wife arranges her husband's assignation with another woman, whom he has pursued. She then substitutes herself in bed.

In Florence, Bertram has been leading a life of excess. He has been fruitlessly pursuing Diana, a virtuous young woman. When Helena arrives on the scene and identifies herself as Bertram's wife Helena, Diana, and Diana's widowed mother devise a plot to trap Bertram. Diana promises to sleep with Bertram if he gives her his family ring and if he accepts her silence during the assignation. She, in turn, will give him a ring. He accepts her silence during the assignation. The deception works. Helena takes Diana's place and becomes pregnant with Bertram's child.

Everything comes to climax back at Roussillion. Helena has been reported dead. The King mourns the passing of this deserving lady. But he reluctantly forgives Bertram for his lack of respect for Helena. The faithful courtier Lafeu proposes that Bertram marry his own daughter. Bertram agrees and gives Lafeu a ring, which the old lord recognizes as Helena's. The King supports the identification. Bertram claims it was thrown from a casement window in Florence. The King disbelieves Bertram and has him hauled away.

Into this tense situation come Diana and her mother. Bertram is brought back to face the charge that he has promised to marry Diana. Unchivalrously, Bertram admits his assignation but calls Diana a common "gamester." Just as complications threaten the stability of the court, Helena arrives on the scene and claims she has fulfilled Bertram's conditions. She is pregnant with Bertram's child. She has his ring. In the ensuing joy at this revelation, Bertram declares, "If she, my liege, can make me know this clearly, I'll love her dearly, ever, ever-dearly." He never says another word.

Measure for Measure

Like *All's Well That Ends Well* and *Troilus and Cressida*, *Measure for Measure* is a bleak play with its focus on evil and the contradictions of the human spirit. Yet it is classified as a comedy. Everything turns out right in the end. Evil is overcome and virtue is rewarded.., but only after clever manipulation by two strong women and a determined man. Never among Shakespeare's most popular plays, *Measure for Measure* has enjoyed more favorable recognition in recent times.

Some modern audiences are disturbed by the manufactured happy ending, but others relish Shakespeare's genius in handling light and dark with dramatic skill. The central puzzling character, Angelo, doesn't easily yield the secret of his personality, as it vacillates from noble to the ignoble. What kind of person is he anyway? He is not a typical heroic literary character, one with whom the audience can feel some identification. Yet his downfall at the end, so dearly hoped for by the audience, provides some disquieting elements, as Angelo requests that he be executed for his actions. Nothing human is alien to Shakespeare.

At the beginning of the play, the Duke of Vienna decides to leave the administration of the city to Angelo, his puritanically upright deputy. Trusted old Escalus will be Angelo's second in command. The Duke has regretted his own laxity in enforcing laws of morality. He feels that a more rigid enforcement might be more prudent and effective if exercised by the saintly Angelo. The Duke assumes a disguise and roams the city to take the pulse of the populace.

Unfortunately, the apparently pious, upright Angelo takes his charge too literally. In his zeal to clean up the city's morals, he orders that Claudio be put to death because he has made Juliet pregnant before marriage. Actually, the two had every intention to wed, but the ceremonies were held up over a dowry dispute. Claudio and Juliet are eager to marry, but Angelo says, in effect, "Too late." Angelo reveals early that he is more concerned with the letter of the law than with its spirit. Escalus pleads for mercy, but Angelo is obdurate.

Claudio's sister, Isabella, who is about to enter a convent, hears of her brother's plight and visits Angelo to ask for mercy for her brother. He falls passionately in love with her and offers clemency for Claudio if Isabella will become his lover. She is shocked and refuses. Angelo, a paragon of virtue swears that he will have Claudio tortured if she continues to refuse. He gives her a day to reconsider.

When Isabella visits Claudio in his cell and informs him of Angelo's threats, he at first heartily supports her refusal. As he thinks about it, though, the prospect of death overcomes his scruples, and he pleads with Isabella to yield and save his life. She berates him bitterly and leaves. The conversation has been overheard by the wandering Duke, disguised as Friar Lodowick.

He intercepts Isabella and unfolds a plan to save her brother. Angelo had once abandoned a woman named Mariana after promising marriage. She still loves Angelo and is willing to play a role in the Duke's plot. Isabella is to agree to have sex with Angelo but only if she is silent and the tryst is consummated in darkness. Mariana will substitute for Isabella, and Angelo will have to marry his rejected lover. This "bed trick," so similar to the deception in *All's Well That Ends Well* (p300), is a reversal. Here, the partner is the former lover, not the present wife.

Meanwhile, the hypocritical Angelo has continued to demand the execution of Claudio, requiring his head as proof. The Friar/Duke stops Claudio's execution, planning to send the head of the criminal Barnardine instead. Barnardine (p166) has been in prison so long he has acquired an affection for it. Perennially drunk, he refuses to be executed on the day appointed. Another prisoner has died and his head is sent to Angelo as "proof" of Claudio's execution.

Escalus and Angelo discuss the Duke's parting instructions about the public proclamation of complaints. Angelo finally realizes the magnitude of his sins, but he is still a deceiver. He wears the mantle of sanctity until his villainy is revealed in the final scene.

Another member of the plan, Friar Peter, arrives with Mariana at the city gate to charge Angelo with having had sex with her. Angelo bitterly rejects this charge, saying he hadn't seen Mariana in years. The Duke, as Friar Lodowick, is sent for to substantiate the charge. When the Duke reveals himself, Angelo realizes his guilt and confesses, seeking his own death as punishment. The Duke orders Angelo to marry Mariana immediately. When they return, he orders Angelo put to death, just as Angelo has ordered Claudio's death. After all, this will be "measure for measure."

Mariana pleads for her husband's life. Isabella adds her plea for clemency, demonstrating vividly the triumph of mercy over vindictiveness. The Duke relents. He forgives not only Angelo, but also Barnardine and Lucio. A minor character but a colorful one, Lucio is a witty, obnoxious, unsavory cog in the major plot. At times, he is not without good qualities of loyalty and friendship, but he is treacherous and slanderous, particularly in respect to the Duke, whom he doesn't recognize in his friar's habit. He has boasted of abandoning a pregnant woman and is ordered to marry her, after which he is to be whipped and hanged. In the general spirit of forgiveness and mercy, however, the Duke spares Lucio, who is considered Lucifer in some interpretation.

During the final scene, Claudio is brought in, very much alive, to general rejoicing. The Duke, who has come to know and love Isabella during their joint plotting against Angelo, actually proposes to Isabella as the play ends. Isabella has been silent after earlier pleading in the last scene. Her reaction to the Duke's proposal is assumed by most directors to be favorable, Shakespeare's probable intention. How have Isabella's vows to enter the nunnery been overcome by her realization that she has been, in her own way, as obsessive as Angelo?

The day has colorful minor characters on the fringes of the action, most of them funny but unsavory. They underline the corruption of Vienna and suggest the need for corrective action, presumably offered by the Duke with his new insights. Once again, Shakespeare's handling of the source material reveals the complexity of his mind and his understanding of human faults.

26

The Final Plays

Our revels now are ended. These our actors
As I foretold you, were all spirits, and
Are melted into air, into thin air.

The Tempest, IV, 1, 248-150

The plays Shakespeare wrote shortly before retiring have a special quality. They introduce tragic events, but there is a reconciling peace that mutes the tragedies. The playwright seems more mellow. There are still villains (Iachimo in *Cymbeline*), headstrong, arrogant tyrants (Leontes in *The Winter's Tale* and Cymbeline); there are even ugly monsters (Caliban in *The Tempest*), but their failings are forgiven and peace prevails. Even in *Henry VIII*, the play ends with hope for the infant Elizabeth and before the bloody sequels involving Henry's wives. Like Prospero in *The Tempest*, Shakespeare seems to be saying,

the rarer action is
In virtue than in vengeance.

The Tempest, V, 1, 27-28

There is no discernible deterioration in Shakespeare's powers as he enters the final years of his creative life, indeed of life itself. There are segments in all four plays that reveal the master's skill. Characterization is still masterful. Complex characters like Prospero delight audiences with their humanity and unpredictability. Some of the finest imagery may be uttered by the demonic character Caliban. If this is the twilight of a career, it's a dazzling one.

A word about one more play. *The Two Noble Kinsman* (p197) did not appear in the First Folio. It was long dismissed as non-Shakespearean, but recent scholarship would restore portions of the play to Shakespeare. The first known text is a quarto published in 1634. It's credited to both Shakespeare and John Fletcher (p 56) as authors. The play may have been performed in 1613, the same year as *Henry VIII*.

To decide whether or not Shakespeare actually wrote any of *The Two Noble Kinsmen*, scholars use internal evidence. "Does this passage sound like Shakespeare? Does it resemble passages from other plays? Does the theme sound like a theme that Shakespeare would have liked?" It's suggested that Shakespeare may have written the first scenes of Act I and Act V. At this stage in his life, Shakespeare might find the creation of an entire play too demanding, but some collaboration with younger playwrights might keep his creative juices flowing without the stress of a full play. Shakespeare didn't realize that he'd be writing for the third millennium!

The four plays in this section were written by a mature craftsman whose skill remained undiminished, whose facility with words fulfilled the promise of a lifetime, and whose philosophy of life, though perhaps a bit mellowed and melancholy, contained an acceptance born of long experience.

Pericles, Prince of Tyre

Though not originally included in the First Folio (p 85), *Pericles* is now usually included in anthologies of Shakespeare's work. It was popular in its day, a popularity continuing through the early 17th century. Then it fell into obscurity. It appeared in 1738 in a mutilated adaptation and in 1854, in a greatly abridged version. Victorian tastes insisted that the play be sanitized. Only three other productions are known before World War I—and two of them were German. Five productions in three centuries is scarcely an indication of great popularity. Since then it has been produced occasionally. Perhaps its abstractions are more acceptable to the 20th and 21st centuries.

Pericles is a transitional work between the problem plays and the final romances. The combination of comedy and tragedy comes to flower in plays like *The Winter's Tale*. The plot is absurd, calling upon readers and listeners for that "willing suspension of disbelief that constitutes poetic faith." Directed by conventions of folklore and romances, the events proceed at a rapid rate unhampered by logic. Still, on the stage, *Pericles* is a good show.

Many characters in *Pericles* are symbols of good and evil, not flesh-and-blood human beings. Goodness and love are constantly challenged. The play's pattern has been described as concerned with winter and spring, death and rebirth, finding and losing. Pericles himself has been called an "allegorical protagonist." He is a good man who accepts his fate and is rewarded at the end.

The Prologue sets the stage for the events that follow. King Antiochus has a beautiful daughter. He will relinquish her in marriage only to the suitor who can solve a riddle. Failure to solve the riddle means death. The secret of the riddle is Antiochus's incest with his daughter.

In scene I, Pericles declares his intention to solve the riddle and win the beautiful daughter. Antiochus tries to dissuade him, warning him of the fate suffered by his predecessors. When Pericles hears the riddle, he understands it immediately but realizes that he is in a no-win situation. Exposing the secret is fraught with danger. Refusing will mean his death. Though Pericles doesn't blurt out the answer, the king realizes that Pericles knows the guilty secret. He gives Pericles a 40-day grace period to answer, intending to murder Pericles before the time is up. Pericles senses his danger and flees, pursued by Thaliard, a lord of Antioch.

Back in his own city Tyre, Pericles fears that the powerful Antiochus will devastate his country. He leaves Tyre, putting the faithful Helicanus in charge. The rest of the play is like a picaresque novel, in which the hero goes in and out of danger, experiencing many ups and downs before settling down in peace.

Pericles' first stop is Tarsus, which has been suffering from famine. Cleon, Governor of Tarsus, and his wife Dionyza welcome the grain that Pericles has brought from Tyre. Pericles is happy in his new setting, but his happiness is short-lived. Word comes that Tarsus is no longer safe for him, and Pericles sets forth again.

Pericles runs into a raging tempest and is shipwrecked near Pentapolis, where he is befriended by three fishermen. A rusty suit of armor turns up in the fishermen's net, armor that had once belonged to Pericles' father! In a picaresque novel, coincidences run rife, as here. The fishermen give the armor to Pericles so that he can compete in a tournament honoring Thaisa, daughter of King Simonides.

Not surprisingly, Pericles wins the tournament, the eye of Thaisa, and the respect of Simonides. He and Thaisa are married, conceiving a child. Pericles receives a letter announcing the death of his old enemy Antiochus and calling him back to take his place as the rightful ruler of Tyre. Though pregnant, Thaisa insists on accompanying him.

Another great storm, this time with Thaisa in labor! Supposedly dead in childbirth, Thaisa's body is thrown overboard in a waterproof casket. The little infant is brought to Pericles. Since the ship is nearer to Tarsus than Tyre, Pericles orders a change of course. He leaves the infant Marina in the care of Cleon and Dionyza and proceeds to Tyre.

Meanwhile, Thaisa's floating casket has reached Ephesus, where a doctor determines she is not dead. She revives, examines the articles found in her coffin, but doesn't recall whether her child was born at sea. Hopeless, she becomes a votaress of Diana's temple at Ephesus.

Years have passed. Marina has become a beautiful woman and aroused the jealousy of Dionyza, whose own daughter has been overshadowed by

Marina. Dionyza arranges to have Marina murdered, but Marina is captured by pirates before she can be killed.

Marina is taken to Mytilene by the pirates and sold to Boult, an agent for a brothel. Marina vows to die rather than lose her virginity. Two gentlemen leave the brothel, purified by Marina's chaste example. Her purity attracts Lysimachus, governor of Mytilene. He takes her under his wing and promises to protect her. Bouit and his partner are annoyed at Marina's purity and vow to have her deflowered so that she can be fit for prostitution. Marina convinces the crude Boult that she would probably make more money for him by giving music lessons. She becomes successful as a teacher of singing and needlework.

Pericles has voyaged to Tarsus to see his daughter, but instead is shown her supposed tomb, erected to allay any charges against the governor and his evil wife. When he leaves, sorrowing, he runs into another storm! He eventually arrives at Mytilene, where Marina has been reforming those around her.

Pericles has been overwhelmed by sorrow, not fit company for visitors. To cheer him up, Lysymachus brings Marina aboard in the hope that her bright and cheerful goodness will rouse Pericles from his sorrow. When Marina tells her story, he joyfully recognizes her as his daughter. But there are virtues still to be rewarded.

In a vision, the goddess Diana tells Pericles to come to her temple at Ephesus. He goes, and at the altar, he tells of Thaisa's death in childbirth on the sea. The High Priestess, Thaisa herself, faints, and the pair are lovingly reunited. Marina is joined with her long-lost mother. The noble Lysimachus will marry Marina and rule with her in Tyre, while Thaisa and Pericles will rule in Pentapolis.

Whew! Goodness has prevailed.

Cymbeline

The editors of the First Folio placed Cymbeline among the tragedies, but most modern scholars consider it a romance with some tragic elements, a *tragicomedy*, as some label it. Since there is no available quarto for *Cymbeline*, we must rely on the First Folio for the text.

When the King's Men bought Blackfriars (p 27) in 1608, they sought plays suited to an indoor theater. *Cymbeline* may well have been the first Shakespearean play to be performed in the new home.

The play fluctuates between fantasy and reality. Romantic, fairy-tale elements appear: the wicked stepmother, the sleeping beauty, the radiant put-upon princess, kidnapped children, a decoded riddle, and crucial bodily marks as signs of identification. Interlaced with these are realistic elements, like battle scenes and a conversation between two national leaders, each with a legitimate axe to grind.

Some favorite Shakespearean elements also appear: the banished hero, the disguised heroine (actually a boy playing a girl disguised as a boy), a grieving lover who thinks his love is dead, a final scene of explanation and general reconciliation.

To advance the plot, Shakespeare introduces Iachimo, an Italian gentleman and con man, whose activities almost destroy the main character. Though the name *Iachimo* suggests "Little Iago," Iachimo is no Iago. His villainy is less deadly, his gestures and explanations almost comic.

Shakespeare has woven three different strands into the complicated plot of *Cymbeline*. The plot of greatest interest to the audience is the interrupted love affair of Imogen and Posthumus, so-called because he was born after his father's death. A second plot is the war between Rome and native Britons. A third plot involves two kidnapped boys and their supposed father. All three plots are tied together at the end in good Shakespearean fashion.

Crusty Cymbeline, King of ancient Britain, has strongly disapproved of his daughter Imogen's marriage to Posthumus Leonatus, once a favorite of the King. He insists that she marry instead the loutish Cloten, son of the Queen, his evil second wife. The devious Queen seems to be helping the married lovers, while secretly plotting their downfall.

Cymbeline catches the two lovers together and banishes Posthumus. Imogen continues to rebuff Cloten and to seek news of her beloved Posthumus from Pisanio, his loyal servant.

Complications inevitably follow. In Rome, Posthumus is goaded by Iachimo into a wager on Imogen's virtue. Through a subterfuge, Iachimo is smuggled in a trunk into her room. At night, he comes out of the trunk, inventories the room, slips a bracelet from her wrist, and notes a mole under her left breast. Armed with this information and the bracelet, Iachimo convinces Posthumus that he has indeed seduced Imogen. Posthumus flies into a rage and plots the death of the "faithless" Imogen.

Events proceed rapidly. Imogen leaves for Wales in the company of Pisanio, supposedly to meet Posthumus. Tortured by anxiety, Pisanio shows Imogen the letter ordering him to kill her. She is distraught by the news and asks Pisanio to kill her, but he refuses, urging her instead to dress in boy's clothing for safety. During her wanderings in the forest, she meets the two kidnaped sons of Cymbeline, abducted many years ago when their adoptive father was unfairly banished by Cymbeline. All three have been leading a quiet existence-too quiet for the boys.

Cloten is in the forest, too, searching for Imogen. Always arrogant, he gets into a sword fight with one of the sons, is defeated and beheaded. His head is thrown into a stream, but his lifeless body is treated respectfully and covered before burial. It is his body that Imogen later mistakes for her husband's.

Feeling ill, Imogen drinks the potion given her by Pisanio supposedly for seasickness or any other ailment. In this matter, Pisanio has been deceived by the Queen, who had in turn been deceived by the doctor. She had asked for a poison, but he had given her instead a sleeping potion. It is this potion that the Queen has given Pisanio. When Imogen falls into a deathlike sleep, she is mourned by the three men. Her body is placed next to Cloten's. When she wakes, she thinks the body is Posthumus's.

The political background of the play impinges upon the lives of the two lovers. Because of Cymbeline's nonpayment of the yearly tribute, a Roman army is marching against the Britons. During the ensuing battle, the two sons of Cymbeline also join the fray, along with their supposed father. They play a major role in the British victory.

Posthumus is in the battle, too. Having received a bloody handkerchief from Pisanio as proof of the killing of Imogen, he regrets his stupidity and goes mad with grief. During the battle, he hopes to be killed.

All the plot lines converge in the final hectic scene. Cymbeline is noti-fied of the death of his Queen, who has confessed her evil designs. Imogen, still in page's clothes, gets Iachimo to confess his evil deed. Posthumus urges Cymbeline to sentence him to death for the "murder" of Imogen. Imogen throws herself upon him, is momentarily rebuffed, then joyously grasped in his arms when she reveals her true identity. Posthumus even forgives Iachimo. Cymbeline is reunited with his two lost sons, and their supposed father is pardoned. Britons and Romans reach an amicable agreement. In this general atmosphere of peace, love, joy, and hope, the play ends.

The Winter's Tale

Like *Cymbeline, The Winter's Tale* doesn't fit into easy classifications. Considered by some critics a step up in the manipulation of comic and tragic elements, it introduces characters and events that would make strange bedfellows in plays by lesser authors. The exotic and the magical mingle with recognizable characters and situations.

As one of Shakespeare's last plays, *The Winter's Tale* shows a maturity that combines grim tragedy with wholesome optimism. The play is divided into two halves, each with its own tone and mood, the first essen-tially tragic, the second ultimately joyous.

The source of the play is Robert Greene's *Pandosto* (p 48), but Shakespeare makes many changes, including the creation of the character Autolycus. The idea of the statue brought to life may have come from Ovid's story of Pygmalion. A recorded performance on May 15, 1611, helps date the play.

The opening scene sets the stage, preparing us to meet Leontes, King of Sicilia, and his old friend, Polixenes, King of Bohemia. Polixenes informs his host that he must return home the next day. Deaf to Leontes' entreaties, Polixenes finally yields to the entreaties of Leontes' wife Hermione. Despite the fact that she had acted only at his urging, Leontes becomes unaccountably jealous. He orders his faithful servant Camillo to kill Polixenes and has Hermione locked away.

Camillo, understandably shocked and frightened, informs Polixenes, and they flee the raging tyrant. Leontes takes the flight as proof of his suspicions. He even questions the fatherhood of his lovable son Mamillius. His ultimate insanity is his rejection of his daughter, newly delivered by his wife Hermione.

Paulina, wife of Antigonus, a faithful courtier, brings the new baby in to Leontes to soften his heart. He is further enraged, at first ordering the child killed. His nobles are so shocked by this decision that they prevail upon him to rescind that order-but only slightly. He orders Antigonus to take the child to some far-off place and there abandon her. To prove how right he is, he sends messengers to the oracle of Apollo at Delphos to support his accusations.

The messengers return. Leontes has the full court ready to hear justification for his accusations against Hermione. When the message is unsealed, all Leontes' accusations are refuted. It concludes with the cryptic "The king shall live without an heir, if that which is lost be not found." The audience thinks, "Why is this? Leontes still has his son Mamillius." At the very moment when Leontes is disputing the oracle, a messenger arrives to announce the death of Mamillius, brokenhearted at his mother's ill treatment.

Leontes blames himself for angering Apollo. Hermione faints upon hearing the news, and Leontes does an about-face. Hermione is removed. Paulina returns with the news that Hermione is dead. The scene ends with Leontes expressing the deepest remorse.

The scene shifts to a desert part of Bohemia. Antigonus has brought the infant daughter to be abandoned as he was ordered to do. His speeches end with one of the most famous exits in Shakespeare: "Exit pursued by a bear." This moves Antigonus from the tale.

The bleak tone of the play ends. A shepherd and his slow-witted son find the little girl and take her home with them. At this point, a narrator tells the audience that sixteen years have passed. The abandoned girl, Perdita, has become a beautiful young woman beloved of Florizel, daughter of Polixenes.

Then follow brilliant scenes of country life, with rustic characters adding life and color to the play. At the sheep-shearing, Polixenes and Camillo disguise themselves to spy on Florizel and this young woman. Though they are charmed by Perdita, they denounce this marriage between a prince and a shepherdess. Florizel refuses to give Perdita up, arranges to flee, with the help of Camillo, who wants to return to Sicilia.

At the court of Leontes, now a thoroughly chastened man, everything is resolved. Perdita is revealed as Leontes's daughter, thus fulfilling the prophecy. Hermione is displayed as a marvelous statue, which comes to life into the arms of Leontes. Polixenes and Leontes are reunited as friends. Leontes generously gives good old Camillo to the fiery Paulina. All is well.

Autolycus, Shakespeare's creation, has little to do with the plot, but his actions charm audiences. He adds an extra note of gaiety to the country scenes. He's a rogue, a pickpocket, a thief, always looking for an easy gain. He's in and out in the last two acts, but ironically the two he has deceived, the Shepherd and his son, do very well, with Autolycus's inadvertent help.

In some performances, one actress has played the roles of Perdita and Hermione, an interesting but not insurmountable challenge.

The Tempest

Written near the end of Shakespeare's productive life, this may have been the last play written entirely by Shakespeare: *Henry VIII*, which followed, may well have involved the collaborative efforts of John Fletcher. A still later time is ascribed to *The Two Noble Kinsmen*, a play wholly in dispute. Some scholars refuse to believe that any part of that play was written by Shakespeare, though modern scholars tend to see more and more Shakespearean genius in portions of the play. One argument against *The Two Noble Kinsmen* is that it did not appear in the First Folio (page), but then neither did *Pericles*, though *Pericles*, now accepted, did appear later, in the Third Folio.

At any rate, *The Tempest* is clearly part of the canon. Many commentators have seen in the figure of Prospero the artist-magician, Shakespeare himself. When Prospero breaks his staff and buries his book of magic,

Shakespeare may be saying farewell to the London stage, which challenged his genius for more than two decades.

The Tempest opens with a storm that threatens a ship at sea. On board, are Alonso, king of Naples; his brother Sebastian; and Antonio, evil brother of Prospero. Antonio had deposed Prospero as Duke of Milan, with Alonso's help. These three men of sin will soon be under Prospero's control, for it is he who stirred up the storm that caused the shipwreck. Also on board is Ferdinand, son of Alonso, who is presumed lost by his grief-stricken father.

The scene shifts to Prospero's island. Miranda accuses her father, Prospero, of causing the storm that so terrified those on board the ship. He tells her that on board the ship were those who caused his ruin. He assures her that no one has been hurt, but the evildoers have been brought fortuitously to his island. He bids her sleep and welcomes Ariel.

Ariel is "an airy spirit," who had once been imprisoned in a tree trunk by a witch. Freed by Prospero's magic, he must remain subservient to Prospero, until released by him. Ariel does the bidding of Prospero and helps substantially in the plans designed to chasten the villains.

An opposite spirit, also under the control of Prospero, is Caliban, son of a devil and a witch. Taught by Prospero to talk and function like a human being, Caliban has never been truly civilized, having tried at one point to rape Miranda. He is variously called a "monster," a "born devil," and a "thing of darkness." Yet Caliban generates the audience's sympathy, too.

He is, after all, a prisoner yearning for freedom. Though brutish by nature, he has some of the finest poetry in the play. He refuses to sink to the level of some of the degenerate human beings also cast ashore. When Prospero offers him pardon at the end, Caliban says, "I'll be wise hereafter and seek for grace."

The first castaway we meet is Ferdinand, blameless son of an evil father. Ariel lures him to the side of Miranda, and they fall in love. Prospero secretly approves of the love, but he decides to test Ferdinand before giving his blessing.

Other castaways gather on other sides of the island. As Alonso grieves for the loss of his son, a good old counselor, Gonzalo, tries to comfort him. During the ensuing conversation, Ariel enters and puts all to sleep except Alonso, Sebastian, and Antonio, three principal characters. Alonso at last falls to sleep, while Sebastian and Antonio stand guard. The evil Antonio takes this opportunity to urge Sebastian to kill Alonso and take over the kingdom of Naples. As he urges Sebastian to draw his sword, Ariel awakens Gonzalo, who shakes Alonso to awaken. The villains explain the drawn sword, saying that they had been threatened by wild animals. This episode emphasizes the evil balanced against the good and purity of Miranda, Ariel, Prospero, and ultimately Ferdinand.

Comic relief is provided by Stephano, a drunken bully, and Trinculo, professional jester and submissive follower of Stephano. He, too, is drunk most of the time. Caliban first meets Trinculo and thinks that he is one of Prospero's spirits. Stephano enters and gives each one some of his wine. The alcohol tricks Caliban into thinking that Stephano is a god and resolves to serve him. Caliban urges Stephano to kill Prospero, so that he, Stephano, can rule the isle and have the beautiful Miranda. Ariel overhears the plot and speeds away.

The love affair between Ferdinand and Miranda has been progressing. Gradually, Prospero becomes convinced that the two will make a happy pair. He promises Miranda to Ferdinand, and tells Ariel to prepare a proper spectacle for the two lovers.

Ariel has been busy, working his magic on Alonso, who repents and vows to change his life. The plotters-Stephan, Trinculo, and Caliban-are tormented by spirits in the shape of hounds and goblins. All the others have been held in spell by Ariel, so woebegone that Ariel takes pity on them and asks Prospero to release them.

All plot strands come together. Prospero is convinced that the penitence of his brother is real and accepts his rightful place as Duke of Milan. When the others awaken from their sleep, they recognize Prospero and accept him as the Duke. Prospero renounces his magic and prepares to return to civilization. Alonso, still mourning the loss of his son, is joyfully introduced to

Ferdinand and Miranda. As a final gesture, Prospero says to Ariel, "The elements be free, and fare thou well."

Whatever Shakespeare's full intentions may have been, it is tempting to look upon *The Tempest* as a poignant farewell to the theater and all the magic that the stage provides.

27

The Sonnets

> Why, look you now, how unworthy a thing you make of me! You
> would play upon me, you would seek to know my stops, you
> would pluck out the heart of my mystery.

Hamlet, **III**, 2, 362-365

Hamlet's scolding of Rosencrantz and Guildenstern is a fitting commentary on the search to unlock the mysteries of the Sonnets. Scholars have long been trying to "pluck out the heart" of the Sonnets' mysteries, without success.

The 154 poems that constitute Shakespeare's sonnet sequence have intrigued readers ever since their publication in 1609. The collection included a dedication "to Mr. W. H. The only begetter of these ensuing sonnets." Since the Sonnets were probably published without Shakespeare's cooperation or consent, the dedication may be the publisher's idea, not Shakespeare's. Still, the mysterious "Mr. W. H." has been identified with several of Shakespeare's contemporaries. Two frequently mentioned candidates are Henry Wriothesley (W. H. reversed), the Earl of Southampton; and William Herbert, Earl of Pembroke, but these are not the only candidates. Others include Hamnet Shakespeare, the Earl of Essex, and even Queen Elizabeth.

Are the Sonnets autobiographical? One school of scholarship looks for events in Shakespeare's life, experiences reflected specifically in the Sonnets. The other school insists that the Sonnets are great poems, independent of any specific references. Of course, all life experiences influence creative output, but all attempts to pin down "the dark lady of the sonnets," for example, have been met with skepticism.

Sonnet sequences were popular in Shakespeare's day. Borrowed from the Italian sonnets of Petrarch, the English sonnet changed the rhyme scheme of the Petrarchan (p112). Shakespeare used his own in all 154, as well as sonnets introduced into *Romeo and Juliet* and *Love's Labour's Lost*.

At the time Shakespeare composed his Sonnets, at least 20 sonnet sequences were being published, notably Sir Philip Sidney's *Astrophel and Stella*. There is little dispute about the authorship of the Shakespeare sonnets. Some critics deplore #145, a "poor poem" written in tetrameter instead of pentameter (p110). The final sonnets, 153 and 154, seem to have little to do with the rest of the series. Still, even these three are conceded to be by Shakespeare.

The sonnets seem to divide into clear sections. If there is a central appeal, it is a series of views about love and the power of poetry to immortalize it. The major division is between the first 126 addressed to a young man and the others, addressed to a woman. The two major divisions are often subdivided. The sonnets to the young man speak first of his beauty and his obligation to provide children of his quality. Then the sonnets begin to show disappointment, but later sonnets suggest reconciliation.

The second division comprises those sonnets addressing a woman of dark complexion, the one often referred to as "the dark lady." There is no stranger love poem than 130:

130

My mistress' eyes are nothing like the sun;
Coral is far more red than her lips' red:
If snow be white, why then her breasts are dun;
If hairs be wires, black wires grow on her head.
I have seen roses damask'd, red and white,
But no such roses see I in her cheeks ;
And in some perfumes is there more delight
Than in the breath that from my mistress reeks.

I love to hear her speak, yet well I know
That music hath a far more pleasing sound:
I grant I never saw a goddess go;
My mistress, when she walks, treads on the ground:
And yet, by heaven, I think my love as rare
As any she belied with false compare.

Is this really a love poem? As Helen Vendler points out in *The Art of Shakespeare's Sonnets*, this seems to be a parody, a reply-poem to a poet who has written traditional, hackneyed lines like

My mistress eyes are brilliant as the sun,
And coral's colour matches her lips' red.

Shakespeare is replying that *his* love is a *real* woman as rare as any conventionally praised love. The final couplet says it all. Yet, despite this inverted praise, in other sonnets Shakespeare rails against the lady for betraying him with other men.

Did Shakespeare suffer an unsuccessful love affair? Is he venting his anger in the Sonnets? Was the "dark lady" Mary Pitton, Emilia Lanier, Lucy Morgan, Penelope Rich? No one knows if the lady is merely a figment of Shakespeare's fertile imagination.

Whether or not there is somewhere a key to the Sonnets is unimportant. The individual poems are beautiful in their own right, like one of the most frequently quoted:

116

Let me not to the marriage of true minds
Admit impediments. Love is not love
Which alters when it alteration finds,
Or bends with the remover to remove:
O, no ! it is an ever-fixed mark,
That looks on tempests and is never shaken;

It is the star to every wandering bark,
Whose worth's unknown, although his height be taken.
Love's not Time's fool, though rosy lips and cheeks
Within his bending sickle's compass come;
Love alters not with his brief hours and weeks,
But bears it out even to the edge of doom.
If this be error, and upon me prov'd,
I never writ, nor no man ever lov'd,

Fidelity has never had a better spokesperson.

28

Shakespeare's Poetry

The truest poetry is the most feigning,
Why, thy verse swells with stuff so fine and smooth
That thou art even natural in thine art.

Timon of Athens, V, 1, 83-84

What did a talented young writer do to earn a living in Shakespeare's England? Shakespeare faced the problem and solved it in two different ways: acting and writing. Early in his career, he became an actor. His name can be found in the playbills of certain plays, one of them by Ben Jonson (p 52).

As in today's Hollywood, the A-list actors made an excellent living. Great performers like Edward Alleyn and Richard Burbage (p 27), the darlings of the playgoers, lived well. Other actors made a living of sorts, though sometimes a meager one. Shakespeare ultimately preferred to give up acting for writing, a choice that made him wealthy.

He had two directions in his writing: poetry and plays. The distinction becomes blurred when we realize that Shakespeare's plays are filled with poetry and that his two long poems are dramatic. Writing poems was a survival device during the plagues, when the theaters were closed. Dedicating a poem to a nobleman often brought financial rewards. The dedications tended to be embarrassingly fulsome in praise of the person honored, but poets had no choice. Shakespeare dedicated *Venus and Adonis* to the young Earl of Southampton. The appeal for sponsorship was apparently a successful ploy, since Shakespeare later dedicated the *Rape of Lucrece* to the same young man. Those dedications have plucked the name of Southampton from obscurity and associated him forever with the, immortal. Successful poems lived beyond the original printing, appearing in a succession of quartos or octavos (page).

Venus and Adonis

The long poem *Venus and Adonis* has the distinction of being the first Shakespeare work to be printed with the author's name in the dedication. The poem was a very early work, though possibly not the earliest. Works do not always appear publicly in the order of composition. It's an erotic work, humorous and lusty in turn. Based on the classical myth of Adonis, the poem concerns itself with Venus's obsession with Adonis and the death of Adonis by the attack of a wild boar.

The name *Adonis* has come down to us as a word for a surpassingly handsome young man. Venus, goddess of love, sees in Adonis the perfect male, a suitable lover, but there is a problem. In Shakespeare's poem, Adonis doesn't reciprocate her love.

> Hunting he loved, but love he laughed to scorn.
> Line 4

Venus uses all her wiles to seduce this pure young man, but Adonis resists. There is humor in her continuing efforts, using all the power of her divine charms to woo this reluctant lover. She cries out,

> "Were I hard-favoured, foul, or wrinkled old
> Ill-nurtured, crooked, churlish, harsh in voice,
> O'erworn, despised, rheumatic, and cold,
> Thick-sighted, barren, lean, and lacking juice,
> Then mightst thou pause, for then I were not for
> thee:

> But having no defects, why dost abhor me?
> Lines 133-138

She goes on, extolling her own beauty, pointing out her perfections, but after all the high-powered exhortations, Adonis cries, "Fie: no more of love." And this to the goddess of love and beauty! This reversal of gender roles may be Shakespeare's satire on male aggression.

Adonis prefers hunting, a choice that kills him. He is fatally gored the next morning by a wild boar, and Venus is left to mourn. At the poem's end, Venus flies off to Paphos "to immure herself and not be seen."

Though perhaps not to modern taste, *Venus and Adonis* has some magnificent imagery, brilliant poetic language, and touches of real humor. Critics have toiled over the symbolism, the philosophical underpinnings, and the paradoxes that love always presents. Parts of the poem are just plain funny!

The Rape of Lucrece

Since *The Rape of Lucrece*, like *Venus and Adonis*, is dedicated to the Earl of Southampton, we may assume that Shakespeare was rewarded for the earlier dedication. Though not quite as popular as the earlier poem, *The Rape of Lucrece* was reprinted seven times before 1640.

The Rape of Lucrece is a more serious poem than its predecessor. An intellectual of the time, Gabriel Harvey commented, "The younger sort takes such delight in Shakespeare's *Venus and Adonis*, but his *Lucrece* and his *Tragedy of Hamlet, Prince of Denmark*, have it in them to please the wiser sort."

In the two poems, Shakespeare displayed his technical virtuosity (p101), *Venus and Adonis* is written in six-line stanzas rhyming *ababcc*. *The Rape of Lucrece* is written in rhyme royal: seven-line stanzas rhyming *ababbcc*.

Almost 700 lines longer than its predecessor, *The Rape of Lucrece* tells in lengthy detail the ancient Latin story of the sexual assault on Lucretia, a noble Roman woman. The rapist, Tarquin, is son of the Roman king. Though tormented by a guilty conscience, his lust overcomes his scruples and he satisfies it. More than half of the poem is devoted to Lucrece's anguish, ended by her death. Dishonored, she takes her own life, but she tells others of the crime. The final couplet tells of the banishment of Tarquin and his father. The banishment was followed by the institution of the Roman republic. Lucrece did not die in vain.

The story fascinated Shakespeare. He referred to it in *Macbeth*, *The Taming of the Shrew*, and *Cymbeline*. His strong central character, Lucrece, foreshadows later independent characters like Beatrice and Portia. Though a victim, she ultimately takes charge of her own life in a fashion approved by the morality of ancient Rome. The conflict of good and evil was a theme dear to Shakespeare. Here it is detailed with brutal simplicity but at great length!

Shakespeare's imagery begins to show the range and depth of his powers. His description of Lucrece is lyrical and sensuous. "Her hair, like golden threads, play'd with her breath." Though sometimes a bit overblown for modern tastes, the descriptions enchanted his readers.

> Her lily hand her rosy cheek lies under,
> Cozening the pillow of a lawful kiss.
> Lines 386-387

Other Poems

Two other poems are generally ascribed in whole or at least in part to Shakespeare: "The Passionate Pilgrim" and "The Phoenix and the Turtle." The former is an anthology apparently assembled without Shakespeare's participation or knowledge. The first two poems in the collection are actually Shakespearean Sonnets 138 and 144. Other poems are versions of passages from *Love's Labour's Lost*. Still other poems in this catchall collection have been traced, ascribed to Christopher Marlowe and Walter Raleigh. Without copyright constraints, the publisher, William Jaggard, published later editions with more pirated poetry. An offended victim of the theft, Thomas Heywood made a public protest, asserting that Shakespeare, as well as he, was "much offended" by Jaggard's high-handedness.

Though now generally accepted as a work by Shakespeare, "The Phoenix and the Turtle" still arouses some skepticism. It is a fairly short allegorical work on the mystical nature of love. The phoenix and the turtle-dove have burned themselves to death to be joined together in love forever:

> Death is now the phoenix' nest;
> And turtle's loyal breast
> To eternity doth rest.
>
> Lines 56-58

Critics have attempted to link the poem with actual persons: Sir John Salisbury and his wife, even Queen Elizabeth and the Earl of Essex. Whatever its origin, "The Phoenix and the Turtle" remains a powerful invocation of idealized love.

Fragments of poems, literary "discoveries" continue to be made: authenticating a poem as a work of Shakespeare's is a hazardous activity.

Afterword

What sees thou else
In the dark backward and abysm of time?
The Tempest, I, 2, 49-50

What If?

In a perceptive short story by Stephen Vincent Benet, "The Curfew Toils," an ambitious young Corsican army officer is frustrated at every turn. Though filled with grandiose schemes equaled by his military expertise, the officer is doomed to obscurity. At the end of the story, his name is *Napoleon Bonaparte*. In the story, he has been born in 1737, not 1769 as was the actual Napoleon. When this fictitious officer died, events presaging the French Revolution were heating up in Paris. He had been born at the wrong time.

What would have happened if Shakespeare had not been born in 1564? How would he have expressed his genius? If he had been born in 1514, fifty years earlier, he might have been a poet like Thomas Wyatt and Henry Howard Surrey, but he would not have been a dramatist. There would have been no theater to stimulate his genius. Even the poetry of the early sixteenth century signaled no major renaissance and flowering.

The timing was just right for Shakespeare. Up to that time, the classical drama of Greece and Rome had been opposed and exterminated by the church. Ironically, however, it was the church that fostered the birth of Renaissance theater. *Miracle* and *mystery plays*, as they were called, presented Biblical stories and morality sermons in embryonic dramatic form. These plays grew in scope, often forming cycles of plays dealing with the religious history of the world. One of these plays, *Everyman*, had a profound effect on British drama. These plays had no named authors.

Just as Napoleon was a product of his time, so Shakespeare was a product of his. The late Elizabethan period saw a flowering of the drama unique in the history of English literature. Toward the end of the sixteenth century, there was an explosion of plays and playwrights. Writers turned to plays for self-expression and economic survival. Playwrights were not guaranteed success, however; most teetered on the edges. Relatively few were successful enough to make a living. Shakespeare was one of those.

The pioneer English comedy was *Ralph Roister Doister* (1553) by Nicholas Udall. It was a far cry from *As You Like It*, but it was a beginning. The pioneer English tragedy was *Gorboduc* (1561). This was the result of an unusual collaboration. Thomas Norton wrote the first three acts, and Thomas Sackville, the last two. These sparks were ignited shortly before Shakespeare's birth.

At that birth, conditions for the drama couldn't have been more favorable. English had survived dynastic squabbles, foreign wars, and threats to the monarchy. A feeling of optimism permeated the land. Theaters for presenting plays were built, sometimes despite the efforts of authorities to curtail the growth of the drama. Competition for the audiences influenced the quality of plays, as well as the quantity. Some plays were revived again and again. Into this most promising atmosphere came the greatest dramatist of them all: William Shakespeare. What would he have created in another period of English history?

The nineteenth century was the time of the great novels. Dickens, Thackeray, Eliot, Hardy, Gissing, Meredith, Brontë-the names roll on and on. If Shakespeare had lived toward the end of that century, would he have concentrated his talent on writing novels? What kind? Would the novels have been greater than those of Dickens and the Brontës, or would he have found the novel medium less suited to his talents?

What if Shakespeare lived today? Would he expend those prodigious abilities on screenplays, television sitcoms, or avant-garde literature? Some find that thought depressing.

Fortunately Shakespeare lived when he did, when English drama was coming into its greatest flowering, when the English language was exuberantly coming into its own. To be sure, there were bright spots in drama after the time of Shakespeare: the Restoration and the early eighteenth century, for example. But there has never been a period so perfect for Shakespeare's genius as the period of Elizabeth I and James I.

A Further Look

Of the multitude of books consulted in the writing of this book, the following were most helpful and most readable.

Abbott, E., A. *A Shakespearean Grammar*, 1966, New York
A classic study of the differences between Elizabethan and modern English. Comprehensive and detailed, it's for students of language.

Ashley, Mike (ed) *Shakespearean Wodunits*, 1997, New York; *Shakespearean Detectives*, 1998, New York
These are imaginative tales, just for fun: professional mystery writers create detective stories combining ingenuity and Shakespearean scholarship. Cases are solved by Hamlet, Henry V., Falstaff, and even Shakespeare himself.

Barton, John, *Playing Shakespeare*, 1984, London
For an understanding of how a director and actors cooperate in interpreting Shakespeare, there is no better book. Videotapes present the original BBC programs on which the book is based.

Bate, Jonathan, *The Genius of Shakespeare*, 1998, New York
What makes Shakespeare different from all his great contemporaries and all the dramatists that have followed? Bates isolates those elements that set Shakespeare apart.

Bertram, Paul, *Shakespeare and the Two Noble Kinsmen*, 1965, New Jersey
Is *The Two Noble Kinsmen* Shakespeare's in whole, in part, or not at all? Bertram considers all the possibilities and provides a complete text of this disputed play

Bloom, Harold, *Shakespeare, the Invention of the Human*, 1998, New York
A fascinating, at times curmudgeonly, book that evaluates all the plays, often from a fresh and challenging viewpoint.

Boyce, Charles, *Shakespeare A to Z*, 1990, New York
Like the Campbell volume below, this is a handy volume for reading play summaries, refreshing faulty memories, and confirming suppositions.

Browning, D. C., *The Complete Dictionary of Shakespeare's Quotations*. 1986, London
A handy book for browsing and for tracking down those elusive quotations that tease the mind. A helpful index alphabetizes key words

Campbell, Oscar James(ed). *The Reader's Encyclopedia of Shakespeare*, 1986,New York
A readable, comprehensive reference book covering the plays, the characters, the rivals, some of the great Shakespearean actors.

Carlisle, Carol Jones, *Shakespeare from the Greenroom*, 1969, North Carolina.
What do actors think about the Shakespearean parts assigned to them? This book provides personal and professional critiques of the four great tragedies, by great names of the past.

Dowden, Edward, *Shakespeare-a Critical Study of His Mind and Art*, 1880, New York
A classic. Dowden's insights more than a century ago are startlingly acceptable to many modern students of Shakespeare.

Elsom, John (ed), *Is Shakespeare Still Our Contemporary?* 1989, London.

The point of Jan Kott's seminal 1969 book *Shakespeare Our Contemporary* is here analyzed by a variety of critics, often from conflicting points of view. Here's an intriguing chapter head: "Does Shakespeare Write Better for Television?"

French, Marilyn, *Shakespeare's Division of Experience*, 1981, New York
How did Shakespeare's attitude toward women change as he matured in his later plays? French clearly demonstrates Shakespeare's growing awareness of the "gender principle," as she labels it and his almost modern approach to feminism in characters like Cordelia and Cleopatra.

Gay, Penny, *As She Likes It Shakespeare's Unruly Women*, 1994, London
Five great heroines-Viola, Rosalind, Katharina, Isabella, and Beatrice-present acting challenges gladly accepted by modern actresses. As the times have changed, so have the interpretations-a tribute to Shakespeare's timeless-ness.

Gielgud, John, *Acting Shakespeare*, 1999, London
One of the greatest actors of modern times demonstrates the sensitivity demanded of any actor playing the great Shakespearean roles.

Holden, Anthony, *William Shakespeare-the Man Behind the Genius*, 1999, London
A lively romp through the known facts of Shakespeare's life, along with some less-than-conservative inferences.

Honan, Park. *Shakespeare: a Life*, 1998, London/New York
A compilation of the known facts about Shakespeare's life woven into an exciting narrative.

Kermode, Frank, *Shakespeare's Language*, 2000, New York
About 1600, something happened to change Shakespeare's language. Like an exciting detective story, this book attempts to explore and explain the subtle transformation toward greater complexity and ambiguity.

Leggatt, Alexander, *Ben Jonson-His Vision and His Art*, 1980, Toronto
Leggatt provides insights into Jonson's life, personality, and art. More than any other rival to Shakespeare, Jonson comes closest (though not too close!) to Shakespeare's genius.

Manvell, Roger, *Shakespeare and the Film*, 1971, London
Though not up-to-date, this provides some excellent discussions as well as over a hundred priceless photographs, from the early Shakespeare films like Max Reinhardt's *A Midsummer Night's Dream*, to the 1970 Paul Scofield King Lear.

Norwich, John Julius, *Shakespeare's Kings*, 1999, New York
The complicated background for Shakespeare's historical plays is skillfully compared with the events as Shakespeare dramatized them.

Rabkin, Norman, *Shakespeare and the Common Understanding*, 1967, New York
An unheralded milestone in Shakespearean criticism, it explores brilliantly the contradictions and paradoxes at the heart of Shakespeare's writing. It forever demonstrates that there is no definitive interpretation of Hamlet or any other great Shakespearean character.

Redfield, William, *Letters from an Actor*, 1967, New York
As Guildenstern in the Richard Burton *Hamlet* (1964), Redfield was in the perfect position to observe some aspects of production rarely touched upon by others. The egos, the tensions, the excitement, the disappointments, and the glories are all related perceptively in the form of letters.

Schoenbaum, S., *William Shakespeare-a Complete Documentary Life*, 1977,New York

An abridged edition of Schoenbaum's monumental study of the documents that have shaped our understanding of Shakespeare's life and possible effect upon his writing.

Spencer, Hazelton, *Shakespeare Improved*, 1963, New York
The song "Anything You Can Do I Can Do Better" might be applied to dramatists of the Restoration (p35). Spencer gleefully reports in detail the "improvements" briefly mentioned in our text.

Spurgeon, Caroline F.E., *Shakespeare's Imagery*, 1935, London
Still the definitive study of Shakespeare's imagery and what it tells us about the mind and heart of Shakespeare.

Stoppard, Tom, *Rosencrantz and Guildenstern Are Dead*, 1967, New York
A tour de force, a romp through *Hamlet* from the point of view of two peripheral minor characters. Portions of Shakespeare's dialogue are interspersed with Stoppard's contributions. Amusing, yet poignant.

Thaler, Alwin, *Shakespeare's Silences*, 1956, New York
At crucial moments in the plays, characters are silent. Thaler evaluates some of the most famous of these silences.

Vendler, Helen, *The Art of Shakespeare's Sonnets*, 1997, New York
An exhaustive but never exhausting study of the sonnets. Though these are a tiny fraction of Shakespeare's total work, Vendler shows how his genius exuberantly illuminates his poetry as well as his plays.

Wells, Stanley (ed), *Shakespeare Studies*, 1986, London
A compendium of articles dealing with various facets of Shakespeare's genius. An example: "Shakespeare and the theatrical conventions of his time." A good way to get a critical cross-section of many Shakespearean achievements.

The Teaching Company presents two lecture series on audiotapes and on videotapes by Shakespearean scholar Peter Saccio:

1. *Shakespeare: the Word and the Action*
A general introduction, often by themes: love and artifice, nature and art, action, history and family.

2. *William Shakespeare: Comedies, Histories and Tragedies*
Concentrates on specific plays; strong on the great tragedies and the English history plays.

Index

A

Admiral's Men, 13, 26

Alleyn, Edward, 26, 323

All's Well That Ends Well, 300-302

Allusions, 148-161

Anglo–Saxon, 118

Antony and Cleopatra, 261-264

Aristotle, 92

Armin, Robert, 32, 61, 283

As You Like It, 278-281

B

Bacon, Sir Francis, 81, 85-86

Beaumont, Francis, 27, 56, 63

Berlioz, Hector, 65

Bernstein, Leonard, 65

Bible, Kings James, 119,122

Blackfriars Theater, 20, 27, 196, 311

Blank verse, 50, 56, 110-111, 115

Boleyn, Anne, 6-7, 18, 254-255

Branagh, Kenneth, 38, 42, 46, 65, 70-71, 96, 207

Burbage, James, 12, 27

Burbage, Richard, 12, 17, 26, 27, 30, 323

Quotations from the Plays and Poems

> Whose words all ears took captive.
> *All's Well That Ends Well,*
> V, 3, p. 17

0-595-19356-0

Printed in the United States
22281LVS00001B/127-141

HOW TO BE
A GREAT
COMMUNICATOR

ALSO BY NIDO R. QUBEIN

COMMUNICATE LIKE A PRO

GET THE BEST FROM YOURSELF

NIDO QUBEIN'S PROFESSIONAL SELLING TECHNIQUES

ACHIEVING PEAK PERFORMANCE

STAIRWAY TO SUCCESS

AUDIO PROGRAMS BY NIDO R. QUBEIN

HOW TO BE A GREAT COMMUNICATOR: IN PERSON, ON PAPER, AND ON THE PODIUM

HOW TO POSITION YOURSELF FOR SUCCESS

SELLING SAVVY

THE 12 ESSENTIAL ELEMENTS TO PROFESSIONAL SUCCESS

HOW TO MARKET YOUR PROFESSIONAL EXPERTISE

HOW TO DEVELOP A WINNING IMAGE

HOW TO MARKET THROUGH DIRECT MAIL

HOW TO PROMOTE YOURSELF THROUGH PUBLIC SPEAKING

HOW TO BE
A GREAT
COMMUNICATOR

In Person, on Paper,
and on the Podium

Nido R. Qubein

John Wiley & Sons, Inc.

New York • Chichester • Brisbane • Toronto • Singapore

This text is printed on acid-free paper.

Copyright © 1997 by Nido R. Qubein
Published by John Wiley & Sons, Inc.

Library of Congress Cataloging-in-Publication Data:

Qubein, Nido R.
    How to be a great communicator : in person, on paper, and on the
    podium / Nido R. Qubein.
       p. cm.
    ISBN 0-471-16314-7 (pbk. : alk. paper)
    1. Public speaking. 2. Self-presentation. 3. Interpersonal
    communication. I. Title.
    PN4121.Q39   1996
    808.5′1—dc20   96-21829

Printed in the United States of America

10 9 8 7 6 5 4 3 2 1

To Cristina,
With love

CONTENTS

     THE BARRIERS   229

         Avoid Impenetrable Barriers   229
         Factors to Monitor   231
         A Dual Medium: Sight and Sound   236
         Overcoming Stage Fright   238

     Epilogue   241
     Notes   243
     Index   245

ACKNOWLEDGMENTS

Occasionally, I forget that I wasn't born in America, that English is my second language, that carving a career in the communication/consulting field is so difficult! By the grace of God, with loving support of family and friends, it has been a mountaintop experience for me. I am so grateful.

Speakers Roundtable is the world's most prestigious group of speakers and consultants. I'm proud to be a member alongside Tony Alessandra, Mark Sanborn, Ty Boyd, Roger Crawford, Jim Cathcart, Danny Cox, Patricia Fripp, Bill Gove, Art Holst, Allan Hurst, Don Hutson, Charles Jones, Jim Newman, Charles Plumb, Naomi Rhode, Cavett Robert, Brian Tracy, Herb True, Jim Tunney, and Tom Winninger. These are all superb communicators and I'm thankful for their friendship.

Robert Henry, my soul brother and confidant, has enriched my life so profoundly. He and his humorist partners—Doc Blakely, Jeanne Robertson, and Al Walker—are dear pals for all time. And so are scores of other fellow professionals in the National Speakers Association.

The most recognized voice on earth belongs to Casey Kasem. An eloquent communicator and an elegant gentleman, he's been such a close friend and an enthusiastic cheerleader of my work. Thank you, Casey.

Art Linkletter, Zig Ziglar, Norman Vincent Peale, Cavett Robert, Og Mandino, DuPree Jordan, and Ben B. Franklin endorsed my work when I was an unknown. They took a risk, and I acknowledge their kindness with love and appreciation.

My publishers bought my work and distributed it to millions in all corners of the globe. My thanks to Vic Conant at Nightingale Conant, who produced eight audiocassette programs simultaneously; to Hal Krause, who translated my management videos into so many languages; to the talented editors at Berkley, who promoted three of my books so well; to Charlie Jones at Executive Books, who, by anyone's standards, represents the epitome of integrity; to John Tschohl at BestSellers, who marketed my work effectively in the United States and abroad; and to PJ Dempsey, my editor at John Wiley & Sons, who's a consummate professional.

If my busy speaking calendar, since 1972, has been the envy of so many, it isn't really a reflection on me. Instead it speaks volumes about seminar promoters, speaker bureaus, meeting planners, and corporate chief executives who believed that I had a message to communicate and invited me so many times to facilitate their meetings. Thank you to John Allison IV, Kerima and Dan Brattland, Michael Jeffreys, Paula Marshall-Chapman, Martie Ormsby, Glenn Orr, Jeff Rives, Eric Worre and Jeff Olson, Joanne Wallace, Bruce Warmbold, and all the good people at Aetna, American Airlines, Amway, Bassett, Broyhill, Con Edison, Dole, GE, Henredon, Marriott, Nynex, Prudential, Realty World, State Farm, USFI, and so many more companies and trade associations. I owe my speaking career to all of you.

When it's all said and done, my life could not have been as meaningful if it weren't for my fellow citizens in my home city (High Point, North Carolina) who accepted me, supported me, and affirmed me with their genuine love. And to the more than two hundred leaders who faithfully support The Qubein Foundation, our Scholarship Fund, thank you from the bottom of my heart for helping educate over three hundred students over the years. You are kind and generous benefactors.

PART ONE

ACQUIRING
THE TOOLS OF
COMMUNICATION

1

COMMUNICATION

The Requirement
of a New Century

On the obstetrics ward at a hospital, a tiny bundle of humanity squirms its way into the world, draws a breath for the first time, and emits a lusty cry that announces its presence to the universe.

The first overt human act is an exercise in communication.

In time, the squall of the newborn gives way to more complex and more subtle forms of communication. The infant will make eye contact with its parents, will learn to beguile them with a smile, captivate them with its cunning, scold them with a scowl.

But most wondrous of all, it will learn to form those neonatal wails into words. Later, it will learn to put those words on paper and log them onto computer disks. It will learn to send them across many miles through fiber-optic cables, through radio signals bounced off orbiting satellites, through feats of technology not yet imagined.

THE GLOBAL TRIBE

These high-tech extensions of the human gift of communication will eventually tie our newborn *Homo sapiens* into a global network that wraps all of us in the folds of humanity.

In primitive societies, hunters and gatherers stayed in touch mainly through spoken language. Their language was the bond that held them together as a tribe, as a people. Interestingly, most primitive tribes refer to themselves by a word that means "the people," whereas they refer to other tribes as "those who talk gibberish."

Today humanity forms a global tribe, and those without good communication skills will find themselves outside the circle of success, among "those who talk gibberish." Those who learn to communicate effectively with people at all levels, of both genders, and from a variety of cultures and backgrounds will be the pacesetters.

Technology helps us communicate with ever larger, ever more diverse audiences, but technology can't provide the message. Communication is one function that can't be performed by machines. Communication is a human activity, the foundation of interaction among human beings. Communication has to do with meanings, with understandings, with feelings, with desires, with needs, and with ideas. You can't communicate with a computer. Computers only store and process data. They don't have needs, desires, ideas, and feelings. Only people do.

The Basics and the Fine Points

This book is designed to help you develop the communication skills required for the global business environment, and to wield them with power and effect. You'll learn not only the basics, but many of the finer points I've picked up during a long and successful career as a professional speaker, author, and adviser to top executives on management and human development.

You'll learn:

- The five keys to successful communication
- How to use words and body language effectively
- How to communicate in the workplace and in the global market with people from different ethnic, cultural, and national backgrounds
- How to speak and write naturally while avoiding sexist language
- How to communicate with power over the telephone
- How to get things done in meetings
- How to communicate effectively from the platform
- How to put power into your writing
- How to make effective use of television and the print media to promote your company and enhance your professional image

Producers Must Communicate

These are no longer "nice-to-have" skills. They are essential to success in the twenty-first century. To produce and market products and services to billions of people worldwide requires a level of communication undreamed of in previous centuries. When the quality of your product depends upon the collective efforts of dozens, hundreds, or thousands of individuals, communication becomes the lifeblood of your enterprise. When the success of your enterprise depends upon the quality of your marketing in China, Turkey, the Netherlands, and Nigeria, communication becomes the lifeline of your company's existence.

The Twenty-First Century Difference

What makes the twenty-first century different from previous centuries is the scope of the communication challenge. The challenge is posed at both the macro and the micro levels.

The Macro Level: Puddles to Ponds to One Big Ocean

At the macro level, the human race, in previous centuries, existed in puddles of humanity.

In time, some of these puddles sent out feeble streams that connected with other puddles. Nearby puddles enlarged until they joined to form larger puddles, and eventually ponds. But until well into the twentieth century, the Earth still consisted largely of separate ponds in Europe, Asia, Africa, the Americas, and islands at sea.

The communication strides of this century have united the ponds and puddles into one great ocean, with currents surging from one region to another, but all interacting as a dynamic whole.

The Micro Level: From Patriarchs to Peers

At the micro level, communication has progressed beyond the simple conveying of instructions from patriarch to tribe, from master to slave, from boss to underling. Communication in the modern world is increasingly a matter of interchange among equals.

In the old-style hierarchical, authoritarian setting, communication was relatively simple. The top person told the underlings to jump, and the underlings only had to ask, "How high?"

In a modern organization, communication requires more finesse. The leader is not a transmitter of commands, but a creator of motivational environments. The workers are not robots responding to switches and levers, but thinking individuals pouring their ingenuity into the corporate purpose. The corporate ideal is not mechanical stability, but dynamic, innovative, continuous change. The leader who can't communicate can't create the conditions that motivate. The genius who can't communicate is intellectually impotent. The organization that can't communicate can't change, and the corporation that can't change is dead.

COMMUNICATION WITH A DIVERSE WORKFORCE

In the old days, the White male was the undisputed master of the American workforce. Although he was a minority in the population as a whole, he was a majority in the workplace, and he monopolized top management.

The White male now represents less than half the workforce. Women and ethnic minorities constitute the majority. By some estimates, only 8 percent of newcomers to the workforce in the year 2000 will be White males.[1]

This new diversity will force us to learn the subtleties of communicating between the genders as well as with people of different racial, national, and cultural backgrounds. Leaders will have to deal not only with different levels of understanding of spoken English, but also with cultural and gender-related differences in nonverbal communication and in the language of motivation.

COMMUNICATION WITH THE MARKET

By some estimates, 85 percent of success in business depends on effective communication and interpersonal skills. People must know about your products and services before they will buy them. If your advertising or public relations messages miss the mark, you've wasted money because you haven't attracted customers or clients. If your salespeople are poor communicators, they won't bring in the revenue. If your customer service representatives are inept at communicating, you'll lose business. When customers of one enterprise take their business to a competitor, the reason in the great majority of cases is poor communication.

COMMUNICATION IN THE WORKPLACE

Today's successful company must be alive, with communications flowing in all directions, through all levels and divisions.

This requires communication skills on the part of everyone—from the CEO to the most junior person on staff.

American executives spend 94 percent of their time involved in some form of communication. They must not only communicate with other executives, customers, clients, and vendors; they must also be able to communicate effectively with the people staffing the offices, running the machines, and delivering the services.

James Kouzes and Barry Posner polled more than 7,500 managers nationwide, asking them what qualities they admired in their leaders. Among the most-mentioned qualities were the ability to inspire, the ability to understand the perspectives of others, and the ability to speak with passion. All three qualities express themselves through communication.[2]

Workplace communication is essential to the process of building quality into goods and services. The Federal Quality Institute listed effective communication among the prerequisites for successful quality assurance. Without communication skills, workers can't learn the techniques of statistical process control and other quality measures, much less put them into practice. Quality circles and self-managed teams are ineffectual without good communication skills on the part of their members. Executives, managers, and supervisors can't nurture qualityoriented corporate cultures unless they know how to communicate ideas and feelings.

Information and Responsibility

The switch from authoritarian to participative management has placed a heavy premium on communication skills. Participatory management demands that each individual in the workforce take responsibility for corporate success. Uninformed people can't take responsibility. But when you give them information, you confer responsibility upon them.

If your company's earnings are dropping because it has lost control of costs, your employees can't be blamed if you fail to tell them about it. If you explain the situation to them, then you invest them with the responsibility to look for ways to cut costs.

Participative management has ushered in the age of teamwork. Companies such as Procter & Gamble, Corning, Levi Strauss, and many others are investing self-managed teams with responsibilities no nineteenth-century tycoon would have dared delegate to line workers.

Line workers decide how to arrange the machinery in a new plant. They draw up job descriptions, determine staffing levels, and take over recruiting. They provide input into budgeting. They decide when to lay off and when to work shorter hours. They maintain their own machinery and do minor repairs. They advise management when new equipment is needed.

These employees could never handle responsibilities like these unless management shared information with them and empowered them to act on that information.

COMMUNICATION IN THE SERVICE ECONOMY

As our economy shifts from manufacturing to service industries, the demand for communication skills grows. A worker who installs door panels as a car moves down an assembly line needs fewer communication skills than a hotel desk clerk or a software designer.

The Hudson Institute conducted a study for the U.S. Department of Labor and concluded that in the early twenty-first century, nearly all new jobs created in the United States will be in the service sector. Only 27 percent will fall in the low-skill category, compared with 40 percent in 1990. The worker seeking a job in the first decade of the twenty-first century will have to be able to read at the eleventh-grade level. During the 1990s the typical high school graduate was reading at the ninth-grade level.

The twenty-first century is going to require an ability to communicate freely, precisely, and clearly. So the American workforce must sharpen its communication skills from top to bottom, from the board-room to the workbench.

This kind of communication cannot be accomplished solely by microchips, fiber optics, and satellite relays. These artifacts of our technology help fill the world with information, but information is lifeless without someone to breathe meaning into it. The greatest need is for understanding—for building bridges across the mental and emotional distances that separate human individuals from one another so that we can live and work together more harmoniously.

The leaders of the twenty-first century must take the initiative in breathing the soul of meaning and understanding into the body of data, in uniting a diverse workforce behind a common vision and common goals. They must teach the people they lead to communicate in all directions and at all levels.

Division leaders and department heads must learn to communicate with their peers in other functional areas. Production must communicate with marketing, marketing with product development, product development with sales, sales with shipping; in fact, everybody must communicate with everybody if the company is to tap the full resources of its work teams.

Communication is the essential tool of the salesperson, too. It is fundamental to the art and science of negotiation. It is a vital component of leadership, the principal role of which, according to Tom Peters, is "organizing meanings for people, providing meaning, providing flags to march behind."[3] It is the tool of corporate intelligence gathering, an essential activity for those who want to remain abreast of the market and of the competition—in short, of those who want to succeed.

I've invested the past two decades in helping organizations solve problems. This book is a culmination of the lessons I've learned, solutions to the problems I've observed, and a summary of the principles I teach. It will equip the business leaders of the twenty-first century to practice that most human of talents—communication—and to communicate success to their staffs and workforces. Learning to communicate effectively is an exciting process. We begin it in chapter 2 by discussing the five keys to the Kingdom of Communication. Let's roll up our sleeves and get on with it.

2

THE KEYS TO THE KINGDOM OF COMMUNICATION

English is my second language, and it has served me marvelously. I'd like to repay my debt by helping others use it with finesse and success. In this chapter I share with you the five keys to the doors to the Kingdom of Communication.

Some people seem to be born with silver tongues. They wield the language the way Joe DiMaggio handled a bat: purposefully, gracefully, and effectively.

But that ability never comes automatically. It has to be learned. The great communicators of history started life just like you and me—with a wordless cry. They had to learn language one word at a time. If you think you don't have what it takes to be an effective communicator, think again. Some of the greatest communicators had to overcome some tough handicaps.

The prophet Moses was, by his own admission, a "meek person, slow of speech." Yet he demanded that the world's mightiest potentate free the conscripted laborers who were making the bricks for Egypt's grandiose building projects. Pharaoh never listened, but six hundred thousand men, with their wives and families, followed Moses out of Egypt through the parted waters of the Red Sea. And they listened when Moses, his face glowing from his encounter with God, descended from Mount Sinai and gave them the law.

You don't have to go up to Mount Sinai to acquire eloquence. All you need to do is acquire and use five keys.

THE FIRST KEY: DESIRE

My wife Mariana and I have reared four beautiful children—Ramsey, Deena, Cristina, and Michael—and we've watched each one slowly acquire the basic tools of language. I can still remember my youngest child, Michael, struggling to tell me he wanted a bottle of fruit juice when he didn't know the words to convey his wishes. It's a frustrating experience for baby and parent.

I experienced that same frustration long after infancy. I came to the United States as a young man with little knowledge of the English language. I had grown up speaking Arabic, a language only remotely connected to English. If I had spoken French, German, Spanish, or Italian, I would have had a substantial supply of common words to get me started. But Arabic and English have few words in common, and the beautiful language that has served me so well in my adopted land was then unintelligible to me.

But I had something in common with the baby struggling to communicate. Human infants have an inborn desire to communicate, and that desire enables them to pick up words quickly and to enlarge their vocabularies continuously. I had that desire, too. With the help of countless friends in America, I picked up the language and used it as an instrument for success.

I became a professional speaker, an author, and an adviser to corporate leaders across America as well as in a dozen other countries. These activities require finely honed communication skills. If I can do it, you can.

In fact, you should find it much easier. I had to invest enormous time and energy in learning the language. If you grew up in America, you already know the language. So if you invest the same amount of time and energy I invested, you should become a virtuoso at communicating.

But to make that investment, you must have the desire to communicate. Moses had it. So did Demosthenes, the Greek statesman whose name has been synonymous with oratory for two thousand years.

Communication Was Greek to Demosthenes

Demosthenes lived during the Golden Age of Greece, when all public disputes were settled by oratory. As a young man, he went before the Assembly in Athens—an unruly legislative body of about six thousand men—to speak on an important issue. To use a modern English expression, Demosthenes bombed. His voice was weak, his thoughts were muddled, and the longer he talked the worse he got. He was hissed and booed off the platform.

Demosthenes vowed it would never happen again.

First, he learned speech writing. Soon he was making money writing speeches for wealthy men.

Then he went to the shores of the Aegean Sea, where he strengthened his voice by shouting into the wind for hours at a time. To improve his diction, he practiced speaking with pebbles in his mouth. To overcome his fear, he practiced with a sword hanging over his head. To clarify his presentation, he studied the techniques of the masters.

Years later, Demosthenes stepped before the Assembly to warn leaders of the great threat posed by Philip II of Macedonia. He inspired his audience with his eloquence and laid before them some clearly reasoned ideas for dealing with the Macedonian. When he had finished, the audience rose and shouted in unison: "Let us go and fight Philip."

. . . And Let Us Go and Fight Hitler

Demosthenes was not alone in having to overcome handicaps. Winston Churchill, who is credited with marshalling the English language and sending it to war against Hitler, suffered from a speech impediment as a child. He had to undergo extensive speech therapy during childhood and early adulthood.

Franklin Roosevelt had to inspire a demoralized nation from a wheelchair. So effective was his communication that few Americans realized that the man who led them so decisively out of a depression and through a global war could not stand up without braces on his legs.

Helen Keller could neither see nor hear, and she spoke with such difficulty that she usually needed an interpreter. Yet she became an eloquent communicator of the highest order.

Sequoyah was a member of the Cherokee nation who believed that the ability to communicate in writing was the key to empowerment for his people. But though the Cherokee had a rich spoken language, they had no written language. So Sequoyah invented one. In a very short time, the Cherokee became a literate people.

Each of these people had a desire to communicate and exerted the effort to fulfill that desire.

So if you feel timid when conversing with other people, tongue-tied when facing an audience, unsure of yourself when putting words on paper, don't give up. Remember Demosthenes, Sequoyah, Keller, Roosevelt, and Churchill. Cultivate the desire, and act upon it.

THE SECOND KEY: UNDERSTAND THE PROCESS

If you want to achieve excellence in communication, you have to cut through the surface and become acquainted with the underlying process. That's what helped Michelangelo achieve greatness as an artist.

Michelangelo wanted to sculpt the human body. He knew the body's outward appearance—the general contours of head, torso, and limbs. But to render the human body in all its subtleties, he needed to understand the underlying structure.

To obtain this knowledge, he would sneak into a mortuary at night and carefully cut through the skin of cadavers to examine the muscles, veins, and bones. It was gruesome work, but it led to some of the greatest art ever to grace the planet.

You don't have to go into a morgue to learn the techniques of communicating, but you must learn the underlying structure of the process.

Communicate Through Images

Language is the primary conveyer of thoughts and ideas. It turns abstract concepts into words that symbolize those thoughts. If the mind can immediately translate the sounds and symbols into mental pictures, communication becomes much more vivid and meaningful. If I say, "I want a desk for my office," my listener has only a vague and general idea of what I want. If I say, "I want a brown walnut desk," the listener has a more vivid mental picture. The more skillful you become at conveying images, the more effective your communication will be.

When Paul Revere began the mission that inspired Henry Wadsworth Longfellow's famous poem, he had to row his small boat past a British warship, the *Somerset*. The poet could have written, "Paul Revere rowed past the British warship *Somerset* on his way to Charles Town." But Longfellow visualized the scene: the dark waters, the ship's ominous hulk swinging wide from its moorings, the moon shining through the ship's rigging. He translated his image into words: "A phantom hulk, with each mast and spar across the moon like a prison bar."

We can't all be Longfellows, but we can do as Demosthenes did: study the techniques of the masters and learn from them. We can learn to translate the images and sounds we receive through our eyes and ears into words that will inform and inspire.

THE THIRD KEY:
MASTER THE BASIC SKILLS

Some people think the first requisite for good communication is an exhaustive vocabulary. Some people think it's impossible to communicate well without first absorbing a heavy dose of grammar, then memorizing a dictionary of English usage.

Words are important. Good grammar is important. And, yes, it helps to know which words and expressions are considered standard and which are considered substandard among educated people. But slavish allegiance to the rules of grammar can actually impede communication. People will sometimes go to great lengths to avoid usage that somebody has pronounced "ungrammatical" or "substandard." In the process, they forget the most important rule of communication: Make it clear and understandable.

Winston Churchill showed his contempt for overweening attention to grammar when he was upbraided for ending a sentence with a preposition. He retorted: "This is the sort of English up with which I will not put."

The purpose of communication is to convey ideas, not to show off vocabularies and grammatical expertise. The vocabulary you use in everyday speech has probably served you well. You use the words that you understand. Chances are, they're the words your friends, colleagues, and employees understand. If you try to use words beyond the vocabularies of the people you're trying to communicate with, you're not communicating; you're showing off.

Read the Gettysburg Address, the Sermon on the Mount, or Robert Frost's poetry. The communications that endure are written in plain, simple language.

Three Basic Skills

Had I waited until I had amassed a large vocabulary of English words and had a grammarian's knowledge of English, it would have taken me a long time to get started in my career. Fortunately, I didn't have to do that. I recognized the three true basic skills in communication: connecting with an audience, conveying messages people can understand, and checking their responses.

These three basic skills are fundamental to the work of any communicator.

THE FOURTH KEY: PRACTICE

No speaker is so good that practice won't improve the presentation. Practice gives confidence to the speaker and polish to the speech.

Practice was particularly important for me because I began my speaking career before I had achieved fluency in the English language. As an undergraduate student at Mount Olive College in North Carolina, I began speaking to people about my native country, and someone would pass the hat.

People in small churches were willing to accept a young foreign student's imperfect English. But my career aims were higher than that. I wanted to communicate my way to success, and that meant learning to use the English language fluently and skillfully. This called for practice. If English is your native tongue, you have a head start on me. But you still need practice to achieve true greatness as a communicator.

Practice Makes Superb

A young musician had listened with awe as a piano virtuoso poured all his love and skill into a complex selection of great compositions.

"It must be great to have all the practicing behind you and be able to sit down and play like that," he said.

"Oh," said the master musician, "I still practice eight hours every day."

"But why?" asked the astounded young man. "You're already so good!"

"I want to become superb," replied the older man.

To become superb, you have to practice. It isn't enough to know what it takes to connect with people, to influence their behavior, to create a motivational environment for them, to help them identify with your message. The techniques of communication have to become part of your daily activity, so that they are as natural to you as swimming is to a duck. The more you practice these techniques, the easier you'll find it to connect with people, whether you're dealing with individuals one on one or with a group of thousands.

Mental Rehearsal

If you're going to give a speech, imagine yourself on the platform, giving the presentation smoothly, clearly, effectively. Imagine what you'll say, how you'll say it, and what gestures you'll use. Imagine yourself feeling confident and energized. And—go ahead—imagine a standing ovation at the end.

You can use mental rehearsal just as effectively in preparing a presentation to a sales force, to a board of directors, or to an annual meeting of shareholders.

You can practice sensitive conversations or sales presentations, too. Imagine what you will say, what the responses will be, and how you will deal with those responses.

If you're planning to write something, get yourself into a relaxed mood and imagine what you would write if you were at your desk at that moment. Many writers get their best ideas while "rehearsing" their writing before falling asleep at night or while commuting to work.

This type of practice can be an immense help to you in progressing from the good to the superb.

THE FIFTH KEY: PATIENCE

Nobody becomes a polished, professional communicator on the first try. It takes patience. A few years ago, William White, a journalism and English instructor, edited a book of early writings by Ernest Hemingway.[1] The young Hemingway was a reporter for a Toronto newspaper, and this book was a collection of his articles written between 1920 and 1924.

The writing was good, but it was not superb. It gave a faint fore-gleam of the masterful storyteller who would emerge in *The Old Man and the Sea*, but it wasn't the Hemingway of literary legend.

What was lacking? Experience. The genius was there all along, but it needed to incubate. The sands of time can abrade or polish. It depends on whether you use your time purposely or let it pass haphazardly.

Hand Rub Your Language

Labor, for the skilled communicator, means constant, careful, loving attention to the craft. Columnist James J. Kilpatrick calls it "hand rubbing" your communication. Hemingway didn't go from cub reporter to master novelist by jotting down words off the top of his head. He looked at what he wrote, analyzed it, compared it to the best writing he had seen, and looked for ways to improve what he had written. In other words, he engaged in self-evaluation.

The cub reporter didn't transform himself into a successful novelist through one blinding flash of literary insight. Nor do people become excellent communicators overnight. Your communication skills can be enhanced through a progressive education program that emphasizes continuous improvement. Most people progress from the "good" to the "superb" through hundreds of tiny little improvements from day to day.

That's the way I developed my speaking and writing style. I listened to the best spoken English I could find and tried to model my pronunciation and diction after it. Although I learned English in a small town in North Carolina, I avoided regional accents as much as possible and worked on developing a speech style that would be at home anywhere in America. It has worked for me.

You can use the keys to the Kingdom of Communication in many settings, under a variety of circumstances. Longfellow was a virtuoso as a poet and Hemingway as a novelist, but the field of communication goes far beyond the literary field. You can be a virtuoso at inspiring your workforce, at negotiating business deals, at marketing your products, and at building a positive corporate image. All these are important communication skills. But always remember: Whatever communication task you undertake, your objective is to connect with people. And that means that your communication must be personal. In the next chapter, we explore ways of communicating so that people will identify personally with your message.

3

ALL COMMUNICATION IS PERSONAL

All communication is personal. A mass audience doesn't have a mind. The individuals within that audience have minds. A speech, a broadcast, or a piece of writing, no matter how polished and professional, will have no measurable effect unless it connects with the minds of individuals. It's like a radio signal beamed at a certain frequency. If no radio receiver is tuned to that frequency, the signal vanishes into thin air.

The message-sender must know how to address the personal concerns of the intended message-receiver.

THE IMPORTANCE OF DIALOGUE

To establish that personal connection, you have to engage in dialogue. Dialogue, according to one dictionary definition, is "an exchange of ideas and opinions."

But dialogue means much more than a swapping of opinions. If I say the United States is a democracy and you say, "No, it isn't," and we both drop the subject, nothing has been accomplished. We have swapped opinions, but neither of us has gained much insight into the other's thinking.

But suppose you explain to me that, by your definition, the United States is not a democracy, in which all issues are settled by popular vote, but a republic, in which laws are made by elected representatives. Then I can respond, "I agree that, by your definition, the United States is not a democracy. But to me, a democracy is a government in which people have a right to choose their representatives by popular vote."

Now we have engaged in dialogue. You understand my definition of democracy and I understand yours. Through dialogue, we learn that the similarity between our views is greater than the difference, and we can move on.

Dialogue, by my definition, is *what happens when your reality connects with your audience's reality and together you move toward a new common reality.*

Dialogue with Mass Audiences

Dialogue doesn't have to take place between two individuals. You can have dialogue with a mass audience, too, provided the message you send strikes a personal note with the individuals in that audience.

One of the most stirring examples of dialogue with a mass audience took place at the dedication of the Gettysburg battlefield on November 19, 1863. The principal address on that occasion was a finely crafted speech delivered by Edward Everett, one of the foremost orators of the day. After he spoke, President Abraham Lincoln delivered a brief secondary speech.

Few people today can recite a single line from Edward Everett's speech at Gettysburg. Generations of schoolchildren have memorized what Lincoln said on that historic occasion.

Lincoln knew his audience. He spoke in simple phrases that nevertheless resonated in the hearts of a nation saddened by civil war. Though the immediate effect on the fifteen thousand people gathered at the battlefield was unimpressive, the president spoke beyond them to the nation at large and, in fact, to posterity. In moments of national crisis ever since, the American people have drawn courage from his words:

> We here highly resolve that these dead shall not have died in vain—that this nation, under God, shall have a new birth of freedom—and that the government of the people, by the people, for the people, shall not perish from the earth.

The words came from the heart of the president and they were aimed straight at the hearts of war-weary Americans. They carried personal meaning for every parent who had lost a son in battle and for every American who despaired for the survival of democracy on the continent. The reality within Abraham Lincoln touched the reality in the hearts of his audience, and together they moved toward a new reality: a stronger, freer America.

Effective communicators know their audiences. They know whom they want to reach and they know how to reach them with messages that touch them personally.

MADISON AVENUE TECHNIQUES

Madison Avenue has become adept at appealing to personal motivations. Watch a new car commercial. It will waste very little time detailing the engineering features of the car. People don't buy cubic inches or compression ratios. They buy driving experiences. They buy image. They buy prestige. The ad writers seek to connect with these desires.

"This is not your father's Oldsmobile" was a line aimed at young people who might once have thought of the Olds as a wheelchair for old folks.

AT&T's familiar line, "Reach out and touch someone," is a personal invitation to everyone within reach of a telephone who has loved ones in distant places.

"You got the right one, Baby, uh-huh" tells you nothing about the flavor of Pepsi Cola compared with that of Coca Cola. But the style and flavor of the commercial clicked with the young audience toward which it was aimed, and soon the youngsters were repeating it and improvising it.

BARRIERS TO DIALOGUE

While the late twentieth century puts a premium on the art of dialogue, it also raises formidable obstacles to it. Physically and technologically, this is the most connected generation in history.

Psychologically, though, we are a disconnected generation. Bombarded daily by communications of every sort and from every direction, we have had to master the art of tuning out most of the information that comes our way. We have learned instinctively to disregard junk mail and focus on the envelopes that bear personal messages. We have learned to regard the sound from our radios and television sets as background noise until we hear something that concerns us personally. This ability to "tune out" is almost a necessity in this age of the information explosion.

But many of us have tuned in technology and tuned out the human factor. We have become so accustomed to being entertained by our television sets, VCRs, stereos, boom boxes, and video games that we have almost forgotten what it's like to interact with other humans.

We've learned the art of channel hopping, flipping remote controls to tune out programming that doesn't interest us. Many people have also developed the art of tuning out the thoughts, ideas, and emotions of other humans. You may notice it when you go into a convenience store and the clerk goes through the mechanics of waiting on you as if it were a transaction between two robots. Salespeople notice it when they call on prospective clients whose attention spans seem to be about as long as the time it takes to switch channels.

Effective communicators must be able to overcome this tune-out tendency and connect with the personal interests of their audiences. The targets of their messages should say, "Aha!" instead of "So what?"

THE FIRST LAW OF
EFFECTIVE COMMUNICATION

This brings us to my First Law of Effective Communication: *No worthwhile communication can take place until you gain the complete attention of your audience.*

In my speaking career, I developed a simple rule for establishing and sustaining contact with my listeners: The audience is top priority. The first thing I do after I've been introduced to an audience is get the audience into the act. I find some device that will elicit audience participation, and I proceed with my talk only when I'm sure I have their undivided attention. I look for signs that the audience's attention is straying, and when I see them, I do something to reestablish contact. For example:

- I ask a question to which the audience can respond.
- I find a way to become physically involved with the audience and to get the audience physically involved with me.
- I use more humor, anecdotes, and audiovisuals.

The principle of involvement doesn't just apply to a speaker addressing an audience. No matter what form of communication you're using, the people you're trying to reach are your audience, and you have to get them involved.

You Have to Get Personal

Whether you're engaged in advertising, marketing, sales, or supervision, you have to get personal. When something becomes personal, it becomes important. You get personal by showing people how they can benefit from listening to your message, or how what you're saying can affect their personal lives.

Lowe's building-supply stores used the personal approach in a series of television commercials showing how ordinary people had made use of Lowe's products in home improvement projects. One commercial described how a family on Elm Street in a small Midwestern town had benefited from using Lowe's supplies. It concluded by saying that Lowe's provided quality products for building projects "on Elm Street and your street." Ordinary homeowners could identify personally with the people these commercials depicted, and the "Elm Street and your street" line reinforced that identification.

When people can make that personal connection between your message and their own lives, good things begin to happen.

When your employees can personally identify with the corporate projects in which they're involved, they will exert themselves to make the projects successful.

One of the secrets behind the spectacular success of the Ford Taurus was the involvement of Ford stakeholders at every level in its design and conception. Team Taurus consulted assembly workers, engineers, salespeople, insurance people, suppliers, and dealers for ideas about the kind of car they'd like to build, sell, and drive. The entire corporate workforce could thus take personal pride in the automobile's success.

Involve the Audience

Successful companies have found that the secret to effective marketing is to involve their audience—the customer—personally and emotionally. Thus, Prudential doesn't sell insurance policies. It offers its customers the security of owning "a piece of the rock." Kodak generated a lot of business not by asking people to buy its film, but by inviting them to "trust your memories to Kodak." What a powerful way to involve people in your product!

Many people are intimidated by computers and their peripheral accessories. They view them as mysterious, incomprehensible, and cantankerous. Therefore, Hewlett-Packard didn't try to sell computers and printers. It advertised, instead, "solutions to unusual problems."

Connect with Employees

If you're an executive leading a corporate workforce, you must always keep the personal interests of your employees in mind. Remember, *people do things for their own reasons—not for yours or mine*. To mobilize their talents and energies behind your corporate goals, you have to show them how their best interests are served by these goals. If they can see personal benefits arising from your corporate goals, then they will become involved in fulfilling them.

But first you have to establish dialogue. That means listening to others. If you listen to individuals long enough, they'll tell you what their concerns and problems are. Take the time to get to know the people you seek to lead—not just their names, but their interests and aspirations. In a friendly way, talk to them about what they did over the weekend, what they plan to do on vacation, what their personal goals are. Then listen. When you listen with open ears and open mind, you'll learn what their interests are. And you'll know how to involve them through personal communication.

4

THE MESSENGER SPEAKS
LOUDER THAN
THE MESSAGE

If you don't believe the messenger speaks louder than the message, consider these two statements:

1. "Haint we got all the fools in town on our side? And ain't that a big enough majority in any town?"
2. "A majority can never replace the man. . . . Just as a hundred fools do not make one wise man, a heroic decision is not likely to come from a hundred cowards."

The first statement says it with rustic humor. The second statement says it in a loftier tone. But both make the same point: The majority decision isn't always the wisest or the noblest one.

Read them again, this time remembering who uttered them. The first statement is from Mark Twain. The second is from Adolf Hitler. How does your knowledge of the sources alter the message you receive? The odium attached to the name of Adolf Hitler negates any positive thing he ever said, and no amount of eloquence will lend it respectability. So if you want to communicate in a positive way, you must cultivate a positive image as a person.

The way people perceive you will depend upon the way you interact with them. We interact with people in one of three basic modes:

- Superior to inferior
- Inferior to superior
- Equal to equal

SUPERIOR TO INFERIOR

The superior-to-inferior relationship can take several forms.

One is the boss–underling relationship. That's the standard relationship between management and employees in the authoritarian workplace. We see it in the comic-strip relationship between Dagwood and Mr. Dithers. Charles Dickens described it in his story of Ebeneezer Scrooge and Bob Cratchett. That relationship has no place in today's workplace. If you approach employees or colleagues with a superior attitude, you can bet that you'll turn them off. Americans have been thoroughly indoctrinated in the philosophy that all people are created equal. Superior position, superior knowledge, superior expertise, and superior experience will win you respect, but only if you display the proper regard for the self-worth of others.

Manipulated Again, Charlie Brown!

The superior-to-inferior mode also manifests itself in the methods of the manipulator. The comic strips provide examples of this relationship as well. Garfield the cat is constantly manipulating Odie the dog. In "Peanuts," Lucy is constantly manipulating Charlie Brown.

Manipulative people are always suspected of having something up their sleeves. Their actions breed attitudes of distrust among the people they work with. The manipulator won't attract a loyal following. Would you trust Lucy to hold the football for you in the big game?

Social Snobbery

Social snobbery is another form of superior-to-inferior relationship. It sometimes comes disguised as noblesse oblige. Webster's defines this as "the obligation of honorable, generous and responsible behavior that is concomitant of high rank or birth." But American society is founded on egalitarian principles. The expression "poor but proud" is a defiantly American one. It captures the idea that wealth and social standing do not confer superiority. If your good deeds are done from the perspective of a superior bestowing favors on inferiors, they will go unappreciated. The recipients will regard you as condescending and patronizing, and will resent you.

Social snobbery often manifests itself on the job as a class distinction between blue-collar and white-collar workers; between degreed and nondegreed employees; between people with advanced degrees and people with bachelor's degrees. It becomes counterproductive when the "superior" refuses to regard the ideas of the "inferior" as worthy of consideration.

The Engineer and the Tool-and-Die Maker

Charles Dygert is a friend of mine who now holds a Ph.D. in vocational education and heads a highly successful consulting business. He began his career as a tool-and-die maker for General Motors. In that blue-collar capacity, he worked from blueprints provided by white-collar engineers.

On one of his first jobs, he discovered a mistake in the blueprint. His fellow tool-and-die makers urged him to follow the blueprint and make the engineer look foolish. They were aware of the blue-collar/white-collar class distinctions and had no love for their "superiors." Charlie was sorely tempted to take their advice, but he decided to correct the error quietly and save the engineer from embarrassment.

Some time later, another engineer approached him with a prototype of a part he wanted to make. He asked Charlie to work with him to design the die to mass produce the part. As Charlie recalls, "I gave him six ideas I wouldn't have thought about before." The white-collar engineer showed respect for the blue-collar tool-and-die maker, and it paid off.

Charlie tells of another plant in which the blue-collar workers came up with a plan that enabled them to retool a major piece of equipment with only fifteen minutes of down time, compared with twelve hours under the procedure set up by plant engineers.

Had the white-collar personnel of that plant practiced social snobbery, the employees would not have gone to them with their idea, and the company would have denied itself tens of thousands of dollars in savings every time it retooled.

Racial or Ethnic Condescension

Another common type of superior-to-inferior attitude is racial or ethnic condescension. We often assume that people with different skin colors, different accents, or different-sounding names have inferior communication and comprehension skills.

The story is told of a Euro-American who sat down at a banquet table next to a man who was obviously of Asian descent. Assuming that his companion was Chinese, the Euro-American turned to him during the soup course and inquired, "Likee soupee?"

When the principal speaker was introduced, the Euro-American was surprised to see the man of Asian descent rise and walk to the podium. He proceeded to give a brilliant address in a fluent, middle-American accent. As he sat down, he turned to the Euro-American and inquired, "Likee speechee?"

Remember: The skin color, ethnic background, or accent of an individual tells you nothing about the individual's native abilities. Nor does your own skin color, ethnic origin, or accent protect you from making a fool of yourself.

INFERIOR TO SUPERIOR

Many gifted people never become all that they could become because they harbor feelings of inferiority. They're afraid to express their own ideas for fear that others know more than they know. They're reluctant to take the initiative because they feel that others are more qualified.

Truman Took Charge

Harry Truman may have felt that way initially when the weight of the presidency fell on him. He had to step into the shoes of the man many regarded as the greatest president since Abraham Lincoln. He had to assume national leadership at a time when the global political order had been shattered. This ex-farmer, unsuccessful haberdasher, and small-time Missouri politician, who hadn't even gone to college, had to negotiate with the likes of Winston Churchill, Joseph Stalin, and Charles DeGaulle. He had to give orders to George Marshall, Douglas MacArthur, Dwight Eisenhower, Chester Nimitz, and Bull Halsey. He had to deal with the question of nuclear weapons, the existence of which had been unknown to him before taking office. Upon his shoulders fell the weight of rebuilding Europe; stopping communism in Greece, Turkey, Iran, and Korea; and reconstituting Japan as a friendly democracy. And at home he had to deal with aggressive labor leaders, defiant segregationists who resisted his efforts to dismantle racial barriers, and virulent red-baiters who were willing to sacrifice democratic principles in their zeal to exterminate communism.

Had Truman communicated with Stalin and Churchill as inferior to superiors, had he allowed Douglas MacArthur free rein in the Far East, had he knuckled under to domestic foes with far greater academic and intellectual credentials, had he doubted his own capacity for decision making, the postwar story would have been far different.

Were all of Truman's decisions the correct ones?

Of course not. Some of them had unfortunate consequences. Some of them are still being hotly debated. But his standing as a leader is unquestioned. In recent elections, presidential candidates of both parties have proudly claimed Harry Truman as a role model.

In whatever field you choose to enter, you will never be any better than you think you are. If you regard yourself as inferior to others, others will regard you as inferior to them. If you confidently assume the role of a leader, others will follow your leadership.

Self-Confidence Can Save the Day

Once a group of hikers in the mountains found themselves engulfed by smoke from a forest fire. The fire threatened to encircle them. The smoke obscured all landmarks. They began to stumble in all directions until one of them said confidently, "Follow me."

Linking hands to stay together, they followed the leader. She led them on a straight path through the smoke to safety.

"How did you know the way out?" one of the hikers asked later.

"I didn't," she said, "but I knew we were goners if we didn't get out of there, so I set a course and stuck to it."

The leader had no more knowledge and skill than any of the other hikers. What she had was self-confidence.

The movie classic *The Wizard of Oz* illustrates the difference a confident attitude makes. The cowardly lion wanted the Wizard to give him courage. The scarecrow wanted a brain. The tin man wanted a heart. And Dorothy wanted to return to Kansas, where she had lived before a tornado swept her away.

The Wizard had a con man's understanding of human nature. He gave the lion a medal, and suddenly the cowardly lion felt brave. He gave the scarecrow a diploma, and at once the scarecrow began acting like a literate person. He gave the tin man a ticking clock, and the tin man took heart. As for Dorothy, he told her that she had always had the power to return to Kansas. All she had to do was to close her eyes and repeat, "There's no place like home," and click her heels together. When she did that, her mind conveyed her out of the dream world of Oz and into the real world she had left when the tornado struck.

In social and business relationships, people often have the feeling that they are powerless to remove themselves from an unwanted situation. Abused spouses stay with their abusers because they have allowed themselves to fall into an inferior-to-superior relationship. Employees tolerate oppressive bosses and sometimes put up with sexual harassment because they see the inferior-to-superior relationship as normal for them. It isn't normal and they aren't helpless. Just as Dorothy had it within her power to return to Kansas, they have it within their power to move out of such situations and into normal relationships.

They don't need a Wizard of Oz. The Wizard performed no magic. All he did was help the four characters recognize the innate qualities they already possessed. He gave them self-confidence.

You Have the Tools of Greatness

Floyd Wickman, one of the nation's leading sales authors and real-estate educators, languished for years in go-nowhere jobs as a Navy enlisted man, a milkman, and a lackadaisical real-estate salesman. Then one day, in a sales workshop, he heard a simple poem that changed his attitude toward himself. The poem, as Wickman recalls it, goes something like this:

> Figure it out for yourself, my lad;
> You've all that the greatest of men have had:
> Two arms, two legs, and a brain to use—
> A brain to use if only you choose.[1]

Wickman went on to build a tremendously successful company. One day, in Las Vegas, I gave the keynote address for his Masters Academy and watched firsthand the transformed—and respected—executive in action.

So when you have feelings of inadequacy in the face of others who seem to be more gifted, remember: You have everything it takes to be a leader—two arms, two legs, a brain, a heart, courage, and the ability to go wherever you wish. All you have to do is recognize them.

EQUAL TO EQUAL

The most effective mode of communicating with people is as equal to equal. That doesn't mean that CEOs have to wear coveralls to work and crawl into the grease pits with their line employees.

It does mean that executives, managers, and supervisors at all levels must respect the dignity of every person in the organization and communicate with employees on a human-to-human rather than a boss-to-underling basis.

Some companies even refrain from referring to people as "employees." They prefer more egalitarian designations, such as "associates" and "team members." But remember: It doesn't help to change the way you designate positions if you don't show respect for the people in those positions.

Elitist attitudes can be communicated in ways other than words. Do top executives get the choice parking spaces, even when they have no more need for their cars during working hours than does anyone else in the organization? Do they ride up to their executive suites on special elevators, eat in executive dining facilities that are off-limits to ordinary workers, and use gold-plated executive rest rooms that other employees never enter?

Then they are saying to their employees: "We're the elite; you're the unwashed crowd."

In companies such as Medtronic, a Fortune 500 manufacturer of medical electronic devices, even the CEO is required to show a badge before entering a manufacturing facility. This helps convey to all employees that the CEO is one of them, not some inaccessible and all-powerful entity.

Guides to the Pecking Order

Executives can also establish an aura of superiority through imposing offices guarded by an army of secretaries. These surroundings can be intimidating to those farther down the corporate ladder.

In some organizations, offices are not designed to encourage a flow of communication among corporate people. They are designed, instead, to show where their occupants stand in the pecking order.

A few years ago, Bell Laboratories took a look at its office layout. It discovered that nonsupervisory personnel usually shared an office with at least one other person. The office had a glass door so that supervisors could always look in to see what was going on.

Supervisors had private offices. They had glass doors, too, but the lower half of the door was frosted, so that you had to stand on tiptoes to see in.

The doors to the offices of department heads had frosted glass from top to bottom. To find out what was going on inside, you had to put your ear to the door and listen.

Executive directors had thick wooden doors. You couldn't see through them and you couldn't hear through them.

Bell Labs redesigned its offices to open up communication channels. The new arrangement had no enclosed offices and no floor-to-ceiling separations of any kind. The work spaces were set off by panels, partitions, furniture, and accessories.

Executives, however, shouldn't have to surrender all their privacy. They need some time in which to concentrate on their executive duties, free of distractions. Many executives, while retaining the privacy of their separate offices, set aside blocs of time each day during which they will receive telephone calls and will talk to staffers and employees who feel the need to confer with them.

Job Skills Versus People Skills

A company today can't be run from the ivory tower. You have to get out and touch people. You have to learn how they feel, think, and respond. You have to learn about their problems, their joys, and their triumphs.

I serve on the board of directors of Southern National Corporation, a regional bank holding company with more than $20 billion in assets. Each of Southern National's corporate executive officers makes it a policy to dedicate one day a month to visiting in the field. They actually go out with their people and meet customers and prospects. They know the people on the front line and the frontline people know them. It has paid great dividends.

This kind of contact gives them great credibility among the people they lead, and this credibility is vital for leadership in the twenty-first century.

Some people think it's enough to develop the basic career skills. But the career skills required for the twenty-first century are likely to change often. The long-term skills that will assure success will be in the area of human interaction. They are skills that will serve you within the family unit, within your social circle, within your community, and within your business organization. They are the skills that will define you as a total person. That totality constitutes a powerful message.

Avoid Relationship Pitfalls

This generation seems to be having a particularly hard time with personal relationships. The family that stays together from wedding bell to funeral knell is becoming increasingly rare. The number of blended families and one-parent households is on the rise. The individual who can negotiate today's obstacle course with relationships intact will hold a major psychological advantage in the race for success.

As I've worked with people at all levels of organizations and in a wide variety of settings, I've observed five common causes of failure in personal relationships, whether in business or at home. They are:

- Preoccupation with self
- Hasty assumptions
- Negative attitudes
- An all-consuming desire to be liked
- A disregard for courtesy

1. *Preoccupation with self.* More than 185 years ago, Sir Walter Scott wrote:

   The wretch concentered all in self,
   Living shall forfeit fair renown,
   And doubly dying, shall go down
   To the vile dust, from whence he sprung,
   Unwept, unhonored, and unsung.

Nobody likes to deal with a person who is afflicted with the "Big I." Self-centered people monopolize the conversation, and always turn the subject back to *their* opinions, *their* abilities, *their* accomplishments, and *their* agenda. They are so concerned about the interests of the "Big I" that they have no time to consider the interests of others.

The word *success* does not contain an *I*. The first vowel is the *U*, and until we learn to think *you* instead of *I*, our batting average in business and in human relations will be close to zero. The best rule for human interaction is still the one pronounced nearly two thousand years ago from a hillside in Galilee: "As ye would that men should do to you, do ye also to them likewise." The surest route to success today is to find out what others want, and look for ways to provide it. This applies whether you're trying to maintain a healthy and harmonious home atmosphere, sell goods and services in the global market, or align a workforce behind an ambitious vision. Being other person-oriented is a learnable trait. It often comes naturally with maturity.

2. *Hasty assumptions.* People who jump to conclusions rarely land in the middle of success. We often prejudge people and circumstances by surface appearances without investigating what lies underneath.

A middle-aged man in shabby work clothes walked into the showroom of a Chrysler dealership in Virginia. The salespeople studiously ignored him.

Finally, the owner of the dealership walked over and asked if he could help.

"How much is that car?" asked the man, pointing to the most expensive model Chrysler offered.

The dealer told him.

"I'll take one," said the customer.

"Very good," said the dealer. "And how would you like to finance it?"

"I'll write you a check," said the man.

And so he did. And as he took delivery of his new car, he turned to the dealer once more.

"By the way," he said. "Do you sell dump trucks?"

The dealer proceeded to sell four Dodge dump trucks to this man, who was the owner of a local construction business.

Looks can be deceiving. Success doesn't always wear Brooks

Brothers suits and Gucci ties. It can also wear jeans and flannel shirts, coveralls and work gloves, or skirts and blouses.

Misjudging Motives

We often jump to conclusions about the motives of others. It's a human tendency to judge ourselves by our motives but to judge others by their actions. We can always convince ourselves that our motives justify our actions. But when we see someone else committing acts that we disapprove of, we're quick to assign improper motives. Often, too, we assume that we know what people are going to say before they say it. So we jump in and complete their sentences, or we respond to what we think they're going to say before they have a chance to say it.

3. *Negative Attitudes.* You may remember the little guy with the unpronounceable name in the comic strip "Li'l Abner," who went around under a perpetual rain cloud. Wherever he went, things went wrong.

Some people are expert rainmakers. They bring on their bad luck through negative attitudes. They know things are going to go wrong, and this faith becomes a self-fulfilling prophecy.

"Cheer up," I once told my friend Bob, who seemed always to be on the losing side of life. "Things could be worse."

"I know," he said. "I once cheered up, and sure enough, things got worse."

"Listen," I said. "If you just have faith that something *good* will happen, something good *will* happen. I want you to believe—really *believe*—that you're going to have a great day tomorrow."

At the end of the next day, I called Bob to ask how his day went.

"Lousy," he said. "Just as I expected."

I had another friend, Charlie, who was just the opposite. If a load of manure fell on Charlie, he'd say, "Boy, think how this is going to help my strawberry plants!"

No matter what the weather was like, and no matter what his circumstances were, if you asked Charlie how his day was going, he'd say, "Today is the best day of my life."

I once asked him: "Charlie, how is it that every time I see you you're having the best day of your life?"

"Well, Nido," he said, "yesterday is gone forever and tomorrow is not yet mine. Today is the only day I ever have, so that makes it the best day of my life."

Charlie died a few years ago, but I'm sure that his reward will be an eternity in which each day is the best day of his life.

People loved Charlie. People avoid Bob. They're afraid lightning will strike them or a tree might fall on them while they're around him. And it just might happen.

4. *The desire to be liked.* It's natural to want people to like you. We draw strength and inspiration from our friends. The warm glow of friendship is a great morale booster. But when you try to buy friendship at any price, you cheapen the product. You end up not respecting yourself, and others don't respect you either.

You win respect by setting high standards and living up to them. The Shakespearean counsel is valid in any age:

This above all: to thine own self be true,
And it must follow, as the night the day,
Thou canst be false to any man.

Subordinates often try to curry friendship with the boss by saying what they think the boss wants to hear. When they do this, they serve neither themselves nor the boss. A good executive knows the difference between a friend and a sycophant. Executives need people who are not afraid to bring them the bad news. They respect those who speak up for what they know and believe. If the boss knows you're a "yes person," how much weight will your opinions and advice carry? What you are will speak much louder than what you say.

People who are promoted to positions in which they supervise their former peers often face situations in which duty appears to conflict with friendship. The answer to that dilemma was provided by the Greek philosopher Sophocles 2,400 years ago: "I have nothing but contempt for the kind of governor who is afraid, for whatever reason, to follow the course that he knows is best for the state; and as for the man who sets private friendship above the public welfare—I have no use for him either."

What's true in the realm of public office is also true in the business setting. Stay true to your principles. Your true friends will respect you for it. The friendships you'll lose because of it are not worth having in the first place.

5. *Disregard for courtesy.* Some people go to the opposite extreme. They interrupt people at will, and they say what's on their minds without regard for other people's feelings. They think the world should run on their schedule, so they show up for appointments when it's convenient, and if they keep others waiting, that's tough. Concessions are for weaklings and diplomacy is useful only as a manipulative tool.

Such people may be able to bulldoze their way to success for a while. But when they encounter reverses and find themselves in need of supporters, they'll find more gloaters than sympathizers.

Courtesy is the oil that lubricates the machinery of commerce. It smooths the path to success in sales, in management, and in personal relationships. For courtesy usually is reciprocated. When you open the door for your companion, your companion will usually open the next door for you. If you listen without interrupting the person who is addressing you, that person usually will listen without interrupting you.

If courtesy isn't reciprocated, don't resort to rudeness in return. The most devastating response to a discourteous act is an act of calm, deliberate courtesy.

You Are a Powerful Medium

You can't find a more powerful medium of communication than yourself—your character, your personality, and your principles.

If you want to send a powerful, positive message to the people with whom you work, follow these principles.

1. *You manage the process, but you lead people.* An organization runs smoothly when its people function smoothly. Dealing with problems in engineering, production, marketing, and sales without considering the human element is like dealing with a flat tire without considering air. The finest steel-belted radial is worthless without

the air that holds it up. The finest engineering, manufacturing, marketing, sales, and servicing systems are worthless without the people who keep them functioning.

In an interview with *Harvard Business Review,* Robert Haas, chair of the board of Levi Strauss, called production management "the hard stuff" and people management "the soft stuff."[2]

Under the old philosophy at Levi Strauss, he said, "The soft stuff was the company's commitment to our workforce. And the hard stuff was what really mattered: getting pants out the door. What we've learned is that the soft stuff and the hard stuff are becoming increasingly intertwined."

So pay careful attention to the human side of your business.

2. *Inspire people, don't just drive them.* We can inspire people by showing them how to be their very best. Ed Temple, the Tennessee State track coach who worked with some of America's top woman track stars, liked to say, "A mule you drive, but with a race horse, you use finesse."[3] Treat your people like Thoroughbreds instead of like mules. They'll get the message and respond.

3. *Be easy to respect and look up to.* You don't gain respect by sitting in an ivory tower and looking down on the work floor. Be accessible to employees and let them see your human side.

Employees are turned off by executives who pretend to be infallible. Observe high standards of personal conduct, but let your employees know that you're human. Talk to them about your bad decisions as well as your good ones. When you blow it, grin and admit it. Your employees will respect you for it.

4. *Be easy to like and get along with.* Employees like leaders who are human—who make mistakes and admit it. It's all right to let them see your vulnerability. If you made a bad decision, talk about it with the people you lead. Let it be a lesson for them as well as for you.

Don't feel that you have to know everything. Acknowledge that the people you lead may know much more than you do about certain things.

5. *Help people like themselves.* Robert W. Reasoner, a California school superintendent who headed a statewide task force on self-esteem, identified five basic attitudes that foster self-esteem. They are:

- A sense of security
- A sense of identity
- A sense of belonging
- A sense of purpose
- A sense of personal competence

Secure people are comfortable with who they are and with what others think about them. They know their roles in the organization and are confident that they can fill them.

People with a *sense of identity* know how they fit into the workplace and how the workplace fits into their lives. To them, work takes its place among family, friends, and community as an important and fulfilling component of their lives.

When employees have a *sense of belonging*, they identify with the company's vision and goals, because these things have personal meaning for them. They personally share in the success and prestige of the company.

Employees obtain a *sense of purpose* from knowing the company's goals and how their efforts contribute toward those goals. Management needs to take employees into its confidence and give them a role in planning and goal setting. You can give employees a *sense of personal competence* by educating them for their jobs and giving them the freedom to succeed or fail on their own.

6. *Help people believe that what they're doing is important.* My friend Stew Leonard, a grocery-store wizard from Connecticut, once told me that he refused to use job titles that he perceives as demeaning. Once he noticed a job listed as "popcorn maker." He immediately ordered a more dignified title.

"How would you feel if someone asked you what you did for a living and you had to answer, 'I'm a popcorn maker'?" he asked me.

Are there any demeaning titles in your organization?

Medtronic, Inc., has a heartwarming way of dramatizing the importance of what its employees do. Each year at Christmastime, the company holds a party for employees. Guests of honor are people whose lives have been prolonged by Medtronic cardiopulmonary devices.

Can you think of ways of dramatizing to your employees the importance of what they do?

7. *Be responsive to people. Listen to people. Read people. Respond; don't react.* Leaders should be accessible to the people they lead. Let your staff and associates know they can come to you with problems, concerns, ideas, suggestions, or complaints. If they bring you usable ideas, adopt the ideas and give the employees credit.

Welcome bad news as well as the good. What you don't know can hurt you. Don't ignore complaints. Listen to them. Find out what you can do to rectify matters. Let the employees know what you plan to do—and do it.

If you put these principles into practice, you will be constantly sending out a powerful and positive message: yourself.

Humans have a variety of ways to send messages. We "speak" with our eyes, our facial expressions, our posture, our clothes, our grooming, our lifestyles, and many other aspects of our persons. But the most familiar and most explicit form of communication is with words. In the next chapter, we'll explore ways to use words for maximum impact.

5

CHOOSING YOUR WORDS

You probably learned in kindergarten that "sticks and stones may break my bones, but words can never harm me."

Yet you can't believe everything you learned in kindergarten. In the world of politics and statecraft, choosing the wrong words can lose elections, precipitate wars, and destroy cities. In the world of business, poor word choices can alienate clients, drive away customers, and land you in lawsuits.

When you write a business letter, draft a proposal, dictate a report, address your employees, speak to a community organization, or negotiate a business deal, words can be powerful tools of success or dangerous instruments of self-destruction.

A Quarantine to Avert War

Ask the Russians. In 1962 President John F. Kennedy was presented with convincing evidence that the Soviet Union was setting up bases in Cuba for nuclear-tipped missiles that could threaten American cities. Soviet ships might soon arrive bearing missiles and nuclear warheads. The president weighed his options. The United States Navy could *blockade* the Cuban coast, but a blockade would be an act of war. A war between the Soviet Union and the United States would surely escalate into a nuclear conflict.

Kennedy declared that no nuclear weapons would be allowed into Cuba. But he didn't call it a blockade. He called it a *quarantine*. That face-saving word allowed the Soviet leader, Nikita Khrushchev, to back down without acquiescing to an act of war. It's possible that one word avoided a nuclear holocaust.

41

THE VALUE OF WORDS

In the world of business, words convey instructions and inspiration to the people who produce goods and services. They are the medium through which merchandise is marketed and sold. They provide guidelines for those who ship and deliver. And they convey directions for assembling and using the products.

The quality of a company's communications can have a significant effect on the image it projects to its customers and clients. Letters that have a professional ring inspire confidence in your organization. And precision in the use of language can save you money when you're making proposals, entering agreements, or quoting specifications.

The way you use words influences the way people size you up as a businessperson. A person who uses language fluently and correctly (proper grammar) is likely to exert much more influence than one who uses it ineptly (mispronouncing and misusing words) and incorrectly (poor grammar).

That doesn't mean that your grammar must be impeccable and that you must know—and use—every word in the dictionary. It simply means that you stand a much better chance of succeeding in the business world if your speaking and your writing identify you as an educated person. In the world of business, as in the worlds of politics and statecraft, the ability to communicate clearly, precisely, and eloquently in spoken and written language is a prime asset. The English language is made up of about 800,000 words. Fortunately, we don't need to know all of them to communicate effectively. We use only about 800 words in our daily conversation. Words must be used with care, however, because their meanings are often slippery. Those 800 everyday words that we use can have about 14,000 different meanings.

Slugging Away

To illustrate: You drink a slug of orange juice in the morning before leaving for work. You read in the morning paper that doctors removed a .22-caliber slug from the shoulder of a robbery victim. As you step outside your front door to pick up your newspaper, you avoid a slimy slug crawling across your lawn. In the cafeteria at your office building, you try to put a quarter into the coffee vending machine, but it won't accept your money. Somebody has dropped a slug into the slot and jammed it. It makes you so mad you want to slug the person who did it.

In that simple story, the word *slug* had five different meanings. Other common words have many more. Webster's Third New International Dictionary lists more than forty meanings for the word *run* and more than thirty for *ring*.

Regional Variations

Meanings of common words may vary from region to region. In most places, if you invite people to dinner, you expect them to arrive sometime after six. But in some places, you'd better expect them around noon. Most Americans refer to the midday meal as lunch and the evening meal as dinner. But in some areas, people have their dinner in the middle of the day and eat supper before going to bed.

A mess is an untidy situation unless you're in the military service, in which case it refers to a meal. In the rural South, a mess refers to the quantity of a commodity required for a family meal.

If you're in Georgia and you're told to "mash the button" for the third floor, don't try to crush the elevator button. You're simply being requested to press it. In South Carolina, a young man might say to his girlfriend's father, "Can I carry your daughter to the picture show?" The father, if he's also from South Carolina, won't throw the young man out. He'll understand him to mean, "May I escort your daughter to the movie?"

So before you speak and before you listen, look around to see where you are.

Standard English Is Always at Home

Despite variations from one locale to another, from one social group to another, and from one ethnic group to another, North Americans generally employ a mutually comprehensible dialect called Standard American English. England, Australia, and New Zealand also have their standard versions of the mother tongue.

For Americans, Standard English is the language of the national television newscast, which communicates to almost every level of society. Wherever you live, if you learn to use the standard dialect of your language, it will serve you in almost every business and social setting you're likely to encounter.

The Multilingual Heritage of English

The English language in all its dialects has been enriched by borrowed words from many different languages, including Latin, German, Greek, Celtic, French, Spanish, Italian, Danish, Yiddish, Arabic, Chinese, and Japanese. It also has drawn on American Indian and African tribal languages. For example, a farmer may raise *swine* (Anglo-Saxon). When he kills and butchers one of the *hogs* (Celtic), he puts *pork* (French) on the table, perhaps accompanied by *succotash* (Algonquian).

The foundation of modern English is the Germanic Anglo-Saxon language. In the year 1066 the French-speaking Normans conquered England, and for the next couple of centuries the French language blended with the Anglo-Saxon, giving rise to modern English. French, in turn, is an offspring of Latin, the language of the Roman Empire.

Today most of the words in the English dictionary are derived from Latin. But most of the words we use in everyday speech are from Anglo-Saxon.

Short and Strong Versus Scholarly and Lofty

As a general rule, Anglo-Saxon words are shorter and more energetic than Latin words. Latin words often are considered more elegant and more scholarly, perhaps because they were the words used by the French-speaking nobility after the Norman conquest. Sometimes Anglo-Saxon words are considered crude whereas their Latin synonyms are considered usable in polite company. Thus "Huxley's Whores" in Leon Uris's novel, *Battle Cry*, became "Huxley's Harlots" in the movie, which was made before Hollywood adopted the policy of "anything goes." Many newspapers refused to advertise Larry King's *The Best Little Whorehouse in Texas*, although they probably would not have objected to *The Best Little House of Prostitution in Texas*. *Whore* is Anglo-Saxon and *prostitution* and *harlot* are Latin.

We *sweat* in Anglo-Saxon and *perspire* in Latin. We *think* in Anglo-Saxon and *cogitate* in Latin. We *talk* in Anglo-Saxon and *converse* in Latin. We *work with our hands* in Anglo-Saxon and *perform manual la-*

bor in Latin. Anglo-Saxon *food* is Latin *victuals*. Anglo-Saxon *cooking* is Latin *cuisine*. Anglo-Saxon *chicken* is Latin *poultry*. You *teach* in Anglo-Saxon; you *educate* in Latin.

You'll notice that most of the Anglo-Saxon words have one syllable whereas most of the Latin words have more than one.

Winston Churchill maintained that "short words are best, and the old words, when short, are best of all." Churchill's language surged with strong Anglo-Saxon terms.

But you don't need to become an expert on Latin and Old English to choose the right words. Use the simplest, most familiar words that express the thought you want to express the way you want to express it. Pretend that you're writing to Winnie the Pooh, who said, "I am a bear of very little brain, and long words bother me."

In his Gettysburg Address, Lincoln used four Anglo-Saxon words for every word of Latin origin, but the Latin words gave his speech dignity and loftiness. The phrase "conceived in liberty and dedicated to the proposition that all men are created equal" contains eight Anglo-Saxon words and only six of Latin origin. But the Anglo-Saxon words are mainly connectors. The Latin words—*conceived, liberty, dedicated, proposition, created* and *equal*—convey the bulk of the meaning and provide the dominant flavor. The expression "of the people, by the people, for the people," however, is pure Anglo-Saxon.

FAD WORDS THAT STICK AROUND

Some people ignore Churchill's advice and shun plain old words in favor of fancy new ones. President Warren Harding promised to return the country to "normalcy" instead of getting us back to normal. During the Eisenhower administration, people stopped completing things and started finalizing them. During the Kennedy administration, people started having judgments instead of opinions.

John Dean, the Nixon staffer who blew the whistle on Watergate, later recalled that during his congressional testimony he was under a great deal of tension because he needed to use the bathroom. Dean would have achieved relief a lot sooner had he avoided the lengthy expressions *at this point in time* and *at that point in time* and said simply *now* and *then*.

Such long, pretentious expressions have become the favorite retreat of the bureaucrat, who follows the maxim "When in doubt, obfuscate." (You could say, "When in doubt, make it hard to understand," but *obfuscate* sounds more bureaucratic.) But, in the office, on the work floor, and in daily conversation, you'll be understood and make a better impression if you choose the most commonly understood words and say them in the most direct way.

WORDS WITH SEMANTIC BAGGAGE

You need to be particularly careful with words that carry meanings that go beyond their dictionary definitions. They come with what we call "semantic baggage."

Let us take the words *denomination, sect* and *cult*. All three have similar literal meanings. Essentially, each refers to a group of people with common religious beliefs. But most people think of a *denomination* as one of the "mainline" and "respectable" religious bodies: Roman Catholics, Baptists, Methodists, Presbyterians, Episcopalians, and Lutherans, for example, within the realm of Christendom. A *sect* is somewhat less respectable. It usually refers to a less popular group whose teachings are not entirely acceptable to the majority. When we hear the word *cult*, we think of satanic worship, the Jonestown tragedy, or David Koresh's ill-fated Branch Davidians of Waco, Texas. Each word carries semantic baggage.

The word *capitalism* has a perfectly respectable pedigree, but for much of the twentieth century it was used in a derogatory sense by adherents of communism. It therefore acquired semantic baggage. Those who practiced capitalism preferred to refer to it as "private enterprise" or the "free-enterprise system."

Propaganda is a neutral term roughly equivalent to *advertising* in most parts of the world, but in the United States "propaganda" is considered to be a shady distortion of the truth.

People often reveal their political and social views through the words they use. *Red China* is a generally pejorative term for the country that calls itself the People's Republic of China. If you call it by its official name, people may think you're a bit leftist in your leanings. *Mainland China* is a more neutral term, and the one preferred by most people who do business with the Chinese. It's one way of avoiding the question of whether the communist government on the mainland or the Nationalist government on Taiwan is the legitimate ruler of China.

Slang Isn't Always "With It"

Some people like to use slang expressions or "street talk" to show that they're up-to-date. In spoken English, slang expressions can make an impact when the right person uses them with the right audience, but there are pitfalls. People who are unaccustomed to using slang may find that some expressions have subtle meanings of which they're unaware. The results can be unintended insults, which can alienate whole categories of people. If slang isn't a natural form of expression for you, don't use it. If you do, it may be as noticeable to the audience as the accent of the Russian native practicing newly learned English.

When writing, remember that slang expressions have short lives. If you don't believe it, go to the microfilms and read newspaper articles from the 1930s and 1940s. The slang expressions that were current then sound quaint and dated today. The average life span of a slang expression is about four years—the length of a high school career.

Don't Be Vague, More or Less

When you speak or write, be as specific and as definite as you can. Words such as *several, many, few, various, recently,* and *in the near future* are vague, and they rob your language of power.

"We will complete the project by August 1" is a much more powerful sentence than "We expect to complete the project in the near future."

The expression *etc.* for *et cetera* or *and so forth* saps your language of power. How would the British people have responded had Churchill told them, "I have nothing to offer but blood, toil, tears, etc."?

Watch out for words that seem to have indefinite meanings but actually mean specific quantities. A *score* is 20. A *myriad* can mean "a large number," but it also refers to a specific number: 10,000. And when using large numbers, be aware of the differences between British and American ways of counting. In the United States, a *billion* means one thousand million (1 followed by nine zeros). In Great Britain, it means one million million (1 followed by twelve zeros). The American billion is called a *milliard* in Britain. The British billion is called a *trillion* in the United States.

Beware also of words that have deceptive meanings. *Presently* can mean *currently*, or it can mean *soon*. To make sure you're understood accurately, use the unambiguous term. A *suggestive* remark is not a simple suggestion; it is a remark tinged with impropriety. *Ingenious* means clever; *ingenuous* means showing childlike candor or simplicity. To *forbear* is to refrain from, or desist; a *forebear* is an ancestor. A *foregone* conclusion is a conclusion known in advance; *forgone* interest is interest that has been forgiven.

It's Best Not to Literally Die

Many people use *literally* as an intensifier to add emphasis to a statement. But to take a word "literally" means to take it at its dictionary meaning. When you say, "I literally died from embarrassment," you're saying that you actually died, although few people have literally died and come back to tell about it.

Other commonly misused words:

To *infer* means to draw a conclusion based on certain information. To *imply* means to indicate indirectly. Remember: The message-sender *implies*; the message-receiver *infers*.

Comprise means to *include*. When you see the expression "comprised of," you know that the word is being used incorrectly. The United States *comprises* fifty states and the District of Columbia. You can also say that the United States is *composed of* fifty states and the District of Columbia.

Unique doesn't mean "unusual" or even "very unusual." It means "one of a kind." Something is either unique or it isn't. A thing cannot be "most unique" or "somewhat unique." Nor can one thing be more unique than another. If it's "almost unique," just say it's *rare* or *unusual*.

POWER ROBBERS

Writers and speakers often rob their language of power by using weasel words or qualifying expressions. Suppose Jefferson had written: "We hold these truths to be more or less self-evident." Imagine Lincoln referring to "the government of the people, by the people, for the people, in a manner of speaking," or Admiral Perry exhorting, "Don't give up the ship, if you can help it."

State your convictions in strong, unequivocal words. That doesn't mean that you must always be blunt and undiplomatic. It simply means that you express your ideas clearly and confidently.

Stability Amid Change

In the era of rapid change, language will change too. The tide of immigrants from other cultures inevitably will add new words to the English language. The advance of technology will necessitate the coinage of new words. At the end of the nineteenth century, words such as *antibiotics, television, microwave,* and *computer* were unknown. If a New York businessperson in 1955 had asked a client in San Francisco to "fax me that information," the client would not have understood. In 1975 only a few initiates would have understood such terms as *microchip, RAM, megabyte, software, hard drive,* and *baud rate.* In 1985 you would have drawn a blank stare if you had mentioned a *CD ROM.*

But if communication is to remain precise, meanings of common words need to remain stable. So Churchill's preference for "short words" and "old words" makes sense. When an old, short word expresses an idea accurately and adequately, use it. Turn to neologisms—new words— only when the old ones are inadequate to the task.

If you use words that are familiar to you and to your audience, the chances of being misunderstood are minimized. And in business, as well as in statecraft, misunderstandings can be costly. If you're offered a chance at a leveraged buyout of a British company for a billion dollars, count the zeros before you sign the papers.

Words are a uniquely human form of communication, but they by no means represent the full range of human expression. In fact, some of our most important communication is wordless. In chapter 6, we look at the many fascinating ways we send messages without words.

6

COMMUNICATING
WITHOUT WORDS

M ost of the communicating you do is wordless. The moment you enter the presence of another person you start communicating. Your
physique, clothing, jewelry, voice qualities, facial expressions, posture,
and many other factors pass along important information about your social, marital, and financial status, your sex, and your personal taste.

Your voice speaks in ways that go beyond words. Your accent may
give away your national or regional origin. Your tone of voice will tell
people whether you feel elated or sad, excited or bored.

Through verbal communication, people learn about your thoughts and
ideas. Through nonverbal communication, they learn about your feelings.

About 93 percent of your communication is nonverbal. Much of it
is unconscious, but you can bring a great deal of your wordless communication under conscious control.

Your media for nonverbal communication fall into four broad categories:

- Voice qualities
- Body language
- Facial expressions
- Clothing and grooming

VOICE QUALITIES

Often, how we say things conveys more meaning than what we say. In
fact, voice quality is said to convey about 38 percent of meaning.

Once G. K. Chesterton, the British writer and critic, went into a fish market and tried an experiment. To the woman waiting on him, he said in a low, endearing voice, "You are a noun, a verb, and a preposition."

The woman blushed, apparently flattered that such a cultured individual had observed these qualities in her.

After buying the fish, Chesterton said in a higher voice, "You are an adjective, an adverb, and a conjunction."

The woman slapped him with a flounder.[1]

Taken literally, Chesterton's words were meaningless. To call someone an adjective—whatever that means—is certainly no more insulting than to call that person a noun. But the tone of voice conveyed a meaning that the woman understood instinctively, and her response was instinctive.

In your daily interactions, it's important to pay attention to voice qualities. You supervise, teach, inspire, encourage, sell, praise, and reprimand with your voice, and much of your meaning is conveyed through media other than words.

When George Bush ran for president in 1988, he hired a voice coach to help him lower his voice an octave. Why? Because the candidate's high-pitched voice had helped saddle him with the "wimp" image, even though Bush had proved his valor as a Navy combat pilot during World War II.

Fairly or unfairly, we impute strength and confidence to the person who speaks with a low-pitched, well-modulated voice. When the voice rises to a high pitch, we sense excitement, panic, and lack of control. That doesn't mean that we should all go around cultivating baritone voices. It simply means that each of us should use the lower end of the voice range when we want to communicate calmness, confidence, and competence.

We convey feelings, moods, and attitudes through a variety of voice qualities, which are sometimes called *paralanguage*. Among these qualities are volume, pace, intonation, stress, and juncture.

Volume and Pace

Volume and pace should be used in a careful, controlled way. These qualities can work in unison to achieve powerful effects, especially when speaking from the public platform. You can let your voice rise to a crescendo, the pace and volume quickening until you reach a peak of excitement. Or you can drop your voice to a dramatic whisper.

Volume should always be loud enough that you can be heard by everyone you're trying to reach with your voice. When addressing a group through a microphone, that generally presents no problem. When speaking without a microphone, keep checking the people farthest from you for signs that they're straining to hear or indications that their attention is straying.

Pace should be adapted to the message. Some simple but telling points can be made effectively in rapid-fire sequence. Others can be made by slowly drawing out the words, or by long pauses to let the points sink in.

We can imagine that Abraham Lincoln spoke in calm, measured tones as he opened the Gettysburg Address with the words, "Fourscore and seven years ago, our forefathers brought forth. . . ." He probably spoke a little faster as he concluded with " . . . the government of the people, by the people, for the people shall not perish from the earth."

We can imagine Patrick Henry's volume and pace increasing as he concluded his famous oration to the Virginia Convention in Richmond:

What is it that the gentlemen wish? What would they have? Is life so dear or peace so sweet as to be purchased at the price of chains and slavery?

Forbid it, Almighty God. I know not what course others may take, but as for me, give me liberty or give me death!

You may never be called upon to dedicate a battlefield or to exhort your comrades to take up arms. But business leaders are constantly called upon to instruct, explain, advise, exhort, and inspire, and the same principles apply. You will use a different pace when explaining your profit-sharing plan to line workers from the one you use when congratulating your sales staff on setting a new record. You'll probably use a slow, calm delivery when explaining the details of an acquisition proposal to your legal staff. You'll be more animated when breaking the news of a promotion to a rising executive. Criticism and reprimands are usually more effective when delivered in a calm, measured voice.

Intonation

Intonation refers to voice pitch. We usually speak in a range of pitches, from low to high. Chesterton used low intonation when he called the woman in the fish market "a noun, a verb, and a preposition." He used high intonation when he called her "an adjective, an adverb, and a conjunction." His intonation provided the meaning that was lacking in his words.

The range between high and low intonations varies from individual to individual, and from linguistic population to linguistic population. The English generally have a greater range than do Americans.

Intonation can enliven your conversation, but don't go to extremes. Linguist Katharine LeMee tells of the Englishman and American who addressed the same Egyptian audience. The Englishman's words were more complimentary than those of the American, but the Egyptians responded more positively to the American. The reason lay in the intonations. The Englishman's clipped Oxford accent was taken as somewhat aristocratic and disdainful, as if he were talking down to the Egyptians. The American's flatter, less modulated intonation came across as more sincere and democratic.[2]

Stress

Stress is another important element of paralanguage. The way you emphasize words can change the meaning of your sentences.

Notice how stress changes the meaning of this sentence:

- *Mary* only takes classes in accounting. (Mary takes classes only in accounting, but others may take classes in other subjects.)
- *Only* Mary takes classes in accounting. (Mary takes classes in accounting, but nobody else does.)
- Mary only *takes* classes in accounting. (Mary doesn't teach the classes; she just takes them.)
- Mary only takes *classes* in accounting. (Mary isn't an accountant; she's just studying accounting.)
- Mary only takes classes in *accounting*. (Mary takes classes in accounting, but in no other subjects.)

As you speak, be conscious of the effects of sense stress on the meaning you're trying to convey. Use stress to help your listener understand the sense in which you use words and to show which words you consider important.

Juncture

Juncture refers to the way vowels and consonants are joined in the stream of speech. If you listen to someone speaking in a foreign language, it sounds like a continuous flow of syllables. That's because you haven't learned to recognize the signs that tell you where one word stops and another begins.

Speakers of other languages have the same problem comprehending English. As I've spoken on different continents, I've formed a great admiration for the translators who have had the task of rendering my speech into other languages. Once I was translated simultaneously into seven different languages. Either my juncture was good or my translators were superb. The audience laughed at the appropriate points and applauded at the appropriate points.

Some combinations, though, will throw even native speakers of English. An elementary schoolteacher once told her geography class, "Malaya is not as big as Siam." One of her pupils went home and told her parents, "Malaya is not as big as my teacher."

So pay close attention to the way you join the sounds of different words, especially if you're dealing with people who are new to the English language.

Juncture will vary from one speaking population to another. To a native of New Jersey, the last syllable in Trenton is pronounced just like the "ton" in "ten-ton truck." A Carolinian would deemphasize the final syllable and call it "TRENt'n." When Britons say "military," they barely pronounce the "a." They join the "t" and the "r" as if they were one consonant. When Americans say it, the "tar" is pronounced clearly, with almost as much stress as is put on the first syllable. To the Briton, it's MIL-i-t'ry. To the American, it's MIL-i-TAR-y.

To take a more extreme example, note the different meanings that emerge when you vary the juncture on the syllables in *notable*:

> The *notable* surgeon was *not able* to perform the operation because he had *no table*.

Inattention to juncture can make your speech indistinct or hard to understand. If you tell a carpenter to build a greenhouse, make sure that you don't end up with a green house. The difference in appearance and cost can be substantial. If you ask your secretary to get you the night rate and have it on your desk the next morning, be sure it doesn't sound like "nitrate." Otherwise, you may find a sack of fertilizer in your "in" basket.

Laughing, Crying, Yawning, Sighing

Other aspects of paralanguage convey important signals during speech. Laughter, crying, and sighing are among the more obvious signals. The meaning of the sentence, "I fell down the stairs," changes dramatically when spoken with a laugh or when spoken through tears. "Tell me how you plan to market that new product you're proposing" sounds much more upbeat when preceded by a sharp whistle than when accompanied by a yawn. "Janet, you misspelled Iacocca again" sounds much less threatening when said with a chuckle than when said with a sigh.

Every language has its little clicks, whistles, and throat noises that don't show up in dictionaries, but which serve useful functions in conversation. When you're talking on the telephone and hear nothing but silence on the other end, you may wonder whether the connection has been broken or the other party isn't listening. An occasional "hmmm," "unh," or "yeah" will assure you that you have the other party's attention.

BODY LANGUAGE

While your tongue is conveying oral communication, your body is talking too.

As soon as you stop to talk to someone, you make a statement. How close do you stand to the person you're talking to?

Each of us walks around in a bubble of space that expands or contracts according to the person with whom we're interacting.

W. H. Auden wrote:

Some 30 inches from my nose,
The frontier of my person goes.

We can assume that Auden spoke to people from a distance of at least thirty inches. Some people move in closer. Some maintain greater distances. Individuals from some Somali tribes in East Africa have personal bubbles seven feet in diameter.

We usually stand closer to friends and loved ones than we do to strangers. So when you're speaking to people on the job or in business relationships, be conscious of their personal bubbles of space. If you notice them backing away from you, don't try to move in. They're establishing a distance that's comfortable for them.

Some cultures tend toward smaller bubbles and some toward larger ones. The animated Italian will move in closer than will the reserved Londoner. Hispanic Texans will move in closer than Nordic Minnesotans. If you move in a rather large bubble and you supervise or manage people who recognize smaller bubbles, you might consider using a larger desk to keep people from crowding you.

Your Posture Sends a Message

After you've established a comfortable distance, notice your posture. Posture can tell your conversational partner a great deal about your attitude. An alert, erect posture signifies interest and involvement. A slouching posture says, "I'm not really interested in exchanging ideas with you." A stiff, rigid posture says, "I don't feel fully comfortable in your presence."

When you stand face to face with an individual, your feet pointed straight toward the feet of the other person, you're signaling to others that this is a private conversation. When you stand so that your bodies form two sides of a triangle, you're inviting others to join you.

Voiceless Signals

A number of voiceless signals can be used to indicate that a conversation is over. If you're seated, you can end the discussion simply by rising. If you're in a crowded room talking to an individual and you're ready to move on to another conversation partner, just direct your eyes away from the person you're talking to.

Talking with Your Hands

Most people talk naturally with their hands. As you speak, your hand movements accompany your words, punctuating them, illuminating them, driving them home. Hand gestures are particularly important when speaking to groups, because they help keep the listeners' attention focused on the speaker. I often use a wireless clip-on microphone when addressing a group. This frees my hands for gestures, and also allows me to walk around and interact with the audience.

You can use two basic types of gestures: *demonstrative* and *emphatic*.

If you're self-conscious about gestures, start with demonstrative gestures. These are gestures that illustrate your words. If your sales staff came within 0.1 percent of reaching its goal, you can illustrate by holding your thumb and pointing finger a fraction of an inch apart and saying, "We missed it by this much." If you're describing the amount of paperwork it takes to file your corporate taxes, you can hold your hand palm-down above your head and say, "It takes a stack that high." You can also use demonstrative gestures to point directions.

As you practice, make sure that your gestures coincide with your words. If the gesture comes before or after the point you're making, it can confuse your listeners. A politician once gave a speech in which he roundly condemned those who advocated a proposal that was contrary to the interests of his constituents. But each time he referred to "they," he pointed to himself and when he referred to "we" he pointed elsewhere. His gestures told the audience that he was with "them"—the enemy.

After you feel comfortable with demonstrative gestures, begin working in some emphatic gestures. These are gestures designed to punctuate your speech. You might make a sweeping, outward movement of the hand, palm opened inward, as you explain a point. You might make the same motion with palm opened outward, to indicate a flat denial or rejection of an idea. You might make a chopping motion, with fist closed, to indicate vigorous determination. You might extend both hands, palms up, in a pleading gesture. Practice emphatic gestures to add power and persuasion to your speech.

FACIAL EXPRESSIONS

The face and eyes are eloquent message-conveyers. Someone has estimated that humans are capable of twenty thousand different facial expressions.

The most pleasant, and usually the most advantageous, is a smile. A smile can be the little bit of sugar that helps the medicine go down. It is always more pleasant to deal with people who smile than with those who frown.

The psalmist tells us that the eye is "the light of the body." The unvoiced testimony it offers is often the most eloquent.

Most people interpret a firm, steady gaze as a sign of sincerity. Darting, shifty eyes are interpreted as signs of untrustworthiness. A quick wink can convey a secret message silently across a crowded room. A coquettish look can set a heart to fluttering.

The ability to look someone in the eye is a sign of high self-esteem. When children fib to their parents, they usually look at the floor. It's hard to have self-esteem while you're telling a lie.

Steady eye contact is also a sign of assertiveness. People who consistently avoid the eyes of those to whom they speak are inviting others to treat them as doormats.

A Baptist minister in Moscow once told an American reporter an interesting story about the Russian poet Evgeny Yevtushenko.

Visiting a wealthy American, the poet noticed a magnificent moose head mounted on the wall of the home.

"How could you bear to shoot such a magnificent animal?" Yevtushenko asked.

"It was easy," said his host. "He didn't look me in the eye. If he had looked me in the eye, I couldn't have shot him."

A word of caution, though: Different cultures respond to eye contact in different ways. A gaze that may seem friendly to an American may be considered intrusive by an Asian.

Even in the American culture, steady eye contact can be overdone. Most people feel uncomfortable when they're the objects of fixed, steady gazes. The most effective eye contact consists of a relaxed, steady gaze that is broken off intermittently. A good way to develop this habit is to look at someone and slowly count (in your head!) to three. This is usually the appropriate length of time to sustain a gaze in one-on-one conversations.

Sometimes, angry conversation leads to mutual glares in which each party tries to outstare the other. Don't be led into this kind of contest. If you find your eyes locked in a stare with an angry person, it's okay to break contact first. In fact, one theory holds that the dominant person will break contact first, since the dominant person takes the lead in all things.

CLOTHING AND GROOMING

Among the first things people notice about you is the way you dress and the way you groom yourself.

Many highly creative people affect a casual indifference toward their personal appearance, but in reality, they are making a purposeful statement. They are saying, in effect, "I'm so good at what I do that I don't have to dress for success."

Henry David Thoreau was such a person.

"Beware of all enterprises that require new clothes," he wrote.

If you plan to spend your life in the seclusion of a place like Walden Pond, follow Thoreau's advice. If you want to make it on Wall Street or Main Street, pay careful attention to the clothes you wear and the visual impact you have on others.

When dressing for the business world, follow the standard advice: Dress for inclusion. Look at what the people one or two steps up the corporate ladder from you are wearing and be guided by their tastes.

That's about the closest thing to universal advice that can be given concerning the realm of dress. Fads and fashions come and go, and what's in today may be passé tomorrow. And the fabric of American culture is quite varied. String ties and cowboy boots for men may be perfectly acceptable business attire in Fort Worth, but they would mark you as eccentric in Boston. Three-piece pinstripes may be the uniform of the day on Wall Street, but may be considered a bit stuffy on Hollywood Boulevard. And if that's true of America, it's even truer of other parts of the world. Wherever you are—in London or Sydney, in Singapore or Luxembourg—follow the fashion lead of the successful people in your business.

The perennial choice for the businessman in the industrialized nations is the gray or blue suit, with lighter shades in warm weather, darker ones in cool weather. Muted pinstripes never seem to go out of style. Brown suits are generally regarded as less authoritative than blue or gray ones.

Women have greater latitude for individuality in fashions, but the general rule still applies. In most businesses, it's best to avoid extremes. Seductive or coquettish outfits may draw admiring stares, but they won't enhance your reputation as a businesswoman.

Solid colors in women's clothing convey a message of seriousness and character. Plaids and prints are more whimsical. In the business office, successful women may be seen wearing suits, dresses, coordinates, and skirts with blazers. Different colors flatter different women. Find your best colors and stick with them.

Shoes should always be shined and in good repair. Adlai Stevenson, the American statesman, may be remembered for the famous photograph showing the hole in the sole of his shoe. But he is also remembered as the loser of two presidential elections.

If your job calls for a briefcase, invest in top quality. It will contribute strongly to your image of success. If you need to have a pen in your breast pocket, make it a high-quality and attractive one. Avoid cheap plastic pens, and never wear pocket liners.

For men, beards are a matter of taste. Make up your mind whether you want one. Don't go around looking as if you've forgotten to shave for several days. It may work for a Hollywood actor or the leader of a stateless people, but not for the average member of the corporate team. If you choose to wear a beard, keep it neatly trimmed.

Both men and women should avoid extreme hairstyles. Again, use the look cultivated by the most successful people in your field as a guide, and adapt it to your own physical features.

Dress for Supervisors

The twenty-first century is ushering in an interesting development in dress for supervisors of blue-collar personnel. In the authoritarian workplace, the difference between firstline supervisors and those who reported to them was usually marked by the presence or absence of neckties. Women supervisors were likely to wear suits as opposed to dresses or slacks. A business suit was a symbol of status and authority. In companies that stress participative management, supervisors and team leaders usually dress in the same fashion as line workers. This implies to the workers that their supervisors are working with them, not over them.

The Friendly Touch

Jim Tunney, a close friend and colleague whom you've known for years as NFL Referee #32, is an eloquent advocate of participative management. He puts great emphasis on one other type of nonverbal communication: the touch of friendship and love.

We are all familiar with the need of children for touching and snuggling. Babies who never feel the loving touch of an adult have been known to die from inattention.

Adults, too, have this need. Tunney, who served for many years as a school headmaster, calls attention to the effects of beta-endorphins. These are substances produced by the body that work on the same segments of the brain as morphine. They kill pain and elevate the mood.

Some people have systems that produce an ample supply of beta-endorphins, so they have a built-in source of good feelings. If you were reared in a comfortable home by supportive parents, and especially if you are the oldest child, chances are you have a good built-in supply of beta-endorphins.

That's because hugging, cuddling, and other physical signs of affection stimulate the production of beta-endorphins. Children who receive this kind of attention develop the ability to produce beta-endorphins, and this morale-producing capacity stays with them.

Children who are not so fortunate grow up with a limited capacity for generating beta-endorphins. They need outside help.

I'm not encouraging supervisors to engage in on-the-job hugging and cuddling. But friendly physical contact can be a great morale-booster. The occasional pat on the back, slap on the shoulder, or sympathetic touch on the arm can help create a sense of loyalty and affection that will pay dividends in quality and productivity on the job.

Giving Communication Another Dimension

The human brain has a unique capacity to form and recognize words, whether they're spoken or written. It also has the ability to send and understand messages through many other media.

Nonverbal language provides dimension to our communication. It supplies feelings to the raw words. The person who learns the art of communication in all its dimensions will have a powerful advantage in the business world of the twenty-first century.

PART TWO

COMMUNICATING IN THE WORKPLACE

7

UP, DOWN, AND ACROSS

In the early twentieth century, lines of communication were neat and clean. Executives told subordinates what they wanted done. Subordinates either carried out their bosses' wishes or delegated them to people below. If the boss wanted information from down below, he asked for it. Communication followed a vertical channel, and most messages flowed from the top down.

The twenty-first-century business will be a sponge that takes in information through countless pores, spreads it throughout the corporate body, and pours it out where it does the most good.

Information will no longer just flow downward from the executive suite and upward through well-defined channels carved through layers of supervision. It will spread:

- From top management down to employees
- From employees upward to top management
- Horizontally among all individuals and departments within the organization

This up, down, and across communication will distinguish the thinking organization of the twenty-first century from the mechanistic organization of the twentieth century.

Formal and Informal Information Systems

Every organization has both formal and informal information systems. A company can control the content, channels, and direction of information through formal systems. Informal systems follow their own dynamics, mostly beyond the control of management or anyone else. Informal systems are also called "the grapevine."

65

More than half the information in an organization travels via grapevine. In some organizations, employees get 85 percent of their information from this informal source. Much of what they hear is accurate, but information from the grapevine is rarely complete. Surveys have shown that most employees prefer to get their information from official sources, such as supervisors, bulletin boards, or the company newspaper.

The grapevine functions by default when management fails to provide full and accurate information through formal channels. Management has the opportunity to promote formal informational channels in upward, downward, and horizontal directions.

TOP-DOWN COMMUNICATION

Top-down communication has traditionally been used to pass along instructions, to inform employees about policies and procedures, to rally employees behind causes that management wishes to promote, and to let employees know how their performance stacks up against the company's norm.

But today's employees aren't just looking to management for directions on what to do. They want to know *what* the company is doing and *how* the company is doing. They want to know how they can help the company and how the company can benefit them.

Here are some of the things a comtemporary company might tell its employees through top-down communication:

- What products the company is producing and how they stack up to the competition's
- What kinds of benefits the company offers and how employees can take advantage of them
- What kind of future the company envisions and how it expects to achieve its vision
- How the company is doing financially
- What the company does with its earnings
- How employees can improve their productivity
- What advancement opportunities the company offers
- What personnel policies and practices are in effect
- What personnel changes have been made

- What community activities the company is involved in
- Where the company stands on current issues

One way of finding out what your employees want to know is to ask them. Conduct a survey to determine what they want you to tell them that you're not telling them now. Ask them where they now get their information about the company and where they'd like to get it.

Options for Top-Down Communication

Modern management has a wide range of options for top-down communication. Here are some of them.

- *Company newsletters.* Advances in desktop publishing make newsletters technically feasible for almost any company. All you need is a word processor and a printer. Newsletters can be as elaborate or as simple as you want to make them, but they should always be informative and enlightening.

  The person ultimately responsible for it must have quick and easy access to top management. The newsletter should contain information that will be interesting and useful to employees, and should be part of a planned communications program.
- *Company newspapers and magazines.* Newspapers and magazines are more elaborate than newsletters. They may require a full-time editor, depending upon how large you want to make them and how frequently you publish them. The newspaper can be an excellent vehicle for up, down, and across communication, especially if it is produced under the direction of a communications professional. The editor should have ready access to top management as well as extensive contacts with people throughout the organization.

  Newspapers and magazines usually are printed outside the company, although advances in desktop publishing technology make in-house printing feasible for many companies. Stew Leonard, who has won nationwide recognition for his management practices at his Connecticut dairy store, makes extensive use of employee publications. He found that the computerized equipment he acquired to print his store signs could be used to print an in-house magazine. His

people produce a weekly newspaper, *Stew's Hotline*, and a magazine, *Stew's News*, which appears every two months.

INA Bearing Company has a superb magazine that captures employees' attention with personal information as well as subjects of
universal interest. The magazine is aptly called *The Rolling Element*.
(INA is the world's largest manufacturer of needle bearings, and
"rolling element" describes the key component of a needle bearing.)

- *Annual reports.* If you use your annual report only as a tool for communicating statistical data to shareholders and other outside stake-
holders, you're missing a good bet. Progressive companies today
make effective use of photographs—of employees producing the
products, of consumers using them, and of top executives interacting with the people they lead. In addition to providing statistics on
financial performance, annual reports promote corporate philosophy, goals, visions, and missions. They can be vehicles for communicating information about the company's products, long-range
plans, and financial progress.

 A professionally produced annual report can promote enormous
pride among employees by emphasizing the tangible and the intan-
gible results of their efforts during the year. Why not consider a
videocassette version of your annual report that can be shown to employees and made available to them for home viewing?

- *Employee handbooks.* An employee handbook can be a valuable
source of information on employee benefits and company policies.
The handbook should be written for quick and easy comprehension.
Steer clear of bureaucratic terms. Make sure company policies are
stated clearly and unambiguously. Explain benefits such as health
care and retirement plans in terms the average employee can understand without resorting to a dictionary. A loose-leaf format will allow for regular and inexpensive updating. A videocassette version
of the handbook can also be a valuable orientation tool for new employees.

- *Bulletin boards.* Strategically placed bulletin boards can provide a
quick and inexpensive communications medium. Communications
placed on the board should be printed or neatly typed. Many word
processor software programs provide a variety of typefaces and
sizes that can be used to produce attention-getting notices. The human resources department can serve as the conduit through which
management passes its messages to the bulletin board.

- *Interoffice memos.* A survey of General Tire employees during the 1980s showed that 44 percent of them preferred to receive information from management via interoffice memos. A memo enables you to target your message to the individual or group you want to reach, and to tailor it to the individuals and circumstances. To be effective, memos should be brief and to the point.
- *Letters.* One of the most overlooked avenues for communication is a letter that is mailed to employees' homes. When you send information to their homes, you reach employees at times and places that allow them to take time to look over the material without worrying about their on-the-job duties. It also makes it easier for them to share pertinent information with their families. Commendations sent to the home can be great morale-boosters.
- *Small group meetings.* Many executives find it helpful to meet with employees in small groups to share information and concerns. Some hold quarterly or semiannual meetings in which they tell employees how the company is doing financially and what changes, if any, are being contemplated.

Long Drug Stores is a West Coast chain of more than three hundred stores that tops $3 billion in annual sales. The store, founded in 1938 by two brothers, Joe and Tom Long, is now run by Joe's son, Bob. Bob Long achieves two-way communications with his employees by holding regional town meetings.

The town meeting concept can be used effectively as an avenue for two-way communication. Not only does it give management a chance to talk to employees; it can also give employees a chance to talk to management in a nonthreatening atmosphere. Make it clear that employees are free to speak out on any topic that turns them on. If they voice complaints, address their concerns on the spot if possible. If that's not possible, assure them that you will look into what's bothering them and get back with them as soon as possible. Then keep your word!

- *Executive speeches.* When employees hear it directly from the CEO's mouth, it gives the message an extra measure of credibility. The CEO can find many occasions during the year to speak directly to employees. Awards banquets, holiday parties, and other special events provide such opportunities. Too often, executives use these occasions to wave to the crowd, utter a few platitudes, and sit down.

Each time you have the opportunity to speak to a group of employees, think carefully about the message you want to present to them. Think about what the company stands for, what kind of future it envisions, and what it will take on the part of the employees to achieve that future. Then think of what you can say that will provide the employees with the information, encouragement, and inspiration to give what it takes.

Executives often speak to local business, civic, and community groups and at professional gatherings across the country. Sometimes these speeches are covered by the local media, but often the words don't carry beyond the room in which they are uttered. General Motors publishes an "Issues Update," consisting of excerpts on selected subjects from executive speeches. The report goes out bimonthly to local communicators and members of management. Smaller companies don't have to produce separate publications for such material, but they can reproduce comments in the company newspaper or, on occasion, distribute copies of speeches to all employees or to key personnel.

Empowerment, Not Control

Remember that the purpose of top-down communications is to empower, not to control. Control limits possibilities. Empowerment expands possibilities. When you communicate *instructions* to your employees, you are limiting their latitude to respond. When you communicate *information*, you are expanding their latitude to respond. Today's corporation needs to be able to respond quickly and flexibly to fast-developing market situations. Therefore, employees at all levels need to know what products the company produces, what products they're competing with in the marketplace, and what they need to do to make their products competitive, if not superior.

Can you imagine a basketball coach taking a team into the second half without letting the players know the score, the identities and weaknesses of the opposing players, the number of personal fouls against them, or the amount of time remaining on the clock? Suppose the players hadn't been told that this game would determine whether they made it into the championship tournament. If the opposing team were minimally competitive, it probably would win the game.

Your employees need comparable information if they're to win in the arena of the marketplace.

UPWARD COMMUNICATION EMPOWERS MANAGEMENT

Top-down communication empowers your employees. Upward communication empowers management by keeping it informed of what's happening on the work floor and in the marketplace.

The first people to know about market trends are the people who make the sales to the ultimate consumer. The first people to know about technical defects in a product are the people who have to make the repairs or handle the complaints. The first people to hear about employee morale problems are the firstline supervisors. These people usually are far down on the corporate charts. What they know may make or break a company. Management needs to provide a way for them to be heard.

GE Erases Boundaries

At General Electric, CEO John F. Welch developed the concept of the "boundaryless corporation," in which information could flow freely up, down, and across the corporate structure. Welch looked for barriers to communication, and when he found them he demolished them.

If you look around, you'll probably find plenty of boundaries in your own company that need to be removed. One of them may be the door to your office, which remains closed to input from your employees. Executives who wall themselves off from the people they lead are depriving themselves of eyes and ears. If the people in your organization have to run an obstacle course of receptionists and secretaries to get into your presence or to gain your ear, you're not going to hear much from them. And what you don't know can hurt you.

Another barrier to upward communication is labeled "NIH," for "Not Invented Here."

Many companies are suffering from the NIH syndrome. Some corporate cultures are hostile to ideas that don't originate in-house. You've heard of "the right way, the wrong way, and the company's way." To paraphrase Vince Lombardi, in many organizations, the company's way isn't the best way; it's the only way. Salespeople, engineers, customer service reps, and others operate at the meeting point of products and customers. They often pick up new ideas from competitors, suppliers, customers, and other sources that their bosses don't encounter. When they bring these ideas home to your company, do the top executives listen to them or turn a deaf ear?

If your attitude is "If we didn't invent it, it ain't worth inventing," then you're shutting out a world of innovative ideas.

An Outside Idea Worth $200 Million a Year

Because GE was receptive to ideas from beyond its corporate walls, it was able to reduce its average inventory levels by $200 million a year. Here's what happened:

Someone from GE discovered an appliance company in New Zealand using an innovative method of compressing product cycle times. The idea was brought back to GE management, who put the method through a trial run in a Canadian affiliate, then transferred it to its largest appliance complex in Louisville, Kentucky. The method, which GE dubbed "Quick Response," enabled GE to respond more quickly to customer needs.

But GE didn't just introduce it in Louisville and forget it. It brought people in from each of its major businesses to study the method and adapt it to their own operations.

GE also dispatched people to Wal-Mart to learn about the management practices that propelled that business to the forefront in retailing.

GE management not only *listened* to ideas brought in by its people; it sent them out *looking* for ideas.

Stifling Layers

Too many layers of management can stifle upward communications. If every communication has to "go through channels" and those channels must wind and twist through a dozen or more levels of responsibility, the chances of a message surviving the trip undistorted are slim to none.

Generally speaking, a corporation should be able to function at peak efficiency with only five layers of management from line worker to CEO. Anything above that turns to fat instead of muscle.

In the old days, management provided people with upward mobility by giving them raises and titles. Soon the corporate workplace was overrun by people with "manager" in their titles and no clear functions other than bottling up ideas and information in petty fiefdoms.

Some years ago I was called to a Midwestern company that was choking on functionless functionaries. Interviews coupled with a needs analysis identified the problem. Despite considerable resistance, the company reorganized and cut out unnecessary titles. Individuals who were not performing functions that contributed to the corporate mission were reassigned to meaningful roles. Today, the company is much more fluid, fluent, and profitable.

Look at your own workplace. How many of your "managers" really need to manage? If you review the job titles and job descriptions in your company, you may see opportunities to reduce the number of management positions by replacing functionaries with leaders. If you do this, you'll be amazed at the way boundaries of authority can be turned into avenues of cooperation.

Cross-Training Encourages Communication

Too many specialized task functions also can impede the upward flow of information. If people are trained to do their own narrowly defined jobs, they have little understanding of the overall corporate process. Therefore, they might not recognize and pass along information that might be highly beneficial to management. As we go into the twenty-first century, more workers will be educated to acquire several different job skills so that they will have broader understandings of where they fit into the total process.

The Pollyanna Syndrome

Another factor that impedes upward communication is the Pollyanna syndrome. Pollyanna refused to see the negative side of anything. It's a charming story, but the "see no evil" attitude can be deadly in the corporate setting. Executives need to know the bad news. Otherwise, how can they possibly deal with the negatives and overcome them? The way you encourage employees to bring you the bad news is to make it clear that you will listen and will do something about it.

The way to make sure you never hear any bad news is to implement the "kill-the-messenger" policy. If you punish the person who tells you there's a bridge out up ahead, the next time there's a bridge out you'll learn about it when you feel the water rising above your ears.

Positive Encouragement of Upward Communication

It isn't enough to eliminate barriers to upward communication. Management also needs to set up systems that positively encourage such communication.

The traditional suggestion box is one such system. When you allow employees to submit anonymous questions, you free them from the inhibitions that accompany more open forms of communication. But if you allow the suggestion box to degenerate into a dead-letter file, you'll do more harm than good. Executives who invite people to put their complaints into a suggestion box should read the complaints, let the people know that they've read them, and tell them what, if anything, can be done about it.

W & J Rives, an apparel-manufacturing firm, uses its suggestion box to obtain feedback from employees. It rewards those who provide it with useful feedback, and where possible, communicates its responses back to the employees.

One way of letting people know that their suggestions are being read is to publish a column on them in the company newspaper or newsletter. The CEO could use this column to address specific suggestions or, if suggestions are too numerous, to summarize them and comment on the more interesting ones.

COMMUNICATING ACROSS THE CHART

Communicating across the corporate chart is a relatively new concept in business. In the past, management has forfeited this function to the grapevine.

Now, business leaders are beginning to realize the importance of cross-functional communication. A large, diversified company may consist of several business units operating, essentially, as separate enterprises. But each unit probably has expertise that could be profitably shared with others. Each has probably developed sales, marketing, and management techniques other units could beneficially adopt.

So corporate management should look for ways to incorporate the benefits of unity while exploiting the advantages of diversity.

One way to do this is to move personnel across divisional lines. This can provide your leaders and potential leaders with fresh perspectives, and your management team with hybrid vigor. People who deal with the challenges of different divisions of the company will develop corporate mentalities instead of departmental mentalities.

Unity in Diversity at the Team Level

The principle of unity in diversity can be practiced all the way down to the team level. If everyone on a work team learns to do several jobs instead of specializing, the team develops a capacity for internal dialogue that can be of tremendous help in solving problems.

The rigid lines between salaried and nonsalaried employees can block lateral communication. Just as a seasoned sergeant or chief petty officer can often impart useful advice and knowledge to a freshly commissioned officer, so veteran line workers can provide valuable insights to engineers, technicians, and managers. Ask the engineer who worked with tool-and-die maker Charlie Dygert on that project at General Motors.

The Boss Takes a Back Seat

Cross-functional teams require and encourage lateral communication. Such teams can be created to address problems and challenges that involve more than one function or department. Ford put together such a team to design the Taurus/Sable automobile. Levi Strauss used one to study the balance between work and family commitments. Chair of the Board Robert Haas himself served on that task force, but only as a member.

"I'm on the task force, but I don't run it," he told the *Harvard Business Review*. "We have everyone from secretaries and sewing-machine operators to senior managers on the task force."[1] Haas realized that these line workers knew far more about the impact of their jobs on their family lives than he could possibly know as their CEO.

When people serve on cross-functional teams, they should answer to the team leader and not to the department from which they were drawn. Their performance should be evaluated on the basis of their contribution to the team effort and not on their contributions to their own department.

WAYS TO ENCOURAGE LATERAL COMMUNICATION

If teams are to function effectively, employees must feel free to communicate with anyone who can provide useful information without checking with higher authority. The old concept of "going through channels" has to be scrapped. If a team that assembles radios finds a pattern of defective parts from a supplier, it should feel free to contact the supplier and work out the problem without checking with department heads and vice presidents.

Using Corporate Media

Management can also encourage lateral communication by providing media through which employees can get to know one another.

Many employees complain: "Things have changed around here. We've lost our personal touch; we're too big. At one time the president knew everyone by first name. Now the company is no longer a family. It's a big business."

The CEO of a large company can't know thousands of employees personally, and the employees can't all be in close personal touch with one another. But company publications can promote a family-like feeling throughout the company.

A company newspaper or magazine does not have to be strictly a tool for top-down communication. It can be a source of general information about the company and its people.

In addition to learning about what the company is doing and how it is doing, employees also want to know what and how other employees are doing. Human interest feature stories in company newspapers provide this kind of information. News of births, birthdays, weddings, and anniversaries promote a sense of community that encourages lateral communication.

An effective company newspaper looks at the company's stake-holders the way a general circulation newspaper looks at the community it serves. It provides people with the information they need and desire, and it seeks, through communication, to provide a sense of community spirit.

Stew Leonard launched his weekly *Stew's Hotline* as a six- to eight-page publication full of stories and photographs about store employees and their activities. He used his store's own printer. The photographs were usually made with instant-developing cameras so that the activities could be recognized while they were still fresh. Stew also inaugurated a bimonthly magazine, *Stew's News*, insisting that no issue go to press until it had two hundred photographs of employees.

The Four Fs Require Good Communication

If a company is to prosper in the twenty-first century, then all barriers to the flow of information and ideas into and through the company must be removed.

Rosabeth Moss Kanter taught us that modern companies must observe the Four Fs, by being focused, flexible, fast, and friendly. A company can't be any of those unless information can flow fast and freely from all corners.

You can't focus the efforts of your entire workforce if your organization is crisscrossed with walls that impede the flow of communication.

You can't be flexible if you have a rigid corporate structure in which every division and department is a closed information loop with no lines of communication to other parts of the organization. You can't respond to the market if you erect barriers to information flowing in from the outside.

You can't be fast if information has to seep slowly through layer after layer of management.

And you can't be friendly if your people don't talk to other people inside and outside your organization.

In the old days, everyone had to "go through channels," and only a handful of people had automatic access to the sending and receiving ends of the channels.

In the new business environment, the channels have to branch into an informational network that reaches every level and every corner of the organization. Not only must management be able to communicate with employees, but employees must be able to communicate with management and—just as important—with each other.

We have already learned that all communication is personal. Communication, reduced to its elemental components, consists of sending mutually comprehensible messages from one mind to another. That means that to become a truly effective leader and communicator, you must learn to communicate one-on-one.

8

COMMUNICATING ONE ON ONE

M ost verbal communication is from one individual to another. This is true whether you're in a family, social, or work setting.

"When you think about it, the only thing a manager does that is visible to the organization is to listen and speak, and to draw and interpret symbols," remarked Ray Stata, CEO of Analog Devices. "Speaking and listening are where it's at." [1]

One-on-one verbal communication affords the greatest opportunity for precision, because immediate feedback can tell you whether you were understood accurately.

But communicating effectively involves more than just accuracy. The purpose of most communication is to influence the attitudes and behaviors of those whom we address. Since the human race is composed of billions of individuals, each with a different way of responding, no one approach is universally effective. So it's important that you learn to express yourself accurately and in a way that will accomplish your purpose concerning the individual you're addressing.

THE BASIC PROCESS OF COMMUNICATION

To achieve precision and effectiveness in communicating, you should understand the basic process of communication. It has four requirements:

- A message must be conveyed.
- The message must be received.
- There must be a response.
- Each message must be understood.

Let's look at these requirements one at a time.

A Message Must be Conveyed

That sounds simple enough. You know what your thoughts are, and you know how to translate them into words. But that's where the simplicity ends.

Each of us has our own mental dialect. It is the common language of the culture in which we grew up, modified by our own unique life's experiences. Our life's experiences add color and shades of meaning to different words.

When you speak, your mental dialect must be translated into the mental dialect of the hearer. The words you speak acquire a different color when they pass through the ears of the person who hears you.

SPOOK OR SPIRIT?

Dr. Muriel O'Tuel, a South Carolina educator, told of the time her young son, Bryant, balked at staying overnight with his grandparents, whom he had always dearly loved.

Asked why, he responded, "I'm afraid of the ghost."

Dr. O'Tuel was mystified. She had grown up in her parents' home and had never seen or heard anything that looked or sounded like a spook.

Some gentle inquiry revealed the source of Bryant's apprehension. He had accompanied his grandparents to church one Sunday, and the sermon had revolved around the Holy Ghost. In the church the O'Tuels attended, the reference usually was to the Holy Spirit. So in Bryant's mental dialect, "Holy Ghost" had a meaning quite different from the one his parents and grandparents understood.

A CUT FROM THE MORGUE

Old-time newspaper people tell about the young copy boy who quit after his first day on the job. The mayor had died in an automobile accident, and the editor had told the young man, "Go down to the morgue and get us a cut of the mayor." The copy boy hadn't learned that in the newspaper parlance of the day, "the morgue" referred to the newspaper's own reference library, and that a "cut" was no more than an engraving of the mayor's photograph, which the newspaper kept on file for quick use whenever the mayor made news. What, in the sender's mental dialect, was a perfectly reasonable and routine request was, in the receiver's dialect, a macabre and perverted demand.

IT DEPENDS UPON WHERE YOU ARE

You can probably think of numerous opportunities for misunderstandings on your job and in your culture. If you tell your travel agent you want a flight to Portland, be sure to specify Maine or Oregon. Otherwise, you may end up on the wrong coast. A colleague of mine once flew to Ohio to keep a speaking engagement in Columbus. Too late, he realized that the group he was to address was in Columbus, Georgia. If someone in my hometown of High Point, North Carolina, asks me, "How did Carolina do in the big game last night?" I know the reference is to the Tar Heels of the University of North Carolina. If somebody in Columbia puts the question in those precise words, I know that "Carolina" means the Gamecocks of the University of South Carolina. In most cities, if you ask a newsstand operator for the *Sunday Times,* you'll be handed a *New York Times.* But in St. Petersburg, Florida, or Seattle, Washington, you're likely to get the local newspaper.

SYNCHRONIZE YOUR VOCABULARIES

When communicating in the work place, be sure that you and the people with whom you communicate are working with the same set of words and meanings. Adjust your vocabulary to the vocabulary of the person with whom you're speaking. And say *exactly* what you mean. In modern speech, we often let our sentences trail off into an expression such as "you know" or "stuff like that." This leaves it up to the hearer to supply the meaning. Your meaning may be quite obvious to you. But if the listener is on a different wavelength, it may be quite different.

The Message Must Be Received

The second basic requirement of the one-on-one communication process is that the message be received and understood. Effective communicators know that they have not conveyed their meaning until they have made sure that the other person has received it exactly as they sent it. They test, with questions and observations, to make sure that the real meaning they wanted to convey has passed through the filters and has been received and understood.

A DANCE THAT WAS TUTU NAUGHTY FOR CHURCH

One businessman neglected to seek the proper feedback when he approached the pastor of his church, and the result was severe embarrassment.

The businessman was looking for ways to raise money for the church softball team, and he approached the pastor.

"Some friends of mine told me about a dancer who is drawing big crowds around the country, and I thought we might bring her here for a benefit performance," he said. "Would you object to a belly dancer for a fundraiser?"

"Of course not," said the pastor. "Go ahead and use the church's Fellowship Hall if you'd like."

So the businessman arranged for the performance and the pastor was on hand for the show. When the dancer came on stage and began her seductive gyrations, the pastor gasped and turned to the businessman.

"How *could* you bring an act like this into the church?"

"But you said it was all right to bring in a belly dancer," the businessman said.

"*Belly* dancer?" said the pastor. "I thought you said *ballet* dancer!"

A few follow-up questions during the initial conversation would have averted this scene. The pastor's unhesitating assent should have thrown up a red flag in the businessman's mind.

"Do you know what a belly dancer does?" he might have asked. Or "I'm told there's nothing lewd about the act, but the dancer will be wearing filmy clothes and she may make some suggestive moves. Do you feel comfortable with that?"

FEEDBACK IS VITAL ON THE JOB

In the business world, too, feedback is important. Serving on the board of the Economic Development Corporation for the city of High Point,

I've learned to nail down every detail when major real-estate transactions are involved. Let's say that you're a developer considering two parcels of land for an office park. So you tell your representative: "Let's go with the parcel on the west end, provided the city is willing to extend water and sewer mains to the perimeter and assume responsibility for maintenance of internal streets and sidewalks. If the city agrees to the utilities but refuses to take over street maintenance, let's try for a relaxation of parking requirements and try to get the purchase price down by 10 percent. If that's impossible, we'll have to opt for the northside tract."

Before your representative goes out the door, briefcase in hand, you'd better get her to repeat those conditions. Otherwise, you may become the victim of crossed signals and end up with the wrong parcel of land.

ASK YOUR LISTENER TO PARAPHRASE

The best kind of feedback is a paraphrased version of your message. Paraphrasing converts the message into your hearer's mental dialect and reflects it back to you. You now have a chance to hear the message the way your hearer received it. You can compare what you hear with what you said, and the two of you can reflect the message back and forth until you're sure that mutual understanding has occurred.

There Must Be a Response

The goal of all communication is to obtain the desired response. You want to say something correctly and have your hearer understand what you mean by it. But you also want the hearer to do something in response.

THE ASSERTIVE APPROACH

Good one-on-one communication calls for an assertive approach. That means letting your hearers know clearly, unambiguously, and courteously what you expect of them as a result of the communication.

Assertive messages make use of the pronoun *I*. When you say, "You ought to make at least three sales calls per day," you're giving the hearer an "out." "Ought" doesn't mean "must," and your hearer may respond with "Yes, but. . . ."

When you say, "I would like you to make at least three sales calls per day," you make clear what your expectations are.

FOCUS ON THE BEHAVIOR, NOT ON THE INDIVIDUAL

When you want to modify someone's behavior, it's important that your message focus on the behavior, not on the individual. It does no good to say, "Bill, you're careless and slovenly and you're going to have to shape up or ship out." Such a message is demoralizing to Bill and gives him no guidelines for meeting your expectations.

A good assertive message begins by describing the specific behavior that you find unsatisfactory. Then it describes the effects that behavior has on you and others in your organization. Finally, it describes the behavior you desire.

So you might take this approach with Bill:

> Bill, I've noticed recently that you're waiting until the last minute to figure your estimates, and they're coming to me with significant errors. I caught a couple this month that could have cost the company thousands of dollars. When your estimates are done hastily, I have to go over them line by line, which is a serious drain on my time. I would like you to organize your time so that you don't have to do your estimates in a hurry. And I want you to go over them twice, double-checking all data, before turning them in to me.

Using this approach, you're not accusing Bill of being careless or slovenly. You're focusing on his behavior, using objective information. And you're telling him clearly what changes you want him to make. Notice, though, that you're not issuing a command. "I would like" and "I want" are quite different from "you must."

A couple of other suggestions: Don't dwell on the past. You can't change yesterday's behavior. You can only aim for the future. And be specific.

FOUR BASIC BEHAVIOR PATTERNS

Be aware, too, that people respond to your words in different ways. Good leaders learn the behavior styles of the people they lead and adjust their approaches accordingly.

If you observe carefully, you'll find that people fall into one of these broad categories:

* *Dominators.* These are your fierce competitors. They are pragmatic, decisive, and intent on winning. When you approach them, forget the small talk. They want you to get to the point. They're not interested in minor details. Give them the big picture. They want to know *how* something works, not *why* it works that way. Be direct and assertive with them. They don't respond to hints. They're likely to challenge you, and if you yield they'll exploit the advantage. Stand your ground and they'll respect you. Dominators don't like to be manipulated, so always be straightforward with them. When you compliment them, praise their achievements and not their personal qualities; Dominators don't want to appear soft. When you discuss problems with them, let them be part of the solution.
* *Interactors.* Interactors are the most sociable of the behavior types. They like to interact with people, and they bask in the admiration of others. They're the people who will know everyone on a first-name basis. Like Dominators, they prefer the big picture to minute details, but small talk is fine with them. They respond to pep talks more readily than the other behavior types do.

    Interactors want to be included in whatever is going on. They don't like to work in isolation. They enjoy compliments and are devastated by public criticism. With them it is especially important that you follow the rule: "Praise in public, criticize in private." But make sure the compliment is sincere. They recognize and resent insincere praise.

    Approach them in a friendly manner, and be aware of your body language. Interactors are very sensitive to nonverbal clues. They'd rather communicate by conversation than by memo, but they have short memories for detail. When you reach an agreement with them, nail it down in writing.

    When you're teaching them, give them an outline, a timetable, or a step-by-step procedure and hold them to it. Interactors like to ad lib, and often overestimate their own competence.

• *Relaters.* Relaters are known for their steadiness and their ability to work well with other behavior styles. They are less aggressive and less decisive than Dominators and Interactors, and prefer to make decisions by group consensus. Relaters dislike conflict and will go to great lengths to get along with others. In the process, they may suppress their own feelings. Relaters may think they're carrying an unfair portion of the workload, but they won't complain openly.

Relaters like comfortable, casual, low-key environments. Like Interactors, they like to be on first-name terms with people. Whereas Interactors want to be liked and admired, Relaters want to be liked and appreciated. They are good listeners, and they are likely to adhere to procedures. They are uncomfortable with change.

When dealing with Relaters, assure them that they're highly valued. When changes are necessary, prepare them well in advance and stress the factors that will remain unchanged. When it's necessary to criticize their behavior, reassure them of your high regard for them as people.

• *Evaluators.* Evaluators are drawn more to logic than to feelings. They are guided by inner standards, which they strive to meet, regardless of whether their efforts are applauded.

Evaluators are the mirror images of Dominators. Whereas Dominators skip the details and cut to the big picture, Evaluators revel in details. If you want somebody to maintain your aircraft or perform open-heart surgery, an Evaluator is an excellent choice.

Whereas Dominators will try to expand their areas of responsibility, Evaluators need to have their roles clearly defined.

Evaluators are interested in how things work, whether they're dealing with mechanical devices or human systems. If you want to know what the rule book says, ask an Evaluator. If you need help interpreting a computer manual, ask an Evaluator.

Evaluators are more interested in quality than in quantity. They're drawn more to reasoning than to imagination. Whereas Dominators and Interactors are action-oriented, Evaluators are methodical perfectionists who won't commit to action until they're certain every detail has been nailed down.

When you communicate with them, skip the small talk. They're interested in practical matters. Don't waste your breath on pep talks.

Just show them how to do a better job. Be very careful when you criticize their work. Evaluators identify very closely with their performance, and when you criticize it you're criticizing them. Put the emphasis on the positive. Don't say, "Pat, I think your site plan is functional, but it falls flat esthetically." Instead, say, "Pat, your site plan meets all the functional criteria. Let me make a few suggestions on esthetics." With this approach, you're not finding fault with Pat's plan; you're providing guidance in improving it. That's what the Evaluator is looking for.

Evaluators share the Relaters' lack of aggressiveness. They'll accumulate a rich store of information and will be glad to share it with others if they're asked. But you have to ask. They also share the Relaters' aversion to conflict. Keep their environment free of turmoil.

Don't play semantic games with them. Be open and straightforward. When they ask questions, give direct answers. The Evaluator is looking for information, not conversation.

Each Message Must Be Understood

Once a message has been delivered, received, and responded to, it's time to take stock of what each person has communicated. The cycle of communication is complete only when you come away with a clearer understanding of the person with whom you sought to communicate. You may not always agree with the other person, and the other person may not always agree with you, but it is important that you understand each other.

Successful communicators learn to recognize and overcome barriers to communication. There are two types of such barriers: those arising from the environment and those stemming from the hearer's resistance.

ENVIRONMENTAL BARRIERS

Barriers arising from the environment include:

- Distractions
- Disturbances
- Diversions

• Discomfort

If you've ever tried to talk with a friend at a crowded and noisy business party, you can readily understand how the environment can present major barriers. If you've ever tried to carry on a conversation in a room where a rock band was going full blast, you can appreciate the noise barrier.

A good general tries not to commit his troops on terrain that presents inherent disadvantages. Good communicators follow similar strategies. They try not to set up conversations in settings that will compete for attention.

If you're planning to discuss an important business transaction, don't do it over drinks in a noisy lounge. If you want to combine business with food and beverage, choose a quiet restaurant, club, or café. If you're going to discuss personnel matters with a supervisor, don't do it on a noisy factory floor. Find a quiet office or conference room. If you're going to go over a set of complicated plans, don't spread them across a table beside a hotel pool. The distractions at a swimming pool may be pleasant, but they *are* distractions. I once spoke to a sales convention in a resort hotel where the meeting room had an open view of the pool. Most of the salespeople were men and the pool was populated with beautiful women wearing skimpy suits. It was hard enough for me to pay attention to what I was saying, and I can only imagine what the audience was going through. You can't really compete with that kind of distraction. Find a setting that will allow you to devote full attention to the agenda before you.

When you are communicating with an individual, that individual deserves your full attention. Choose a time and a place that will minimize interruptions. If you're meeting in your office during business hours, have your secretary hold telephone calls or use your telephone answering device for the duration of the conversation. Many executives set aside certain times of day during which they will receive telephone calls and unscheduled visitors. The rest of the time they reserve for creative thinking, strategic planning, decision making, and other duties of leadership.

When disturbances do occur, try not to talk over them. If the disturbance is obviously temporary, suspend the conversation until the interruption is past. If it's obviously going to be prolonged, try to reschedule the conversation for a more favorable time.

I often teach salespeople where to sit on sales calls or when they're conducting business over a meal. My advice: Put the other person's back to any distractions, so your listener's attention won't be constantly diverted by what's happening in the background.

Finally, pay attention to comfort. Audience discomfort is one barrier you can't overcome: Your only winning strategy is to avoid it. Stay away from settings that are too hot, too cold, or otherwise uncomfortable. Nobody can concentrate while in a state of discomfort. And if the person you need to communicate with is ill, injured, or going through some emotional trauma, it's best to reschedule the conversation. Otherwise, you're going up against impossible barriers to communication.

Monitoring the environment is the task of any person who wishes to communicate, whether as a company leader, a salesperson, a manager, or a letter writer. You just can't ignore such barriers. To do so is to give up and let the competing voices have your audience's attention. If people are distracted, are interrupted, or feel uncomfortable, they're not likely to tune you in completely, understand your message thoroughly, or respond to you positively.

AUDIENCE RESISTANCE

Barriers resulting from audience resistance fall into two categories: external factors that cause people to tune you out, and internal factors that prevent them from giving you their complete attention.

People often form first impressions on the basis of external factors. If the first impression is negative, you won't get the person's attention. Be mindful of characteristics of dress, speech, and actions that may be turning people off. If your dress is too casual, frivolous, or distracting, you may be losing listeners. If your voice is strident, shrill, or guttural, people may find you unpleasant to listen to. In certain areas, regional accents may turn people off. If you speak with a pronounced regional accent and are doing business in a region where that accent is not commonly heard, you may have to look for ways to overcome this barrier. You may want to work on acquiring a more generic accent. Or you may want to spend some time cultivating the listener's confidence.

It goes without saying that good grooming and good personal hygiene are essential to good communication. Body odor, halitosis, or a disheveled appearance will cause people to turn away from you.

Internal barriers to communication may stem from a lack of interest in what you're saying or a lack of understanding.

If you discern a lack of interest, then your task is to find some way to lead your listener to identify with your message. How does it concern your listener personally? What bearing does it have on the listener's job, income, health, family, or security? Once you establish that point of identity, you'll have the listener's attention.

People have a way of erecting defense mechanisms and emotional barriers when they feel threatened by what you are saying or by the way you are saying it. Studies have repeatedly shown that people, like other creatures, feel protective of their territories. Invade those turfs or act in a threatening manner, and you will be sure to turn them off. When your task is to deliver an unpleasant message or to persuade your listener to take some unpleasant action, look for ways to neutralize the negatives and to reassure the person who feels threatened.

BONDS OF MISUNDERSTANDING

Sometimes, it's just a question of not understanding what you're talking about. During World War II, the United States raised money for defense by selling war bonds. In some remote parts of the country, where newspapers, radios, and public schools had not yet penetrated, people were a little slow to learn about the heroic leadership of Winston Churchill, the Japanese sneak attack on Pearl Harbor, and the determined response of Franklin Roosevelt.

So when a bond salesperson approached a farmer who was out in the barnyard slopping his hogs, the salesperson was frustrated at the lack of interest in his patriotic mission.

"Wouldn't you like to help out by buying some war bonds?" he asked.

"Reckon not," replied the farmer.

"Wouldn't you like to join the defense effort with Mr. Roosevelt?

"Nope, reckon not."

"Aren't you upset over what they did to Pearl Harbor?

"Reckon not."

"Don't you want to be on the side of Churchill?"

"Nope."

"So you don't want any bonds?

"Nope."

Frustrated, the salesperson moved on.

The farmer's wife came over and asked what the stranger had wanted.

"This fellow had a story about a guy named Roosevelt who got a woman named Pearl Harbor in trouble over on the side of Church Hill and wanted me to go to his bond."

Sometimes, you have to explain very carefully.

KEEP IT SIMPLE

The most important thing you can do to make sure that you're understood is to keep your communication simple. People don't like to be led through a maze of words and mental meanderings before they reach the main point of your message.

Once while evangelist Billy Graham was flying into Dallas to address the student body of a large seminary, a storm moved in. Visibility at the airport became so poor that the plane couldn't land. So it had to circle over the city for several hours—long beyond the time of his scheduled appearance. But no one on the ground knew that the plane couldn't land.

"It occurred to me while I was up there circling around," he later told a group, "that as preachers, we spend most of our time circling around in a fog, while people are wondering where in the world we are."

It's a condition that plagues people in any business. The high art of plain talk is simply saying something so that it can be understood. And it's the best way to clear away the fog from all your communication attempts. But how do you do it?

SIX COMMUNICATION TECHNIQUES

Here are six techniques you can use to say things simply but persuasively, and even forcefully.

1. *Get your thinking straight.* The most common source of confusing messages is muddled thinking. We have an idea we haven't thought through. Or we have so much we want to say that we can't possibly say it all. Or we have an opinion that is so strong we can't keep it

in. As a result, we are ill prepared when we speak, and we confuse everyone. The first rule of plain talk, then, is to think before you say anything. Organize your thoughts.

2. *Say what you mean.* Say *exactly* what you mean.

3. *Get to the point.* Effective communicators don't beat around the bush. If you want someone to buy something, ask for the order. If you want someone to do something, say exactly what you want done.

4. *Be concise. Don't waste words.* Confusion grows in direct proportion to the number of words used. Speak plainly and briefly, using the shortest, most familiar words.

5. *Be real.* Each of us has a personality—a blending of traits, thought patterns, and mannerisms—which can aid us in communicating clearly. For maximum clarity, be natural and let the real you come through. You'll be more convincing and much more comfortable.

6. *Speak in images.* The cliché that "a picture is worth a thousand words" isn't exactly true (try explaining the Internal Revenue code using nothing but pictures). But words that help people visualize concepts can be tremendous aids in communicating a message. Once Ronald Reagan's Strategic Defense Initiative became known as Star Wars, its opponents had a powerful weapon against it. The name gave it the image of a far-out, futuristic dream beyond the reach of current technology. Reagan was never able to come up with a more powerful positive image.

Your one-on-one communication will acquire real power if you learn to send messages that are simple, clear, and assertive; if you learn to monitor the hearer to determine that your message was accurately received; and if you learn to obtain the desired response by approaching people with due regard for their behavioral styles.

Your finesse as a communicator will grow as you learn to identify and overcome the obstacles to communication. Practice the six techniques I just mentioned, and you'll find your effectiveness as a message-sender growing steadily.

But sending messages is only half the process of communicating. To be a truly accomplished communicator, you must also cultivate the art of listening.

If you're approaching a railroad crossing around a blind curve, you can send a message with your car horn. But that's not the most important part of your communication task. The communication that counts takes place when you stop, look, and *listen*.

9

STOP, LOOK—AND LISTEN

We're all familiar with the warning on the signs at railroad crossings: Stop, Look, and Listen. It's also a useful admonition for communication.

It's easy to think of communication as a process of sending messages. But sending is only half the process. Receiving is the other half. So at the appropriate time, we have to stop sending and prepare to receive. As Marc Antony admonished the Romans in Shakespeare's *Julius Caesar*, "Be silent that you may hear."

A sign on the wall of Lyndon Johnson's Senate office expressed Antony's thought in a more down-to-earth way: "When you're talking, you ain't learning."

Something Clicked

Many years ago, a young man went to a Western Union office to apply for a job as a telegrapher. In those days, messages were still transmitted in Morse Code through audible clicks.

The young man had no experience in telegraphy, but he had studied it at home and he knew the code.

His heart sank as he walked into the office and looked over the crowd of people filling out application forms.

As he sat down with his own form, he heard a clicking noise in the background. He stopped filling out his form and listened. Then he dashed into the nearby office. Moments later, a man emerged and told the other applicants they could go home. The job had just been filled.

What got him the job?

The clicking noise was the sound of a telegraph receiver. The young man listened and translated the clicks into words: "If you understand this message, come into the office. The job is yours."

LISTENING PAYS

Listening pays off daily in the world of business. When you interview a candidate for a position with your company, you normally spend about 80 percent of your time listening. Smart salespeople have learned that you can talk your way out of a sale, but you can also listen your way into one. They listen to their customers to find out what their needs are, then concentrate on filling those needs. Skilled negotiators know that no progress can be made until they have heard and understood what the other side wants. Enlightened employers listen to their employees and learn about their wants and needs.

Listening to Sausage Grinders

Ralph Sayer brought twenty-first century management into the world of sausage grinding as CEO of Johnsonville Foods in Sheboygan Falls, Wisconsin. Sayer became a strong believer in management by listening. He went out into his plants and opened his ears.

One of the complaints he heard was that new employees were poorly trained. This put a burden on the other employees, who had to rectify their mistakes and compensate for their low productivity.

"We gotta fix it," they told their CEO.

"You're absolutely right," Sayer responded, "and you guys know what these people need to know when they come in. . . . Train them."

Sayer reasoned that the employees themselves knew more about the job requirements than the human resources department did, so he put the employees in charge of hiring, firing, and training.[1]

When his employees complained about co-workers who brought "boom boxes" into the plant and played loud music, Sayer didn't tell them what to do. He asked them for solutions, and he listened.

I would replace the training element of Sayer's formula with a system of comprehensive, integrated employee education. This would provide his workers with the skills to meet their expanded responsibilities. But his willingness to listen to the people on the work floor is exemplary, and other executives would do well to emulate him.

Listening Requires Thought and Care

Listening, like speaking and writing, requires thought and care. If you don't concentrate on listening, you won't learn much, and you won't remember much of what you learn.

Some experts claim that professionals earn between 40 percent and 80 percent of their pay by listening. Yet most of us retain only 25 percent of what we hear. If you can increase your retention and your comprehension, you can increase your effectiveness in the twenty-first century's Age of Information.

The Benefits of Listening

Skillful listening offers these benefits:

- You will learn from what you hear.
- You will show the people to whom you listen that you're interested in them.
- You will gain insight into the way others perceive their individual needs, desires, and motivations.
- You will give others a chance to let down their guards so that they can hear what you have to say.
- You will actively involve others in the communication process.
- You will clarify misconceptions.

Listen with Your Eyes

If you listen only with your ears, you're missing out on much of the message. As we learned in chapter 6, some of the most important communication is done without words. Good listeners keep their eyes open.

Look for feelings. The face is an eloquent communication medium. Learn to read its messages. While the speaker is delivering a verbal message, the face can be saying, "I'm serious," "Just kidding," "It pains me to be telling you this," or "This gives me great pleasure."

Some nonverbal signals to watch for:

- *Rubbing one eye.* When you hear, "I guess you're right," and the speaker is rubbing one eye, guess again. Rubbing one eye often is a signal that the speaker is having trouble inwardly accepting something.

- *Tapping feet.* When a statement is accompanied by foot tapping, it usually indicates a lack of confidence in what is being said. If a vendor says, "We can deliver the goods within six weeks," while moving toes or heels up and down, better allow for a couple extra weeks.
- *Rubbing fingers.* When you see the thumb and forefinger rubbing together, it often means that the speaker is holding something back. It may be a signal for you to ask some penetrating questions.
- *Staring and blinking.* If you've made your best offer and the other person stares at the ceiling and blinks rapidly, your offer is under consideration. Allow time for a decision to be made. If you hear a deep breath and a sigh, the decision has probably been made.
- *Crooked smiles.* As Shakespeare wrote, "One may smile, and smile and be a villain." Most genuine smiles are symmetrical. And most facial expressions are fleeting. If a smile is noticeably crooked or if it remains for more than a moment or two, you're probably looking at a fake smile, and you're quite possibly listening to an untruth.
- *Poor eye contact.* Poor eye contact can be a sign of low self-esteem, but it can also indicate that the speaker is not being truthful. Most people find it hard to look you in the eye while lying to you. But before you judge a person's motives by eye contact, remember that in some cultures direct eye contact is considered rude.
- *Forced eye contact.* Just as lack of eye contact can be a sign of lying, so forced eye contact can be a sign of faking it.
- *Frequent rubbing of the nose.* This can also signal a lack of candor.

It would be unwise to make a decision based solely on these visible signals. But they can give you valuable tips on the kind of questions to ask and the kind of answers to be alert for.

Good Listeners Make Things Easy

People who are poor listeners will find few who are willing to come to them with useful information.

"No one cares to speak to an unwilling listener," said Jerome, the scholar of the fourth and fifth centuries who translated the Bible into Latin.

Good listeners make it easy for speakers. They make it clear that they're interested in what the other person has to say.

When you're ready to listen to someone, eliminate all the competition for your attention. Put aside whatever you've been working on. Listening can't be a part-time activity. Turn off the radio, television set, or stereo. Assume an alert posture, facing the speaker squarely and at eye level. Show that you're ready to listen by leaning toward the speaker. Keep arms and legs uncrossed. Be respectful of the speaker's "bubble of space," positioning yourself neither too close nor too far away.

As the conversation proceeds, you can guide it with body language. A single nod keeps the conversation going. A double nod encourages the speaker to elaborate. A triple nod may make the speaker hesitate, change the subject, or gradually wind down.

A listener's verbal response can either ignite a conversation or squelch it. Figure 9–1 contains examples of igniter phrases and squelcher phrases.

Monologues in Duet

Remember that conversation is an interactive process. In a truly productive conversation, two or more minds are engaged in a mutual enterprise—the interchange of thoughts. This process, however, often degenerates into a monologue in duet: We're thinking about what we're about to say instead of listening to what the other person is saying. When we do that, we often miss out on key points or misunderstand what has been said.

The process of listening involves interpretation, evaluation, and reaction. Listen carefully to what the other person is saying. Put yourself in the speaker's shoes and try to interpret what you hear from the speaker's point of view. What is the speaker thinking and feeling?

Fit what you hear into the framework of what you already know, and evaluate it against your present knowledge. Ask questions for clarification, and listen carefully to the answers. Then give your reaction.

I often use three exercises to demonstrate to audiences the value of listening carefully and evaluating what is being said.

In one, I ask the audience to repeat the word *joke* each time I hold up my hand.

IGNITERS	SQUELCHERS
I like that . . .	The problem with that is . . .
Keep talking, you're on track . . .	No way it will work here . . .
Go ahead, try it! . . .	Impossible under our current system . . .
We can do a lot with that idea . . .	It's not a bad idea, but . . .
That's great, how can we do it? . . .	We've never done it that way before . . .
That's neat! What else do we need? . . .	You haven't considered . . .
How can we get support for it? . . .	We have too many projects now . . .
I think it will fly . . .	It won't work . . .
Gee, why not? . . .	We haven't the time . . .
Hey, that's a great idea! . . .	We're not ready for it yet . . .
How can we build on that idea? . . .	It's all right in theory, but not in practice . . .
I agree! . . .	Let's be practical . . .
How can we help you? . . .	Why start anything now? . . .
This is going to be fun! . . .	You know, I think you really are dumb . . .
I love challenges like this . . .	Has anyone else tried it? . . .
That would be interesting to try . . .	It's been the same for ten years. Why change now? . . .

Figure 9-1

After they've responded with "joke" several times, I ask, "What do you call the white part of an egg?"

The audience invariably answers, "yolk." Which leaves me wondering what they would call the yellow part of an egg.

In another exercise, I begin by saying, "Imagine you are a bus driver and it is your mission to drive your bus due north four miles, due east three miles, due south two miles, and due west one mile."

While my listeners are trying to track the bus's route in their minds, I ask the question: "How old is the bus driver?"

Few people remember that I began by saying "Imagine *you* are a bus driver. . . ."

In the third exercise, I ask the audience to give me a four-letter word beginning with *s* that describes what you do when you go to a mall.

That one's a piece of cake: *Shop.*

Now, I say, give me a four-letter word starting with *s* that describes what you do when you return merchandise to exchange it for something else.

Most of the audience responds: *Swap.*

Now (listen carefully), think of a word that describes what you do when you come to a green light.

If you said, "Stop," you need to go back for a remedial driving course—or perhaps you need to take a course in listening.

Note that I didn't specify the number of letters in the last word, and I didn't say what letter it began with.

These are more than cute exercises designed to draw chuckles from an audience. They clearly illustrate the value of interpreting and evaluating before responding to what you hear.

Wait Your Turn to Talk

When you sit down to listen, don't try to seize the floor before the speaker is ready to yield—unless you are trapped in the presence of a nonstop talker and you have to interrupt in the interest of time. Busy executives don't have to become captives of long-winded bores. When you find yourself in the presence of such a motormouth, you may have to break in at strategic points and try to keep the conversation focused.

But in normal conversations, the speaker will let you know when it's time for you to speak. The signal could come in the form of a question, an expectant look, or a pause that gives you a chance to step in without interrupting.

As you listen, don't prejudge. Wait until you've heard all the speaker's ideas before you make a final evaluation. While the speaker is talking, focus your full attention on what is being said. Don't tune out the speaker as you frame your own response. When it's time for you to speak, you can take a moment to collect your thoughts. There's nothing wrong with an interlude of silence.

Don't Be Presumptuous

Good listeners don't presume that they know what the speaker is going to say. But they do try to anticipate the direction of the speaker's thinking. They ask themselves, "Where is this line of reasoning going?" and they follow the speaker through the thinking process.

Questions should be used to help the speaker provide the information you want. They should not be used to grill or cross-examine. Keep your questions brief and open-ended.

Good listeners provide the speaker with feedback. An occasional nod, an "unh huh," and an "I see," tell the speaker that you're still paying attention. When it's your turn to speak, paraphrase the speaker's message as you understand it. This gives the speaker a chance to correct any misinterpretation.

Taking notes is a good sign that you're interested in what you're hearing—unless, of course, the speaker is sharing confidential information.

"He listens well who takes notes," wrote the Italian poet, Dante, more than 670 years ago. Indeed, the palest ink is better than the most remarkable memory.

Over the years, I've watched how people take notes in my seminars. Some write down everything. Others pick and choose, based on their needs.

Note taking is an art. If you try to transcribe the whole conversation, you'll be so engrossed in note taking that you won't have time to absorb, interpret, and evaluate the ideas. Just jot down the key points as you listen. The important question is, "How will I use this information later, and how easily can I retrieve it?"

WHY PEOPLE DON'T LISTEN

All of us have experienced occasions when we wished we had listened more closely to what was being said. Usually, good listening requires self-discipline, and sometimes it demands self-examination. If you sometimes have problems listening to what others say, some of these factors may be behind the difficulty:

- *Prejudice.* You may conclude—either before or during the speaker's remarks—that the speaker has nothing significant to say. The reasons for such prejudice are many. They may include the speaker's appearance, age, actions, voice, race, religion, and nationality. All of us carry around petty biases. It's easy to say that we should get rid of them, but prejudices are emotional, not rational, and they can be insidious. It's best to overcome our prejudices, but while we're *overcoming* them we must learn to *override* them when our best interests are involved. You do this by taking charge of your thoughts. Force yourself to seek out the value in what is being said. When you're lost and asking for directions, you don't let your attention stray because the person giving directions is wearing overalls instead of a business suit. You listen for the information you need to get to your destination. When you're inclined to tune out a speaker because of some prejudice, remind yourself of the purpose of the conversation. Keep that purpose in mind, and listen for the words that bear on that purpose.

  I once was the victim of such prejudice without knowing it. It wasn't anything I said or did, and it had nothing to do with who I was. It was something my host had said. I was at a Colorado resort, speaking to a group from a Japanese company, and I was the only outside speaker. It was Saturday evening, and my speech was the final event of a program that had begun Monday morning.

  I was giving it my best, and I thought I was doing a good job. But something wasn't clicking. The audience wasn't showing the high level of enthusiasm I had expected.

  Later, I found out why. These people were tired after a grueling week of meetings, and many of them would have preferred to be somewhere else. But their boss had told them that afternoon that they were to hear a professional consultant that evening and that they were to give him the courtesy of listening to him. The boss's remarks made them angry, and built up a prejudice against the "outside consultant." As a result, many of them just sat in self-imposed boredom without bothering to listen to what I had to say.

- *Jumping to conclusions.* You may decide that what the speaker is saying is too difficult, too trite, too boring, or otherwise unsuited to your needs. Therefore, you feign attentiveness while your mind is elsewhere. When you encounter this situation, bring your mind back to the here and now. Accept the challenge of drawing from the speaker some ideas and information that will be valuable to you personally. If the messsage is too trite or too boring, use questions to probe for more interesting and stimulating material. If the information is too difficult, ask the speaker to simplify. Just say, "You're a pro at this, and I'm not. Give it to me in layperson's terms." Then don't be afraid to ask questions for clarification. The speaker will be flattered by your interest and will be eager to help you understand.
- *Assumption.* You may assume that you already know what the speaker is going to say, so your attention drifts elsewhere. As a result, you miss any new information the speaker may give. When you find yourself thinking this way, make it a game to look for something new to take away from the conversation.
- *Inattention.* If you're like most people, you speak about 125 words per minute, but you think more than 400 words per minute. As a result, you may use the "spare time" to think of what you're going to say next. In the process, you may miss out on much of what the speaker is saying. The remedy is to use the "spare time" to evaluate and interpret what the speaker is saying. You can frame your own response when it is your turn to speak.
- *Selective listening.* You may sometimes hear only what you want to hear. Once again, the solution is to evaluate and interpret. Look for information and ideas that challenge your own ideas. Compare them with what you know and what you feel. Think about how you might deal with this information or these ideas. Should you reconsider your own position? Should you devise new strategies in light of the information?
- *Excessive talking.* If you insist on monopolizing the conversation, you're not going to hear very much. Be conscious of the amount of time you spend talking, and be alert for signs that your listener has something to say. Be willing to yield the floor at reasonable intervals.

- *Lack of empathy.* Good listeners try to see things from the speaker's perspective. If you listen strictly from your own perspective, you may miss out on the relevance of what is being said. The speaker's vantage point is an important part of the message.
- *Fear.* When you suspect that what is about to be said will reflect unfavorably upon you, fear may result. Many people will stop listening then and find ways to start arguments, or use some other means of escape. Patrick Henry, the fiery patriot of the American Revolution, had the right idea: "Whatever anguish of spirit it may cost, I am willing to know the whole truth; to know the worst, and to provide for it."

Rate yourself as a listener by taking the Listener Quality Quiz in figure 9–2.

HOW GOOD IS YOUR LQ?

You can test your self as a listener by taking this Listener Quality Quiz. In the blanks at the end of each listening quality, score yourself on a scale of 1 to 5, with 5 as a high rating and 1 as a low rating.

1. I always try to give every person I talk with as much time to talk as I take. (_____)

2. I really enjoy hearing what other people have to say. (_____)

3. I never find it hard to wait until someone else finishes talking before I have my say. (_____)

4. I listen, even when I don't particularly like the person who's talking. (_____)

5. The sex and age of a person make no difference in how well I listen. (_____)

6. I assume every person has something worthwhile to say and listen intently to friends, acquaintances, and strangers alike. (_____)

7. I put away what I am doing while someone is talking. (_____)

8. I always look directly at the person who is talking and give that person my full attention, no matter what is on my mind. (_____)

Figure 9-2

(*Continued on the following page*)

9. I encourage other to talk by giving them verbal feedback and asking questions. (_____)

10. I encourage other people to talk by my nonverbal messages, such as gestures, facial expressions, and posture. (_____)

11. I ask for clarification of words and ideas I don't understand. (_____)

12. I am sensitive to the tone of the speaker's voice, expressions, and gestures that convey meaning. (_____)

13. I never interrupt a person who is talking. (_____)

14. I withhold all judgments and opinions about what a person is saying until I have heard it all. (_____)

15. I listen past the words to the feelings and meanings the person is expressing, and test to see whether I am understanding correctly. (_____)

16. I make mental outlines of the main points of what a person is saying. (_____)

17. I look mainly for points on which we can agree, not mainly for points on which we disagree. (_____)

18. I respect all people's rights to their opinions, even if I disagree with them. (_____)

19. I view every dispute or conflict as an opportunity to understand the person better. (_____)

20. I recognize that listening is a skill, and I concentrate on trying to develop that skill in my daily life. (_____)

Scoring: **Add up your total points and figure your LQ as follows:**
90–100—You're all ears.
80–89—You're a pretty good listener.
70–79—You're missing a lot.
Below 70—You need to follow Shakespeare's advice: "Give every man thy ear but few thy voice."

Once you've mastered the basics of sending and receiving written, spoken, and nonverbal messages, you're ready to start applying these skills in specific areas of your life.

Starting in chapter 10, we'll cover one of the most sensitive areas of human interaction: communication between the sexes.

10

AVOIDING
THE GENDER TRAP

During the latter half of the twentieth century, women entered the American workforce in strength. Rosie the Riveter, who moved into the vacant shoes of the men who shipped off to fight World War II, spearheaded the movement of women into the workplace. After the war, women refused to go back to the kitchen. They stayed, they called for reinforcements, and they insisted on equal rights. Slowly, but surely, they have won those rights and have justified their place in the workforce.

This means that more and more business communications are directed toward women and more and more of them originate with women. If differences exist in the way women communicate and the way men communicate, people of both sexes can increase their effectiveness by learning about these differences. If sexism has permeated the language we speak, it's important that we clear it out and render our communication gender-neutral. This calls for several adjustments in traditional patterns of communication. Three, in particular, stand out.

First, there's the language. The English language had its origins in a male-dominated society, so the concept of male superiority is embedded in the language. This has to change.

Second, because women and men have filled different cultural roles throughout human history, they have developed different manners of communicating. Each has its strengths and drawbacks.

Third, when men and women began working side by side, the issue of sexual harassment entered the workplace.

So the advances of women in the business world—in numbers and in stature—pose these communications challenges:

107

- Using the language in a graceful, grammatical, gender-neutral way
- Learning to understand the communicating style of the opposite sex and to use it yourself when appropriate
- Developing guidelines for interaction that allow conscientious men and women to work comfortably with one another without worrying about the issue of sexual harassment

THE LANGUAGE CHALLENGE

Some language students infer that the Anglo-Saxon progenitors of our language assumed that men were the norm for the human race and women made up a subcategory. Hence, when the language referred to people in general, it used masculine terms. When it referred to women in particular, it used feminine terms.

We encounter gender problems most often when we are dealing with personal pronouns. For those who put away their English textbooks a long time ago, let me explain what I mean.

We have three sets of pronouns that refer to people:

1. The first-person pronoun refers to the speaker or writer. First-person singular pronouns are *I*, *me*, *my*, and *mine*. First-person plural pronouns are *we*, *us*, *our*, and *ours*.
2. Second-person pronouns refer to the person to whom the communication is addressed. They are the same in both singular and plural form. They are *you*, *your*, and *yours*.
3. Third-person pronouns refer to third parties. Third-person singular pronouns are *he*, *she*, *it*, *him*, *her*, *his*, *her*, *hers*, and *its*. Third-person plural pronouns are *they*, *them*, *their*, and *theirs*.

Notice that only one set of pronouns—the third-person singular—makes a distinction between males and females. The rest of the pronouns are gender-neutral—that is, they can apply equally to either sex or to both sexes.

The problem arises when we need a singular pronoun that can refer to either or both sexes. The only third-person singular pronouns we have that are gender-neutral are *it* and *its*, and we usually use those words to refer only to animals or inanimate objects.

The traditional answer to this dilemma has been to use the masculine pronoun to represent either or both sexes.

Abe the Sexist?

To illustrate the problem—and to dramatize the way times have changed—let's look at a highly sexist statement by a man whose name is still synonymous with equality and justice: Abraham Lincoln. Lincoln once made this observation:

> It is difficult to make a man miserable while he feels he is worthy of himself and claims kindred to the great God who made him.

Any politician who uttered those words today would be greeted with cries of outrage: "What about women? Aren't they, too, kindred to the great God who made them?"

Some people would have edited the statement to read:

> It is difficult to make a person miserable while she or he feels he or she is worthy of herself or himself and claims kindred to the great God who made him or her.

Abe would have been caught in a bind. On the one hand, his statement would have satisfied the requirements of gender neutrality by using both masculine and feminine pronouns and by alternating them so that half the time the feminine pronoun came first and half the time the masculine pronoun came first. It also would have met the grammatical requirements. But the statement would have been hopelessly awkward and worthless as a literary effort.

GENDER-NEUTRAL PRONOUNS

What does one do?

At the turn of the twenty-first century, there are two alternatives. One is to draft plural pronouns for double duty as singular pronouns when you refer to either or both genders.

Following this procedure, Lincoln would have said:

It is difficult to make a person miserable while they feel they are
worthy of themselves and claim kindred to the great God who
made them.

In this case, Abe would be letting the plural pronouns *they, themselves*, and *them* stand in for the singular *person*. That's what most people do in everyday conversation, but the usage still sets the grammatical
purist's teeth on edge.

It can be argued that it is far more logical to use a plural pronoun to
stand in for a single person than to use a masculine pronoun to stand in
for a feminine person. This logic is likely to prevail in the twenty-first
century, and it's my prediction that by the end of the first decade of the
new millennium *they, them, their*, and *theirs* will be perfectly acceptable
as singular neuter pronouns. The question of whether we'll use *themselves* or *themself* is up in the air, but I'm betting on *themselves*.

In the meantime, if you want to be gender-neutral and avoid the
awkwardness of *he/she* and *him/her* while remaining perfectly grammatical, there is a way. As we've seen, any plural pronoun can refer to
either or both genders. So can any pronoun in the first or second person.

Therefore, you can usually solve the gender dilemma by switching
to the plural or to the first or second person.

Abe could have reworded his remarks this way:

It is difficult to make people miserable while they feel they are
worthy of themselves and claim kindred to the great God who
made them.

Or, if he preferred, he could have switched to the first person:

It is difficult to make us miserable while we feel we are worthy
of ourselves and claim kindred to the great God who made us.

Or he could have followed the common—and grammatical—practice of using the second-person pronoun to refer to people in general:

It is difficult to make you miserable while you feel you are worthy of yourself and claim kindred to the great God who made you.

Most situations that call for gender-neutral pronouns can be handled through one of these devices. So if you're running a restaurant, you can post a sign saying, "All who handle food must wash their hands after using the bathroom," or "If you handle food, you must wash your hands after using the bathroom." But if the sign says, "Everyone who handles food must wash their hands after using the bathroom," the Health Department won't complain; nor will the servers and customers, unless they happen to be English teachers or fussy writers.

CONSCIOUSNESS RAISING

The other problems of gender neutrality are relatively easy to fix. They usually call for nothing more than consciousness raising.

Here are some areas for attention.

•   *Find substitutes for compound nouns that contain "man" or "woman" as part of the word.* A common strategy is to substitute *person* for *man* or *woman*. If you choose this strategy, be sure that you don't use *person* only when referring to women or to people of both genders. If you refer to a woman as a *spokesperson* while you refer to a man as a *spokesman*, you're still being sexist.

   Figure 10–1 shows some examples of sexist words and their gender-neutral equivalents.

SEXIST	GENDER-NEUTRAL
Spokesman	Spokesperson, Representative
Policeman	Police officer
Fireman	Firefighter
Congressman	Representative, Member of Congress
Chairman	Chairperson, Chair
Postman	Mail carrier
Repairman	Repairer
Workman	Worker
Craftsman	Artisan
Alderman	Board member
Salesman	Salesperson
Businessman	Businessperson

Figure 10-1

The same rule applies to words such as *forefathers* and the expression *city fathers*. I hate to pick on Honest Abe, but when he stated that "Our forefathers brought forth on this continent a new nation . . . ," he ignored half the population of the American colonies. "Ancestors" and "forebears" are terms that embrace both forefathers and foremothers. *City leaders* is a gender-neutral way of describing the mayor and governing body of a municipality.

- *Avoid other words that tend to stereotype male/female roles.* For some reason, English-users have a hang-up about using words ending in -er and -or to refer to women—even though the suffixes were originally applied to women. When the word describes an occupational function or role, we seem compelled to add an -ess, an -ette, or a -trix to the root word. What difference does it make whether the aircraft is flown by an *aviator* or an *aviatrix*, so long as it takes off and lands safely? Can you look at a statue and tell whether its creator was a sculptor or a sculptress? Does a steak served by a *waiter* taste different from one served by a *waitress*? Do authors punch the keyboard differently from *authoresses*? (Fortunately, we don't have to refer to a woman radio or television journalist as a *broadcastress*.)

  When recruiting personnel, in particular, businesses should be careful to use gender-neutral terms. Usually, there's a handy non-sexist term that serves very well in place of the sexist term. If you balk at calling both men and women *aviators*, call them *pilots*. Most restaurants now call the people who bring your food *servers*. Patricia Aburdene and John Naisbitt are both authors. They're also *writers* (nobody ever refers to a *writress*).

- *When referring to both sexes, alternate between mentioning males first and females first.* Sometimes, even when they're making an obvious effort to be gender-neutral, people show a bias toward the masculine. This applies to female as well as male communicators. When we're trying to avoid using the masculine pronoun to refer to either sex, we almost invariably substitute *he or she*. We refer to *men and women*, *husbands and wives*, and *boys and girls*. The expressions *bride and groom* and *ladies and gentlemen* are exceptions. In common practice, we place the masculine term first. To be gender-neutral, alternate the terms.

- *When using stories and illustrations, use female as well as male examples.* The female has been slighted in literature and folklore, and so we have fallen into the habit of slighting her in our portrayal of workplace situations. I learned this lesson firsthand while speaking at a management conference for AT&T in New Jersey a few years ago. The audience consisted of men and women. During the break, a woman executive reminded me that all my examples were masculine-oriented. Since then, I've included feminine and masculine examples in my repertoire of yarns. And I try to avoid sexist stereotypes. I don't automatically assume that an executive or manager is a *he* and a stenographer or bookkeeper is a *she*.

- *Remember that women are adults.* Modern women often resent it when men refer to them as *girls*. The male executive who says, "I'll have my girl type up the report" is being blatantly sexist. "Secretary" is a perfectly good term, and it's gender-neutral: We call the head of the federal Commerce Department the secretary of commerce, regardless of whether the post is filled by a man or a woman. The male boss who casually invites "the girls and guys at the office" to a cookout at his home may get away with it. But it's always safer to say "women and men" or "the whole gang."

Men often show distinctions by referring to men by last names and women by first names. If an executive says, "Johnson, I want you and Pat to collaborate on that project," you can bet that Johnson is a man and Pat is a woman. If you refer to men by last names only, refer to women the same way. Personally, I prefer the more casual first-name approach in workplace situations and other informal settings, and the use of courtesy titles on more formal occasions. All my friends, associates, and employees—including my secretaries—call me Nido when we're interacting at work, and I call them by their first names.

The Way Men and Women Communicate

Men and women have traditionally communicated in different ways. This has led to misunderstandings, both in the workplace and in the home. Even today, the legacy of cultural conditioning can be detected in the communication habits of men and women. Members of both sexes should be aware of the differences and learn to take them into account.

We could easily fall into the trap of stereotyping masculine and feminine communication styles, and that would be unfair to both sexes. Men are often stereotyped as the forceful communicators, though I've known women on all continents who speak as forcefully as any man without sacrificing their femininity. Women are often assumed to be more nurturing and caring in their choice of language, but I've known men who are secure in their masculinity yet speak as gently as any woman. As time goes by, I suspect that men and women will become more alike in the way they express themselves. I don't think this will be a case of women learning to talk like men. I expect to see men and women emulate the best in both styles of communication so that we finally arrive at a truly gender-neutral style of communicating.

Who Said It?

To illustrate the characteristics traditionally associated with male and female language, read these quotations and guess which sex they suggest:

- Dammit! I broke my fingernail.
- Oh dear! I just broke my nail!

- That's a nice-looking little statue on your bookcase.
- That's an adorable figurine on your bookcase.

- You'll have to go back and refigure that bid.
- Shouldn't you go back and refigure that bid?

- Fifty percent is too big a markup for that product.
- A 50 percent markup is a bit high for that product, don't you think?

Most people would identify the first statement in each pair as masculine in tone and the second as feminine, even though a man or a woman might have uttered any of them without sacrificing sexual identity.

Casey Miller and Kate Swift, two women who studied the language habits of males and females, characterize the differences between male and female communications this way:

Males adopt a more direct, forceful way of talking; females a more tentative, questioning approach. What one typically phrases as a statement or command the other formulates as a request.[1]

University of California linguist Robin Lakoff attributes this to cultural conditioning:

Discouraged from expressing herself forcefully, a girl may acquire speech habits that communicate uncertainty, hesitancy, indecisiveness and subordination.[2]

Different Expletives and Adjectives

Other students of male/female conversation maintain that women traditionally have used different expletives from men. They are more likely to shun profanity and to favor polite language. Men are more likely than women to use *Damn! Son of a gun! Holy mackerel! Great Caesar!* and *By thunder*! along with other, more explicit expressions. Women are more likely to say *Darn! Oh dear! Mercy! For goodness sake!* and *Good heavens!*

But these are broad generalizations. Some women are capable of salty speech, and some men shun even the mildest profanity.

Women traditionally have used adjectives that reflect deeper feelings than the ones men use. What's *good-looking* to a man will be *lovely* to a woman. What's *nice* to a man will be *adorable* to a woman. What's *great* to a man will be *wonderful* to a woman.

That doesn't mean that a man who thinks a rose is *lovely* is somehow effeminate or that a woman who says *Holy mackerel!* is being "mannish." It's just that one sex has historically shown a preference for one type of adjective and expletive while another sex has preferred another type.

Women shouldn't worry about using the terms that come naturally to them, regardless of which sex these terms are associated with. And neither should men.

When a Question Becomes a Statement

But notice two other sentences in that group. The statement, "You'll have to go back and refigure that bid," is associated with masculine communication, while the question, "Shouldn't you go back and refigure that bid?" is associated with femininity. The assertive statement, "Fifty percent is too big a markup for that product," is assumed to come from a man, while the tentative statement, "A 50 percent markup is a bit high for that product, don't you think?" is assumed to be from a woman.

According to students of male/female communication differences, the man is more likely to put his communication in the form of an assertive directive. Many women (and some men) prefer to put it in the form of a tentative question.

Women, says Lakoff, are more likely to use the "tag question" such as "don't you think?" at the end of their opinions. Even when she doesn't conclude with a question, a woman may raise her voice at the end of the sentence so that "Meet you at 7?" becomes a question rather than a statement.

"By seeming to leave decisions open and not imposing a viewpoint on others, women's language comes off sounding more polite than men's," she observed.[3]

Dr. Deborah Tannen, linguistics professor at Georgetown University in Washington, D.C., did extensive research into the way men and women communicate. She maintains that men usually grow up in a world based on a hierarchical social order. In their world, she says, "conversations are negotiations in which people try to achieve and maintain the upper hand if they can, and protect themselves from others' attempts to put them down and push them around. Life, then, is a contest, a struggle to preserve independence and avoid failure."

A woman, however, approaches the world "as an individual in a network of connections. In this world, conversations are negotiations for closeness in which people try to seek and give confirmation and support, and to reach consensus. They try to protect themselves from others' attempts to push them away. Life, then, is a community, a struggle to preserve intimacy and avoid isolation. Though there are hierarchies in this world too, they are hierarchies more of friendship than of power and accomplishment."[4]

We don't have to agree with Tannen's conclusions about the motives behind the different styles of communicating. It's enough to recognize that differences do exist, and that some of the differences correlate to a greater or lesser degree with differences between the sexes. The differences do not mark one style of communication as superior and another style as inferior. All they tell us is that when an executive says, "A 50 percent markup is a bit high for the product, don't you think?" she is not necessarily asking your opinion. She is probably making a statement in a style traditionally associated with women.

Tannen likens conversation between the sexes to cross-cultural communication. Even body language is different, she found. Women tend to align themselves face to face and maintain eye contact; men and boys tend to sit at an angle, or even parallel to each other, and look around, glancing at each other occasionally. To a man, a woman's direct gaze may be taken as flirtatious while a man's direct gaze may be taken as challenging.[5]

Tannen attributes the differences to the woman's search for intimacy as opposed to the man's search for independence. Because of these differences, she says, a woman is likely to listen politely to conversation that doesn't particularly interest her, while a man is more likely to try to take control of the conversation rather than allow the other person to get the upper hand.

"What is the hope for the future?" she asks. "Must we play out our assigned parts to the closing act?"

Her answer:

Although we tend to fall back on habitual ways of talking, repeating old refrains and familiar lines, habits can be broken. Women and men both can gain by understanding the other gender's style and by learning to use it on occasion.

Women who find themselves unwillingly cast as the listener should practice propelling themselves out of that position rather than waiting patiently for the lecture to end. Perhaps they need to give up the belief that they must wait for the floor to be handed to them. If they have something to say on a subject, they might push themselves to volunteer it. If they are bored with a subject, they can exercise some influence on the conversation and change the topic to something they would rather discuss.[6]

Women Don't Have to Sound Like Men

Women don't have to sound like men to be forceful and assertive. But they do need to be aware of the way men might perceive some of their communication characteristics.

This awareness can be invaluable in the marketplace when women are trying to sell to or buy from men. It can also be highly useful for women corporate leaders who must manage or supervise men and who must deal with male peers on the management team.

What a woman perceives as politeness, a man might interpret as indecisiveness or reluctance to make a commitment. The twenty-first century woman needs to cultivate assertiveness, just as the male with the macho self-image needs to cultivate tact. There's a good middle ground that will serve both sexes well.

Women need not sound like "one of the boys" to convey self-confidence and poise in a business setting. They need only speak as if they believe firmly in what they're saying. When they give instructions, they can phrase them tactfully, but give them in a confident voice, as if they expect them to be carried out.

The Strong Female Voice

A woman's voice is different from a man's voice, and there's no need for women to try to change. The late twentieth century brought a healthy crop of successful women broadcasters to the television news shows. Network stars such as Barbara Walters, Diane Sawyer, and Connie Chung demonstrated that the female voice could speak with authority. Remember Barbara Jordan, who held the 1976 Democratic National Convention spellbound and went on to become a federal judge? Dallas columnist Molly Ivins wrote, tongue-in-cheek, of Jordan that she "can't help sounding like God Almighty."[7] Yet Jordan spoke in a rich, feminine voice. Ann Richards, who went on to become governor of Texas, keynoted the 1988 Democratic National Convention in a decidedly feminine voice. Elizabeth Dole, George Bush's secretary of labor, spoke effectively and authoritatively in her soft North Carolina accent. There was nothing weak or tentative in the communication styles of any of these women.

The point is: Whether you're a man or a woman, a strong, low-pitched voice conveys calmness, confidence, and authority. A lower voice range is the best for assertive communication. A higher pitch signals excitement, and sometimes nervousness and fear.

SEXUAL HARASSMENT

When women began filling positions formerly reserved for men, some men clung stubbornly to the notion that women were created for the gratification of men and were therefore fair game for sexual advances. Some women still clung to the notion that their femininity was an asset to be exploited, and were willing to use it to gain workplace advantages.

Sexual harassment became a workplace issue. When Anita Hill, an Oklahoma professor, accused Supreme Court nominee Clarence Thomas of sexual harassment while she was working with him, the harassment issue was dramatized on the American national stage. Everybody talked about it.

Both men and women began to wonder where the line was to be drawn between friendly patter and sexual communication. Women became more ready to draw the line, and even some men began to come forward to complain about harassment from female bosses and associates.

Imagine Your Spouse Is There

A simple rule should suffice in governing behavior between the sexes in the workplace: Always conduct yourself as you would if your spouse or the other person's spouse were in the room with you. Even if neither you nor your co-worker of the opposite sex is married or committed to someone else, conduct yourself as if both of you were. This applies particularly when you're dealing with people under your supervision.

People vary in their acceptance of sexual patter. Some enjoy it. Some are embarrassed and even intimidated by it. Be safe—and considerate. Avoid off-color jokes and sexually suggestive remarks. Don't flirt on the job and never suggest—even in jest—that sexual favors might lead to more favorable treatment on the job while sexual indifference might hold back advancement.

Every business should draw up a policy on sexual harassment. Both men and women should play a role in drafting it. It should set clear guidelines for what behavior is acceptable and what is unacceptable. It should provide a specific procedure for reporting and resolving harassment charges. It should also outline specific penalties, and those penalties should be enforced.

ETIQUETTE BETWEEN THE SEXES

Attitudes are communicated through the little courtesies we show to other people, but in the changing world of gender relations, little courtesies can be misinterpreted. Actions that once communicated a sense of courtesy and a concern for proper etiquette may now be regarded as signs of condescending and patronizing attitudes.

Should men open doors for women? Should men light women's cigarettes? Should men and women shake hands with each other in social situations?

The rule of thumb: If you normally provide a courtesy for a person of the same sex, provide the same courtesy for a person of the opposite sex. Don't expect a member of the opposite sex to do things for you that you wouldn't expect a member of your own sex to do.

In business settings, women want to be and expect to be treated as fully equal to men. If you're walking side by side with a client or business associate and you reach the door first, it's common courtesy to open the door and hold it for the other person—regardless of gender.

Most women no longer expect male business associates or clients to get out of the car, walk around, and open the door for them. And it's no longer mandatory, in a business setting, for a man to light a cigarette for a woman. In social settings, the rules vary according to the individuals involved.

The presence of women has enriched the workplace, greatly enlarged the pool of talent, and increased the level of justice and equity in our country. The company that takes full advantage of the talents of both sexes doubles its prospects for success. And the individuals who learn to communicate effectively across gender lines in gender-neutral fashion are powerfully positioned to share in that success.

The gender factor, though, is not the only element of diversity in the modern workplace. The American population is becoming a kaleidoscope of cultures, and this variety is being reflected in the workplace. The European workplace is also becoming more diverse as people from North Africa, Asia, and other former colonial areas look for opportunities on the Continent, and as southern Europeans go job hunting in the industrialized north. In the next chapter we explore avenues of cross-cultural communication in the workplace.

11

CROSS-CULTURAL COMMUNICATION

Those who lead the American workforce of the twenty-first century must learn to communicate with a variety of cultures. The workforce has changed because American demographics have changed. The monochrome, predominantly male environment of the early twentieth century is gone, never to return. In its place is a colorful demographic brocade, drawing together people from nations and cultures around the globe. Out of this ethnic and cultural mixture will be drawn the leaders of tomorrow. Today's leadership must find ways to bring non-White and nonmale employees into the circles of leadership. It is not just a matter of fairness; it is a matter of necessity.

THE CHANGING WORKFORCE

The character of the American workforce is changing. In 1980 there were 41 million Americans in their twenties. The twenty-something population for the year 2000 is projected at 34 million. The *Training and Development Journal* projects that between now and 2020, the size of the working-age population will increase by less than one percent a year.[1] The growth rate for the working-age minority populations will be much higher; the growth rate for non-Hispanic White males will be somewhat lower. If the economy grows by about 2 percent a year, business can expect a growing deficit in the labor pool. There won't be enough White men to fill the ranks. This means that, even without Equal Employment Opportunity legislation, and setting aside all considerations of fairness and ethics, businesses will have to hire, develop, and promote women and minorities. In the twenty-first century, women and minorities will constitute the great majority of the workforce.

Even in the mid-1990s, White men made up only 44 percent of the workforce, while they constituted less than 40 percent of the total population. By the year 2000, their percentage of the working population will have shrunk significantly because of immigration and higher birth rates among minorities. In addition, a new generation of women will have grown up in the ranks of business, eager for the challenges of leadership and unwilling to be relegated to subordinate roles.

The American heritage is no longer a European but a global heritage. At the outset of the 1990s, our population included 30 million African Americans. If they occupied a separate country, it would have more people than forty-eight of the fifty-two African countries. The 22.4 million Hispanics in the United States outnumber the total population of all but three of the Spanish-speaking countries of Latin America.

The 7.3 million Americans of Asian or Pacific island descent outnumber the populations of more than half the countries in Asia and the Pacific. You'll see more Oriental faces in America than you will see in Cambodia, Laos, Hong Kong, or Singapore.

Within our boundaries are about 2 million American Indians—close to the population of Panama.

What's more, their numbers are growing. As figure 11–1 shows, the Asian/Pacific population of the United States nearly doubled between 1980 and 1990. The Hispanic population grew by more than 50 percent, while the African American population expanded by 13.2 percent. Meanwhile, the population of non-Hispanic Whites grew by 5 percent.

Non-Hispanic Whites still constitute the majority of the American population, but at some point during the twenty-first century this will change. Non-Hispanic Whites will simply be the largest of several minorities in the nation and in the workplace.

This means that corporate leaders, from CEOs to supervisors, must learn to deal with and motivate a workforce that springs from a variety of cultures. They must also learn to do business in the global marketplace, which demands a knowledge of and sensitivity to the ways of other cultures.

Language Instruction

In many cases, companies have found it advantageous to offer their employees courses in English as a second language. California Literacy, organized to provide literacy training through community colleges in the state, emphasized English as a second language. Its approach was to use

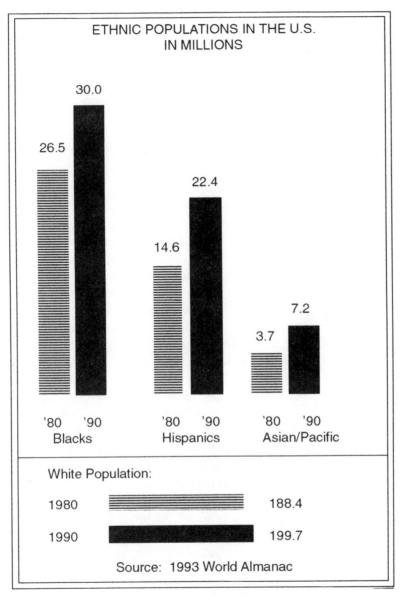

Figure 11-1

manuals, training materials, and other written materials taken from the workplace itself.

The Honeywell Corporation carried its language instruction one step further. It discovered that Minneapolis, the site of its headquarters, had the second largest concentration of Southeast Asians in the United States. Many of these Asians were finding jobs at Honeywell, and the language barrier was becoming a problem. Honeywell not only provided English-language courses for the Vietnamese, Laotians, and Cambodians in its workforce; it also provided instruction in Asian languages for its American-born personnel.

FEELING AT HOME WITH DIVERSITY

If you want to obtain top performance from your workforce, you can't afford to have a substantial percentage of employees feeling like outsiders. Businesses must look for ways to make people from diverse backgrounds feel comfortable working with one another. This means providing environments in which people will be respected regardless of gender, skin color, language background, or national origin.

Honeywell began with awareness training for its personnel. It looked for similarities rather than differences, and focused on cultivating attitudes of respect. Then it provided more skill-based education, teaching the techniques for managing a diverse workforce.

Too often, people tend to look at other ethnic and cultural groups through stereotypical lenses. All races and cultures have been affected by the forces of history, but we also share common human characteristics. The more we get to know one another, the more we recognize the similarities and the more we see people as individual humans instead of members of some special group. We come to recognize the absurdity of stereotyping and the dangers it entails.

The best way to understand people from another culture is to establish lines of communication. You'll learn a lot more by asking than you will by observing. One way to ask people about themselves is to organize special-interest groups for ethnics within the workforce. Then meet with them and let them tell you about their problems and concerns.

Find Out What Offends

It's up to the company to create an environment that is congenial to all racial, ethnic, and national groups. That environment is nourished through countless day-to-day interactions between management and employees and among peers.

These interactions will be more harmonious if we understand that communications are sent and received through cultural filters. I've had to adjust my cultural lenses repeatedly as my consulting work has taken me to the Middle East, the Pacific Rim, Australia, and New Zealand, as well as across Europe.

I've learned that words, expressions, and gestures that mean one thing in one culture may mean something else in another culture. A term that may seem perfectly harmless to you may be offensive to someone from another ethnic group. A gesture that may be offensive to you may be a friendly communication to someone from another culture.

People who deal with persons from other cultures, including those who supervise them, should be sensitive to the attitudes that go along with the culture.

How can we know what to do and say when dealing with people of other ethnic and cultural groups?

First, find out what terms and expressions are offensive to the ears of others. Never use derogatory terms to describe racial, ethnic, or national minorities, even in joking.

Sometimes it may be difficult to find out what is or is not offensive to minorities. The word *Negro* was once perfectly acceptable to Americans of African descent, since it is derived from a Latin word meaning "black." "Colored people" was a euphemism that became enshrined in the name of one of the most active and effective organizations for African Americans, the National Association for the Advancement of Colored People (NAACP). But today those terms are considered passé at best and patronizing and insulting at worst. The corrupted, slovenly pronunciation of Negro is deeply offensive to most American Blacks. During the Civil Rights revolution, "Black" became the preferred descriptive, and "African American" gained acceptance during the 1980s and 1990s.

"We People" Versus "You People"

But don't be patronizing. Many White Americans wear their racial tolerance on their sleeves and go out of their way to demonstrate that they're not bigots. Black Americans have fought long and hard for equal treatment in the workplace and in society at large. Most of them don't want special treatment. They want to be treated as Americans, not as *Black* Americans. While they may take great pride in their cultural roots, they still regard themselves as part of the American fabric—as indeed they are.

When presidential candidate Ross Perot addressed a Black audience as "you people" in 1992, he lost points, even though he was trying to assure them that he was in sympathy with their aspirations. The preamble to the American Constitution begins with the words "We, the people of the United States of America." Today, "We, the people" embraces citizens of all races, cultures, and national origins. There should be no such thing as "you people" when addressing other members of the corporate family. If you can't say "we people," you need to brush up on your intercultural communication.

What Is a Navajo?

No one has developed a completely satisfying name for the people who were inhabiting the Americas when Columbus arrived. Columbus called them "Indians" because he thought he had found the Indies of the Orient. If you use that name, you have to be sure to distinguish the American Indians from natives of India. "Native American" is a recent term, but what does that make people of European, African, or Asian descent who were born in the United States?

When the Europeans first came to America, the native inhabitants didn't perceive themselves as one people. They perceived themselves as Algonquins, Iroquois, Cherokee, Apache, Dakota, Navajo, and Aztecs. It's quite acceptable to refer to people by tribal name, but if you have to use an all-encompassing name, listen to the individual's conversation and be guided by the preference you observe. Or just ask.

Beware of Ethnic Slang

Some words that may be considered innocent by native-born White Americans may be offensive to minorities. Most Asians don't want to be called "Asiatics," because the term harks back to the days of colonialism.

"Chinaman" and "Jap" are unacceptable in any context. So are such derogatory nicknames as "Gook," "Chink," "Wop," "Mick," "Paddy," "Span," "Dago," "Hymie," and "Hebe." These words should be entirely banished from the vocabularies of twenty-first century leaders.

English Is Precise But Blunt

English is a precise language, but it is perceived as blunt by many speakers of other languages.

Americans often pride themselves on "straight talk" and "telling it like it is." This is a turnoff to Japanese workers, who practice "ishin-denshin"—communication by the heart. To the Japanese, the truth lies in the things you imply, and is not openly stated. Vagueness is preferred to precision. If you're too explicit with the Japanese, they take that as the mark of a know-it-all.

This highly diplomatic approach is common among Asian cultures. In some languages, diplomacy is taken to such an extreme that there is no word for "no."

Facial expressions can be deceptive, too. The Japanese are taught not to burden other people with their problems. Therefore, the bright smile on a Japanese face may mask a heart full of disappointment or despair.

But the face can often be a more accurate message-carrier than the tongue.

Knowing When You're Getting Through

Suppose you're trying to give Mei Ling, your Chinese accountant, some technical on-the-job instructions.

If you say, "Do you understand?" Mei Ling will probably say "Yes" even though she is totally in the dark. Why?

Mei Ling doesn't want to lose face, and she doesn't want you to lose face. If she says "No," it can only mean one of two things to her: She is too dense to comprehend or you are a poor instructor.

In such cases, it's important to watch the face. It's hard to disguise puzzlement, and it's usually easy enough to see comprehension.

Be alert for indications that you're not getting through. Ask for feedback. If your listener repeats what you've said exactly in your words, you probably didn't get through. Listen for questions. People who are following your thoughts usually ask pertinent questions to expand their understanding. If there are no questions, there's likely to be no understanding. And be suspicious when you encounter too much nodding agreement. A person who understands what you're saying will usually find something to elaborate on or to disagree with.

Use Standard English

It didn't take me long, after I came to America, to discover that the English language is full of bewildering idioms. In idioms, words take on meanings that are quite different from their dictionary definitions. For instance, when you say, "I give up," you mean "I surrender," "I quit," or "I yield." But the newcomer to the English language may be puzzled. What does it mean to make a gift in an upward direction?

Not long after I came to this country, I went into a drugstore, made a purchase, and was on my way to the door.

"Come back," said the cashier, in a friendly North Carolina accent.

I turned and went back to the counter.

"What did you want?" I asked.

"Nothing," she said.

"But you told me to come back."

The people in the store went into hysterics.

In the Southern United States, "Come back" is a friendly parting expression that means "Come back to see us sometime" or, in a commercial setting, "I hope you'll do business with us again."

"How are you?" was another expression I had to get used to. I soon learned that this is seldom an inquiry into your health or circumstances. It's another way of saying "hello," and the only response called for is "Fine, how are you?"

You won't be able to clear all idioms from your speech when you address foreign-born workers on the job; nor should you. Idioms are important tools of communication, and newcomers to English must learn them just as they must learn individual words. But be aware that you may occasionally have to explain carefully what you mean. When you ask, "Can you run this machine?" your listener may think you mean "Can you pick up this machine and run with it?"

Slang or jargon should be avoided until the employee has become fluent in English. Use simple, standard-English expressions and you'll communicate more effectively.

Provide Good Orientation

When you're dealing with people from another background, learn as much about them as you can. Go to the encyclopedia or to the card catalog at the library. Find out whether there are ethnic organizations that might provide some information. Ask for help from a member of that ethnic group who has already fully adapted to the American culture. And ask the newcomers themselves: "Ishaq, I know you're going to find things different here from the way they are in Pakistan. I want to be as helpful to you as I can. Please come to me with any questions you have, and let me know if the way we do things conflicts in any way with your customs and beliefs."

Mentoring can also be used as an adjustment tool for immigrants. The ideal mentor would be one who is familiar with both cultures. If such a person is not available, then look for someone with an abundance of friendliness, tolerance, and tact. Give mentors good orientations into the other culture and let them know what to expect in the way of behavior or reactions.

You can give employees from other cultures a sense of belonging to the group by seeking their suggestions and comments. The special-interest groups mentioned earlier can provide useful insights. But some people may be reluctant to provide open criticism, even in the non-threatening environment of a focus group. So the wise executive will provide a system whereby employees can make comments and suggestions anonymously. That way, you get the benefit of feedback and nobody loses face.

Administering Discipline

Sometimes members of the majority culture may feel uncomfortable about disciplining someone from an ethnic or cultural minority. We should certainly be sensitive to the way our words and actions might be perceived. Yet it is entirely proper to expect people to measure up to reasonable standards of performance and conduct.

Make sure that all employees understand what is expected and know the consequences of failure to measure up. This should be spelled out clearly in written policy. This policy should be explained in clear language upon hiring.

When the standards are not met, the first step should be a courteous and helpful reminder, delivered in private. When sterner measures are required, it's wise to confer with someone who is familiar with the culture and ask for advice. Plan your approach and follow it.

THE LANGUAGE OF CULTURE

While human nature is basically the same no matter what culture you're dealing with, the language of words, gestures, and customs—the language of culture—differs widely.

American soldiers in Vietnam often stood casually with hands on hips when talking to each other or to native Vietnamese. This body language could be unsettling to a Vietnamese. In their culture, standing with hands on hips means that you're very angry and are getting ready to throw a punch.

When Nikita Khrushchev held his hands aloft at the United Nations and seemed to be shaking hands with himself, many Americans interpreted that as boorish behavior. Russians recognized it as a friendly gesture.

If you're introduced to a French person who gives your hand one quick shake, then drops it abruptly, don't be offended. That's the standard handshake in France. If your new French friend clinches his right hand into a fist and jerks his thumb toward his mouth, don't walk away in a huff. You're being invited to have a drink.

If you call to a Japanese worker across a crowded room and she puts her finger to her nose, she is not giving you a gesture of disrespect. She's just asking, "Are you talking to me?" An American would point to the chest, not to the nose.

Different Perceptions

If an American salesperson talks to an English client over lunch, the Briton will probably speak in a low voice that can be heard only by the salesperson. The American's voice will become louder as enthusiasm grows. The Briton doesn't want to intrude on the privacy of others in the restaurant. The American wants to demonstrate sincerity and commitment. What the American perceives as openness, the English person perceives as thoughtlessness. What the Briton perceives as being discreet, the American perceives as being timid.

The Japanese are more like the British. Americans have a saying, "It's the squeaky wheel that gets the grease." The Japanese have a saying, "The pheasant that doesn't cry won't get shot."

Americans are a gregarious people; to them silence is something to be avoided. Dr. Edward T. Hall, professor of anthropology at Illinois Institute of Technology, once told of an American family that was host to an Arab student. The family became upset with their guest at one point and decided to give him the "silent treatment." The cold shoulder went unnoticed. In the Arab culture, you don't have to go off into another room to be alone. You can simply fall silent, and people will grant you your privacy without taking offense. So the young Arab had no way of knowing that his American hosts were upset with him. [2]

Invisible Bubbles

Different cultures move in "invisible bubbles" of different sizes. The "invisible bubble" refers to the distance we normally keep from other people when we're interacting. You will normally stand closer to an intimate acquaintance than to a stranger.

Latin Americans have small invisible bubbles. They like to move in close and talk animatedly.

On the other hand, hearty back-slapping behavior that might go over well among Americans of European and African descent might embarrass people from Asian cultures, who are accustomed to more formality.

Eye Contact

Eye contact is perceived in different ways in different cultures. The English will gaze steadily into the eyes of their conversational partners as a sign of interest and involvement. Americans, having been taught that it's impolite to stare, will look the other person in the eye, but will look away occasionally. The Japanese will look down as a sign of respect.

If you're the supervisor and you stop to make friendly banter with some workers from the Orient, they may suspect that you're checking up on them. In some Eastern cultures, socializing on the job is taboo.

What all this means is that you must be aware of cultural differences when you're dealing with people in the workplace and the marketplace.

Cultural Profiles

If a number of different cultures are represented in your workforce, it might be helpful to prepare cultural profiles for each employee from a minority culture. Make this profile part of the employee's personnel records. The profile might contain information on language, religion, food customs or restrictions, the political system in the homeland, national and religious holidays, and customs that might affect work habits.

This same type of profile can be vital to executives and salespeople who must deal with peers in other cultures.

One reason the Japanese have been so much more successful in the American market than Americans have been in the Japanese market is that the Japanese have studied our culture. They know our language and they know our behavior.

Americans have not yet learned to communicate effectively with the Japanese. We expect our democratic, egalitarian behavior to go over well in other cultures. When two American CEOs sit down to negotiate, with their respective management teams beside them, everybody tries to be comfortable with one another. The CEO's staff may address her by first name, and may even argue with her good-naturedly. In many other cultures, including the Japanese, rank has its privileges, and among them is the respect and deference of those of lower rank.

SELLING ACROSS CULTURES

Sales approaches will differ from culture to culture. Americans like to exchange preliminary pleasantries, then get down to business. To the Japanese, the pleasantries are the heart of the procedure. A deal an American might close within twenty-five minutes could stretch into hours for the Japanese, for whom a night on the town might be a part of the process.

Americans, of course, are no strangers to the practice of conducting business on the golf course. But whereas an American would try to turn in an impressive performance, the Japanese would take pains to lose the match rather than humiliate the other person.

You cannot learn, in one chapter of one book, everything you need to know about every culture you will encounter in the American workplace or the global marketplace. Nor will I try to make this chapter the single reference source for this subject. It's just a quick reminder that the diverse workforce and the global marketplace require a global perspective and a willingness to get to know and understand people from other backgrounds.

All of us must become aware that the American style of communication is not the only style, and that it is possible for people with the best of intentions to be misunderstood in embarrassing and offensive ways when communicating with people of other languages and cultures.

Two-Letter Words

When you're dealing with people of other cultures, make a conscious effort to learn as much as you can about the culture. Listen to the people with whom you communicate. Look for ways to obtain feedback. And remember, the ways of other cultures may seem strange to you, but they're normal to the people who practice them. And the ways that are familiar to you may be strange and bewildering to others.

We must understand and accept the fact that all cultures, including our own, have their peculiarities, but that humans in every culture are basically similar. That's why I can conduct seminars in Auckland, New Zealand, Frankfurt, Germany, Montreal, Canada, and Kuala Lumpur, Malaysia—all in one month—and still get warm responses from each audience. People are people. Their similarities outnumber their differences.

To achieve excellence, though, we must exert a genuine effort to understand the variety of cultures we will inevitably encounter.

The American population has always been a blend of cultures. To continue the success story that has been running for more than two centuries, we must keep looking for the qualities that unite us. We are indeed a nation composed of Anglo Americans, Italian Americans, German Americans, African Americans, Asian Americans, Arab Americans, and many other groups. But we have always achieved success as a people by distilling all those terms into the two-letter words, *We* and *Us*.

We cannot succeed as a business or a society if we regard people who look and talk like us as "we" and those who look and speak differently as "they." This nation has never been homogeneous. If it had been, America today would be just a bigger, stronger England. But we are not England. We are the United States—a splendid alloy of metals drawn from the whole of the earth, forged on the anvil of hardship and challenge, shaped by the hand of freedom. We can make the alloy even stronger by learning to communicate with our compatriots—in all their varieties—effectively and respectfully.

Fortunately, the twentieth century has given us a vast tool kit of technology to facilitate our communication efforts. This technology will enable us to communicate in innovative ways that would astound the people who saw the nineteenth century give way to the twentieth. At that time, the telegraph, the telephone, and the wireless radio represented the cutting edge of communication technology. In the next chapter, we'll take a quick look at what's ahead in communications technology and how it might affect the businesses of the future.

12

POWER THROUGH TELECOMMUNICATION

In addition to presenting us with a variety of communication challenges, the twenty-first century also provides us with a wide range of communication tools. These tools place the entire globe within range of our messages. Our skills at bridging cultural differences are rendered even more useful by the technological advances that make it possible to bridge geographical distances.

We began the twentieth century with the telephone and the telegraph, and they were soon followed by the radio. We begin the twenty-first century with a smorgasbord of communication devices.

Hey, Ma Bell! Look what your little black telephone has grown into!

Cellular phones, voice mail, and automatic dialing don't even scratch the surface. The twenty-first century promises to add the dimension of video and computerized data to the traditional voice phone, making it a combination telephone, television, and computer—and lots of other things.

The wedding of telephone and computer has a name: computer-telephone interface, or CTI.

This new couple will take advantage of digitized data—data transmitted in computer language that can be received by a variety of devices. With the proper equipment, a television set can receive and display computer text and a radio can receive a telephone call.

PREPARING FOR NEW TECHNOLOGIES

These advances are either here now or are just around the corner, and it isn't too early for business leaders to begin preparing for those yet to come. An official of GTE Telephone Operations in Dallas makes these suggestions:

- Look at the way your office is wired. The next generation of telecommunications equipment will require the enhanced capacity of fiber optics or other broad-band technologies. Check with your telephone company for suggestions on preparing for these advances.
- Inventory your telecommunications equipment. Find out what possibilities exist for present equipment that you may not be aware of. Determine in what ways you might be able to take advantage of services that require greatly enlarged capacity. The videophone could be your next step into the world of telecommunications.
- Rethink the way you communicate. You can make a telephone call with your feet on your desk, wearing jogging shorts, or still dripping wet from the shower. The videophone will not be so forgiving. Your dress, environment, posture, gestures, and facial expressions will all be part of the message. If you use the videophone for sales transactions, you'll need to provide your salespeople with additional education to enable them to make maximum use of this new medium.
- Look for ways in which you can develop new products and services to take advantage of this technology. Do you have a database that others might pay to use? Could you offer a new service? The opportunities are unlimited.[1]

ALLY OR NUISANCE?

Meanwhile, back in the primitive 1990s, the telephone in its present incarnation is one of the strongest allies and greatest nuisances businesspeople have.

Salespeople have learned that the telephone can save on tires and shoe leather. By using a city directory that is cross-indexed for telephone numbers and street addresses, they can locate and reach the people they want to reach. If they spend three minutes on each call, they'll reach twenty prospects an hour, which is hard to do if you're communicating by car, cab, or plane.

Executives have learned that conference calls, even without the video dimension, can often eliminate the need for meetings that require people from far-flung places to converge on one spot.

You Can't Fax a Smile

The voice phone remains the businessperson's communications medium of choice while we await the technological refinements that will enable us to debut before the eye of the videophone. And it is a powerful and useful medium.

Fax machines and computer modems have expanded our options for transmitting information, but they still haven't eliminated the need for the immediacy and the intimacy of voice communication. Nor are they likely to eliminate the telephone call—with or without pictures—as a preferred method of getting in touch across distances. Telephone conversations don't have to be typed or punched into word processors. And you can't fax a smile, though you can convey one over the telephone by voice quality.

As a matter of fact, phone calls can often eliminate the need for writing. You'll usually save time by picking up the telephone instead of the dictaphone. You'll certainly save time for your secretary, which means that you're saving your company money. After you've made your call, make notes of what you discussed and keep them organized for ready reference.

With all its advantages, though, the telephone can become a tyrant, monopolizing your time, interrupting your transactions, and breaking your concentration. But only if you let it.

Let's look at some ways to make your telephone your ally instead of your nemesis.

There's No Substitute for a Live Voice

First, remember that for a good, positive impression by telephone, nothing beats the sound of a live voice that speaks from a knowledgeable mind.

Answering devices can fill in on weekends, on holidays and after hours, but they can't provide the warmth and flexibility of a good telephone receptionist. Nothing is quite so frustrating as to dial a business number and get a synthesized voice that runs down an itemized list of people or departments you can reach if you "touch 1 *now*." What if the answer is *none of the above*? Your caller has wasted a lot of time listening to the entire list and must still press a button to reach a live person who can route the call to the proper party. Many people resent it when they call long distance and find themselves at the mercy of an answering system.

Even when the videophone marries computer and telephone technology, it's a good bet your callers will welcome a live face and voice to welcome them to your corporate world.

Have Your Calls Screened

That doesn't mean that you have to be at the beck and call of your telephone every hour of the day. Your secretary or receptionist can screen your calls, connecting you immediately with the people you need to talk to and holding other calls for you to return at a more convenient time. (It goes without saying that your secretary or receptionist should be articulate, friendly, and familiar with your organization.) Designate a certain time of day for returning telephone calls, and at that time answer all the phone calls that have come in. You may have to make adjustments for callers who are several time zones away and exceptions for callers who are in other parts of the world. But a good secretary or receptionist can make those judgments for you.

Take Control of Your Time

When you do place telephone calls, take control of your time. If you have a lot of frequently dialed numbers, an automatic dialer can save you time and money. You can punch a single button to dial the number without having to look it up. If you use a desktop computer, you'll find many software programs that allow quick and easy retrieval of frequently called numbers.

Decide what you want to accomplish with the call and make a list of the important points you want to cover. When you reach your party, get quickly to the heart of the subject, cover the points efficiently, and end your call as soon as you can without being discourteous.

Body Language by Phone

When you communicate by sightless telephone, remember that your voice must convey meanings that would be conveyed by a variety of visual clues in a face-to-face conversation. So make full use of the voice qualities covered in chapter 6: power, pitch, pace, intonation, stress, and juncture.

Here's a suggestion: When you speak by telephone, act as if you were speaking face to face. Stand as if you were facing your caller across the room. Smile, just as you would in the presence of the other party. Practice the same body language you would practice in direct conversation. When you do this, your voice will automatically convey the nonverbal nuances.

Your voice conveys more power when you speak from a standing position. It is more natural and less strained when you're not using your neck and shoulder to cradle a telephone. The telephone picks up on smiles and scowls and conveys them through subtle nonverbal clues.

Start your conversation with a rising inflection. This injects a note of warmth and cheerfulness at the outset of the call.

Identify yourself promptly. This applies whether you're the originator or the recipient of the call. If you're calling someone you know, don't assume that your voice will be recognized. Your voice may sound different over the telephone than it does in person.

Identify Yourself Fully

Identify yourself fully, pronouncing your name slowly and distinctly. Don't say, "Hi, George, this is Julie." While you're going into your message, George's mind will be racing as he tries to recall all the Julies he has known and trying to decide which one you are.

Assuming that you and George are on first-name terms, say, "Hi, George, this is Julie Gladstone at Cosmic Enterprises." If George doesn't recall you immediately, at least he'll know what company you represent.

Speak directly into the mouthpiece, using the natural volume you'd use for a person sitting across the desk from you. This gives you the latitude to vary your volume to suit the message you're trying to convey.

Use the other person's name frequently. This provides a personal touch that compensates for the lack of eye contact.

Know What You Want to Accomplish

As you talk, keep in mind the reason you're on the telephone:

- You want the person on the other end to hear you and understand exactly what you mean.

- You want your conversational partner to agree with you, or at least give you a sympathetic ear.
- You want to accomplish something. You want the other person to understand what you want done, why it should be done, and when it should be done. And you want your listener to act on what you're saying.
- You want to understand the person at the other end of the line.

Think about these objectives each time you speak by telephone. It will help you in planning your calls and in making them both effective and efficient.

Closing the Conversation

If you're the recipient of the call, use questions to determine quickly the purpose of the call and what the caller expects from you. When the call has accomplished its purpose, bring it to a close quickly and courteously. Summarize what you've discussed and the conclusions you've reached. Review the things each party has agreed to do. End with a friendly comment such as "It's been nice talking with you." And let the other person hang up first.

Don't Let It Bug You

When you're off the phone, be sure you've actually hung up. Laying an open receiver on your desk is like bugging your whole office. And don't assume, while talking on the telephone, that a hand over the mouthpiece will keep your voice from carrying to the other end of the line. Always assume that the other person can hear everything you say.

Technology also means that secrets can pass through electronic cracks. Most executives have little reason to fear electronic eavesdropping, but reasonable precautions should be taken to keep sensitive communications away from prying eyes and ears. Make sure that your incoming and outgoing fax messages are not exposed to unauthorized eyes. Remember that cellular telephones rely on radio transmissions, which can be intercepted by anyone who has a radio tuned to the proper frequency. And hackers consider it a challenge to penetrate corporate computer networks and feast on confidential data. The modern executive need not be paranoid, but it's always wise to have somebody on staff who keeps abreast of the latest technology and can advise you on the best ways to use it effectively while avoiding its pitfalls.

The revolution in telecommunications is so fast and comprehensive that it takes your breath away. But remember: The technological advances are simply means of conveying your voice and image across distances. Learn and practice the verbal and nonverbal skills that serve you well in person-to-person interaction. They'll provide the basis for the skills you'll need in tomorrow's high-tech world.

Not all twenty-first-century communication will require space-age technology to convey messages across oceans and continents.

Much of the work in the business world is still done by people sitting in the same room, often around the same table, sharing information and ideas. The ability to conduct effective meetings is a powerful leadership trait—one we'll explore in the next chapter.

13

GETTING THE MOST FROM MEETINGS

In the twenty-first-century workplace, emphasis is on teamwork instead of individual efforts. That means that decisions must be made and problems must be solved by group action. So the effective leader must be skilled at conducting meetings.

Meetings can be caldrons of creativity and fountains of energy, or they can be exercises in wheel spinning and utter wastes of time. It all depends on how you conduct them.

IS THIS MEETING NECESSARY?

The first step in planning meetings consists of a series of questions. The most important one: "Is this meeting really necessary?"

Often a leader can achieve consensus and teamwork simply by taking a cup of coffee and walking from workstation to workstation. If you can get the job done that way, why interrupt everyone's routine by calling a formal meeting?

Sometimes meetings are scheduled at regular intervals, and everybody gets together regardless of whether there's anything to talk about. These meetings usually produce little besides yawns.

What's the Purpose?

Assuming that the meeting is necessary, the next question to ask is, "What's the basic purpose?" The basic purposes of most meetings fall into one of these categories:

- Gathering information

- Providing information
- Fostering motivation
- Exchanging ideas and solving problems

Other Questions

Here are some other questions to ask about your meeting:

- What is its goal? What do you want to accomplish through this meeting?
- Who should attend? Who are the people who would benefit from the meeting? Who would contribute the most to it?
- Who should conduct it? Who would be most likely to guide the group toward its goal? The highest-ranking person in the group isn't necessarily the best choice for group leader. Often, executives should take a back seat when serving on cross-functional teams and defer to a team leader who has more knowledge and expertise in the subject being explored.
- What procedures and rules will be followed? You may want to stick strictly to parliamentary procedure, with the group voting up or down on each proposal. But it's usually easier to obtain a team's commitment when the decision is reached by consensus.
- Where should it be held? The meeting site should be as free of distractions as possible. It should be comfortable, but not too comfortable. And it should have all the resources you need to make your presentation and obtain your decision.
- What information should be sent to participants in advance? Don't wait until you convene the meeting to distribute reading materials. The meeting should be taken up with discussion, not reading. If the participants need certain information to accomplish the purpose of the meeting, distribute that information well in advance of the meeting date. This will make it possible for all participants to be familiar with the material and to discuss it intelligently.
- What audiovisuals do you need for the meeting and who should prepare and present them? Audiovisual presentations should be well planned. Make sure the materials are in the proper order and that the person who presents them is familiar with them.
- When should the meeting begin and end? Set definite times for starting and concluding the meeting and stick to them. Late starts are an-

noying. Meetings that drag on past the allotted time interrupt schedules and result in fidgeting and inattention. Meetings that end abruptly while decisions are still up in the air are frustrating and unsatisfying. Set an agenda. Include only those items that need to be discussed at this meeting. Start on time and end on time.

CHOOSING A LEADER

The choice of a leader is important. A leader must be strong enough to keep the meeting on track and to make sure that everyone has an opportunity to participate. When the purpose is to provide information, the leader should take firm control of every facet of the meeting. In such a meeting, the role of the participants is not to provide input but to absorb output. Their function becomes a passive one.

When the purpose is to gather information, solve problems, or take advantage of opportunities, you want active participation from the group. In such cases, the leader must be someone who is able to guide a discussion, elicit comments, and synthesize the ideas that are advanced. The leader doesn't dominate this type of meeting, but becomes a facilitator.

SEATING ARRANGEMENTS

The purpose of the meeting will determine the best seating arrangement. If you're aiming for an interchange of thought, with everyone encouraged to join in, arrange seats in a circle. If you plan to make use of a panel, arrange the seats in a horseshoe or a T. This focuses attention on those at the head. If the leader is to do all the talking, arrange the seats in rows, as in a theater.

A podium, by elevating you above your audience, will give you greater prominence as a leader, but it will also make you less approachable. A leader who sits around the table with participants or stands at their level is more likely to achieve effective interaction.

If you want to make a formal presentation from a raised platform and later initiate an interchange with participants, step in front of the lectern or, better yet, step down from the platform. Assume an informal pose, and invite discussion.

GROUP BRAINSTORMING

Brainstorming is an effective method for group decision making. When you embark on brainstorming, these guidelines will help you.

- *Keep the group small.* The larger the group, the harder it is to obtain consensus. A group of seven to twelve people usually is the optimum size for decision making. Such a group is large enough to generate a good supply of ideas yet small enough for everyone to provide significant input.
- *Come prepared.* If you're the leader, you should know what you want to accomplish and should have in mind or at your fingertips the things you need to accomplish it. The participants will look to you for the basic information and will base their decisions on the facts as you present them.
- *Make the purpose clear.* Participants should understand why they're there and what they're expected to accomplish.
- *Create a relaxed atmosphere.* People interact better when the mood is informal, the setting is comfortable, and they feel that they can relax.
- *Don't prescribe; listen.* If you already know the answers, what's the use of calling the meeting? Encourage the group to contribute ideas freely.
- *Encourage discussion.* Make it clear that there is no "wrong way" or "right way" and that good decisions result from a thorough examination of all alternatives.
- *Discourage ridicule.* Make it clear that criticism is welcome but ridicule is off limits. People should feel free to offer novel ideas without fear of looking foolish. No idea is too exotic for consideration and none is above criticism. In fact, unconventional ideas should be encouraged.
- *Prepare for follow-up.* When decisions are reached, make sure that the tasks involved in implementing them are assigned and that the individuals understand and accept their assignments.

Static and Dynamic Judgments

When we hear a new idea advanced, we have a natural tendency to ask, "Will it work? Is it practical?" When we try to answer these questions, we are making *static* judgments.

Static judgments should be suspended during group brainstorming. The proper question is, "How might we make this idea work?" Answering that question requires *dynamic* judgments. It stimulates creative thinking. Each dynamic judgment is itself a creative idea, so that one idea triggers several others.

As these ideas are examined, modified, and combined, the group progresses toward a consensus. When it reaches that consensus, it will have produced a creative solution, with the feasibility and practicality thoroughly examined.

Bringing Problems into the Open

Meetings can sometimes be useful in bringing problems into the open. Situations may be simmering just beneath the surface. The leader knows something is wrong but can't quite pinpoint the cause. That's when it's time to sit around the table with staff members and say, "I'd like to hear what's on your minds. What isn't going the way it should be going, and what can I do about it?"

If the response is timid, try going to a flip chart. Pick up a pencil and ask, "Who'd like to start it off?" The blank page will be like a vacuum demanding to be filled. While you're at the flip chart, keep your back to the staff. They'll feel less intimidated when they don't have to look you in the eye.

Let your staffers talk. Answer any direct questions as well as you can, but remember that your main function is to take notes so that you can review the feedback. At the end of the session, summarize what you've heard, make any necessary corrections and clarifications, and promise to respond to the feedback. Then be sure to keep your promise.

SITUATIONS THAT CALL
FOR INTERVENTION

No meeting proceeds smoothly without course corrections. The leader who isn't prepared to intervene may have to stand helplessly by while the meeting gets out of hand.

Here are a few situations to watch for and suggestions for dealing with them.

- *Group fragmentation.* The group may break down into a number of private conversations.

This often happens when controversial issues or actions arise and participants begin discussing them among themselves. When this happens, ask the person who has the floor to stop until order has been restored. Call the group to order and ask those who are involved in the individual conversations to share their thoughts in an orderly fashion with the entire group. If the problem persists, call the talkers by name and ask them to join the group. If this doesn't stop the talking, calmly suggest that those involved might want to carry on their discussions in some other place so that the rest of you can get on with the meeting at hand.

- *Aggressive takeovers.* Sometimes aggressive, extroverted people will try to take over the meeting.

You can exert some control by seating such people next to you and admonishing them through whispers. Another technique is to give the aggressive, outspoken person a formal role in the meeting that will satisfy the need to be heard. If the takeover attempt still seems to be getting out of hand, impose a rigid rule governing the time when each person can speak.

- *Too many clams.* Some people are timid about speaking up in a group.

You can draw such people into the discussion by asking them specific questions. Then pose follow-up questions to persuade them to elaborate. Assure them that their opinions are valid and welcome.

- *Uninvited guests.* People may show up who were uninvited and unanticipated.

If it's an open meeting, or if the guests are welcome, acknowledge their presence and invite them to join the discussion. Otherwise, politely (and privately, if possible) ask them to leave.

- *Late arrivals.*

Always arrange the room so that the door is to the rear, and leave extra seats near the door. Then let the latecomers straggle in. You don't have to interrupt the meeting to acknowledge their presence.

- *Distractions.* Sometimes the setting and room arrangement make it difficult for people to pay attention.

Distractions can be minimized through advance planning. Arrange in advance for a room that has a comfortable temperature. Err on the cool side. The human body is a space heater, and a room full of people will warm up quickly. Try to avoid rooms with outside views—especially if the outside view is a swimming pool, a beach, or some other eye-catching attraction. Make sure the lighting is adequate: Too much is better than too little. Select chairs that are comfortable enough to keep people from squirming but not comfortable enough to lull them to sleep. Make sure that everyone can see and hear you and anyone else in the room.

AFTER THE MEETING

A meeting is productive only if the decisions reached result in concrete and positive actions that lead to the desired goal. The most common failure of meetings is that, when they are over, nothing happens.

You can avoid wasted time and missed opportunities resulting from meetings that get nothing done if you follow these suggestions:

- Make sure all participants understand their assignments.
- Distribute the minutes as soon after the meeting as possible.
- Help all participants with their individual assignments.
- Check to see that all deadlines are met.
- Plan follow-up meetings when they are needed.

Some executives complain that they spend most of their time attending meetings and shuffling papers. It's true that communication of one type or another tends to monopolize the business day, but then communication is the essence of business. The answer to the challenge is not to stop communicating but to manage communication.

PART THREE

FOCUSING YOUR COMMUNICATIONS

14

FOCUSING ON THE RIGHT AUDIENCE

You can't communicate with everyone in the world, even if you think you have a message everyone ought to hear. Skilled communicators learn to direct their messages toward the audiences they can realistically expect to reach.

Let's make it clear what we mean by an audience. We're not necessarily talking about a group of people sitting in an auditorium listening to you give a speech from a platform. That's just one kind of message and one kind of audience.

For our purposes, your message may take the form of spoken words, written words, or graphic representations. It may be delivered in person, on paper, on tape or computer disk, via audiovisual equipment, or through electronic transmission.

AIM FOR YOUR AUDIENCE

Your audience is *anyone you want to reach with a message*, whether customers, employees, government, or the community at large. Identify your audience and aim for it.

For instance:

- If you have products and services to sell, you're spinning your wheels if you're directing your sales message to people who have no interest in or need for what you're selling, or who lack the means to buy it.
- If your business serves a specific metropolitan area, you're wasting your money and time trying to reach a statewide, regional, or national audience.

153

- If your clientele is drawn from a specific professional category, a professional journal or trade publication may be a more effective medium than a general circulation publication with much wider distribution.
- If the communication vehicle you're using doesn't reach the audience you're aiming for, the most compelling of messages will have no effect. The classic example is the billboard that read: "If you can't read, call 1–800-GET HELP." You can't reach illiterate people through written messages. You can't communicate with the blind through videotapes. And you can't communicate with the deaf through audiocassettes.

Aim your communications toward the people who are most likely to be influenced by them.

There are numerous advantages to choosing your audience. Here are some of them.

- *You can concentrate all your energies and resources on one focal point.* When I was a little boy, my brother gave me a small magnifying glass. I knew what its main purpose was. When I held it at a certain distance from an object, the object looked bigger and I could see it much more clearly. But I soon learned that the magnifying glass had an unsuspected power. It could focus the sun's rays on a tiny spot and, if I held it there long enough, it would burn a hole in the substance on which I focused it.

  Communication works on the same principle. Focus your message on the specific audience you want, and you can concentrate and intensify your power. You will be able to gain a clearer, more thorough understanding of the people you want to reach, give them more of yourself, and bring to bear the full power of all you have and all that you are.
- *You can provide purpose and direction to your communications efforts.* At the dawn of the twenty-first century, the mass audience is shattering into a myriad of small audiences. There was a time when all America was united during prime time in its attention to three major television networks. We all watched such classics as "Gunsmoke," "All in the Family," and "The Mary Tyler Moore Show."

  The days are gone when three networks catered to a large, undiversified audience. Instead, we have a smorgasbord of offerings from cable and satellite television—network programming, locally produced and syndicated programs, full-length movies, round-the-clock news, round-the-clock weather, round-the-clock current affairs, and a variety of other types of programs. If we can't find what we want among those offerings, we can always go down to the video store and rent a videotape on just about any subject under the sun.

The same is true of the print media. The nation no longer reads *Time*, *Life*, and *Saturday Evening Post* in unison. Instead, we go to the newsstands in search of the specialty publications targeted toward our particular interests. The armchair traveler can read *National Geographic*. The outdoor person can read *Field & Stream*. Golf enthusiasts can read *Golf Digest*. Epicures can read *Food & Wine*. Dieters can read *Weight Watchers*. There are specialty publications for stamp collectors, coin collectors, boaters, skiers, hang gliders, chess players, bridge players, and Bingo players. There are trade and professional publications for every profession imaginable.

This diversity makes the scattergun approach expensive and ineffective. But it makes it easier for you to pick your target. You can now determine what groups are most likely to respond to your message and choose the media that will reach them.

Direct-mail advertisers have developed this into a science. They know which mailing lists will yield the most prospects for time-share condos, which will yield the most buyers of supplemental health insurance, and which will have the customers lining up for the latest in audio and video equipment.

If you concentrate your efforts on smaller groups with high percentages of prospects, you'll achieve more success at less cost than by appealing to large groups with a low percentage of prospects.

• *You'll become known by those you would reach.* Successful real-estate agents have developed a sales strategy that can provide a model for other types of communication. They have learned the value of "listing farms." These are neighborhoods or subdivisions that agents adopt as their personal prospecting grounds. The agent tries to become known to the people in that area so that when home owners are ready to sell their property the agent's name will be the first to pop into their minds. Telephone prospecting, canvassing, and targeted newsletters all come in the inventory of tools for the listing farmer.

The most successful agents know that a small farm worked intensively will yield better results than a large farm worked less intensively. Why? It's easier to get to know and to be known by the people in the smaller area.

The underlying strategy applies to all types of communication efforts. Get to know the people you're trying to reach. Become acquainted with their likes and dislikes. And make sure that they are acquainted with you and the ideas you stand for, so that when people make decisions on matters of interest to you, your position will be prominent in their minds and will be clearly associated with your name or the name of your business.

- *You can save your most valuable asset: time.* When you choose the specific audiences you want to reach and concentrate on just those audiences, you control your time rather than allowing your time to control you.

  Again, salespeople provide an example of the futility of trying to reach everyone with a message. Many of them work long hours at a feverish pace and never seem to encounter success. They buttonhole everyone they encounter and go into their sales pitches. If you're standing in line with them at the supermarket, they try to sell to you. If they run into you at the neighborhood tavern, they try to sell to you. If you're sitting beside them on an airplane, they turn on the sales pitch.

  Why don't they succeed?

  They're not identifying their best prospects and concentrating on them. They're not targeting their audiences. Truly accomplished salespeople identify the prospects who have a logical reason for buying and the resources and authority to make the decision to buy. They spend their time with the people who can give them the response they desire and who are most likely to do so.

  The same technique can be followed in nonsales situations. If you're an executive looking for people to put on your management team, do you spend your time mentoring everyone on your staff? Or do you spot the people with real management potential and work closely with them?

  Target your audience, focus your communication, and save yourself time.

- *You can practice what you do enough to become really good at it.* When producers want to work the kinks out of a stage production before exposing it to the scrutiny of Broadway critics, they take it on the road. There, before a variety of crowds in different cities, they can learn what the audiences appreciate. By the time they reach Broadway, they may have dropped certain musical numbers, modified some dialogue, and rewritten whole scenes. The performers have learned what facial expressions, body language, and voice intonations draw the proper response. They have perfected their timing so that they automatically make the right moves at the right time.

As a professional speaker, I have learned what types of stories draw good response from certain audiences, what kinds of exercises draw them into my presentations, and how to cope with the most common interferences I encounter. Thus, I am able to eliminate those stories and exercises that I know won't work and practice those that will work until I can do them automatically. This frees me to concentrate entirely on the people in my audience and the way they are responding to what I'm doing.

This principle holds true with other types of audiences. Just as you become familiar with the house or apartment you live in day after day, so you become acquainted with the people you spend your time with day after day—but only if you concentrate on a limited number of audiences.

• *You can multiply your effectiveness by expanding to similar audiences.* Find a category of customers or clients you click with and stay with it. Look for similar audiences that will respond to similar approaches. This allows you to become better and better at the things that yield success with the people you're trying to reach.

I count on invitations for return engagements and additional projects for clients as the backbone of my professional speaking career. If I had to spend a percentage of my time cultivating new clients and developing new approaches for reaching audiences I know nothing about, I would be wasting my most creative energies.

In other types of business, it's more cost-effective to cultivate repeat business with customers whose needs you're familiar with than to be constantly scouting for new business among customers whose needs you don't know as well.

That doesn't mean that you should develop one line of products and stick with it without change. That's a recipe for sure failure in the twenty-first century. Your customers' needs will be constantly changing. To serve them successfully, you'll have to change with them. But it's much easier to adjust to the needs of customers you know and are already serving than to learn about the changing needs of new customers. It's like trying to follow a moving train. If you're already aboard, a sweeping curve represents only a gentle change of direction, and you feel no great jolt or stress. But if you're running alongside the train at a different pace, trying to grab hold and pull yourself aboard, the curve could jerk you under the wheels and into disaster.

• *You can invest your life where you have the highest interest level.* Most people do best at the things they enjoy doing most. I love speaking to an audience. When I speak to a receptive audience about a subject dear to my heart, I am happiest and at the peak of my effectiveness. To me, public speaking is not work. It's enjoyment; it's play.

Play has often been defined as doing something you enjoy doing. According to this definition, you can play your way through life, and still be very successful, if you carefully target your audiences.

Your audience may be quite different in nature from mine. I'm a speaker and a consultant. Someone else may be a writer, a musician, or an actor. We tend to associate audiences with the performing professions, but everyone plays to an audience. If you're a plumber, your audience is the customer who monitors your work and pays your bill. If you're a member of a workplace team, your audience may be your co-workers. If you're a supervisor, your audience may be the people you supervise. If you're on the management team, your audience may be your colleagues or your staff. If you're a salesperson, your audience is your prospects. If you're in the direct-mail business, your audience may be the people on a mailing list.

CULTIVATE THE RIGHT AUDIENCE

Communication is the life force of every vocation, and your enjoyment of that vocation depends upon the satisfaction you get from the communicating. If you're getting no satisfaction or fulfillment from your efforts, then you may be communicating with the wrong audience. Your interest just isn't there. Find an audience that turns you on, and cultivate it.

How do you do that?

Here are five questions that will help you.

1. *What do you want to do?* One of the most common reasons for the failure of communication efforts is that the people who initiate them don't know what they want to accomplish. They may have a general idea of what they want, but their goals are so vague that no one can understand them. Therefore, they have no logical audience.

   Be specific. What do you want to accomplish? One way to focus your thoughts on that question is to write one concise sentence describing precisely what you want to do. This will lead you to the next question.

2. *Who can help you get it done?* The best audience for your communication is the one that can give you the most help in doing what you want to do. If you've just bought a stereo that delivers sound from only one speaker, you won't get it fixed by telling your tale of woe to the entire neighborhood. You'll achieve it by describing your problem to the person who sold you the stereo.

   If you want to start a new department of innovation in your company, you don't take your idea to the people in the company cafeteria. You take it to the executive who has the authority to make the decision, or to someone who is in position to influence the people in authority.

   If you want to get maximum performance from your sales team, teach the members to target their audiences. Some of the hardest-working salespeople I've met in my seminars were dismal failures because they hadn't learned to target their audiences. They were articulate, personable, and knowledgeable about the products they sold. But they didn't pick their prospects well. They wasted most of their time talking to people who could not buy what they had to sell. When they learned how to determine who could best make the decisions they wanted them to make, they were able to sell more in less time, with less effort, and often at a higher profit.

   Don't look for the person who will listen sympathetically. Look for the person who can give you the results you want.

3. *Who would want to help you do it?* People do things for *their* reasons, not yours. If you want people to help you accomplish what you want to accomplish, look for the people who have the strongest reasons for helping you.

   The salesperson who sold you the defective stereo has a stronger reason for helping you than does the manager of the store's garden department. Why? Because the stereo salesperson stands to lose if you return the item for a refund, and if you take your business elsewhere.

A direct-mail corporation put zip into its sales performance by targeting the audience that had reason for wanting its product.

I looked over the company's very specialized product line and suggested that it rent a mailing list of people who had bought similar products from other companies.

At first management demurred. The specialized lists cost more than the lists they were renting.

Yes, I pointed out, but the specialized lists contained the names of the people who would help them: the people who would like to buy their products.

Management took my advice and was delighted at the results. The more expensive lists produced a higher percentage of people who wanted to buy the products. Sales improved dramatically.

The advice delivered two millennia ago from the hillside in Galilee remains valid: Don't cast your pearls before swine. In other words, don't waste your breath telling your story to people who feel no need to hear it. Go to the people who are likely to give you the response you desire.

4. *Why would an audience listen to you?* Remember that this is the age of communication. We are bombarded with messages everywhere we go. So why should anyone listen to your message in particular?

Answer that question as candidly and objectively as you can. Don't be overly modest and don't be egotistical about it. What qualifications do you have to ask people to do what you want them to do?

The answer may lie in your position of authority, the influence you exert over your audience, or the specialized knowledge that you have and they need. It may lie in your superb eloquence—your strong persuasive powers. Or it may lie in fortuitous circumstances.

5. *How accessible is this audience?* If you want to run a full-page ad in the *Wall Street Journal*, it's going to cost you plenty. The *Journal*'s huge, widely dispersed readership is accessible only to those who have the resources to market nationally. You can reach *Journal* readers with your message if you're willing to fork over the cash or if you can persuade the editors that your message is worth printing in the news or opinion columns. But if you run a neighborhood gro-

cery, the readers are inaccessible to you, for all practical purposes, because even though you can reach them with your message, they can't respond by buying your products.

Even the readership of the daily newspaper serving your city may be inaccessible to you if you draw your clientele from only a small corner of the metropolitan area. But many metropolitan papers carve their circulation areas into smaller segments and publish zoned editions. These zoned editions offer attractive advertising rates to merchants who need only to reach readers within their areas of coverage.

There are other ways of reaching targeted audiences. Do you know of other people who have contact with the audience you want to reach? If so, do they have reason to help you contact that audience? Book or magazine publishers may be selling printed materials regularly to an audience you want to reach. They may find it worthwhile to publish something you've written to appeal to their audience. Radio and television talk show hosts are always looking for guests who have something interesting to say to their audiences.

People with common interests often form associations, and these organizations can serve as vehicles for reaching their members. Such organizations frequently publish newsletters, newspapers, and magazines that accept articles from outsiders. Don't overlook the possibility of speaking to these groups at chapter meetings or conventions.

Analyze a potential audience and determine how accessible it is. If it can be reached without overtaxing your resources and if it appears likely to respond to your message, go for it.

EVALUATE YOUR AUDIENCES

Once you have narrowed your choice of audiences through these five questions, your next step is to evaluate them to see which you want to reach.

Here are some criteria for evaluating them.

• *The targeted audience should have the power to do what you want it to do.* The executive vice president for operations may have the *authority* to authorize the purchase of a fleet of trucks, but she may lack the *power* because the board of directors failed to budget enough money for the purchase.

Your boss may have the *authority* to grant you a raise, but someone higher in the organization may have the *power* to overrule the decision. If you're unhappy with your 5 percent raise, to whom do you appeal? Your boss, who may have recommended 10 percent, or your boss's superior, who might have cut the recommendation in half?

- *The audience should know that it needs to hear what you have to say.* If the audience is not aware of its need to listen, it probably won't listen. You can take the time and make the effort to educate it about its need to listen, but that will take an extra investment of time and energy. Could that investment be made more productively elsewhere?

- *The audience should want to hear what you have to say.* An audience must be able to see the benefit in the message you're sending, and must be ready to hear it. Had I gone to Erfurt, Germany, in 1983 to speak on the subject of entrepreneurship, I probably would have spoken to an empty house and very likely would have received an official government invitation to leave the country.

But when I went there in 1993, on the third anniversary of German reunification, some five hundred business owners drove through bad weather for up to six hours and paid hard-earned Deutchsmarks to hear me speak. Why?

Erfurt was a part of communist East Germany in 1983, and communism suppressed private enterprise. Learning how to succeed in a market economy was useless information to people who did not live in a market economy. By 1993 Erfurt was part of a unified Germany, and businesspeople who had grown up grappling with the communist system now needed to learn the ropes of capitalism. They were hungry for what I had to say.

I found similar enthusiasm in Luxembourg, the small principality that serves as the capital of the European Community. With opportunities beckoning in this populous common market, more than eight hundred European business leaders showed up at the EC's Parliament House, where my speech was translated into six languages.

Impressive things happen when the right message reaches an audience that wants to hear it. When the audience isn't ready to listen, you can save your breath.

When John Kennedy took office as president, he challenged his fellow citizens with these words:

> Ask not what your country can do for you; ask what you can do for your country.

The people were ready to listen; it was something they wanted to hear.

When Jimmy Carter spoke of a national "malaise" and called for individual sacrifices, the people were not ready to listen; it wasn't something they wanted to hear.

It takes extraordinary eloquence to overcome an audience's unwillingness to listen. Even the great Winston Churchill had to sit out of power for six years following World War II because the people he had led to victory didn't want to hear his message that the Tory Party was best fitted to lead the postwar reconstruction.

- *The audience should fit into your life's goals.* If you know who you are and where you're going, an occasional detour to reach out to an audience might help fulfill some of your goals. However, one detour can lead to another until you find that you're investing your best resources in audiences that are not leading you toward your goals.

  Using these criteria, you should be able to determine which audience has the best potential for giving the response you desire for the least amount of time and resources invested.

One More Question

Now there's one other question to ask: *Are you the best person to present this message to this audience?*

In some cases, it might be more productive for you to get someone else to say what you want said. I have turned down many speaking engagements because I knew there were others who could deliver a particular message to a given audience much more productively than I could. Remember, as a communicator, your goal is not to stroke your own ego, but to get the response you desire. If others can do that better for you, look for a way to get them to do it.

Focusing on the right audience is just the first step. To achieve the desired results, the right message has to reach the right audience. So it's necessary to focus your message for the audience you have in mind. The next chapter will show how it's done.

15

FOCUSING YOUR MESSAGE

You know what audience you want to reach and what response you want. Now your task is to focus your message.

Focusing your message means finding the precise message to persuade your audience to do what you want it to do, then presenting the message in the most appealing way.

WATCH THE MAIN TITLES

The best examples of such targeting at work are the "main titles" television shows use to lock in their audiences. These are the fifteen- to twenty-second grabbers at the beginning of each show. They're designed to make you pause in the midst of your channel hopping to watch the opening scenes from the program, or to prevent you from flipping to another channel to sample its wares. The networks reason that if they can get you to watch for just a few seconds, they stand a better chance of hooking you for the duration of the show.

Networks will pay well into six figures for a good "main title," because they know that the millions spent on producing the show will go down the tube if the viewers don't stick around to watch. The bigger the audience, the more commercials they can sell and the more they can charge for them.

What the networks look for in main titles, you should be looking for in the way you launch your messages. Here's what a main title is supposed to do:

- Gain attention immediately and hold it.
- Introduce the subject to be covered.

- Set the tone, pace, and mood for the show.
- Introduce the characters and convince the audience that they are good people to spend time with—people you can identify with.
- Dispel any fears the audience has about watching the show.

Take a couple of evenings to relax with your remote control and watch the main titles carefully. Note the techniques and think about ways you can adapt them to your communications, whether you're giving a speech, trying a case in court, writing a memo to your staff, or proposing marriage to your true love.

FIVE BASIC STEPS IN FOCUSING YOUR MESSAGE

You can follow five basic steps in focusing your message for maximum effect: (1) Target your subject; (2) collect all the materials you need; (3) select the materials you will use; (4) let your message ripen in your mind; (5) organize your message.

Target Your Subject

Decide what you want your audience to do in response to your communication. If you're making a speech, do you want to have your audience laughing, crying, patting each other on the back, or charging into the field bent on setting new sales records? You might want them to do several of those things, but one objective should predominate. Otherwise, your audience will be confused.

Remember that the subjects of communication are related to needs and wants and the satisfaction of needs and wants. If you don't need or want anything, there's no reason to communicate. Sometimes, communication itself is the principal need. If you've been isolated from human companionship for a long time, you have a strong and urgent need to communicate. In the workplace, communication usually centers on the things needed to accomplish the job and produce a product or service at a profit.

If you build your message on the needs of your audience, you are choosing the strongest possible subject. If you can address people's needs in a way that lets them know that you'll satisfy them, you immediately get their attention. Identify people's needs and wants, then convince them that the actions you propose will satisfy them, and you'll get the response you desire.

STICK TO SUBJECTS YOU KNOW

You may have heard the story about the deacon who attended a meeting called to decide whether the church should spend the money to buy a new chandelier. The deacon listened to the arguments, then rose to have his say.

"Brethren," he began, "I'm firmly opposed to this church spending its money on a chandelier, for three solid reasons: First, nobody in the church knows how to spell it; second, nobody here can play it; and third, what this church needs is more light."

On another occasion, a man who professed to be an authority on every subject walked into a barber shop and saw a scruffy owl perched on top of a cabinet. The man proceeded to belittle the taxidermist for doing such a poor job of stuffing the bird. He held forth on the finer points of ornithology, noting how the owl's wings hung at the wrong angle, its head was askew, and the color of the feathers indicated that the taxidermist had touched up his work with some cheap hair coloring.

When the man had finished talking, all eyes were on the owl. The bird blinked a couple of times, stretched its wings, then flew to the opposite side of the room.

Both stories illustrate the truth of the adage: It's better to keep your mouth shut and let people think you're ignorant than to open it and remove all doubt.

If you're a speaker or facilitator, your audience rating goes up in direct proportion to your knowledge of the subject. I'm often invited to speak to audiences on subjects about which I know little or nothing. Unless I can easily learn enough about the subject to speak intelligently on it, I suggest another topic, recommend another speaker, or decline the invitation. I respect both my audience and my career too much to run all over the world showing my ignorance.

Usually, the subjects you know the most about are the ones that reflect your deepest interests. You'll always be more impressive and more effective when you're communicating about subjects in which you have a vital interest.

In the workplace, too, it's important that you know what you're talking about. Good leaders know where their expertise begins and ends. They don't mind sharing their expertise with the people they lead, but they're not too proud to admit when they don't know the answers. Leadership in the twenty-first century doesn't consist of knowing all the answers. It consists, rather, of knowing where to go or whom to go to for the answers.

SPEAK TO SUBJECTS THAT ARE MANAGEABLE

Don't take on a subject that you can't deal with adequately in a reasonable amount of time. This often requires nothing more than determining what people want to know or what they need to know, and confining your message to those points. Or it may require that you break your subject down into manageable subtopics and deal with them one at a time.

Don't be like the mother of six-year-old Robyn, when asked, "Mom, where did I come from?"

Mom proceeded to explain to Robyn all the details of human biology: how the mother's body produces an egg, which descends from the ovary down the Fallopian tube to the uterus, where it meets sperm cells from the father, which have swum up through the vagina until they reach the egg, penetrate it, and fertilize it; how the genetic code works to construct an entirely new human out of the seeds of the two parents; how the cells divide to form an embryo, which develops within the placenta; and how at full term a fully developed baby appears.

By the time Mom was finished, Robyn's eyes were glazed.

"Does that explain it to you?" asked Mom.

"I guess so," yawned Robyn. "But my friend Todd says he came from Florida."

Mom could have skipped the details and answered Robyn's question in one word. Instead, she tried to compress a biology textbook into one lesson.

We often do that in our communications. We try to tell everything in one session. In the process we confuse our listeners and lose their attention.

Don't try to tell it all in one sitting. If your subject is a broad one, break it down into manageable segments and focus on one segment at a time.

For Robyn, it was enough for the time being to know that she came from Virginia. She could be told later how her mother carried her for approximately nine months within her body. A later conversation could deal with conception. We learn in small increments. So it's best to communicate in small, focused increments.

Collect all the Materials You Need

The more you know about a subject, the more forcefully you can present your message. So your first step is research.

On some subjects you may already be up to speed. Your research will only fill in the nooks and crannies and refresh your memory.

On other subjects, you'll need to do extensive research. Cast a broad net. You'll want to focus your information later, but initially your task is to gather all the facts that you can. Assume nothing. Be sure of your facts. This is especially true if you're critiquing someone.

As you gather information, keep in mind the main thrust of your communication. Assemble everything you need to make a strong case. Collect quotes, specific examples, research data, and anything else that will support your position or help you clarify it. Gather more information than you plan to use, so you can select the strongest pieces.

Then study the material. You won't be able to deliver your message effectively until you get it off the page or out of your word processor and into your mind.

Select the Materials You will Use

The most effective materials are those most likely to get the response you want. If your objective is to persuade a prospect to become a customer, look for the thing you offer that will provide the most powerful motive to do business with you instead of with someone else. This is what advertising copywriters call the "unique selling proposition."

Whether you're trying to make a sale, inspire greater productivity, or persuade your true love to meet you at the altar, look for your unique selling proposition and concentrate on that.

In most forms of communication, you can count on making only one good point. I have found it helpful to boil down the most important point I want to make in a brief sentence that expresses it concisely. That's true whether I'm dictating a letter or memo, preparing a speech, writing a book, or structuring an action plan for a prospective client. Once I have a clear focus on what I want to say, I'm better able to convey the message to the audience.

Having selected your most compelling point, look for the materials and arguments that present it in the clearest light and support it most emphatically. If there's something that needs clarifying and explaining to your audience, find the simplest, most comprehensible way to do so. Select the information, materials, and arguments that add the most credibility to your main point. If you know your audience, you can select the supportive materials you feel it will find most convincing. Keep cutting away the fluff until only the essential points, ideas, arguments, and supporting data remain.

Let Your Message Ripen in Your Mind

Horace, the ancient Roman poet and satirist, uttered a truth that people of all ages have learned to their chagrin: "Once a word has been allowed to escape, it cannot be recalled."

That's why it's wise to sleep on important communications. Give them time to ripen in your mind. Give your intuitive mind a chance to examine them and respond to them. How will it sound to the audience you're trying to reach? Are you sure that's the best way you can say it? Are you sure the results it will bring are the results you want?

We've all had the experience of dropping a letter in the mail and almost immediately regretting that we mailed it. We've all said things in anger that we immediately wish we had left unsaid. We've all gotten into arguments and, hours and days later, thought of just the right words that might have made the point we were trying to make.

There are times when you have to respond on the spur of the moment. But why respond in haste when it isn't necessary? Sometimes, when I have a very important letter to write, I will dictate a draft. Then I will let it incubate for several days, using that time to question everything I have said. If it's really important, I will test my statements on some people whose judgments I value. Once I feel that I have really digested what I want to say, I dictate a final draft. This process has helped me avoid the consequences of poor communication in many situations.

Organize Your Message

Every communication springs from a process of organizing. You have to organize your ideas, then express them in sentences, which consist of words assembled in an organized fashion.

Casual conversation is only loosely organized. We speak spontaneously as ideas form in our minds, giving very little thought as to how
we will express ourselves.

This loose-jointed method of assembling and expressing ideas
works very well when we're making small talk. But when it comes to
expressing important ideas, much more preparation is necessary. That's
why the U.S. president's staff will spend weeks researching, writing, and
rewriting a State of the Union message. No president would go before
Congress and deliver a State of the Union message spontaneously, off
the cuff.

So when you have something important to say, whether it's giving
directions to your staff, a performance appraisal to an employee, or a report to the board of directors, it pays to organize.

Here are some tips for organizing your communications.

* *Organize around your most compelling points.* Recall the two stories I told earlier in this chapter, about the deacon at the church meeting and the owl in the barber shop.

  Did you chuckle when you read the deacon's words, " . . . what
  this church needs is more light"?

  By itself, there's nothing funny about the line. If I had begun my
  story with that statement, you wouldn't have chuckled. The organization made the difference. Every sentence in the story led up to the
  punch line.

  And in the story about the owl, what if I had revealed in the first
  sentence or two that the owl was alive and not stuffed? The effect
  would have been lost.

  The principle applies whether you're telling a joke or negotiating a merger. Your most compelling point has more impact when
  you set it up. That doesn't mean that it has to come at the end of your
  message, like the punch line of a joke. But your whole communication should be organized with a view toward presenting your compelling point in the most powerful way.

  Sometimes the most powerful way is to state boldly and clearly what you want at the outset of your message, then follow with
  statements that explain and support it. This grabs the audience's attention and makes it receptive to the supporting points that follow.
  This approach works best when you know the audience will be open
  to your ideas and will perhaps be enthusiastic about them.

If you expect audience resistance, the best approach might be to start on common ground. Begin by stating the ideas that you know your audience will agree with. Then gradually, logically, build toward your compelling point.

This technique can work, too, when you want to build suspense toward a dramatic climax—as when you're unveiling a revolutionary new product.

At times you might state your most compelling point repeatedly throughout the message, each time using supportive material to set it up.

The number of ways to organize your message is limited only by your imagination. But for maximum impact, you have to organize.

- *Use three major components.* Regardless of which type of organization you use, your message will consist of three fundamental parts: an introduction, a body, and a conclusion.

THE INTRODUCTION

The introduction should be an attention-getter. Newspaper and magazine writers are taught that the most important paragraph in any story is the first paragraph—the lead. The headline writer usually derives the headline from the lead. Readers may be drawn to the story by the headline and accompanying illustrations, but it's the lead that determines whether they'll read on or go to the next headline.

An introduction has to be more than an attention-rouser. It must lead the audience directly into the body of the message. If it doesn't do that, you're likely to find yourself in the position of the absent-minded pastor who visited another church and was impressed by the opening words of the pastor's sermon: "I spent the best years of my life in the arms of another man's wife." The congregation was immediately awake and ready for the next line: "She was my mother."

The absent-minded pastor decided to use it on his own congregation.

"You know, I spent the best years of my life in the arms of another man's wife," he began. The audience came to shocked attention. And the pastor forgot the next line. After several seconds that seemed like an eternity, he finally stammered, "I can't remember who she was."

I sometimes hear speakers open by saying "Sex! Now that I have your attention, I want to talk about. . . ."

That introduction may be effective if your subject is, indeed, sex. But if it's a report to stockholders on your third-quarter performance, you're still stuck with the task of introducing your *real* subject.

Somebody somewhere in the dim reaches of time began telling students in Public Speaking 101 that a speech should begin with a good joke. The first cave man to rally the clan to an elephant hunt probably started his speech with an elephant joke, and thus was born the cliché.

The twenty-first century is a good time to scrap that advice. A good joke at the start of a speech may get the attention of the audience and put it in a good mood, but it gives you a tough act to follow. Unless the joke has direct relevance to your most compelling point, its effect is lost as soon as the laughter dies. You now have to figure out how to direct the attention away from the jollity and toward your central message.

A good introduction must always alert an audience to the fact that what is about to be said is something it should hear. If it contains a humorous note, fine. But the humor should oil the skids that lead into the main body of the communication. If it doesn't, you'll slide smack into a wall of inattention.

THE MAIN BODY

The main body of communication presents the most compelling point in the clearest and most stimulating light. It must make your message *SING*. That means it must do four things:

1. *Scintillate.* That's a five-dollar word for sparkle, excite, and entertain.
2. *Inform or instruct.* The audience should go away with the feeling that it has gained new knowledge, new understanding, or new insight.
3. *Nudge toward action or agreement.* In other words, persuade or influence.
4. *Give inspiration.*

A strong communication doesn't perform these four functions one at a time. Each function is interwoven throughout the body of the talk.

If you try to progress from scintillating to informing to persuading to inspiring, you'll leave your audience behind. They'll listen so long as you're being entertaining, but when you switch from a humorous to a serious vein, they'll tune you out.

If you're going to use humor (and it's an effective form of entertainment), sprinkle it throughout your communication. An effective technique is to make a point, then wrap it up with a humorous illustration. The illustration adds to the impact of the point and makes it memorable.

The three-point body is the simplest form of organization. Decide how you want to present your most compelling point and use the two other points to set it up or explain it. In one type of organization, point 1 might be your most compelling point. Point 2 could explain it, and point 3 would persuade the audience to take action on it.

Suppose you've had a good quarter and you're announcing the results to your employees. You might organize your communication this way:

1. *Performance-related bonuses are 20 percent higher this month.* (Your most compelling point).
2. *This is because of the success of our continuous quality-improvement process, which resulted in a reduction in defects from twenty-five per thousand units to nine per thousand. This meant lower production costs and a healthy rise in net earnings.* (Supporting point).
3. *If the employees can bring defects down to the level of four per one thousand, they can look forward to even larger bonuses next quarter.* (Persuading to act).

Suppose you're introducing your newest product line to a group of retail dealers. Your organization might be something like this:

1. *Most young people who are just starting households are well educated, with sophisticated tastes in home furnishings.* (Setting up.)
2. *However, few of them have the income to buy costly originals, and many of them are looking for furnishings that will be able to survive their child-rearing years.* (Explaining.)
3. *Our new line of furniture has the look of authentic originals, yet it is made of inexpensive materials designed to resist stains, scratches, and tears.* (Unique selling proposition.)

Experiment with different arrangements. But always aim to present your most compelling point in its most convincing setting.

THE CONCLUSION

A conclusion does more than ring down the curtain on your message. It is your final opportunity to make your message accomplish what you set out for it to accomplish.

A good conclusion can accomplish these things.

- *A conclusion can reinforce what you have said.* One good way to do this is to summarize the main points briefly. Distill the essence of your message into three or four short, memorable sentences so that the audience leaves with your ideas ringing in its ears.
- *A conclusion can invite people to act.* Salespeople know that their presentation isn't complete until they've asked for the order. Your message isn't complete until you've told the people in your audience clearly, precisely, and persuasively what you want them to do.
- *A conclusion can inspire your audience.* You might do this with a challenging question, a glowing promise, or a strong statement of your most compelling point.

   One caveat: Be sure that you're inspiring them to do what you want them to do.

   A group of hunters who wanted to hunt doves on a farmer's property sent Charlie to the door to ask the owner's permission. The farmer agreed, but asked a favor in return: "I have a sick mule down in the pasture, and I need to put him out of his misery. But I just don't have the heart to do it. Would you mind taking care of that sad chore for me?"

   Charlie agreed, but when he saw the sad old mule standing by the farmer's faithful milk cow, he, too, lacked the heart to dispatch the animal. So he told his fellow hunters: "That farmer was so rude, I can't believe it. He called us every name in the book and told us to get off his property pronto or he'd shoot the tires off the van. I think we need to teach this guy a lesson. Judy, you've got your gun loaded. Why don't you shoot his mule?"

Judy took careful aim, and quickly and mercifully dispatched the ailing animal.

By this time, Hank had taken his gun out of the van and loaded it.

"I'm fighting mad too," he fumed as he took careful aim and squeezed the trigger. "I think I'll kill his cow!"

Charlie's message had inspired his listeners to act—but in a way that he hadn't bargained for.

• *A conclusion can set the stage for future communications.* Sometimes your entire purpose can't be accomplished with one communication. So your conclusion can prepare your audience for what's to come: ". . . So as you can see, our proposed new facility will have minimal impact on the air quality for the region. We are confident that the same will be true of water quality, and we will submit the appropriate data as soon as our environmental analysis is complete."

YOUR HOUSE OF COMMUNICATION

Like a house under construction, a communication does not emerge fully formed. A house starts with a foundation. The framework is erected on this foundation. Then follow the walls, roof, and floor. Partitions are erected. Finally come the finishing touches: paint, plaster, wallpaper, carpeting, and fixtures.

A communication in any form must start with a foundation. It is built upon a central purpose.

The framework consists of an outline—the main points listed in the order that they will be presented.

The outline is partitioned into an introduction, body, and conclusion. Into this shell, you move your information, ideas, arguments, and explanations.

The introduction is the entrance to your house. It should be inviting and functional. It should lead smoothly and conveniently to the other areas of the building, with a theme that is echoed throughout.

The main body is your living space. You'll take your audience through your living room and den for entertainment. You'll present food for thought in your dining room and kitchen. You'll go into the library for information. The information, ideas, arguments, and explanations form the furnishings. Your anecdotes, images, and illustrations form the decor.

The conclusion takes your guests out of the building and into the garden of inspiration and contemplation, where they can reflect upon the things they encountered within and apply them in their own lives.

Let's suppose that you're in charge of drumming up attendance for the annual convention of your trade association. You want to send a letter that will motivate people to attend. Here's how you might outline it:

   I. Introduction
      A. Give the date and site of the convention.
      B. Cite the advantages of the timing.
      C. Paint an attractive picture of the setting.
  II. Main Body
      A. Give details of the program.
      B. Show the advantages to the attendee.
      C. Give details of hotel rates and registration fees.
 III. Conclusion
      A. Suggest that the convention be combined with vacation plans.
      B. End with a hearty invitation to attend.

Following the outline, you might compose the following letter:

Dear [Name of Member]:

Come join us in New Orleans April 15–18 for the annual convention of the National Plant Nursery Association. At this time of year, the historic old city puts on its spring finery and reveals what a delightful place it can be. The charming Bourbon Orleans Hotel is an ideal base from which to explore the exciting French Quarter and to sample the food and entertainment in this city that blends the cultures of America, Europe, and Africa.

Our featured speaker will be Dr. Rose la Fleur, professor of botany at Tulane University, who will show blooms from the three new varieties of roses she has developed and will tell how you can make them a money-making part of your inventory for next spring.

Dr. I. B. MacIntosh, professor of computer science at Louisiana Tech, will demonstrate how computers can help you build more profitability into your business at minimum capital expense. A panel of your fellow members will share with you some of the ways they have used computers to enhance profits.

J. P. Hedgerow, president of Hedgerow and Boxwood Nurseries of Richmond, Virginia, will describe ways of expanding your business by developing and nurturing new market areas. A complete program is enclosed.

There'll be opportunities for golf and tennis, of course, at the city's splendid recreational facilities, and a chance to partake of the food, entertainment, and excitement of the famed French Quarter.

We still have rooms available for $90 a night per couple, and registration is only $250 per member and $125 for spouse or companion.

What an excellent opportunity to combine a business trip with a pleasure excursion! I know you'll want to attend. If you'll return the enclosed registration form by March 15, we'll hold a place for you. See you there!

> Daisy Larkspur
> Convention Chairman

The introduction opens with the most compelling point: the time and place of the national convention. It paints an inviting scene and beckons the reader into the body of the letter for more information.

The body provides the pertinent information: a list of the topics and speakers with suggestions on how they can help the business owner, and a summary of hotel rates and registration fees.

The conclusion suggests that the member combine the business trip with vacation plans and asks that the registration form be returned. The writer tells the recipient what she wants done and when she wants it done.

A message, of course, can't accomplish its purpose until it has been presented to the receiver. The next chapter will help you focus your presentation.

16

FOCUSING YOUR PRESENTATION

Once you have focused on your audience and have focused your message, it's necessary to turn your attention toward your presentation. Your presentation is the means by which you deliver your message to your audience. Focusing it requires that you choose the right medium, use it to best advantage, and aim for the right response.

Let's say that you're a musician and you were called upon to provide some diversion for a group of business executives after a demanding round of conferences.

You chose to play Debussy's *Afternoon of a Faun*, and it bombed.

There was nothing wrong with the message. It was the same great composition that has thrilled audiences for a century or more. There was nothing wrong with the audience—a group of cultured business executives gathered in the lounge of a top-flight hotel. But the presentation wasn't focused. It used the wrong medium to poor advantage. It also aimed for the wrong response.

The medium was a tenor banjo—the wrong strings for Debussy. If you had been presenting a medley of tunes from *Showboat*, you would have been using the medium to good advantage. But for Debussy, a concert piano would have been more appropriate.

Even had you given an accomplished piano performance, your communication still would have fallen short. After a grueling round of conferences, these executives were interested in some lively stimulation, and this was the night for game 6 of the World Series. The executives were gathered around a large-screen set watching the baseball action. They might have enjoyed a round or two of "Take Me Out to the Ball Game," and some appropriate fanfare during exciting moments of play. But nobody wants to listen to Debussy when there are two outs, the ty-

179

ing run is on second, and the count is three and two. Debussy induces reverie. The response you were after was excitement.

Whatever message you're trying to deliver, no matter how skillfully you deliver it and no matter how appropriate the audience, if the presentation isn't properly focused, it will flop.

A Wide Selection of Media

The plethora of media available today makes it technically easy to reach an audience two feet or two continents away. You can send a note via computer network to your secretary in the reception area or you can send a fax to your company's geologist in the rain forests of Indonesia.

But that doesn't mean that your message will be heard or heeded. The globe is saturated with messages, and each of us has to decide which one we'll pay attention to for the moment. A television ad aimed at business executives is likely to receive little attention if it's aired during the mid-morning hours. An advertisement for a Rolls Royce, no matter how skillfully crafted, is not likely to generate showroom traffic if it's published in *Boy's Life*.

WHICH MEDIUM IS BEST?

Message-senders must decide which media are the most effective avenues to their audiences under the given circumstances. A good presentation by itself doesn't assure success. It succeeds only when it gets the desired response from the targeted audience.

How do you determine which medium to use?

Here are some suggestions.

- *Choose a medium that fits the image you want to project.* The medium should reflect your personality or the corporate image. You don't present your annual report in a comic-book format. You don't advertise your designer originals in *Mad* magazine. Take the time to browse through some magazines. Note which companies advertise in which magazines, and how the messages vary from publication to publication.
- *Choose a medium that fits the audience you want to reach.* To make that choice, you need to know what kind of people are in your au-

dience. You need to know what they read, what television programs they watch, what radio stations they listen to, their tastes in music and clothes, their reaction to visual messages, their accessibility to the telephone, and the types of mail they get.

Telemarketing, for instance, might work fine if your audience is working couples who can be reached and sold to at home. But if your audience consists of business executives who must be reached and sold to at their offices, telemarketing might be disastrous.

- *Choose a medium that fits your purpose in sending the message.* If you're soliciting small donations from a mass audience, a form letter may be effective. But if you're looking for big-ticket contributors, willing to contribute $10,000 or more, steer clear of the form letter. Personal visits are a must.

A number of factors should govern your choice of a medium. Cost is important. The results must be worth the expenditure. Simplicity is another. If the medium depends upon extensive use of graphics and you lack the expertise or the resources to prepare the graphics, it's not the medium for you. Your plans for follow-up will also affect your choice. But the most important consideration is whether the medium fits your purpose.

- *Choose a medium that fits your message.* If you're trying to explain to your employees why wage increases are going to be cut back or to your stockholders why you're skipping the quarterly dividend, don't send your message in a slick, four-color brochure. You can't plead austerity while traveling first-class. Ask yourself: How complex is the message? What is its tone and nature? What will the medium say about the message?

- *Choose a medium that fits the occasion.* Once a newspaper editor carefully planned his editorial page for Christmas day so that it would be inspirational to those of the Christian and Jewish faiths. He wrote an editorial that called attention to the traditions of Hanukkah as well as those of Christmas, and pointed out the significance of the events celebrated by each festival. He chose Biblical passages respected by both faiths. What he didn't do was choose the editorial cartoon for the facing page. The cartoon was chosen by another editor. It featured a caricature of Menachem Begin, then prime minister of Israel, flying over conquered Arab territories with a scroll in his hands and shouting "Torah, Torah, Torah." The presentation was a clever criticism of Israel's actions in annexing the Golan

Heights from Syria. It alluded to the famous war cry of the Japanese pilots attacking Pearl Harbor: "Tora, Tora, Tora."

But the cartoon was preeminently the wrong medium for the wrong occasion. Jewish readers interpreted it as an affront to their sacred writings, delivered at a particularly inappropriate time of the year.

Presentations can be poorly targeted in less emotional ways. Many meeting planners lose sight of circumstances and attitudes when they arrange their programs. In the early morning, after a night of partying, it's no time to hit an audience with a complex audiovisual presentation. In the late evening, after a heavy meal complete with dessert, it's no time to schedule a deep lecture on economics.

The right medium for any presentation is the medium that will convey most effectively the message at the time it is to be sent to the audience. The mood of the audience, the tempo of the presentation, the nature of the occasion, and the audience's attention level at the time of the presentation are all major considerations in choosing the right medium.

- *Choose a medium that has the capacity to convey the message you wish to present.* This is a factor too often overlooked in the business world. An executive applies for a $125,000 a year position and sends off a one-page photocopied resume. The medium is inadequate. The resume for such a position must showcase the applicant's capabilities, and it must reflect quality and class.

We often overestimate the power of written communication, however. A client once noted that his semiskilled workers were leaving his company for other companies that paid only marginally better wages and offered far less in employee benefits. When benefits were factored in, they were earning less in their new jobs than they earned in the old ones.

"Do they know that?" asked one of my associates, who was consulting with the company.

"Sure," replied the executive. "We give them a booklet that explains it all as soon as they're hired."

The consultant checked into it and found that few employees actually read the booklet, and few who read it could understand it. The booklet was inadequate for the task.

Each medium has its strengths and weaknesses. Use its strengths and bypass its weaknesses. If your message relies heavily on visual impact, don't try to convey it by radio. Words can never describe adequately what the eye can perceive with ease. Television is your preeminent visual medium. But television is stingy with its time. It has thousands of messages to deliver each day, with only twenty-four hours in the day and only four hours of prime time. If your message is too complex to fit into a thirty-second spot or even into a ten-minute segment of a talk show, you may want to consider one of the print media. Remember, too, that television aims for the broad audience. If you want to reach a small audience with specific interests, a specialty publication may be your medium.

Radio stations do aim for specific audiences. Some target their programming toward youthful audiences, some toward the Baby Boomer generation. Different stations may aim toward audiences at different educational and income levels. In some areas, you'll find stations that target different ethnic and linguistic groups. But complex messages rarely play well on radio. The average listener's attention span is relatively short.

General circulation newspapers offer many vehicles for your message. You may submit a news release, pay for an advertisement, write a letter to the editor, or submit a column for the editorial or commentary pages. Newspapers also can display photographs and drawings—often in color—though, of course, they can't match the visual impact of television. Most subscribers to general circulation newspapers are over thirty years of age, and though different sections appeal to different groups, newspapers can't provide the pinpoint targeting of specialty publications. In considering a newspaper as a medium, take into consideration the newspaper's circulation: How many households does it reach? Where are these households?

Public speaking can be a powerful medium if properly used. Let's say that you're a developer who wants to build town houses adjacent to a single-family neighborhood. The people in the neighborhood are opposed. Your most effective approach may be a public presentation before a neighborhood audience in which you explain your project, using visuals, and answer questions from the audience.

Public speaking can also be the doorway to other media. If you're invited to address a civic club or other group on a timely subject, ask the program chair whether it will be all right to invite the media. If the media send reporters and cameras, your message may carry well beyond the walls of the meeting room.

MAKE MAXIMUM USE OF THE MEDIUM

Once you've chosen the medium, look for ways to make maximum use of it. Each medium has its distinctive characteristics. Learn them and use them to obtain the desired response.

Six tips will help you target your presentation for the desired response.

1. *Be sensitive to the way your audience will experience the presentation.* Put yourself in the shoes of the person who is receiving your message. How would you respond if the message came to you?

   Each day my desk is the target of a blizzard of paperwork. Some of it is important, some of it is trivial, and some of it is worthless. Separating the important stuff from the trivial stuff is time-consuming. Many executives experience the same problem. This means that you should try to handle as many details as possible in person or by telephone. A telephone call can save time and eye strain, and it's easier on the landfill.

   If I do have to communicate important matters on paper, I don't want my communication to get lost in the blizzard that descends on the recipient's desk. So I send it by a commercial air express service. It costs more than regular mail, but offers some significant advantages. I know that the package will be handed to the client personally. The client will open it and find an attractive presentation and a request for immediate response. My communication will get priority over the other written materials that arrive by regular mail. By being sensitive to the way my clients experience my presentation, I can tailor it for maximum impact. It works.

2. *Don't overload your presentation.* Sometimes we expect a presentation to accomplish too many things at once. You can't use a van simultaneously as a pickup truck, a mini-bus, and a camper. You have to choose the function you want it to serve.

   Correspondingly, you can't use a brochure simultaneously to promote, explain, remind, build prestige, and provide a source of exhaustive information. A brochure can handle any one of these functions, but not all of them at once. Concentrate on a few compatible functions for your presentation.

3. *Make your presentation attractive.* People judge you by the quality of your presentation.

Go before an audience of business executives in old, wrinkled, misfitting clothes with your hair disheveled and your face showing a lack of acquaintance with a razor (if you're a man) or a makeup brush (if you're a woman). See how many people listen.

Send out a brochure with small, hard-to-read type jammed tightly onto pages of cheap paper. See how many people read it.

Market yourself using a videotape with faded, shaky, fuzzy images in a dull, nondescript office. See what kind of results you get.

A poor presentation is worse than no presentation at all. Going first-class costs some bucks, but it pays dividends. If you're preparing a brochure or other written communication, invest in commercial art, color printing, and enough paper to permit an attractive layout. If you can't afford the extra paper, cut back on the length of your copy, not on the quality of your presentation.

4. *Develop a strong sense of timing.* Before the days of round-the-clock television coverage, a major morning newspaper decided that its subscribers in the hinterlands would read the results of the national election in the next morning's edition, come hell or high water.

The presses were put on hold and a story was prepared so that all that was needed to make it complete was one paragraph: the opening paragraph telling who won.

The news came in, the story was completed, and the presses rolled.

So did the train that carried the newspapers to the hinterlands. But it rolled minutes before the circulation truck arrived with its cargo of newspapers. Not only did the subscribers in the hinterlands miss the story about the election results; they also missed every other story carried in the paper that day.

Timing was the crucial factor.

Timing is a major factor in business communications as well. Direct-mail merchandisers have learned that the response to a mailing is heavily dependent on timing. If you're selling Christmas cards, you don't send out your catalog on December 10. If you're selling weekends at Niagara Falls, you don't time your promotion for December. Holidays, seasons, and even the days of the week on which your presentations arrive can have a profound effect on the response. So can the length of a presentation. If it takes too long to read a presentation, the recipient is likely to toss it before your message gets across.

5. *Cultivate a sense of pacing to sustain interest.* Most people's attention span is on the order of two or three minutes. Whether they're reading or listening, they'll switch mental channels unless there's a change of pace.

Notice the programming pattern on your favorite radio station. The average song will last about three minutes, unless you're listening to a classical work. The music companies know that's about the limit of the average listener's attention span. The tempo will change from one recording to another. A vocal selection will be followed by an instrumental; a pulsating rock beat by a mellow "oldie"; a lively polonaise by a soothing sonata.

Professional speakers pace their points, using pauses, stories, and audience exercises to sustain attention. And they know just when to conclude.

Pick up a novel and thumb through the pages. Which ones look more inviting? Probably the ones with lots of dialogue, because dialogue breaks up the paragraphs. Long paragraphs lend a solid, unbroken appearance to the page. Short paragraphs promise a constant change of pace. That's why newspaper writing is characterized by short paragraphs. Good writers use dialogue, similes, metaphors, analogies, subheadings, and other devices to provide a constant variety of pace.

6. *Stage every presentation to create the mood you want.* Remember television's "Jackie Gleason Show"? It opened each week with an elaborate and colorful dance number by the June Taylor dancers. The dance and the music set the stage for the grand entrance of the flamboyant comedian.

On Broadway, the splashy opening number was a standard feature of musical productions until Richard Rodgers and Oscar Hammerstein II broke the mold. They had a lone cowboy ride slowly across the stage, with its quiet, pastoral backdrop. Out of the hush that filled the theater, the opening number rose like the voice of a lark breaking the morning silence, and the audience heard for the first time the haunting Hammerstein lyric perfectly attuned to the Rodgers music: *There's a bright golden haze on the meadow.*

Oh what a beautiful morning it was! *Oklahoma!* took off like a frisky colt, and musical history was made. The opening number set the perfect mood for the production that followed.

Staging gets the audience ready for your presentation. One of the most effective examples in my experience was General Electric's national sales convention in Honolulu's Sheraton Waikiki Resort Hotel. GE invited me to speak to the group.

The staging began well in advance of my presentation. These were GE's top salespeople—the folks who put the power into the bottom line. Nothing was too good for them. Each time they went to their rooms, they would find a treat of some kind—some exotic food or interesting wine.

Months in advance, GE's planners had hired a musical group, which delivered announcements in songs it had composed. Everything was designed to set a positive, upbeat mood. When I stepped onto that stage to speak, the audience had been well prepared to hear what I had to say.

This generation has grown up with professionally staged presentations. It expects to be approached with flair and excitement. If you don't provide it, your audience will sense that something is lacking.

This is true all over the world. Graeme Clegg owns a company based in Auckland, New Zealand, which sells products through direct distributors in more than a dozen countries in Asia, Australia, and the Pacific Rim. Each of the meetings Clegg holds for his distributors is a major production, with music and dance numbers as part of the presentation. Even the decor is designed to capture the audience's attention.

The art of presentation has become more sophisticated at the dawn of the twenty-first century. Newspapers and magazines once used screaming headlines to draw people into their presentations. Now they use creative layouts, graphic art, and plenty of color.

Television uses colorful backdrops, technical legerdemain, and mood-setting music to launch its presentations. Radio heralds its announcements with musical lead-ins. Direct-mail houses use sweepstakes, and stores use displays, lighting, and other attention-getting devices to bring people in. Shopping malls compete to see which can provide the most exciting setting for shoppers to make their purchasing decisions. No matter what type of presentation you're making, set the stage with imagination and flair.

The time and resources spent on the message and the presentation would be wasted, of course, without a concrete purpose in mind. The object of your message is to obtain results. In the next chapter, we show how to focus on the results you want to achieve.

17

FOCUSING YOUR
RESULTS

The object of a communication is to make things happen. If nothing happens, the communication has failed. Often, we become so involved in making a superb speech, creating a literary gem, or producing a smashing layout that we forget to ask ourselves: What results are we seeking?

We become like the surgeon who brilliantly made an incision, excised the tumor without damaging surrounding organs, and closed the wound cleanly and expertly, only to find a dead patient on the table. It was small consolation for the family that "the operation was a success, but the patient died."

The history of commerce is replete with comparable stories.

The Model A Fizzled

The Model A Ford is regarded today as one of the most memorable automobiles ever built. Like its sturdy predecessor, the Model T, it was tough and reliable. Unlike the homely "T," it had style and flair. It was a good performer for its day, and even after World War II it was still commonly used as a family car. It was a good car and a good-looking car. But it was not a successful car.

The Model A could not regain for Ford the sales lead that had been snatched from it by upstart Chevrolet. The Model A lasted only four model years before it was replaced by the famous Ford V-8.

The Steamship That Sailed Too Late

The SS *United States* was a beautiful ship—fast, luxurious, and well-designed. It brought to the United States the world speed record for transatlantic steamship crossings, beating earlier records set by Cunard Lines' *Queen Mary* and *Queen Elizabeth*. But it was launched at the dawn of the jet age, and soon the jumbo jets rendered it obsolete.

The Nuclear Ship That Sailed Too Soon

The NS *Savannah* was another beautiful ship, and a technological marvel in the bargain. It was the world's first nuclear-powered merchant ship. Designwise, it was eminently successful. But disputes with maritime unions over the manning of the vessel led to its early retirement.

An Innovative Flop

The Chevrolet Corvair was an innovative automobile, with a rear-mounted, air-cooled aluminum engine. It was comfortable, good-looking, and reasonably priced. But it could not compete for sales with the more conventional Ford Falcon, and Chevrolet eventually had to junk it in favor of the Chevy II, which evolved into the Nova.

In each of these examples, the operation was a success, but the patient died.

Why?

Results Are What Counts

The efforts, though brilliantly executed, failed to produce the desired results.

We may spend a lot of time and talent crafting a superb message and delivering it in a compelling manner to an audience eager to receive it. But if we have given no thought to the *results* we're seeking, the audience won't respond in the way we want and the message will fail. Results don't happen. They have to be programmed.

When an audience fails to respond to a message in the desired way, it's usually because they never knew what response was desired. And usually, the reason the desired response is unclear to the audience is that it's unclear to the communicator too.

So before you make your presentation, ask yourself: "What if the audience did exactly what I want it to do? What would that be, and how would I know it?"

TWO KINDS OF SUCCESS

Before you answer these questions, think about the kinds of success you're seeking. There are two kinds as far as communication is concerned. There is *short-range success* and there's *long-range success*.

When the audience lets you know that it enjoyed the presentation and understood the points you were making, you've achieved short-range success. When the communication moves the audience to take the action you wanted it to take, you've achieved long-range success.

The Understanding Didn't Go Far Enough

Let me give you an example.

The investors in a franchise operation wanted to sell franchises in a certain part of the country. They knew the proposition was complex, so they invited prospects to regional meetings and carefully outlined the details. They used visual aids and handouts and held question-and-answer sessions.

The short-term results were excellent. After the first round of presentations, 80 percent of the people who attended said they would buy franchises. All who attended were given two weeks to respond.

At the end of the period, none of the prospects was on board. When the investors looked into the reasons, they learned why. The prospects who attended the meeting understood the proposal. But they were unable to explain it adequately to their spouses, lawyers, and accountants. So in the long term, the investors' communication had failed.

The investors tried again. This time they asked prospects to bring their spouses and at least one adviser. By explaining the proposition to each person involved in the decision making, they achieved long-term success.

When the prospect says "yes" to the job offer, you have achieved short-term success. When the spouse is also sold on the job, the company, and the location, then you are far more likely to achieve long-term success because you've increased the likelihood of a satisfactory, lasting relationship.

TWO KINDS OF FEEDBACK

To achieve both kinds of success, you need two kinds of feedback: *presentation feedback* and *message feedback*.

Presentation feedback tells you whether your audience heard and understood what you said. Message feedback tells you whether the audience responded the way you wanted it to respond.

The amount and type of feedback you seek depend upon your goals for making a presentation.

Let's say that you're launching an advertising campaign for your new line of personal computers. Since you're aiming for the household market, you've decided to use newspaper advertisements. What kind of feedback might you seek?

You might want to know which newspapers draw the best responses. You might want to know which wording is most effective, what day of the week is best to advertise, how frequently your ads should run, and what size ad is most cost-effective. All this is presentation feedback.

Advertising agencies have complex systems for obtaining this information. You can get it by including in the ads coupons with coded symbols that tell you which newspapers they were clipped from and the day of the week the ad was published. Or you can have responses directed to a post office box with code letters in the number to let you know which ad was being answered. Use your imagination to come up with other ways of obtaining feedback.

Now let's suppose that you've just inaugurated a continuous quality-improvement process, and you've just explained it to your employees, perhaps through an article in your company publication, through a letter to employees, or through a speech.

Now you're not so much concerned about how well the presentation went over as you are with the level of understanding among your employees. How do you gauge it?

A simple questionnaire might do the job. If the questionnaire shows that the program is well understood, you need only follow through with your implementation plans. If it shows that the employees are confused about certain aspects of the plan, you can devise additional communications addressing those specific areas.

Expect Surprises

When you seek feedback, expect surprises. It's been said that the Chevrolet Nova experienced sales resistance among Spanish-speaking people, not because the product lacked the qualities they were looking for, but because the expression "No va" in Spanish means "No go."

Don't look for the feedback that strokes your ego. And don't look for the kind that reinforces your biases. If feedback is going to help you, it has to come with the bark off. If the feedback is unfavorable, don't dismiss it as ignorant or unfair. Look for ways to change your presentation so that it yields positive feedback.

Recognizing the Desired Response

How will you know when the audience gives the response you desire?

The time to ask that question is *before* you go into your presentation. I've found it useful, early in the preparation stage, to write out a succinct statement specifying the response I desire, then planning the feedback that will tell me whether I've gained that response.

In some cases, you may find that the presentation you've planned just doesn't have the power to give you the desired response. If that's the case, you can do one of two things: You can plan another presentation that has the power you need. Or you can lower your expectations.

In other cases, you may spot some weak places in your presentation, and you can adjust to take care of the weaknesses.

Strategies for Obtaining Feedback

Here are some time-tested strategies for obtaining feedback.

- *Test your presentation and message, not the audience.* If the message isn't getting through, it's rarely the fault of the audience. Sure, some audiences are more savvy than others, and some are friendlier than others. But part of your challenge as a communicator is to know the audience you're facing and to design your presentation to appeal to that audience.

If your feedback tells you that you didn't connect, find out why and look for ways to make the connection the next time.

- *Test your effectiveness, not your abilities.* Don't ask your audience, "Did you enjoy the presentation?" Few people are going to look you in the eye and say, "You really bombed." Most people will tell you that you did fine. Some will heap glowing praise on you. That may be great for your ego, but it won't help you improve your presentation.

A local television talk show host once opened a new series of shows and found that he was getting a new kind of feedback.

"When I was doing another show, people would come up to me and tell me they'd seen the show and enjoyed it," he said. "Now they stop me on the street to give me their opinions about the subjects we're discussing."

You can obtain this kind of feedback by asking specific questions about what you had to say. When people pay you compliments, draw them out with questions to determine whether they understand what you've said.

- *Ask your audience for feedback.* If you're giving a speech, make it clear that you're not evaluating the audience, but that you're interested in its opinions.

"I've been telling you what I think; now I'd like to hear what you think about this subject," is a good way to introduce your request for feedback. On radio or television, you can ask your viewers or listeners to respond by telephone or letter. If you're running an ad in a print medium, a brief invitation to respond or a brief questionnaire that can be clipped and mailed can elicit feedback. Coupons accompanying an ad can tell you how many customers are responding to a specific message.

- *Devise a way of evaluating the feedback you get.* Direct mailers know from experience how many responses they should receive from their mailers. When there's a money-back guarantee, they set an acceptable quota for returned merchandise. When they get more responses and fewer returns than they expect, they know they've been successful. If the responses are too low and the returns too high, they know to make adjustments.

- *Tailor your feedback and evaluations to your ultimate goals.* Let's say you have a product that is popular with the Baby Boomers, and you want to extend its appeal to the younger generation. So you develop an advertising campaign aimed at the younger generation. Your feedback from the younger consumers is favorable. They're turning on to your product. But remember your ultimate goal. It isn't to sell your product to young consumers. It's to *broaden* its appeal to all age groups. So while you're congratulating yourself on your success with younger consumers, you might want to see how your advertising message is affecting your older customers. If it's turning them off, then some adjustments need to be made.

Feedback Is Useless Unless Used

Feedback is useless unless it's used, and there are a number of ways to use it.

If your feedback indicates that your presentation was a resounding success, there's a tendency to sit back and bask in the accolades. But remember that a successful presentation is not an end in itself. You're looking for long-term results. Your presentation may have resulted in brilliant solutions to long-term problems, but devising solutions isn't enough. You have to implement them. What long-range response were you seeking?

Use Failures to Build Success

If feedback is negative, don't go away depressed. Use your failures to build toward future successes. Analyze what went wrong, and look for ways to prevent it from happening again.

Remember how Demosthenes bombed when he first went before the Assembly in Athens? Instead of letting the hoots discourage him from ever taking the platform again, he analyzed his weaknesses and then corrected them. When he returned, he gave a stellar performance.

You can use negative feedback just as effectively. Did your audience go to sleep? Look for ways to enliven the subject or to stimulate the audience the next time around. Did your jokes bomb? It may be that you were poking fun at somebody's sacred cow. Find out. Ask people you can trust to give you friendly but candid criticism, and listen to them. Ask them specific questions about your presentation and their reaction to it.

You may think a certain line or turn of phrase is the greatest piece of work since Mark Antony's eulogy of Caesar. But the line is only as good as your audience's perception of it. If the audience didn't respond to the line, you may have been using it on the wrong audience. Or it just may be a bad line. If it doesn't work, toss it out and find something that *does* work.

Negative criticism is like a sander: It cuts away at the surface, but it polishes. Use negative feedback to polish your presentation. It can be your key to constant improvement.

Use What Works Best for You

Good communicators use their experiences to learn what works best for them. The self-effacing style of Wendy's founder Dave Thomas wouldn't work for hard-charging GE executive Jack Welch. Actor Eddie Murphy's racy street-flavored humor wouldn't work for the suave Johnny Carson. My style might not work for you. The important thing is to develop your own style and learn what works best for you. I listen and analyze my feedback so that I can fine-tune every presentation for maximum effectiveness.

When I'm asked for my card, I usually ask, "Was there something in particular that interested you?" If the answer is "Yes," I find out what it was. Then I say, "I'm often hard to reach by telephone. Give me your business card and I'll see that you get the information you want." On the back of the card, I note what the person was interested in. Then I make sure the information is provided. Later I call to see whether the individual was satisfied. This personal attention often opens doors for future opportunities. It's easier to get through to busy people when you're giving them information they've requested than it is to reopen a door they've closed.

As you learn to focus your communication efforts, you'll find yourself growing in effectiveness as a leader of people and an influencer of events. People will not only receive your message; they will also understand it and act on it.

PART FOUR

PLATFORM POWER

18

PREPARING FOR YOUR SPEECH

With all the technological wonders of the twenty-first century, business executives will still find one of their most effective communications media to be the one employed with such skill by Demosthenes 2,300 years ago: the art of public speaking.

For reaching a widely dispersed audience quickly and economically, telecommunications will be indispensable. But telecommunications media cannot present the message in the flesh. They can't put communicator and audience in a shared ambience. Only the live public speech can do that, and nothing can stir the emotions like a live speech, eloquently crafted and superbly delivered.

Occasions for Public Speaking

A public speech can be used to communicate a corporate vision to employees. It can be used to guide employee motivation in the direction an executive wants it to go. It can be used to create favorable images of the company and the executive in the community. It can be used to persuade public bodies to take action in harmony with the company's best interests. A public speech can exhort, entertain, explain, or persuade. While it reaches only a limited immediate audience, its secondary audiences can be immense. People go back to their homes and offices and tell others what they've heard. The media may listen and publish excerpts from the speech and the gist of what was said. Television and radio stations may extract sound bites.

So the art of public speaking is well worth cultivating, and the preparation for a public speech deserves careful attention.

199

Three Types of Speech

The type of preparation you undertake will depend upon the type of speech you give. There are three basic types of public speech:

1. Impromptu
2. Written text
3. Extemporaneous

IMPROMPTU SPEECHES

The impromptu speech usually is the most intimidating for the speaker, though it need not be. This is the speech you have to give on the spur of the moment, without benefit of notes or outline.

It may happen when you're recognized from the platform at a public function and you're called upon to give "a few appropriate remarks."

It may happen at a board meeting when you're unexpectedly called upon to explain a project you're in charge of or a proposal you've made.

Or it may happen when you're the program chair for a service club meeting and the scheduled speaker fails to show up.

Stay Calm

Two words are important to keep in mind under such circumstances: *Don't panic.*

If you're frequently called upon to speak in behalf of your company, it pays to keep a "generic speech" on hand. This speech might contain your core message—the essence of what you want people to know about your organization. It should contain information that you're familiar with and don't have to look up. If you can't keep a copy of this speech in your briefcase, at least be familiar with its general outline, so that when you are called upon unexpectedly you can quickly organize your thoughts.

When the call comes, take a moment to think. Make a quick mental outline of the points you want to make. Don't worry about the words you'll use. Just organize the ideas. The words will come to you, just as they do when you're engaged in ordinary conversation.

WRITTEN TEXTS

A young minister once asked his outspoken grandmother for a critique of his first sermon.

"I saw only three things wrong with it," she said, to her grandson's relief.

"What three things were wrong?" he asked.

Her answer dispelled his relief.

"First, you read it. Second, you didn't read it well. Third, it wasn't worth reading."

If you can help it, don't read from a text. Unless you're an excellent reader, and something of an actor, you'll sound stiff and unnatural.

However, there are occasions when it's necessary to read a speech. When it's critically important that the information be delivered precisely and accurately, reading may be your only choice. If you're dealing with touchy legal issues, for instance, one stray ad lib could cost you dearly.

The procedure for developing and organizing a written text is similar to that for an extemporaneous speech. In an extemporaneous speech, you organize your ideas. In a written speech, you go one step farther and put the ideas into the actual words you'll be speaking.

As you write, remember that written language has one style and spoken language another. Write for the spoken language. Express your thoughts the way you would express them in a conversation, not the way you would write them in a letter or essay. Remember, too, that the eye can glide over words that tie up the tongue. Read the text aloud and make sure there are no tongue-twisters or difficult-to-pronounce combinations.

When delivering the speech, don't read word for word. Let your eye take in clusters of words, so that your mind is dealing with ideas, not syllables. This will make it easier for you to express the ideas naturally and fluently.

A smooth, natural delivery will be easier if you are thoroughly familiar with the text. Don't try to memorize it, but know how it's organized and know what points you want to stress. You may want to underline the words you wish to emphasize and note the places you want to pause.

Thorough familiarity with the text will enable you to maintain eye contact with the audience without fear of losing your place. If you do lose your place, don't worry. Calmly scan the page until you come to the right line. It will take only a moment, and you won't lose your audience.

EXTEMPORANEOUS SPEECHES

Extemporaneous speeches are usually the most effective. When speaking extemporaneously, you are guided by a carefully prepared outline without being tied to a specific text. The outline provides you with the ideas you want to express. You can then form these ideas into words in a natural, conversational way. This type of speech combines the advantages of spontaneity and good organization.

Since the majority of experienced speakers use the extemporaneous approach, most of the material that follows deals with preparing an extemporaneous speech. However, most of the suggestions are equally applicable to the written text.

SHOULD YOU ACCEPT?

A good speech demands careful and creative preparation. The preparation begins before you decide to accept the invitation to speak. Your decision should be guided by the answers to these questions:

1. Why should I speak to this audience in this place at this time?
2. What should I speak about?
3. How can I make my speech enjoyable, interesting, informative, and persuasive?
4. How should I organize my speech?
5. How can I prepare myself to make a good delivery?
6. How can I keep calm and avoid stage fright during my speech?
7. How can I connect with my listeners and keep them involved?
8. What barriers to communication might I experience and how can I deal effectively with them?
9. How can I clarify complex ideas, be convincing on controversial claims, and inject interest in otherwise dull material?
10. How will I get the response I want from my audience, and how will I know when I get it?

Why You and Why Now

The importance of question 1 should be obvious. If you have nothing to say that will be useful or interesting to this group, then you shouldn't speak. If you are scheduled at a time and place and in a context that will make it difficult if not impossible for you to deliver your message effectively, then you should decline the invitation.

Before you accept, learn as much as you can about the organization that has extended the invitation. Know its background, history, and purpose. If you accept the invitation to speak, will others interpret your acceptance as an endorsement of its goals? If so, are the goals ones you can comfortably endorse?

Find out about the interests of the people you're invited to address. What do they already know about the things you speak on? What can you tell them that will add to their useful knowledge? How much time will you have in which to tell them?

Who else is on the program and what are their topics? In what order will they speak? How will your speech and your message fit into the overall program? Will you follow a dynamic or a boring speaker? Will the speech preceding yours be informative or inspirational?

Identify the Barriers

Identify the barriers you may have to overcome to get your message across. Will this be a sympathetic, hostile, or neutral audience? Are you opening the program? Are you closing it? What kind of room arrangements will you find? Will you be the last speaker before lunch or the first after lunch? Will your audience come to you directly from a cocktail hour?

All these considerations are important in deciding whether this speech is likely to advance or retard your purpose. Don't go into a situation in which you know it will be hard to look good. If the deck seems stacked against you, pass.

Reasons to Accept

With most invitations, you'll probably find plenty of reasons to accept. Here are some good reasons for saying yes:

- You have some valuable information or insights you want to give to the group.
- Now is an appropriate time, and this is an appropriate place to share your ideas.
- This audience will accept your leadership, provided you earn it when you speak.
- You have something important you want this audience to do.

Choosing a Topic

Once you've decided to accept the invitation, your next task is to choose your topic. Here are some criteria for selecting a topic:

- It should be something you know about or can find out about.
- It should be a subject the audience knows at least a little about but wants to know more about.
- It should be timely and appropriate for the audience.
- It should be narrow enough that it won't be confusing.
- It should be instrumental in achieving the response you want.

Gathering Your Materials

After you've chosen your topic, analyze what you already know about it and decide how much additional information you'll need. You're now ready to research your speech.

Use the library, periodicals, your own files, and any other appropriate resources to fill in the gaps in your knowledge of the subject. Then, to make it truly your own speech, draw upon your personal experiences to provide vivid illustrations or use your imagination to produce original stories.

Organizing Your Speech

A lot of complicated formulas have been advanced for organizing speeches and other communications. It doesn't have to be complicated. It can be a simple matter of choosing the material you want to use and following your mind's natural selection process. Here's how I do it:

1. I go through all my material and select only those points that are relevant to my audience and my speech.
2. I write out one concise sentence that clearly tells what I'm going to say.
3. I reduce my ideas to three or four sentences that clearly present the idea expressed in my topic sentence. I arrange them in the most convincing order. This becomes my outline.
4. I flesh out the outline with explanations, supportive statements, funny lines and stories, and persuasive points.
5. I select a humorous related story to use as my introduction and a brief summation of main points to use as my conclusion. I end my speech with a clear, convincing challenge for specific action.
6. I let my speech ripen in my mind and heart until I understand the implications of everything I will say, feel it very deeply, and am sure every point is as clear and convincing as I can make it.

Now I'm ready to deliver the speech in words that are spontaneous, but that spring from well-organized, deeply felt thoughts.

When You Use a Speechwriter

Speech writing is a communication specialty in itself. It is also time-consuming. Not all executives have the time or the inclination to devote to the craft. That's why corporations often have a staff of speechwriters, or delegate the task to members of their public relations departments.

This works fine, so long as the speechwriter knows the executive's thoughts and speech patterns. If the speechwriter doesn't know you well, you could find yourself looking at a speech that distorts your viewpoint and uses a style of expression that is not natural for you.

The better the speechwriters know you, the better they can express your ideas in your kind of language. If the speechwriters don't report directly to you, they should report to someone who knows you very well, and that person should edit the draft very carefully.

Make sure the writing staff has a clear understanding of your position on the issues you plan to address. If you have company literature or correspondence that states the official position, make it available to the writers. Your writing staff should have a library of corporate literature, including annual reports, sales and marketing literature, external and internal publications, and a file of executive speeches. When you come across articles or quotations that you find especially relevant or cogent, have your secretary clip them or copy them and send them to the writing staff.

It will help the writers to have samples of your speaking or writing on hand. This can take the form of audiotapes, videotapes, speech manuscripts, and copies of correspondence. Such resources will enable the writers to familiarize themselves with your speech patterns and your word choices.

If you have trouble pronouncing certain words or word combinations, the writers should know about it.

Competent writers will provide you with a well-organized and well-written script. Your task is to personalize it.

Never go to the platform with a speech you haven't read before. Take the time to read the draft while you are not rushed and are not distracted.

Read the speech first for content. Has the writer included all the points you want to make? Is all the information factual? Does it express the viewpoint you want to express? Does it reflect your priorities?

Next read it for style. Does the writer use any words that are unfamiliar to you? objectionable to you? incompatible with your style of expression?

Next read the speech aloud. Do the words flow smoothly and naturally? Are there any tongue-twisters? Are there any sentences that you can't speak in a single breath?

Don't hesitate to second-guess your writer on the wording. This is *your* speech and it should say what you want to say the way you want to say it. Change any words necessary to make it conform to your natural form of expression.

As you read the speech, be alert for opportunities to add personal stories and anecdotes that will put your imprint on the speech. Stories and images can add life, interest, and inspiration to your speech. In the next chapter, we provide suggestions on finding and choosing these elements.

19

COMMUNICATING THROUGH IMAGES AND STORIES

If communication were just a matter of passing along information and ideas, speakers could save their breaths. All they'd need to do would be to pass out copies of their outlines. But when people come to hear speeches, they're looking for more than raw information. They expect to be entertained or inspired as well as informed and persuaded. Information and ideas must be passed along with a skillful leavening of humor, pathos, and captivating illustrations.

That's why experienced speakers have learned to employ images and stories to bring their speeches to life. Stories and images enable them to make their speeches enjoyable, interesting, informative, and persuasive.

CHOOSE YOUR STORIES

Storytelling is an art, but you can learn it. The first thing you have to learn is how to choose your stories. Select each story with these criteria in mind.

- *The story should be one the audience can relate to.* Probably the most effective storyteller of all time was Jesus of Nazareth, whose parables still make their points nearly two thousand years after they were first uttered. The stories he told revolved around the everyday lives of the people in his audience.

  When he told the parable of the lost sheep, he knew he was addressing an audience familiar with the routine of the shepherd.

When he told the parable of the Good Samaritan, he knew that his audience had grown up in an environment of animosity between Jews and Samaritans, and would grasp the moral significance of a Samaritan man stopping to render aid to a Jewish stranger. When he spoke about dough and leaven, he knew that in his audience were women who made bread by mixing sour dough with fresh dough for leavening, confident that "a little leaven ferments the whole lump."

When you use stories, follow Jesus' example. Make them stories people in your audience will be able to connect with through their common experiences.

And make sure they will relate to each story in a positive way. Once I was invited to address the annual sales meeting of Borden's, Inc., in Houston. I immediately began to think about all the stories I'd heard about Elsie the Cow. But, following my usual practice, I checked with someone at Borden's to find out whether it would be appropriate to joke about Elsie.

"Heavens no," replied my contact. "We consider Elsie almost sacred."

The story must be clear and able to stand on its own. There's a truism about jokes and anecdotes: If you have to explain them, don't bother. If the audience doesn't immediately grasp the moral or the punch line, the story has bombed and no amount of explaining will rescue it. A story may resonate among people who share your specific knowledge and expertise, but it will fall flat among the uninitiated. Avoid stories that require special knowledge or special vocabulary unless you know that your audience has that knowledge and is familiar with that vocabulary.

If I say, "A jumbo shrimp is an oxymoron," the line will fall flat with an audience that doesn't know that an oxymoron is a contradiction in terms, like a square circle or a straight curve.

Before I use a story with an audience, I tell it to several people. By observing their responses, I can tell which stories click and which ones flop.

The story must relate clearly to the point you wish to make. It isn't enough that a story is funny or poignant or captivating. It must also contribute toward the purpose of your speech. Its relationship to your message should be clear immediately. The audience should have no trouble figuring out how the story relates to the point you're making.

Some speakers like to start out with a joke: "A funny thing happened to me on the way to the hotel. . . ." They tell it, wait for the laughter to die, then say, "But seriously, though. . . ."

The joke has added nothing to the speech. Instead of leading the audience compellingly into the subject of the talk, it has flashed the message: "You've had your dessert. Now it's time to eat your spinach." The good part is over; the dull part begins. That's no way to capture and hold an audience's attention.

- *The story must be one you can tell well.* You may have heard the story about the new prison inmate who was puzzled by what happened after the lights went out. Someone called out a number, and suddenly the whole cellblock erupted in laughter. As the laughter died, someone called out another number, and again the inmates roared.

"What's going on?" the newcomer asked his cellmate.

"We're telling jokes," came the reply. "We don't hear many new ones on the inside, so we end up telling the same ones over and over. Everybody knows them all, so to save time we've just numbered them. When I call out 'Number 76,' everybody knows which joke I'm talking about, so everybody laughs."

The new inmate wanted in on the fun, so he called out "Number 76." He was greeted by dead silence.

"Why didn't they laugh?" he asked.

"Some people can tell 'em and some can't," replied the cellmate.

It's true. A joke that goes over big when told by one speaker will be a dud when told by another. That's because the personality and background of the teller impart a certain flavor to the joke. My buddy Robert Henry can tell jokes about Southern Baptists and get away with it, because he springs from Southern Baptist soil and the aura clings to him. A Jewish comedian can crack Jewish jokes that would be offensive coming from a non-Jew. A Black comedian can crack jokes that might be considered racist coming from a White person. A joke that works for a fast-talking, gregarious personality might bomb when used by a more subtle, low-key personality. A story must be suited to the personality of the teller and must fit in with the mood of the speech.

- *The story must fit into the allotted time.* Sometimes, when you're building toward a major point, a story can be stretched to obtain full impact. If you're making a minor point, you'll want to make it short and sweet. Be sure the length of the story is appropriate for the point you're making and for the length of your speech.

Practice Telling Your Story

Many speakers spend hours rehearsing their main points and neglect to practice the storytelling. That's a mistake.

If a story is worth telling, it's worth telling well. The only way you can be sure you're telling a story well is to practice it repeatedly.

A good story has rhythm and flow, and it has a mood. The only way you can give a story these qualities is to make it a part of you. Tell the story over and over. Listen to yourself telling it on audiotape. Better yet, *watch* yourself telling it on videotape. Look for ways you can improve the way you tell it.

Let the Audience Respond

If a story is to be effective, the audience must have a chance to respond to it. Use pauses to build anticipation for your punch line. After you've delivered your punch line, pause again to give the point a chance to sink in.

INVOLVE THE AUDIENCE

A good speech achieves interaction between the speaker and the audience. A good speaker looks for ways to involve the audience. A good story provides an avenue.

As I tell a story, I often ask questions that keep the audience responding. I'll reach a key point in the story line and will ask something like, "What do you think he did next?" If the audience is really with me, the answer will immediately pop into their minds, and I can tell, just by watching them, that I've connected.

The best way to involve the audience in funny stories is to tell the stories as if they were about people in the audience. If the people you choose are well known to the group, the results can be hilarious. It works on the same principle as the celebrity "roast." You may pick on a top executive, or a member of the group who is known as a cut-up, or a highly respected person in the audience.

There are four important rules for using the technique properly:

- Always make sure you clear it with the individual who will be the subject of your humor, or at least with someone who knows the individual well enough to tell you whether the person may be offended.
- Keep it good-natured. Always make sure that your punch line doesn't land in a sensitive spot. Bob Hope liked to poke fun at Gerald Ford during Ford's presidency. But he always ribbed the president about his golf game, never about his foreign policy.

  Most audiences will resent it if an outsider is perceived as attacking one of their group. Gene Perret, who once served as head writer for Bob Hope and Carol Burnett, remembers ruefully a speech he gave at a company function. He devoted an entire routine to making fun of a blueprint machine that never worked. In the middle of his speech, the manager of the department that made the machine walked out angrily.[1]
- Keep it short. If you run on and on about the same individual, people tend to get bored and the individual involved may be embarrassed.
- At the end, thank the person, by either shaking hands or conveying a compliment.

ILLUMINATE WITH IMAGES

In chapter 2 we learned that one of the keys to the Kingdom of Communication is the use of images. Images can illuminate your stories and your arguments.

Before you can use images, you must be able to see them—first with your literal eyes and then with your mental eyes.

You can't describe something you haven't seen, and you haven't really seen something until you've examined it carefully. Therefore, a good communicator must be a keen observer.

The poet Robert Frost was a meticulous observer.

"The Vermont mountains stretch extended straight," he wrote. "New Hampshire mountains curl up in a coil."

Who but a person intimately acquainted with the New England land-scape could have written that description?

"Like a piece of ice on a hot stove, the poem must ride on its own melting," he wrote in a preface to his collected poems.

Frost had not only seen ice melting on a hot stove; he had keenly observed it.

When you're watching a movie or a television show, notice how the cameras pan the scene for a general view, then focus in on the specific thing the director wants you to notice.

Many of us go through life panning the landscape. We get a general view of our surroundings, but we seldom look at things up close. Those who do are rewarded with glimpses of uncommon beauty in little things.

The American Indian, before surrendering to the Europeanization of the continent, was a keen observer, because life and livelihood depended on close observation. Crowfoot, the Blackfoot warrior and orator, used poignant imagery derived from close observation in his memorable last words:

> What is life? It is the flash of a firefly in the night. It is the
> breath of a buffalo in the wintertime. It is the little shadow which
> runs across the grass and loses itself in the sunset.

That's imagery employed by someone who looked at his world closely and saw its vivid details.

If you take a keen interest in the little things happening around you, you'll find a wealth of images to employ in your communication.

After you've seen the image, your next challenge is to convey it to your audience in words that will accurately describe what you mean. This can get tricky, because members of the audience must fit the image into the pattern of their own individual experiences.

The possibility of misunderstanding is multiplied if your audience happens to come from a cultural or linguistic background different from the one you're familiar with. When Soviet leader Nikita Khrushchev visited the United States during the 1950s, he used a bit of imagery that got hyped in the translation. Americans read that the flamboyant Communist had boasted, "We will bury you." What Khrushchev had said—and what his Russian hearers understood him to say—was "We will surpass you."

Before you use imagery with a group, ask yourself two questions:

1. *How might this audience misinterpret my imagery?*
2. *What can I do to prevent misunderstanding?*

Images, like stories, must be chosen carefully with your audience and your message in mind. Here are some criteria to use in choosing images.

• *Your images should be clear and understandable to your audience.* An acquaintance of mine who grew up on a Southern farm that lacked modern conveniences was once trying to describe a romantic scene to a young woman who was a generation younger and had grown up in a middle-class urban setting.

"The moon," he told her, "was big as a wash tub."

To him, the image was clear. But the young lady looked puzzled.

"How big is a wash tub?" she asked.

• *Your images should be ones that your audience can identify with.* Your images should resonate among the day-to-day experiences of the audience.

An old textile mill hand once announced to his workmates, "My son just doffed off a set of twins."

To anyone unacquainted with textile-mill lingo, the announcement would be almost incomprehensible. But textile workers were familiar with the image of a "doffer" working his way up and down the rows of spinning frames, rapidly snatching the full bobbins of yarn from the spindles, tossing them into a box, and replacing them with empty bobbins. He was "doffing off" the bobbins from the spindles. The old hand was announcing that his son had become the father of twins.

A farmer might have said, "My son just harvested a set of twins."

A salesperson might have said, "My son just closed on a set of twins."

Use your imagination, and your knowledge of the audience, to produce images that illuminate.

The classic example of failure to identify with an audience involved Marie Antoinette, wife of King Louis XVI of France. When told that the poor people of Paris were angry because they had no bread, she responded, "Let them eat cake."

The lady, born to royalty, could not identify with people whose options were bread or starvation, not bread or cake.

- *Your images should be useful.* The image you use should accomplish a purpose in relation to your speech. Imagery used just for the sake of being cute serves no purpose.

In 1946 an invisible line running from the Baltic Sea to the Adriatic Sea separated the communist world from the free world. Winston Churchill gave it a name that captured its significance and fixed its image in the minds of the world. He called it the Iron Curtain. The term became a highly useful shorthand for the boundary between two conflicting ideologies.

Imagery can be used to inspire. When General Barnard E. Bee of South Carolina saw his troops about to buckle before the Union onslaught in the First Battle of Manassas, he pointed toward General Thomas Jackson of Virginia.

"Look at Jackson!" he cried. "There he stands like a stone wall. Rally behind the Virginians!"

General Jackson was forever immortalized as Stonewall Jackson, and the name provided inspiration for the men who served under him.

Imagery can also be used to explain complex ideas by likening them to something the audience is familiar with. One writer, explaining the workings of a nuclear reactor, likened the nucleus of an atom to a rack of balls on a billiard table, ready to fly apart when struck by a speeding cueball.

- *Your images should be vivid.* William Shakespeare was a master of imagery:

"O tiger's heart wrapped in a woman's hide."   (*King Henry VI*)

"These words are razors to my wounded heart."   (*Titus Andronicus*)

"She hangs upon the cheek of night like a rich jewel in an Ethiop's ear."   (*Romeo and Juliet*)

"He doth bestride the narrow world like a Colossus." (*Julius Caesar*)

Choose images that vividly call attention to your message or its meaning.

- *Your images should be concise.* Think of the commercial images that sell: "Reach out and touch someone" (AT&T), "Like a rock" (Chevrolet trucks), "The best part of waking up" (Folgers Coffee).
- *Your images should be memorable.* Memorable images are not only vivid; they capture the essence of the message like a fine camera capturing the essence of a moment.

John McCrae immortalized the fallen American soldiers buried in a Belgian graveyard with this simple, vivid, and memorable imagery:

> In Flanders fields the poppies blow
> Between the crosses, row on row

Recall, too, the memorable words of astronaut Neil Armstrong as he stepped from the lunar module and planted the first human footprints on the moon: "That's one small step for a man, one giant leap for mankind."

Think of the vivid image Dr. Martin Luther King Jr. used in his "I have a dream" speech: "little black children and little white children playing together on the red hills of Georgia."

These images are easily visualized. They capture the spirit of the message. They leave in the minds of the audience mental pictures that will help them remember the messages they adorn.

Images painted with words must be interpreted by the audience. If the audience doesn't "see" the same image that you see, the imagery goes for naught.

You can help your audience with the interpretation through four devices: *repetition, reinforcement, feedback,* and *application.*

Repetition

You may have been taught in school that good speakers never repeat themselves because repetition bores audiences.

I've found the opposite to be true. Generally, the people in your audience will appreciate the restatement of images because it helps them fix those images in their minds. The key is to repeat the ideas, but to frame them and state them differently. This is a powerful aid to learning.

The experts tell us that more than two-thirds of what we hear vanishes from our minds after twenty-four hours. The percentage of information that sticks goes up markedly, however, when we hear it repeated several times.

You can use several different devices for repetition.

One is to *restate or review what you have just said.* Begin with the phrase, "In other words. . . ." The audience will know you're about to repeat the image in another way. The repetition will either help people focus on the image more clearly or fix it more firmly in their minds.

You can *summarize what you've said by repeating significant points.* If the people in the audience remember the main points, they will find it easier to recall the details.

You can *interpret what you've said.* "Just as a cueball sends a rack of billiard balls flying in all directions, so a stray neutron from one atom of uranium can send the protons and neutrons of another atom flying apart."

You can *call attention to special things that should be remembered.* This is done by restating what you've already said: "Remember what I said earlier: A reactor in a nuclear power plant is just another device for boiling water."

Reinforcement

Reinforcement can come in visual or verbal form, and it can be presented as images or as supporting data.

You can provide *visual reinforcement* through slides or transparencies, through objects the audience can examine, or through images on handout sheets. Charts and graphs help people visualize statistical information. Diagrams help them understand how things are put together, how devices work, and how things are laid out.

You give *verbal reinforcement* by painting other word pictures that emphasize the image you wish to convey. For example, during a talk I often say, "Now when I told that to an audience in [another city] they. . . ." Then I recreate the image as I described it to the other audience and detail their reaction to it.

Supportive data provide raw facts that reinforce the message conveyed by the image.

"If the pipes produced by this plant in a year's time were laid end to end, they would form a pipeline stretching from New York to San Francisco," you might say, displaying a map of the United States with a drawing of a pipeline stretching from coast to coast.

Then you could provide the supporting figures, listing the number of feet of each category of pipe the plant produced.

Feedback

Feedback lets you know whether the audience has understood your image the way you intended for it to be understood. The question should not be, "Do you understand what I said?" The proper question is, "What did you understand me to say?"

So if you're explaining how a nuclear power plant works, lead your audience through the process with questions designed to determine whether they understood your imagery.

"So if the nucleus of the atom is a rack of billiard balls, what do we call the cueball that comes flying into the rack?

"A neutron! You got it.

"And what happens when the neutron hits the nucleus?

"Right! The nucleus flies apart and produces energy. Now what do we use that energy to do?

"Boil water and make steam. So now you know how a nuclear plant works."

Don't be surprised if the audience sometimes misses the point. That's the value of feedback. It lets you know when your audience has received the wrong image, and gives you the opportunity to go back and set the picture straight.

Application

Perhaps the most effective method of assisting an audience in understanding your image is to make them participants in its application.

Once a speaker was cautioning his audience against compromising its stand against nudity and violence in movies. "Many times," he said, "it's tempting to say, 'This movie is all right; it only has one or two questionable scenes in it.'"

To dramatize his point, he held up a glass of clear water. "This water," he said, "was taken from a pure mountain spring." He took a drink to demonstrate its purity.

Then he held up another glass, this one filled with a dirty-looking liquid.

"This water," he said, "was taken from a puddle in a pig sty."

His listeners crinkled their noses.

Then the speaker used an eye dropper to extract some of the filthy water from its glass. He put two drops into the glass of clean water and stirred it until there was no visible trace of the filth.

"Now," he said, passing the glass among his audience, "who would like a drink from this glass?"

It was a point the audience would not forget. The speaker had drawn his listeners into the experience. The application was unmistakably clear.

Finding the Right Image

At first, you may find it hard to come up with stories and images to illustrate the points you make. But keep your eyes open. As you read, make note of stories and illustrations that may be applicable to the things you want to say. Listen to the stories and images others use. Borrow shamelessly. Do you think John F. Kennedy or his speech writer, Theodore Sorensen, came up with the expression, "Ask not what your country can do for you; ask what you can do for your country"? Oliver Wendell Holmes Jr. used very similar words in an address to Union army veterans in 1884.

Do you think Franklin Roosevelt originated the expression, "The only thing we have to fear is fear itself"? A century earlier, the Duke of Wellington said, "The only thing I am afraid of is fear." More than two hundred years before Wellington, Francis Bacon wrote, "Nothing is terrible except fear itself."

So listen, read, borrow, and adapt—but always acknowledge the source of the material you've borrowed (it's both unethical and illegal to plagiarize the work of others).

Be a keen observer of the ideas, events, and scenes that make up your world, and let your communication sparkle with reflections of the things you've seen, heard, and experienced. You'll find your speeches taking on new life.

Your speech gains its ultimate effectiveness when you are at one with your audience—when your listeners follow your every word, thought, and movement willingly and effortlessly. You can achieve this kind of oneness with your audience if you practice the suggestions found in the next chapter.

20

CAPTIVATING YOUR AUDIENCE

Perhaps you have watched with envy as a skillful speaker strode confidently to the platform and immediately played the audience like a fine instrument.

Such performances don't just happen. They're the result of careful planning. You can achieve the same effect if you follow the right strategies. Let's look at four effective strategies.

BE SENSITIVE TO YOUR AUDIENCE

You may have heard of the tough sergeant who was told to break the news gently to Private Jackson that the recruit's mother had died. The sergeant called his unit together and told them: "I want all you guys whose mothers are still alive to take one step forward." As most of the recruits stepped forward, the sergeant quickly added: "Not so fast, Jackson."

A lot of speakers are just as insensitive as that sergeant when they communicate with their audiences. They deliver the message without worrying about how their hearers might receive it. Such speakers have a hard time establishing rapport with an audience.

Skilled communicators try to understand their audience. They want to know what their listeners think and feel, and they design their presentations to appeal to the particular audience they're addressing.

This doesn't mean that they try to tell the audience what the audience wants to know. There was no way Private Jackson could welcome the news that his mother had died. But there was a way that the sergeant might have approached him gently and paved the way for the unsettling news.

Good speakers work to establish common ground with their audience, even when they know an audience may disagree with some of the things they have to say. That common ground is vital, even with friendly audiences. Audiences are always more receptive to speakers who demonstrate respect for their attitudes and thoughts.

The Christian apostle Paul demonstrated an ability to establish common ground when he addressed an audience of polytheistic Greeks on Mars Hill in Athens. How was he going to persuade them to look into a religion that worshiped only one God, and an unseen one at that?

Paul began by calling attention to all the gods to which the Greeks had erected altars. Then he noted that one altar was dedicated to an "unknown god." This unknown, unseen God was the one he wanted to tell them about.

The good speaker plays the role of the host. It's no accident that the master of ceremonies on a television show is identified as "your host." The job of a host is to anticipate people's wants and needs, to take care of them, and to make people feel comfortable and at home.

That's the job of a good speaker, too. The pros remember the purposes behind their presentations, but they also look for ways to make the audience feel comfortable and unthreatened.

It's a poor speaker who comes before an audience behaving like a guest—as if it's up to the audience to adjust to the speaker's wavelength. It's up to you to adjust your wavelength to the audience.

Like a good host, a good speaker will respect the audience's comfort zone. Let me illustrate. Have you ever gone into a store to buy a specific product and had the salesperson pounce like a lion rising to the prey? It makes you want to turn around and look for the same item in another store, doesn't it? You know that the salesperson has one thing in mind: making that sale. Your wants and needs are secondary considerations, if they're considered at all. You're wary, because even though the salesperson can sell you what you want and need, you're not sure that your best interests are going to be served. Your comfort zone has been violated. Your confidence in the salesperson has been diminished.

You'll respond favorably, though, to the salesperson who approaches with a friendly smile, takes the time to find out what you need, then looks for ways to help you fill your needs.

It's the same with a speaker. Audiences have their comfort zones, which they tend to protect from intruders. And they regard as intruders those speakers who come on too fast and too strong, more intent on proving themselves right than in sharing ideas and feelings with the audience.

For some people, sensitivity comes naturally. Others have to cultivate it. If the speaker is well prepared, you can't tell the difference. Whether it's natural or acquired, the sensitivity manifests itself in subtle ways. Sensitive people don't talk down to their audiences. They don't ignore the physical needs of people. They don't crack tasteless jokes that are likely to offend people. They don't put people down or hold them up to ridicule in front of the audience. And they speak to their audience, large or small, as though to one person at a time.

PAY ATTENTION TO YOUR AUDIENCE

The person who is sensitive to an audience is responsive to its needs and wants. The person who is aware of the audience knows what factors are having impact on the audience at a given moment and is able to adjust his or her presentation accordingly.

When you're the speaker at a meeting or a conference, find out what the audience has been experiencing. Does your speech follow a significant business session at which the organization has made major decisions? Are you addressing a corporate audience that has just been told about a major reorganization? Have figures just been released showing that the company experienced a banner sales year? a disastrous sales year? Has the weather affected travel plans or interrupted recreational activities? Has there been a major local or national news event that is weighing on everyone's mind?

Your awareness of circumstances such as these will help you adjust your presentation to the mood of the audience and thus achieve maximum impact.

I remember one morning in 1978 when I was to address an audience in Indianapolis, Indiana. The night before the world had been horrified by a stunning piece of news. The bodies of 911 followers of cult leader Jim Jones had been discovered in the jungle of the small South American nation of Guyana. They had been victims of mass suicide and executions. It so happened that Jones was originally from Indianapolis.

I had planned to begin my presentation with my usual style of warm-up—a humorous introduction that got the audience to chuckling while I worked at building bridges of understanding. But I knew on this day that a light-hearted introduction would be totally inappropriate. Clearly, I had to address the issue that was on everyone's mind.

So I began by letting my audience know that I shared their sadness and concern. I expressed the hope that this event, as sorrowful as it was, might in some way contribute to a better understanding of human motives and feelings.

Eventually, I reached a point in the address when I could develop my original outline and share the humor that I had planned for the occasion. But first, I carefully laid the foundation, recognizing the trauma that the Jonestown tragedy represented for them.

UNDERSTAND YOUR AUDIENCE

Understanding your audience can mean the difference between triumph and disaster in persuading it to act. Two American presidencies illustrate the difference this understanding can make. Jimmy Carter came to the presidency in the aftermath of Watergate and Vietnam, and found a nation yearning for honest, effective leadership. As the negative consequences of the war were reinforced by the impact of the oil crisis, the president faced the nation and, in a candid and sincere address, spoke of the "malaise" that had settled on the country. He told his fellow Americans that the country faced a period of austerity.

Carter didn't understand his audience. Americans didn't want their president to tell them they were suffering from a sense of ill ease and would have to tighten their belts. They wanted a leader who would tell them that things were going to get better and that he was ready to lead them toward better times.

After a generation of taking it on the chin, Americans were ready for an upbeat message. When Ronald Reagan brought it, they listened and responded—and they stayed with him, even through a deep and painful recession. Reagan understood his audience.

Different audiences will respond in different ways. You wouldn't give the same address to the Chamber of Commerce that you would give to the United Mine Workers. You wouldn't speak to a Shriners convention the way you'd speak to the American Association of University Women, or to the Jaycees the way you'd speak to the American Association of Retired People.

You gain considerable insight into an audience by answering some basic questions about the people that compose it:

- *What do they want out of life?* It isn't enough to know what the people in your audience need. You also must know how they perceive those needs.

    Some people are known as motivational speakers. That's a misnomer. A speaker can't motivate an audience. The audience is already motivated. It is motivated to do what it wants to do, not what you or I want it to do.

    People are like water in a faucet. The water is motivated to flow out of the faucet, but it doesn't have the opportunity until you open the tap. Many people are just as strongly motivated, and they're waiting for the opportunity to follow their motivations. The speaker who shows them that opportunity is instrumental in releasing a gush of energy.

    Some people, too, are like mountain streams, which flow swiftly but follow their own channels. A good speaker shows them how to channel their motivations toward the results the speaker desires.

- *What do they fear?* Knowledge of what people fear can be a powerful tool in channeling motivations. Sometimes you'll need to neutralize the fear. A drowning person, terrified at the prospect of dying, will thrash and flounder, preventing the lifeguard's rescue efforts. But if the lifeguard can remove this fear of death, the victim will relax and cooperate with the rescuer.

    On the other hand, a person who is inclined to get behind the wheel after imbibing too many martinis needs a healthy dose of fear—the fear of tragic death, of either the driver or those in the path of the driver.

    The more you know about your audience's fears, the better you will be able to establish effective communication.

- *What do they know?* If somebody from out of town calls and asks directions to your place, the first thing you normally ask is, "Where are you now?"

    You have to know where people are before you can tell them how to reach their destination.

    The process is similar in communication. There has to be a point of origin and a destination.

The point of origin is what the audience already knows, understands, or believes. The destination is what you want the audience to know, understand, or believe after you've finished talking.

So when you speak to an audience, you must start on common ground. You must be aware of what the audience knows or believes. Otherwise, you won't have a clue as to where to begin the presentation.

After you've established that common ground, you have to retain it throughout the presentation.

Some people, when they're speaking on their area of expertise, like to impress their audience with how much they know. That's a sure way to lose an audience. Your purpose is not to impress people with your knowledge, but to communicate your knowledge in such a way that they will be influenced to do the things you want them to do.

Speakers shouldn't worry about whether they know more than the audience or the audience knows more than they. If you think you know more than your audience, you may come across as condescending. If you think your audience knows more than you, you may feel intimidated.

It's best to think of yourself as neither inferior nor superior to your audience—just different. You know things your audience doesn't know, and the individuals in the audience know things you don't know. Neither is inferior or superior to the other.

• *What do they understand?* There's a big difference between knowing and understanding. When you're driving, it's not enough to know that the traffic light is red. You must also understand that a red light means you must stop.

The American audience that saw Nikita Khrushchev hold his clenched hands above his head knew what the Soviet leader was doing. But the audience didn't understand that it was a gesture of friendliness and not an act of braggadocio. Other incidents of international misunderstanding are more humorous.

Let me relate one other example of the difference between knowing and understanding.

A small community in a poultry-growing region was holding a festival to celebrate the industry that was the backbone of its economy. As part of the festivity, 4-H youngsters entered a poultry contest. The chickens they had raised were on display, all plucked and cleaned and ready for the cooking pot. Representatives of the area's supermarkets were there, vying for the honor of offering their customers the prize-winning product while reaping some favorable publicity.

An out-of-town visitor arrived late just as the bidding was reaching its climax.

"I'm offered $9; who'll make it $10?" chanted the auctioneer.

The visitor looked at the boxes of high-quality poultry—about thirty pounds of it. Ten dollars seemed like a steal.

"Ten dollars," he called, and the auctioneer said "Sold."

The visitor came forward, taking a crisp bill from his wallet.

"That'll be $300," said the auctioneer.

The visitor was mortified. He *knew* he had bid $10 for the poultry. He *understood* that he was bidding $10 for the whole batch. Had he arrived at the start of the auction, he would have known that he was bidding $10 *per pound*.

So when you're speaking to an audience, be alert for any misunderstanding and be prepared to deal with it promptly. When you're asking $10, make sure your audience understands that you mean "per pound."

IDENTIFY WITH YOUR AUDIENCE

If you want to captivate your audience, you must be able to see through the eyes and hear through the ears of your listeners. That means identifying with the audience. When members of your audience perceive you as one of them instead of as an outsider, you've arrived as a communicator.

If you can use the word *we* to embrace yourself and the audience—and your listeners accept the embrace—then you have their attention.

The framers of the Constitution of the United States faced a huge communications task. The people of the former colonies thought of themselves as New Englanders, New Yorkers, Virginians, or Carolinians first, and as Americans second. In the public consciousness, "United States" was a plural descriptive and not the name of a nation. How were the founders of the Republic to promote the idea that the settlers from Maine to Georgia were a single people and not thirteen different nationalities?

The preamble to the Constitution helped set the tone. It read:

We the people of the United States, in order to form a more perfect union, establish justice, insure domestic tranquility, provide
for the common defense, promote the general welfare, and secure the blessings of liberty to ourselves and our posterity do or-
dain and establish this Constitution for the United States of
America.

The phrase "We the people" (as opposed to "We the peoples")
helped establish the oneness of Americans, though it took a civil war to
establish once and for all that this was "one nation, indivisible." The
framers didn't present the Constitution as a gift from them to the people, but as a creation of the people themselves. Instead of guaranteeing
freedom for "you and your posterity," they undertook to "secure the
blessings of liberty for *ourselves* and *our* posterity" (emphasis mine).

As a speaker, look for ways to achieve oneness with your audience.
The more you identify with the circumstances, needs, and feelings of
your audience, the easier it is for your audience to identify with you.

On the way to achieving this oneness, however, you will encounter
many barriers. Some of them can be avoided and others can be overcome. The next chapter shows you how to deal with them.

21

CONQUERING THE
BARRIERS

Every speaker hopes for the perfect occasion. The layout of the room is perfect; every seat in the house is the best. The audience is alert, receptive, and friendly. The sound system works splendidly and the acoustics are ideal. There are no visual or auditory distractions while you speak. Your voice is great, your timing is perfect, your audiovisual materials are in the right order and right side up, and the equipment works. Your introduction is an attention-grabber, the audience stays involved throughout the presentation, and your smashing conclusion brings the whole room to its feet.

When you encounter all these conditions, mark the date on your calendar. Break out the champagne and celebrate it year after year. You're not likely to encounter such an experience again in your lifetime. In public speaking, as in most other endeavors, Murphy's Law is alive and well: If anything can go wrong, it will. (O'Toole's Law says that Murphy was an optimist.)

That doesn't faze accomplished speakers. They know that unexpected glitches will occur, and they're prepared to deal with them.

AVOID IMPENETRABLE BARRIERS

Many barriers can be anticipated and sometimes removed in advance. Some barriers are impenetrable, however. A good football coach knows that when it's the fourth down and nine yards to go on your own twenty-yard-line, you don't run the ball unless you're in desperate straits. The best strategy is to fall back and punt.

Good speakers, too, know when to punt. Dr. Martin Luther King Jr. was a courageous man, but he didn't waste his breath preaching racial harmony to Ku Klux Klan audiences.

Never Speak Following a Long Cocktail Hour

I once spoke at a banquet in a beautiful resort hotel in Hilton Head, South Carolina. When I arrived, I noticed a cocktail party in progress. It had started at 3 P.M., and the waiters were still taking orders for drinks when I was introduced. The audience was drunk, and people were throwing bread rolls from one table to another. There was no way I could inform, persuade, or inspire this audience. The experience taught me never to accept an engagement in which I'm scheduled to speak immediately after a long cocktail party.

Don't Try to Beat the Band

Congressman Jim Wright of Texas, when he was speaker of the U.S. House of Representatives, encountered another impossible situation when he addressed the annual meeting of the National Conference of Editorial Writers in Fort Worth, Texas. Immediately behind the platform from which he spoke was a partition that divided the large meeting hall into two rooms.

The speaker made a few preliminary remarks, then opened the floor for questions. Just as the meatier questions were coming in, the room exploded with noise. On the other side of that partition was a rock band, which was providing music for a dance. The band had agreed to keep silent until 9 P.M. The editorial writers' program went a few minutes past 9, and the band refused to wait any longer.

The noise was so loud that people sitting at the tables couldn't hear each other, much less the speaker. The meeting planners tried to persuade the band to hold off for a few more minutes, but the band refused. Wright did the only thing he could do under the circumstances: He threw up his hands and sat down.

Competition and Resistance

The barriers to communicating from the platform fall roughly into two categories: competition and resistance.

The crusader who tries to sell gun control to a group of National Rifle Association members is encountering resistance. This takes the form of an emotional or intellectual reluctance to hear what is being said. Jim

Wright was encountering competition: The noise from the band successfully competed against his voice for the ears of his audience.

The best way to confront these barriers is to avoid them. Don't accept an invitation to address an audience that you know you have no chance of reaching or persuading. And work with the program chair in advance to head off any possible competition for your presentation.

FACTORS TO MONITOR

Here are some environmental factors to monitor in advance.

- *Physical layout.* The size and shape of a room can be critical factors in the success of your speech. I once spoke to a group in the expansive ballroom of the Dunes Hotel in Las Vegas. The room could have accommodated a group four times as large as the one I addressed. The audience did what audiences normally do: The people moved to the rear of the auditorium. This created a distance between me and those who came to hear me.

  When this sort of situation arises, you have to remember the proverb: If the mountain won't come to Mohammed, then Mohammed must go to the mountain. In this case, the ballroom was equipped with spotlights and long microphone cords. I was able to move to the audience and to interact with it.

  A room that is too small can be as bad. When people are crowded into a small space, they feel packed in and it's hard for them to give you their full attention.

  Acoustics have a major effect on the way your message is perceived. In some rooms, if you turn down the sound system, the audience can't hear you. If you turn it up, it sounds like you're in a cave. If you have anything to say about the choice of settings, choose a room appropriate for the size of the group, with acoustics appropriate for your presentation. If you have to speak under unfavorable circumstances, innovate as I did in the case of the Dunes engagement.

- *Temperature and lighting.* When people get warm and the lights are dim, they tend to get drowsy—especially if they've just been wined and dined. When the room is too cool, people get fidgety; their minds are focused more on their discomfort than on anything you might have to say. When the lights are too bright, they can destroy any feeling of intimacy between speaker and audience. Bright lights, too, can cause people to become edgy and tense.

The best time to check out these conditions is before you stand up to speak. When you're ready to speak, your mind should be free to concentrate on your message and your audience. Remember that when you stand up to speak, your excitement will probably make you warmer than most people in your audience. Monitor your audience as you speak. If you sense that the people are physically uncomfortable, stop and try to do something about it. Isn't that what all good hosts would do for their guests?

- *Faulty equipment.* It's amazing how many conference centers will spend millions on an auditorium, then balk at spending a few hundred dollars for a decent public address system.

In most cases, you're at the mercy of the public address system when it comes to conveying your words to the audience. So arrive early and check it out. Take care of any problems before you mount the platform. Talk to the people who will be operating the equipment. Make sure they understand your needs and wishes.

If you're using audiovisual aids, make sure the equipment is functioning before you get up to speak. If you're going to be operating it, be sure you know how it works.

- *Visual distractions.* Maybe you think what you have to say is more interesting than anything that could possibly be going on around you. But don't tell that to an audience within clear view of a swimming pool populated with shapely mermaids in revealing attire or muscular Adonises with pectorals on display. You're quite likely to lose out.

So if you have any influence over the setting, get a room with no competing views to contend with.

You may have to deal with other types of distractions. It's hard for a speaker to maintain rapport with an audience while waiters are bringing in the flaming dessert or are removing dishes from the tables. It's hard to compete with bright photographic flashes or television klieg lights.

If possible, arrange for these distractions to take place at a time when you're not speaking. If any of them interrupt your speech, it's usually best to stop until the distraction has passed.

- *Noises.* When you're speaking, your voice should be the loudest sound in the room. If other noises compete, you'll struggle to retain the audience's attention. I've competed with jackhammers breaking up concrete, with kitchen workers playing or fighting, with low-flying aircraft, and with other meetings or parties nearby.

Sometimes you have to compete with pleasant sounds—soft, piped-in music or a band performing in the next room.

It's best to find out about your competition in advance, do what you can to eliminate it, and, if that's impossible, develop a strategy for dealing with it.

Monitor the Audience

When you're addressing an audience, keep a close watch on everything your listeners do. Be alert for signs that you're losing their attention or that they're having trouble following you. Are the people in the back rows straining to hear you? Can everyone see you clearly, and can they see any visual aids you might be using?

If the people in your audience start out alert and attentive but later start fidgeting and slumping in their chairs, it usually means that the environment is uncomfortable for some reason. Find out why, and take care of the problem before you proceed.

If you know your listeners have been sitting in one position for a long time, perhaps in uncomfortable chairs, give them a break. Involve them in a stand-up exercise or call a short recess to give people a chance to visit the rest rooms.

Overcoming Audience Resistance

Barriers resulting from audience resistance can be just as formidable as those resulting from environmental conditions.

I once spoke at a major meeting of the Diamond Shamrock Corporation in Florida. I didn't know until I arrived that my audience would include people from all over the world. Many of them knew little English. A fast-paced speech full of witty colloquialisms would have forfeited the attention of a significant proportion of this audience. So I developed a strategy. I spoke slowly and distinctly. And I wove into my speech some stories about my own experiences in learning the language and customs of the American people. The strategy enabled me to gain and hold the attention of the foreign visitors and further enhance the international flair of the meeting.

On another occasion, I was asked to give an inspirational speech to the sales force of a large air-brakes manufacturer in Saginaw, Michigan. What I didn't know when I accepted the invitation was that just before I spoke the company was to announce a major shake-up in the sales division. I therefore found myself speaking to many people who had seen their territories restructured and some who had seen their incomes reduced.

Since I was there at the invitation of management, it was natural for the audience to assume that I was somehow involved in all the changes, or at least knew about them.

Under such circumstances, don't pretend you don't know what has happened and don't stand up and crack jokes about other people's misfortunes. Let the audience know that you care and look for positives in the situation.

Diagnose Audience Response

If you look and listen carefully, audience response will tell you whether you are encountering emotional or intellectual resistance. Audience response is to the public speaker what symptoms are to a doctor. Sensitive speakers know what audience response to expect, and when they don't get it, they look for the reasons.

One technique for testing the degree to which you're getting through to the audience is to ask a question periodically that can be answered with one word. If the audience shouts back the answer, you know you've connected. If only a few respond, you need to find out why you're losing your audience.

Become Physically Involved with the Audience

It's an unusual day when I don't get up and speak to some group. Over the years, I've learned a few secrets for breaking down the barriers to communication between speaker and audience.

One of the most effective is to become physically involved with the audience. You may feel safer hiding behind the dais or standing with several rows of empty seats between you and the audience. But you can't carry on dialogue with an audience that is isolated from you.

Poor Me Versus the Great Gipper

One of the toughest pieces of competition I had came at a meeting of the Associated General Contractors of America. I was scheduled to speak in the afternoon. The mid-morning speaker was a man named Ronald Reagan, who at the time was living at 1600 Pennsylvania Avenue in Washington, D.C.

There are worse fates than following Ronald Reagan on the platform. I discovered one of them very quickly. For some reason, the president had to reschedule his speech for the exact time that I was to speak. So guess who most people went to hear? I've overcome some tough obstacles, but I can't match the president's clout. Instead of an audience of several hundred, I faced an audience of about thirty.

But what an audience! These people had to be committed if they were willing to pass up a speech by the Gipper in favor of one by Nido Qubein. So I tried twice as hard to please them. I called them to the front of the room, and we sat around in a circle. The speech turned into a group discussion. The audience became so involved that it was hard to break it up at the appointed time.

Get the Audience Physically Involved with You

Another technique is to get your audience physically involved with you. You can do this with any number of simple devices that don't require intense mental effort or manual dexterity. One of my favorites is the hand-clapping game.

I used it to good effect once when I shared the platform with Dave Thomas, founder of Wendy's, and Bill Leonard, then president of CBS News. The occasion was the Western Kentucky University Free Enterprise Fair, and the audience was made up of several thousand high school and college students who were there for a good time.

I had spoken six times that week to major corporate and association groups. This definitely called for a change of pace.

So I asked the students to clap their hands when I crossed my hands, but not to clap when my hands weren't crossed. At first they acted on signal. But when I began faking the crossing of my hands and speeding up the tempo, they soon became confused. I kept working at it until everyone in the audience was involved.

This may not work as well with the stockholders of IBM, but with the appropriate group it's a good warm-up exercise that can grab the attention of your audience and prepare them to listen to you.

Older audiences can be captivated by equally simple devices. Once, speaking at the River Oaks Country Club in Houston, I asked how many of the men present dominated their wives. Only one held up his hand. That brought a laugh. But when his wife stood up and pushed his arm down, she brought down the house.

Obviously, a routine can be staged if you set it up with the right person. Involving an individual from the audience can be an effective way of catching the attention of everyone—especially when the individual involved is well known and well liked. But remember the words of caution I passed on earlier: Make sure the individual involved has a good sense of humor and is a willing participant. And avoid embarrassing or putting down the individual. The people in the audience identify with the individual chosen from their ranks more than they do with you. Send the person back into the audience with a word of commendation on being such a good sport, and ask the audience to applaud. This will make your confederate from the audience feel good and will identify you with the audience.

When you use an exercise to involve the audience, follow these guidelines:

- Keep it simple.
- Make it move.
- Make it short.
- Make it fun for everybody
- Make it fit your audience and situation.

A DUAL MEDIUM: SIGHT AND SOUND

A platform speech is a dual medium. It communicates through the ears and it communicates through the eyes. So when you're addressing an audience, look alive. Be relaxed but enthusiastic. Let your face, hands, and posture communicate mood and meaning to your audience.

The audience will read meaning into your body language whether you are conscious or unconscious of what you're doing. If your hands hang limply by your side, the audience infers that you're scared. Hands folded across the chest tell your listeners that you're defensive. Hands nervously fidgeting with your glasses or notes inform everyone that you're self-conscious. Use your hands for natural, purposeful gestures, the way you do when you're holding an enthusiastic conversation with an individual.

And let your face and voice come alive. A monotone drones people to sleep. A blank expression says, "Nothing I'm saying is worth getting excited about."

Speak in a lower voice range to convey a feeling of confidence, but modulate your voice to show various degrees of excitement, concern, anger, or conviction. And let your face reveal your emotions. Don't try to fake it; just let your feelings show.

When you're in front of an audience, let yourself unwind. You have an appealing personality. Let it come through. Use every natural charm at your disposal to captivate the audience.

Let your style fit your audience. I used the hand-clapping routine with the high school students from Kentucky, not with the contractors who chose to hear me instead of President Reagan.

Good communicators are so attuned to their audiences that they can make every individual think, "These words are meant just for me."

Use Visual Aids

Audiences today have grown up with television, movies, and video-tapes. They're even adding the sight dimension to their phone conversations. They are more visually oriented than any previous generation. When they come to hear you talk, they bring their eyes as well as their ears. If they were there only to listen, they could get it all from an audiotape.

So visual aids can be the battering rams with which you break down walls of resistance to your message. They can help you get the audience completely involved with your presentation.

One method I sometimes use is to display several common items— perhaps a key, a paper clip, a cup, or a pencil, on an opaque projector. After I've given members of the audience a minute to observe them, I turn off the projector and ask them to write down a list of all the things displayed. This leads into a discussion of how little we tend to observe the common things around us and how hard it is to remember even a few things.

When you use visual aids, keep these suggestions in mind:

- Keep them simple—never more than three lines on a slide.
- Convey only one message per visual.
- Make sure the visual calls attention to you and your message and doesn't distract your audience.
- Practice using the visuals until you can do it naturally and comfortably.
- Before you begin the presentation, make sure the audiovisual tools are all in working condition.
- Keep your visual aids short.
- Apply them to what you're saying.
- Test the audience's response to them.

OVERCOMING STAGE FRIGHT

For many people, the greatest barrier to communication from the public platform is in their own minds. About 40 pecent of Americans suffer from "performance anxiety," also known as stage fright. It's believed to be the most widespread phobia in the United States.

Stage fright can be overcome. Part of the remedy is changing your attitude toward the speech.

According to Dr. Michael T. Motley, stage fright is most common among people who look upon a speech as a performance rather than an exercise in communication. They go to the platform convinced that the room is full of critics who will be evaluating their gestures, language, and posture. This anxiety leads them to assume the role of actors, adopting formal, artificial language and behavior that they assume to be better than their normal, natural ways of expressing themselves.[1]

You can overcome this tendency by looking upon your speech as an opportunity to communicate your thoughts and ideas to the audience. Concentrate on the message, not on the performance. Think of the main ideas you want to communicate and how you want to get them across.

Practice your speech before one or two individuals. Talk as if you're conversing with those individuals. Use your notes to remind you of what you want to say. You'll probably feel silly delivering an oration to just one or two people, so don't orate. Talk to them conversationally, using the language, inflections, and gestures you use in ordinary conversation.

When you get on the platform, follow the same technique. Look at specific individuals in the audience and speak to them one person at a time. When you're talking to individuals, you keep your language natural and you overcome the feeling that you're giving a performance.

Motley provides these additional tips:

- Put yourself in your audience's place. Be aware that your audience consists of individuals with differing interests and attitudes and different degrees of familiarity with your topic. Speak to them in their terms and in their language.
- Don't memorize and don't read. Use the extemporaneous approach.
- Forget about your hands and facial expressions. Concentrate on the message you want to convey and let your nonverbal communication take its natural course.
- Adopt a calm, unhurried pace. You're there to impart understanding, not to "get it over with."[2]

Burton J. Rubin, author of *The Stagefright Handbook*, notes that many speakers get into trouble by thinking ahead to what *might* happen. Their fears of "going blank" or committing some verbal blunder become self-fulfilling prophecies.

The remedy is to "stay in the present." One way of doing this is to select some object in the room—a table, chair, sofa, or lectern—and concentrate on it. This will keep your mind from becoming crowded with "what ifs."

Another technique is to concentrate on the words you want to stress and the way you're going to interpret your material. If you're thinking about these things, you won't have the mental capacity to think ahead and worry about the "what ifs."

If you should go blank, don't panic. It happens to everybody. The ideas and words you want are in your brain; you just need to take a moment to find them. So pause for a moment. A little silence never hurt anyone. Forget the audience, forget your anxiety, and just concentrate on remembering. Retrace your train of thoughts, one thought at a time. It'll come.[3]

Nervous or Not, Be Yourself

The advice to "be yourself" applies regardless of whether you suffer from stage fright.

Adopt a style that accords with your personality. If you're normally a quiet, dignified individual, don't hop, skip and jump to the platform as if you can't wait to fire up your audience. The best way to approach the podium is with calm, confident strides. Face your audience and smile. Then begin your speech.

Establish good eye contact at the outset. Effective speakers don't speak to the crowd. They speak to the individuals in the crowd. Don't look at the back of the room and don't let your gaze wander vaguely over the audience. Look individuals in the eyes. Look for people who return your look with friendly, interested expressions. Maintain eye contact long enough to achieve mutual understanding, then move on to the next person.

Public speaking can be one of the most rewarding forms of communication. When you find yourself firing up an audience, the energy flows both ways. Master the medium. The skills you develop in addressing a live audience will serve you well in the twenty-first century.

EPILOGUE

Throughout this book, we've demonstrated that words are more than sounds entering the ear, more than ink patterns on paper.

They convey meaning. They convey instruction, information, and inspiration. They convey power. And in business, they have a strong effect on the bottom line.

To inform people is to equip them for success, because in any competition, the informed person has an edge over the uninformed. And information can be acquired only through communication.

So, as you can see, the ability to communicate with precision has a tremendous impact on corporate profits.

Educate, Don't Train

In other times, management could rely on repetitive training to equip the workforce to carry out its tasks. But today's workplace requires thinkers, not robotic performers. You train dogs to fetch sticks, seals to balance balls on their noses, and lions to jump through hoops. You have to educate people to carry out the mental tasks required in today's jobs.

Today's workforce needs more than training in how to turn screws and how to pull levers. It must be educated to communicate properly. An organization's success depends heavily on the ability to achieve alignment among all the people who work for it. That alignment cannot be achieved without effective communication to unify the people toward a common vision, a common mission, and common goals.

An organization is also dependent for its success on the ability to innovate and to change. Innovation and change flow from powerful ideas that germinate within the workforce and are communicated across functional boundaries and up and down through management levels.

We've spent entirely too much time in the past teaching people what to do instead of concentrating on how they think and how they feel and how they behave; far too much time getting a job done instead of producing excellent results; far too much time conforming instead of creating.

Successful corporations need workforces made up of people educated in such skills as goal setting, problem solving, decision making, conflict management, and other communication skills.

Penetrating the Barriers

A human organization is a collection of minds. It functions only when information flows from mind to mind. Each mind is a barrier that encloses its own thoughts and information. The great task of communication today is to penetrate the barriers so that the information can flow.

If you analyse the management problems in any business organization, you'll find that the majority result from breakdowns in communication.

Efficiency experts claim that at least 40 percent of the average worker's time is spend doing tasks that are either unnecessary or have to be done over because they were not done according to instructions.

Executives can increase their influence by learning the techniques of persuasive communication. High-powered communicators learn to focus words the way a laser beam focuses light.

At the Heart of Everything

Communication is at the heart of everything we do. It is the foundation for interaction among human beings. Communication has to do with meanings, with understandings, with feelings, with desires, with needs, and with ideas.

Our world is filled with information, but that isn't enough. We need understanding, and that calls for transcending that "immutable barrier" between one person's thoughts and another's; for bridging the distance between human beings so that we can better live together, work together, get along with each other, and make this earth the best possible home for the human race.

It is my hope that this book will help you build bridges to your staff, your employees, to your customers, and to everyone who plays a meaningful role in your career and your life.

NOTES

Chapter 1

1. Lennie Copeland, "Four by Four: How Do You Manage a Diverse Work Force?" *Training and Development Journal*, February 1989, p. 18.

2. James M. Kouzes and Barry Z. Posner, "The Credibility Factor: What Followers Expect from Their Leaders," *Management Review*, January 1990, p. 29.

3. Tom Peters, *Thriving on Chaos: 45 Tactics for a Mangement Revolution* (Chicago: Nightingale Conant, 1987), audiocassestte #5.

Chapter 2

1. Ernest Hemingway, *Dateline: Toronto* (New York: Charles Scribner's Sons, 1985).

Chapter 4

1. Floyd Wickman, *The Wickman Formula: Seven Steps to Achieving Your Full Potential* (High Point, N.C.: Executive Press, 1991), p. 96.

2. Robert Howard, "Values Make the Company: An Interview with Robert Haas," *Harvard Business Review*, September–October 1990, p. 142.

3. Ed Temple with B'Lou Carter, *Only the Pure in Heart Survive* (Nashville, TN: Broadman, 1980), p. 94.

Chapter 6

1. In Mario Pei, ed., *Language Today: A Survey of Current Linguistic Thought* (New York: Funk & Wagnalls, 1967), pp. 102–5.

2. Ibid.

Chapter 7

1. Robert Howard, "Values Make the Company: An Interview with Robert Haas," *Harvard Business Review*, September–October 1990, pp. 134–42.

Chapter 8

1. Michael Rothschild, "Want to Grow? Watch Your Language," *Forbes ASAP*, October 25, 1993, p. 20.

Chapter 9

1. "Face-to-Face: Managing the Journey," *INC.*, November 1990, p. 46.

Chapter 10

1. Casey Miller and Kate Swift, *Words and Women: New Language in New Times* (Garden City, N.Y.: Anchor Press/Doubleday, 1976), p. 108.
2. Ibid., pp. 109–10.
3. Ibid.
4. Deborah Tannen, *You Just Don't Understand* (New York: William Morrow, 1990), pp. 24–25.
5. Barbara Gamarekian (New York Times News Service), "Book Looks at Poor Communication between the Sexes," *Raleigh News and Observer*, June 30, 1991, p. 10E.
6. Tannen, *You Just Don't Understand*, pp. 24–25.
7. Molly Ivins, *Atlanta Journal-Constitution*, August 29, 1993, p. D5.

Chapter 11

1. "Four by Four," *Training and Development Journal*, February 1989.
2. In Mario Pei, ed., *Language Today: A Survey of Current Linguistic Thought* (New York: Funk & Wagnalls, 1967), p. 123.

Chapter 12

1. David Russell, director of custom communications for GTE Telephone Operations in Dallas, as quoted in *Nation's Business*, May 1993, p. 28.

Chapter 19

1. Dyan Machan, "How You Can Get a Few Good Laughs," *Reader's Digest*, December 1991, pp. 79–80, as reprinted from *Forbes*, October 15, 1990.

Chapter 21

1. Michael T. Motley, "Taking the Terror Out of Talk," *Psychology Today*, January 1988, p. 47.
2. Ibid., p. 49
3. Burton J. Rubin, *Stage Fright Handbook* (Saratoga Springs, N.Y.: Decision-Making Systems Ltd., 1986), p. 2.

INDEX

ABOUT THE AUTHOR

Nido Qubein is chairman of an international consulting firm and recipient of the highest awards given for professional speakers including the Cavett (known as the Oscar of professional speaking) and the Council of Peers Award of Excellence. He has served as president of the National Speakers Association, which has a membership of 4,000 professionals. He holds a Doctor of Laws degree from his alma mater along with dozens of other honors and distinctions.

Nido has written many books and recorded scores of audio and video learning programs, including a best-seller on effective communication published by Nightingale-Conant and Berkley. He is an active speaker and consultant, addressing more than one hundred business and professional groups around the world each year. He doesn't just talk business, he lives it. He is an entrepreneur with active interests in real estate, advertising, and banking. As a "business insider" with extensive boardroom exposure, he's in touch with the challenges confronting you and your team every day.

Money magazine claims, "Qubein puts on a memorable program, gliding from one anecdote to another. Nearly 70 percent of his business comes from companies that have utilized him before. His client list is a 'who's who' of blue chip corporations."

Business Life magazine says, "He coupled his charismatic style and positive nature with his acquired knowledge of human relations and communication . . . and built a multimillion dollar, multifaceted consulting enterprise—proving the American dream is still alive and well."

For information on Nido Qubein's speeches,
books, cassettes and consulting call or write:

Creative Services, Inc.
806 Westchester Drive
P. O. Box 6008
High Point, NC 27262 USA
Telephone (910)889-3010
Facsimile (910)885-3001